UNRULY
RHETORICS

COMPOSITION, LITERACY, AND CULTURE

David Bartholomae and Jean Ferguson Carr, Editors

UNRULY RHETORICS

PROTEST, PERSUASION, AND PUBLICS

EDITED BY JONATHAN ALEXANDER, SUSAN C. JARRATT, AND NANCY WELCH

University of Pittsburgh Press

An earlier version of Nancy Welch's chapter originally appeared in the *Community Literacy Journal*. An earlier version of Jonathan Sterne's chapter appeared as "Bodies-Streets" in *wi: Journal of Mobile Media* (June 2012) and as "Quebec's #Casseroles: On Participation, Percussion, and Protest" in *Sounding Out* (June 4, 2012).

Published by the University of Pittsburgh Press, Pittsburgh, Pa., 15260
Manufactured in the United States of America
Printed on acid-free paper
10 9 8 7 6 5 4 3 2 1

Cataloging-in-Publication data is available from the Library of Congress

ISBN 13: 978-0-8229-6556-5
ISBN 10: 0-8229-6556-9

Cover illustration: iStock / soberve
Cover design: Joel W. Coggins

CONTENTS

PART III
LIMITS AND HORIZONS

ACKNOWLEDGMENTS

In addition to acknowledging the work of our contributors, the editors also thank Jasmine Lee and Jens Lloyd at the University of California, Irvine, for their assistance in preparing various versions of this manuscript.

UNRULY RHETORICS

INTRODUCTION

JONATHAN ALEXANDER AND SUSAN C. JARRATT

Political activity is whatever shifts a body from the place assigned to it. . . .
It makes visible what had no business being seen, and makes heard a discourse
where once there was only place for noise; it makes understood as discourse
what was once only heard as noise.
> —Jacques Rancière, *Disagreement: Politics and Philosophy*

In the civil rights movements of the 1960s in the United States and elsewhere, bodies shifted from their assigned places and made noise that they intended to be heard as political discourse: the student movements in the United States and Europe; in South Africa, especially after the 1976 Soweto massacre, large-scale street demonstrations featured the singing and dancing called toyi-toyi; the 1977–1978 civil resistance against the Shah in Iran; the Poland Solidarity movement of the 1980s and the fall of the Berlin wall in 1989; the first Palestinian intifada in the late 1980s/early 1990s. These few selected cases from the final decades of the last century suggest the global vitality of social protest in this period.

From a US perspective, however, beginning with the election of Ronald Reagan in 1980, activism seems to have subsided in an era of capitalist growth,

3

trickle-down economics, and cultural quietism. Other influential factors include the enactment of civil rights demands into law, the backlash against feminism, a move toward cultural conservatism, the 1990s cultural wars (fought largely in the press and in the halls of academe), and the move into a neoliberal era with its all-encompassing economies and smooth affects. For many social protest scholars, then, the so-called Battle in Seattle marked a turning point. The 1999 protest against the World Trade Association at its meeting in Seattle was a demonstration that brought together multiple constituencies against a global agent; it played out over several days with considerable performative creativity. There followed soon after the contentious election of George W. Bush, the events of 9/11, and then in the spring of 2003 massive worldwide protests against the impending US war in Iraq—millions of people marching in New York, London, Paris, and Rome. Fast forward to the spring of 2011, and we have the uprisings in Tunisia, Libya, and Egypt; in the United States, rowdy labor protests in Wisconsin; and by the fall, Occupy Wall Street. A case can be made that protest movements and cultures of activism in the United States and across the globe have come to life in the twenty-first century. A number of analytic frames have been called upon or created to make sense of this upsurge and to foster speculation about its causes: globalization and its networks, the influence and availability of new media, a revival of interest in performativity and the carnivalesque, and others.

As activists respond to changing economic and global conditions, questions arise: What accounts for these ebbs and flows? Are we seeing new modes of protest? Jacques Rancière's observation, published in 1995 in France, inspires further questions along these lines: What makes it possible for people to gather together to express a public will? What provokes bodies to shift from assigned places? What is the process of translating the often unruly noise of protest into discourses of democratic participation?

While the digitally and televisually mediated nature of much contemporary activism has drawn significant recent scholarly attention, we approach activism and protest here as a complex mix of bodies, technologies, discourses, and even histories that need to be considered collectively so as to guide a new understanding of contemporary rhetorical interventions within and across numerous spheres. For instance, during Quebec's mass student strikes in 2012 that fought off tuition hikes and toppled the provincial government, student unions turned to social media to publicize key days of action. But it was the sea of red-shirted college students filling the boulevards, joined by thousands of residents in traditional pot-banging protest that repeatedly transformed the city of Montreal into a public space for broadcasting the students' demands.

Quebec's "Maple Spring" thus joins a long history demonstrating how—by definition—protest puts bodies disruptively in public space. Indeed, when current examples are examined closely, we find technology and embodied protest complexly intertwined. From this angle we can consider how many twentieth- and twenty-first-century protests are grounded in long histories of activism and lively interanimations of old and new rhetorical means.

Consider, for example, the Egyptian phase of the so-called Arab Spring (known locally as the January 25 Revolution)—mass demonstrations in Cairo's Tahrir Square beginning in January 2011 and reaching a climax on February 11 with the resignation of Hosni Mubarak from his thirty-year run as president. One narrative circulating about the uprising features "an oppressed people who have suffered passively suddenly decid[ing] that enough is enough and, thanks to Western technology and inspiration, spontaneously ris[ing] up to reclaim their freedom" (Bishara ix). This "world media narrative" (Bishara ix), highlighting the crucial role of social media and other new technology, needs to be assessed in the context of a longer history of struggle and a clear-eyed account of the role of new media in recent years. Revolutionary movements of 1881, 1919, and 1952 laid the ground for more current protests from 1998 forward based on dire economic conditions. When the Egyptian government crushed a strike by textile workers on April 6, 2008, a group of young activists connected through Facebook and other social networking sites and formed the April 6 Youth Movement in solidarity with the strikers. This movement propelled the massive popular protests in January 2011—the assembly of bodies in Tahrir Square that finally could not be ignored by the Mubarak regime. In a fascinating and detailed calculation of the role of social media and oppositional movements in Egypt leading up to the January 25 Revolution, Merlyna Lim finds that face-to-face communications such as contacts at coffeehouses and in cabs played as strong a role as social media in bringing masses of people to Tahrir for those fateful eighteen days.

In a similar fashion, an analysis of the 2011 University of California, Davis, "pepper-spray incident" highlights the combination of historical, embodied, and technologized factors. In "Toward an Economy of Activist Literacies in Composition Studies: Possibilities for Political Disruption," Caroline Dadas and Justin Jorry analyze responses arising out of the pepper-spraying by police of a group of student protesters at UC Davis, who had organized a peaceful sit-in to call attention to tuition hikes across the system. Dadas and Jorry link the incident at Davis to other protests across the globe:

> Incidents like Davis—as well as those that played out in other contexts such as
> Occupy Wall Street and the Arab Spring—indicate that political disruption is

carried out and sustained through complex systems of situated literate activity that occur over time and across myriad locations. As participants in these systems of literate activity, activists are compelled to navigate and manage a network of semiotic resources in which the potential of any given resources—its political value—is relative to its position in the network and not always readily apparent. In this way, such phenomena raise interesting questions about the available means of disruption and, more specifically, how individuals determine the affordances and limitations of the semiotic resources that enable disruption and challenge the status quo. (144)

Turning their attention to one "available means of disruption," Dadas and Jorry focus on semiotic remediation by analyzing remixed photos of the pepper-spraying; for instance, we see the cop spraying the Declaration of Independence, or assaulting a reclining female figure in an Andrew Wyeth painting. The remixes, which circulated widely on social media, constitute an attempted disruption of official narratives. The unruliness of the parodic images creates shock through juxtaposition. In the process, such images channel and amplify the original unruliness of the bodies of the protesters themselves in refusing to be removed from campus. Dadas and Jorry point out that such images, including video footage of the original pepper-spraying, put into circulation images of actual bodies under attack: "when [such images are] juxtaposed with administrative messages, the videos materialize the bodies of students and officers" (148).

From the vantage point of just these two examples, contemporary practices of protest seem a lively mix of bodies, technologies, and historically proven practices. Yet the technologically mediated dimensions of activist work have perhaps drawn the most scholarly attention, with some commentators arguing for new media as the leading factor in a new age of activism. In *Networks of Outrage and Hope: Social Movements in the Internet Age*, Manuel Castells focuses attention on many current activist projects, arguing that "the networked social movements of the digital age represent a new species of social movement" precisely because they "have been dependent on the existence of specific communication mechanisms" (15). Castells asserts that "multimodal, digital networks of horizontal communication are the fastest and most autonomous, interactive, reprogrammable and self-expanding means of communication in history" (15). His analysis becomes technologically determinist when he argues that "characteristics of communication processes between individuals engaged in the social movement determine the organization characteristics of the social movement itself: the more interactive and self-configurable communication is, the less hierarchical is the organization and the more participatory is the movement" (15). We take the force of his argument here, acknowledging the important role that technologies of communication have played in facilitating protest. But Castell's formulation obscures the role of other dimensions of contemporary protest. For instance, he maintains that the "faster and more interactive the process of communication is, the more likely the formation of a process of collective action becomes, rooted in outrage, propelled by enthusiasm and motivated by hope" (15). The speed of protest is important, surely, but Castell's gesture to affects, many long-standing and developing over decades, suggests histories of deeply felt and embodied desires to disrupt the status quo. As such, we might ask, what are the relationships among histories of protest, affects, technologies, and spontaneous assemblages? We are indebted to such studies for the ways they call attention to different forms of protest. Yet fascination with new technologies can obscure how much, as labor economist Kim Moody suggests, seemingly "new" forms of organization and resistance aren't "new in history" but, instead, are reclaimed as "new" for this era, foregrounding the technological element (7).

In this collection, then, we attend to such "networks of outrage" as they are vectored across different times and spaces via old and new media. It is possible to read scholarship like that of Dadas and Jorry, Castells, and others as attempts to translate unruly protest activities into (postmodern) forms of political argument (see DeLuca). If anything, though, these valuable amplifications suggest to us a more fundamental role for disruption in conceptualizing political activity and the need to analyze further the power of disruption and the unruly vis-à-vis politics. In this volume we give priority to unruliness as it disrupts what appears or is taken to be the normal flow of life. In the complex mix of histories, bodies, and technologies at play in each case examined by our contributors we collectively ask, What do we make of unruliness as political force? In recent events such as Occupy Wall Street and the Arab Spring, the extended span of time and mix of voices and media pose particular challenges for rhetorical analysis. Other cases—such feminist performances as SlutWalk and the interventions of Pussy Riot, for example—raise questions about participation, representation, and purpose. It is tempting to see unruliness as a kind of amorphous force breaking into the decorous and orderly spaces of public life. But as Tim Markham comments, "The valorization of amorphousness in protest cultures and social media enables affective and political projection, but overlooks politics in its institutional, professional and procedural forms" (94). Perhaps there is a problem with Markham's opposition between amorphousness and "politics." What is needed is an address to the "unruly" and the "political," and their relationship to, or undoing of, rhetoric as communication, at a more fundamental level.

THE UNRULY AND THE POLITICAL

The unruly permeates discussions of contemporary protest, including forms of argumentation, technologized and multi-mediated activism, and bodies on the line. Our genealogical gestures above begin to suggest the history and persistence of the unruly: its ability to inhabit various spaces and to link technologies, past and present, to bodies. Might the unruly, in fact, not take shape as just one of many rhetorical strategies within political activity but, perhaps, be constitutive of the political itself?

Recent rhetorical scholarship is pushing the inquiry in precisely this direction. Robert Cox and Christina R. Foust, for example, in their 2009 overview of social movement rhetoric track the development of a critical conversation in communications studies that calls into question social movements as already constituted entities whose members participate on the basis of stable identities and, through deliberation, arrive at coherent demands (610). The emergence of the term "counterpublic" in the 1990s out of Habermasian public sphere theory seems to open the critical terrain to some degree (see Cox and Foust 613; Warner), but even this analytic is at risk of losing its capacity to decenter "social movements" when its use marks recognizable group identities or issues as ontologically prior to the events at which they are called forth. As the critical language turns toward performance, resistance, and bodies in their materiality, it seems better able to capture the complexity of unruly events as we envision them. Critics such as M. Lane Bruner have shifted critical attention from the specific strategy goals of the demonstration or rally to an appreciation for states of liminality or the carnivalesque, created through complex and multi-stage events such as the Seattle World Trade Organization protests. Pursuing the extra- or nonsymbolic dimensions of protest opens up the possibility for understanding the phenomenon of assembly beyond the limits of the "political" defined in modernist terms as a structure of rational exchange between groups variously empowered or disempowered along the lines of constitutionally defined rights. Under these newer frames of understanding, assembled bodies have not only semiotic meaning, as Dadas and Jorry suggest, but material force exceeding the symbolic (see DeLuca).

As resources for reimagining the relationship between unruly rhetoric and the political, we turn to two theorists of continental political philosophy whose recent work on democratic/popular sovereignty—despite some differences—offers insights on rhetoric: Jacques Rancière and Judith Butler. In brief, for Rancière, unruliness is constitutive of politics; for Butler, unruliness speaks to and from the pervasive condition of the precarity of life. For each, existential conditions of inequality or unlivability are the inescapable conditions of the "political" and can be addressed rhetorically.

Jacques Rancière asserts that politics itself "revolves around what is seen and what can be said about it, around who has the ability to see and the talent to speak, around the properties of spaces and the possibilities of time" (*The Politics of Aesthetics* 13). Rancière's understanding of the democratic polis is deeply rhetorical. He begins by exploring the processes and mechanisms through which certain kinds of ideas come into view and who can talk about them. But such processes seem inevitably to result in the exclusion of many different voices and views. So Rancière redefines the argumentative process of democracy itself, not as rational actors meeting at a table to debate but, rather, as the process that "makes visible what had no business being seen, and makes heard a discourse where once there was only place for noise; it makes understood as discourse what was once only heard as noise" (*Disagreement* 30). For Rancière, democracy is a "rupture in the order of legitimacy and domination," dependent on subjects engaged in perpetual dissensus, or "the making contentious of the givens of a particular situation" (Panagia and Rancière 124). While Warner figures a counterpublic as a space of alternative scene-making that may one day be transformative for how the dominant public sphere conducts its business, Rancière imagines democracy itself as ongoing disruption, as those subjects who had not even been capable of being seen breaking into the frame of vision, their voices once heard as noise making themselves heard in the conversation. Such a view departs radically from the conventions of deliberative rhetoric with its "desires to have well-identifiable groups with specific interests, aspirations, values, and 'culture'" (Panagia and Rancière 125). Rancière actually understands consensus as the "negation of the democratic basis for politics" (Panagia and Rancière 125) and imagines in its place democracy as perpetually unruly.

For Rancière, inequality is the given condition of the political: "Politics, as we will see, is that activity which turns on equality as its principle. And the principle of equality is transformed by the distribution of community shares as defined by a quandary: when is there and when is there not equality in things between who and who else? What are these 'things' and who are these whos?" (*Disagreement* ix). Arendt imagines democracy through a similar figure: "To live together in the world means essentially that a world of things is between those who have it in common as a table is located between those who sit around it; the world, like every in-between, relates and separates men at the same time" (xx). But because her world is peopled only by those who do not labor, there is never an issue about who shows up at this table. For Rancière, on the other hand, "The struggle between the rich and the poor is not social reality, which politics has then to deal with. It is the actual institution of politics itself. There is politics when there is a part of those who have no part, a part or party of the poor" (*Disagreement* 11). And as such, politics demands or expects spatial disruption: "Political activity is whatever shifts a body from the place assigned to it or changes a place's destination" (30). We come to understand the rhetorical implications of such a reorientation as Rancière marks the difference between "the discursive articulation of a grievance"—that is, a conventional agonistic discourse—and "the phonic articulation of a groan" as the primal or disruptive expression of inequity (2). Rancière explains his foundational conception of how "protest" comes into being: "Spectacular or otherwise, political activity is always a mode of expression that undoes the perceptible divisions of the police order by implementing a basically heterogenous assumption, that of a part of those who have no part, an assumption that, at the end of the day, itself demonstrates the sheer contingency of the order, the equality of any speaking being with any other speaking being. Politics occurs when there is a place and a way for two heterogenous processes to meet" (30). Rancière makes clear that protest does not arise out of a periodic recognition of "wrongs"—those exceptional occasions on which things are going badly and *people* rise up and correct wrongs, returning the state to its normal order. But, rather, "The concept of wrong is not linked to any theater of 'victimization.' It belongs to the original structure of all politics" (39). Thus Rancière makes it possible for us to reorient our analytic questions. A conventional rhetorical analysis would ask, Why now? Against which wrongs? Or with what technology? Or with what arguments, groups, and goals? Instead we ask, How does this particular emergence of the unruly give expression to the fundamental inequality grounding the political?

Similarly, Butler begins her recent work *Notes toward a Performative Theory of Assembly* by noting a disjunction between "the political form of democracy and the principle of popular sovereignty" (2). In her formulation, the latter designates a more primal political condition, one that "has to precede and exceed any form of government that confers and protects that right of assembly" (160). Freedom of assembly, asserts Butler, "may well be a precondition of politics itself" (160). It is a "performative power that lays claim to the public in a way that is not yet codified into law and that can never be fully codified into law. This performativity is not only speech, but the demands of bodily action, gesture, movement, congregation, persistence, and the exposure to possible violence. How do we understand this acting together that opens up time and space outside and against the established architecture and temporality of the regime, one that lays claim to materiality, leans into its supports, and draws from its material and technical dimensions to rework their functions?" (75).

Questioning the term "we the people," Butler speculates, "Perhaps 'the people' is that designation that exceeds any and every visual frame that seeks to capture the people, and the more democratic frames are those that are able to orchestrate their porous character" (165). She asserts that democratic freedom demands "plural acts and pluralities of bodies" (182).

Perhaps more forcefully (or vividly) than Rancière, Butler is attuned to the precarity of life unrecognized by conventional political theories. She holds that there is "an irreducible fact of politics: the vulnerability to destruction by others that follows from a condition of precarity in all modes of political and social interdependency" (118). Emphasizing the dependencies of bodies on each other, Butler observes that "vulnerability is also not just a trait or an episodic disposition of a discrete body, but is, rather, a mode of relationality that time and again calls some aspect of that discreteness into question" (130). Differentiating her position from Arendt's, for whom the unbearable is the difficulty of entering into a political relation with others, Butler acknowledges that people assembling will have differences from one another. Political struggles—scenes of protest—are, for Butler, not solely about meeting specific demands: "After all, even if we come to understand and enumerate the requirements of the body in the name of which people enter into political struggle, are we claiming that political struggle achieves its aims when those requirements are met? Or do we struggle as well for bodies to thrive, for life to become livable?" (133). For both Rancière and Butler, politics or protest is not caused by the temporary failure of systems and structures to enfranchise people or groups but, rather, erupts periodically out of the pressure to respond to the fundamental inequality and persistent precarity of life. Its temporal, spatial, and technological reach is unlimited.

Such insights emerge not only in continental philosophy but also from other lines of thought in recent rhetorical analysis. In an influential essay from the late 1990s, Kevin Michael DeLuca works with the embodied quality of radical environmental and queer protests. He argues for images of the protesting body as making arguments but also notes that the body in such events functions as a site of incoherence (20). He sees the body as being both socially constructed and excessive, and he highlights "public arguments that exceed the bonds of reason and words" (20). Expanding the range and modalities of protest seems a hallmark of activist work at the turn of the century. Marking the twenty-first century as an era with new rhetorical challenges, Kevin Mahoney argues, "The current assault upon all forms of democratic participation . . . makes it necessary to engage in a very different kind of project" (152). Citing Michael Hardt and Antonio Negri's *Empire*, Mahoney observes that "the most intense and broad-based political movements/rebellions within Empire are 'all but incom-

municable'" (154). Echoing this trope of "incommunicability" as well as Butler's precarity, Kelly E. Happe sees rhetoric in Occupy as "an extension of an
already existing vulnerability" (211). Her analysis draws on Foucault's reading
of *parrhēsia* not as a "free speech, dependent on conventions of intelligibility"
but, rather, as an opening or rupture (216–17). From many philosophical and
rhetorical perspectives, then, the political is the collective groan of deeply felt
precarity and vulnerability sounding out as unruly protest.

The line of theorizing we have laid out here would suggest that unruliness breaks out spontaneously, driven by existential conditions, and certainly this is so in many scenes of political protest. But unruliness can also
be staged as a rhetorical tactic. In our 2014 article "Rhetorical Education
and Student Activism," we examine a staged disruption of a talk by the Israeli ambassador Michael Oren on the University of California, Irvine (UCI)
campus. Students from the Muslim Student Union (MSU), who later became known as the Irvine 11, stood up at different points during Oren's talk
to shout out slogans that called into question his honesty and ethics, citing
his participation in the relocation or even death of many Palestinians. What
seemed an unruly even hostile eruption of anger was, rather, a carefully
choreographed protest that had taken months of planning, debate, and self-
sponsored education to enact. Students in the MSU investigated different strategies of protest, considered multiple options, and debated tactics. Their goal
was not just to critique Oren but also to bring to attention how they believed
their views had not been heard or attended to in previous forums and platforms for debate about the Middle East at UCI. As we put it, the "students
focused more on the modality of the exchange itself—the genre or structure of
the event—and less on the message" (535). Such conscious attention to framing, we assert, characterizes unruly rhetoric as rhetorical practice.

Rhetorical preparation for such unruliness can be fostered within as well as
outside the curriculum. Nancy Welch has for over a decade advocated for rhetorical pedagogies that pay attention to bodies engaged in political action, particularly at a time when the mass circulation of information about politics can
seem overwhelming. In *Living Room: Teaching Public Writing in a Privatized
World*, she worries that students are developing a reduced notion of the complexity of argument, debate, and protest, particularly when compared to the
vibrancy of contemporary forms of civil unrest: "we should be collectively concerned about the disturbing gap between actual demonstrations of mass public
argumentation and what many of our students, in their classrooms and in the
wider culture, learn about leaving arguments to the experts or until the next
election" (143–44). She proposes potential remedies in her article with Tony
Scott, "One Train Can Hide Another: Critical Materialism for Public Com-

position," in which she and her coauthor call for "enacting pedagogies that embrace . . . public rhetorical work in full, embodied form" (575). Arguing for critical materialism as a counter to the dematerializing tendencies (leaving the body behind) of public composition pedagogies and approaches to rhetoric, they state, "Just as one train can hide another, when our conceptions of public rhetorical practice prioritize discursive features and digitized form over—and to the exclusion of—historical context and human consequences, we miss how texts may mobilize meaning not to upend but to reinforce relations of power" (565). Recognizing how the bodies of protesters themselves are often on the line and at risk when protesting connects the circulation of abstract ideas with the lived realities of people fighting injustice, the authors note that such recognition is a "materially challenging task given the urgency of social and environmental conditions plus the speed, volume, and insistence of new media texts vying for attention" (575). But Scott and Welch insist that thinking carefully through those conditions is necessary to create a more informed—and potentially engaged—citizenry.

RHETORICS OF THE UNRULY

We believe that current projects in rhetoric and writing studies can be brought into fruitful contact with new political philosophies. Toward this end, we ask, how do we articulate the unruly within the political? Butler herself frames such a question: "I'm using one word after another, searching for a set of related terms as a way of approaching a problem that resists a technical nomenclature; no single word can adequately describe the character and the aim of this human striving, this striving in concert or this striving together that seems to form one meaning of political movement or mobilization" (133). We propose that "unruly" might be one word that, while hardly totalizing or encompassing all political striving, marks how speech, action, and bodies coalesce in time and space, enacting the work of politics in the ways Rancière, Butler, and contemporary rhetorical critics have imagined.

Out of what does such unruliness coalesce? As we saw in Alexander and Jarratt's analysis of the Irvine 11 and the students' staged protest of Michael Oren, some unruliness is tactical, a conscious strategy deployed to interrupt existing norms of political debate and discussion. In a way, the very presence of visibly nonwhite, likely Muslim bodies at the scene of the speech might itself have seemed to some to be potentially unruly, an incursion of (unwanted) presences. Indeed, some bodies in particular contexts are prone to being constituted as unruly, such as the bodies of women or racial minorities. And even other unruliness, following Rancière, arises as an un-premeditated groan, a deeply perceived if not fully conscious sense of needing to be heard in situations and in conversations in which one's voice is either actively elided or not yet legible. Those groans might constitute the political, but they do so as pre-articulate expressions across multiple political positions, from left to right. Given the different origins of unruliness, then, an ethics of unruliness based on its ontology may be less useful than a consideration of ethical action in the aftermath of unruliness. What do we do after we hear the groan? As rhetoricians, we are inclined to favor those unrulinesses that are then followed by an opening of the field of discussants and attention to the previously illegible.

Readers might note that many of the examples here, as well as those discussed throughout the chapters of this book, focus on left-leaning and progressivist forms of activism. These choices reflect the orientations of the authors and editors of this volume. But we acknowledge that a left-leaning disposition may not be a requisite for ethical unruly rhetorical practice. For instance, students in the Muslim Student Union described in Alexander and Jarratt's article may not consider themselves "left-leaning" per se, and they might hold religious views that others would consider "conservative." Further, recent events during the run-up to the 2016 presidential election, such as protests that turned violent outside rallies for Donald J. Trump, certainly suggest a kind of unruliness. In Rancière's parlance, we might understand the violence outside a Trump rally as "noise" arising out of a sense of precarity and outrage; unruliness becoming rhetorical is the process of "mak[ing] understood as *discourse* where what was only heard as noise" (*Disagreement* 30, emphasis added). At the same time, though, we might assert that an *ethical* unruly rhetorical practice, while not inherently left-leaning, is one that aims to bring to light an inequality (in Rancière's terms) or precarity (in Butler's) by disrupting routinized exchange within the public sphere. Contemporary examples of unruly rhetorical protest are pitched at disrupting local and global structures of social and political inequality, racial and gender-based injustice, and governmental overreach and abuse. The progressivist nature of such unruly rhetoric is part of our sociopolitical and cultural moment. In contrast, some Trump supporters, seeking an authoritarian figure to resolve their political problems, turn to the violence of unruliness to seek security (in Butler's terms) and "policing" (in Rancière's) as solutions to inequities; thus democratic exchange of any kind is unwelcome. As Butler puts it, "The opposite of precarity is not security, but, rather, the struggle for an egalitarian social and political order in which a livable interdependency becomes possible" (69). Trump supporters who hit, spit on, and violently expel protestors, urged on to such violence by their leader, are enacting just the opposite of livable interdependency, their unruliness arising from a reactive impulse to exclude and silence any voices other than that of the demagogue.

Even more recent unrulinesses might serve as examples when considering what kind of unruliness turns toward the generative and which does not. Close to home in 2016, Jonathan stumbled across a sign on his campus announcing an upcoming talk by former Brietbart correspondent Milo Yiannopolous. The handmade poster proclaimed in large block letters, "Who are we to let such dangerous faggotry go unpunished?" The provocation, particularly the use of the word "faggotry" on a college campus in southern California, which is more hospitable than not to queer people, was intended to be tactically unruly in getting attention and provoking comment. Such unruliness was likely intended to bring to the fore a view about homosexuality that was at odds with attitudes held by many students and faculty on a fairly liberal-minded campus and thus is a use of unruly speech *seemingly* to expand the conversation and include other voices about controversial topics. But while Jonathan didn't necessarily object to Yiannopolous's appearance on campus, he felt, as a queer man, the verbal assault of both the word "faggotry" and the implied need for queers to be punished. Many others, especially queer students, felt similarly, seeing not a call for discussion but an attempt to silence—and particularly, to silence those who have only just begun in the last half century to find a voice, to turn the groan of homophobic oppression into articulate claims for civil rights.

More dramatically, the confrontations among police and protestors at neo-Nazi and white supremacist marches in Charlottesville, Virginia, on August 11–12, 2017, resulting in at least one death, speak to another example of right-wing unruliness attempting to call attention to its racist views. And while one might argue that such views might deserve a hearing in an open and democratic society, we can't help but see the use of Nazi salutes and gestures simulating lynching as forms of psychic terrorism intended to belittle, demean, and threaten. Again, white supremacists' unruliness might signal their desire to be heard, but its ultimate aims are pitched at the silencing of others—at the raising of one set of voices at the expense of others. In contrast, we want to draw attention to unruly rhetorical practices that highlight both the precarity of lives and conditions of being as well as the insufficiency of prevailing or dominant platforms for public conversation. At times, these are not just disruptions that happen to have rhetorical force but, rather, are disruptions that have drawn attention to oppressive structures and walled-off attitudes; as such, they are in service not of the mob (*ochlos*) but of the *demos* (Rancière, *Politics of Aesthetics* 84).

Our contributors take up our call to consider the role of the unruly in the complex matrix of bodies, technologies, and histories that animate political protest in service of the "livable interdependence" evoked by Butler. While not every author posits the unruly as constitutive of politics, as Rancière and Butler seem to do, they all explore how the unruly moves through many different ways of understanding contemporary political protest and its historical roots. For some scholars of composition, rhetoric, and communication studies, the ideals of discursive rationalism, stakeholders-at-the-table mediation, or dematerialized circulating discourses still hold sway, but many intermingle older and newer modes of analysis. Recognizing the ongoing importance of named collective goals and modes of representation to political activity, the contributors to this volume stage fresh encounters with the unruly as a flexible tool of analysis. In the process, contributors variously consider how new platforms of dissemination as well as long-standing rhetorical assumptions about civil discourse and effective argument might be informed and complicated by unruly bodies and gatherings. Along such lines, they ask, What threats do unruly rhetorics stage to the body politic and what role do ideals and pedagogies of civil discourse play with reference to the vulnerable body of the citizen? How can historical examinations complicate analyses that might otherwise be drawn from single moments of upsurge? How do interactions of embodied rhetoric and other rhetorical means re-create public space and public hearing? And what does a fuller understanding of unruliness bring to the teaching of rhetorics?

In the fifteen chapters that follow, scholars analyze specific cases of unruliness in public scenes ranging from street demonstrations to encounters in state houses and on university campuses to staged performances and occupations. To contextualize and deepen our understanding of bodily assemblage and performance, a number of chapters take up historical precedents and literary articulations of unruliness. Mediated encounters are tracked in chapters on an alternative newspaper, social media agonistics, and projects for writing and teaching unruly rhetorics. The chapters are grouped in three sections, "Bringing Back the Body," "Civility Wars," and "Limits and Horizons," with each part designed to explore unruliness as an outbreak of political expression or as a form of rhetorical action or as a complex merging of force and tactic that mobilizes bodies, technologies, and histories in civic protest. The three sections call attention to three manifestations of or approaches to the notion of the unruly. Essays in each section highlight a particular aspect, but as you will see, there are overlapping elements in many.

PART I: BRINGING BACK THE BODY

It is the body that suffers precarity, and it is through the assembly of visible and audible bodies—often in unexpected and unsanctioned places—that the "people" claim a share in the communal (Rancière, *Politics of Aesthetics* 84). Thus we begin with Dana L. Cloud's essay "Feminist Body Rhetoric in the #unrulymob, Texas, 2013," which analyzes the 2013 "people's filibuster" in the Texas state legislature—an uprising against a draconian antiabortion bill that also produced backlash rhetoric naming women as an "unruly mob" that might use tampons and feces as weapons. Cloud traces how women's bodies are both the site of public ideological and political contestation *and* the repository of the unruly: everything regarded as private, dangerous, disgusting—ruling women out of public political bounds. In a similar vein in "Walking with Relatives: Indigenous Bodies of Protest," Joyce Rain Anderson insists on a continuing tradition of Indigenous resistance to the colonial forces that have sought to eradicate Indigenous bodies for centuries in order to claim and exploit the land. In particular, Anderson focuses on Idle No More, a US and Canadian movement against the Keystone XL and Dakota pipelines, hydraulic fracturing, mass hydropower projects, and more. She discusses the hunger strike, "flashmob" style dance, and occupations that bring Native bodies into public focus, and in so doing, make visible Indigenous strategies of protection and maintenance—long-term practices built on continuity rather than the short-term impulse of protest.

We turn next to a dramatic claim of embodied audibility: Canadian media and sound studies scholar Jonathan Sterne's "A Groove We Can Move To: The Sound and Sense of Quebec's *Manifs Casseroles*, Spring 2012." For some hundred days in the spring of 2012, Montreal university students, joined each night by the city's Francophone residents, carried out a raucous pot-banging social strike, part of a province-wide struggle against austerity cuts to university education and a draconian anti-protest law. In this essay, Sterne draws readers into the sound and sense of the *manifs casseroles*. In addition to providing in-the-moment snapshots of a movement that resulted in the (temporary) victories of overthrowing the provincial government and staving off tuition hikes, Sterne connects the pot-banging protests to the history of charivari or "rough music" and its uses in contemporary protests, from Quebec and Argentina to Iceland and Spain, to counter neoliberal austerity, atomization, and alienation with a public, embodied, and mass "politics of possibility."

But what *is* possible when a body is unruly or when calling attention to unruly bodies? Matthew Abraham, in "Steven Salaita's Rhetorical Refusal: Taking to Twitter as a Form of Political Resistance and Protest," offers an examination of scholar Steven Salaita's tweets during the summer of 2014 as an example of unruly rhetorical practice powerfully drawing attention to bodies in peril. While roundly criticized in some quarters for being uncivil, Salaita's public comments allow Abraham an opportunity to explore how rhetorical refusals to play by the rules of normative discourse can throw into stark relief the ongoing precariousness of Palestinian bodies. And finally, returning us to women's bodies in "SlutWalk Is Not Enough: Notes toward a Critical Feminist Rhetoric," Jacqueline Rhodes examines the viral SlutWalk protests as both a rhetorically savvy blend of real bodies, sex, and social media needed to challenge entrenched patriarchal culture and, simultaneously, a continuation of mainstream (white) feminism's complicitous relationship to white supremacist patriarchy. The SlutWalk wave of in-your-face protests against slut-shaming, victim-blaming, and rape culture marks a much-needed continuation and updating of Take Back the Night and other forms of feminist street theater of the past half century. At the same time, the protests mark a continuation of white feminist privilege and exclusions. In a reading that both appreciates this twenty-first-century manifestation of feminist critical action and cautions that it is "not enough," Rhodes argues for an antiracist, critical feminist consciousness characterized by performance, virality, and a constitutive intersectionality that not only expand feminism's methods but challenge its goals.

PART II: CIVILITY WARS

In the next section, authors focus on the ways the standard of civility comes under scrutiny and containment by various forces: the state, the status quo, or the forces of so-called security (what Rancière would term "policing") but also the seemingly neutral or innocuous surrounds of middle-class sensibilities and professional organizations. Nancy Welch, in "Informed, Passionate, and Disorderly: Uncivil Rhetoric in a New Gilded Age," juxtaposes historical and contemporary disputes over "civil" modes of protest. Just as a prominent contemporary antinuclear activist chastises other nuclear power protestors for their "incivility" and "mob mentality" in protests of the Nuclear Regulatory Commission, the turn-of-the-twentieth-century settlement movement condemned the now celebrated 1912 Bread and Roses strike in the same terms. Welch demonstrates how, in the last Gilded Age as well as in our own, a ruling class enlists middle-class sentiments to defend a civil order—not for the good of democracy but against it. The next chapter, "Circulating Voices of Dissent: Rewriting the Life of James Eads How and *Hobo News*," by Diana George and Paula Mathieu, takes us to another turn-of-the-twentieth-century medium for dissent: the *Hobo News* published by "hobo millionaire" James Eads How. George and Mathieu use the case study of How's curious personality and his mainstream reception in order to highlight the pathologizing of homelessness as well as the potential for forming coherent counterpublic vehicles through which radical views could meet and ideas circulate. Through material analysis —not of typeface and design but of the embodied means of distribution and dissemination—George and Mathieu trace the multiple, shifting, and always mass collaborative tactics of dissident groups to circulate ideas in the face of power structures that would seek to shut them down.

In a personal testimony, Kevin Mahoney tracks the crosscurrents of two contemporary movements, testing their implications for teachers and scholars of rhetoric in "We Are Not All in This Together: The Case for Advocacy, Factionalism, and Making the Political Personal." While a National Task Force on higher education produced *A Crucible Moment* calling for civility as the antidote to the toxicity of public discourse that followed the election of the United States' first African American president, Republican governor Scott Walker's unbridled assault on Wisconsin's public universities and collective bargaining rights demanded a bolder response: "throwing one's body on the gears of the machine." Mahoney reclaims Thomas Paine's critical stance on civility, including the tactical and necessary uses of factionalism, as necessary to defending democracy's project. Reporting from within the crucible of a university protest, Yanira Rodríguez and Ben Kuebrich chronicle their experiences with an eighteen-day sit-in at Syracuse University in "The Tone It Takes: An Eighteen-Day Sit-In at Syracuse University." They document the ways that institutional rhetorics of free-market neutrality, coupled with academic ideals of civility and scholarly detachment, attempted to neutralize resistance to the corporate restructuring of higher education. Ultimately, the authors call for recognition that the result of embodied dissent is not division but proximity, the proximity on which deliberation and exchange depend. In a third essay focused on the university scene, John Trimbur attempts to make sense of why the Conference on College Composition and Communication and the National Council of Teachers of English, unlike other professional associations, failed to issue a statement protesting the University of Illinois at Urbana-Champaign's firing of newly hired Stephen Salaita in 2014. In "The Steven Salaita Case: Public Rhetoric and the Political Imagination in US College Composition and Its Professional Associations," Trimbur speculates that the position might be understood as emblematic of the organizations' shared ethos of decency, sincerity, and responsibility, which have made them prey, on one hand, to neoliberal "responsibilized accountability" and leery, on the other hand, of the unruliness of the political imagination as seen in Situationist, punk, and performative styles.

PART III: LIMITS AND HORIZONS

Essays in this final section highlight the complexities of unruly performances while simultaneously recovering and celebrating the unruly—the sexual, the profane, the playful, and the persistent—as interventive forms of political behavior. Drawing on a literary resource, Deborah Mutnick in "Answering the World's Anticipation: The Relevance of *Native Son* to Twenty-First-Century Protest Movements" analyzes twenty-first-century activist responses to structural racism and endemic police brutality in light of Richard Wright's powerfully influential novel. Adopting conceptional lenses from Marx and Bakhtin, as well as Wright's own language regarding his novel's "x-ray vision," Mutnick traces Wright's dialectical understanding of black life and white power structures. This dialectical understanding and the x-ray vision that enables it, Mutnick argues, can help rhetoricians see more clearly how the rhetoric of liberal democracy—the rhetoric of "the open hand"—masks the violent means by which white power structures control and destroy the Bigger Thomases of the world. Moving from race to language in "*Dignitas* and 'Shit Shovels': Corporate Bodies and Unruly Language," Jason Peters asserts that bodies and a body politic are constituted through linguistic regimentation. Peters reads the unruly (and even profane) rhetorical style of a 1920s New England French-language activist whose use of immigrant working-class French to challenge Catholic Church English-only policies is suggestive of an alternative, hybridized, local needs–inflected conception of language. At the same time, Peters draws out the ways linguistic fluidity—in this and other language-rights movements—is enlisted for an argument that would protect the purity of a national language and ultimately suppress alternate language practices and values.

In "Remix as Unruly Play and Participatory Method for Im/Possible Queer World–Making," Londie T. Martin and Adela C. Licona introduce another medium for the emergence of unruliness. This chapter features the efforts of teens in an Arizona social justice summer camp through their digital video remixes to speak back to punitive state forces and laws that would herd students through a school-to-prison pipeline and pathologize their sexual identities. The videos, Martin and Licona observe, are indeed haunted by normative, neoliberal, and utopian discourses. Such discourses, however, exist in a playful and productive tension with the videos' queer world–making tactics—creating through what Lauren Berlant terms "aspirational normativity," the insistent and persistent hope for a better life through which a queer futurity can be glimpsed. Working with the power of a different set of voices in "On Democracy's Return Home: The Occupation of Liberty/Zuccotti Park," John Ackerman and Meghan Dunn take inspiration from one of the authors' participatory study of the Occupy Wall Street movement and their collective interest in the *chora*, a place that acts as a kind of receptacle holding the potential for a different form of living to take place. Offering the results of fieldwork conducted during the Wall Street occupation, Ackerman and Dunn argue that Occupy provided—and continues to provide—the fertile ground for the emergence of new ideas and alternative democratic modalities. They invite us to attend to the time of the political, recognizing that "voices will fall silent" for a time, returning to "the residua of the everyday," but that this waning can also be met by a "slow, yet vital, recovery"—a reclamation of the demos, multi-sited, without demands other than the possibility for a livable life, for plural existence in public space.

The final chapter in the volume returns us to bodies on the line—in this case those of educators and activists from the Middle East and North Africa (MENA) seeking to carry forward the Arab Spring's rhetoric of hope in the face of the grim and de-democratizing conditions—including military usurpation of power in Egypt and devastating civil war in Syria—that have followed. In "Then Comes Fall: Activism, the Arab Spring, and the Necessity of Unruly Borders," Steve Parks and his coauthors challenge US rhetorical scholars to understand how they are implicated in and should be hailed by the life-and-death tasks undertaken by MENA educators and activists, including grasping the connections between the barbarous acts perpetuated upon a civilian population and the seeming logic of academic writing. Introducing the work of Syrian activist Bassam Alahmad, Parks traces the alternative rhetorical framings that academics might deploy as they attempt to write, publish, and teach in solidarity with those struggling for a geographically and culturally specific survival.

Nancy Welch's "Afterword: Science, Politics, and the Messy Arts of Rhetoric" concludes the volume with some of the probing questions that we hope our readers will continue to consider—in both activist and scholarly work. What are the implications of unruly rhetorics as we have theorized and analyzed them here? Can the practice of unruliness be learned and repeated? Should unruly rhetorics be taught? One of the strong implications of this work is that rhetoric as a theory and practice of conventional deliberation—including the solid principles of reasoning, argumentation, and persuasion taught in many rhetoric classes—exists in an uneasy or tenuous relationship with other forms of political expression, both historically and in today's contemporary political scene. Numbers of rhetoric and writing teachers are committed to activism and have devised creative ways of incorporating activist elements into their curricula. Do such efforts lead to "unruliness"? The diversity and complexity of the cases laid out in the preceding chapters suggest that any attempt to formalize or regularize the unruly as we present it would do an injustice to the spontaneity, creativity, and local specificity of such outbreaks. Indeed, the idea of teaching unruliness seems like the opposite of the unruly.

That said, we recognize ways that political actors have learned from each other, often outside of educational settings (see, for example, Logan, *Liberating Language*). Martin Luther King Jr.'s adoption of Mohandas K. Gandhi's practices of nonviolence is a classic example. More recently, we note the way Gene Sharp's 1973 primer for nonviolence was translated into Arabic and circulated as a plan of action by Egyptian activists in the early days of the January 25, 2011, movement (Madrigal). As teachers of rhetoric, we can use the approaches and examples here to help students inquire deeply into the contexts of and pressures on rhetors in any and every moment where the inequality postulated by Rancière breaks out. Such analyses will lead to a more profound appreciation for the precarity from which people express their sovereignty and a sharper awareness of those forces that drive them to assemble: the threat to life and safety of intellectuals in the Middle East (Parks et al., this volume), of black citizens in US cities (Mutnick, this volume), of women anywhere and everywhere in public (Rhodes, this volume), as we are being reminded so vividly in the wake of Trump's bragging about sexual assault.

Perhaps the most compelling finding here comes from the insights concerning the time and place of "the political" or of popular sovereignty as free assembly. As Anderson observes about the Indigenous peoples responding to the pipeline projects, they have not gathered for a one-time protest but see themselves as perpetual protectors. Similarly with Ackerman and Dunn's observations about the Occupy "movement," we can use the "unruly" to rethink the time and space of the political itself, of assembly, and of rhetorical action.

WORKS CITED

Alexander, Jonathan, and Susan C. Jarratt. "Rhetorical Education and Student Activism." *College English* 76, no. 6 (July 2014): 525–44.

Arendt, Hannah. *The Human Condition*. University of Chicago Press, 1958.

Bishara, Marwan. *The Invisible Arab: The Promise and Peril of the Arab Revolutions*. Nation Books, 2012.

Bruner, M. Lane. "Carnivalesque Protest and the Humorless State." *Text and Performance Quarterly* 25 (2005): 136–55.

Butler, Judith. *Notes toward a Performative Theory of Assembly*. Harvard University Press, 2015.

Castells, Manuel. *Networks of Outrage and Hope: Social Movements in the Internet Age*. Polity, 2012.

Cox, Robert, and Christina R. Foust. "Social Movement Rhetoric." *The SAGE Handbook of Rhetorical Studies*, edited by Andrea A. Lunsford, Kirt H. Wilson, and Rosa A. Eberly, 605–27. Sage, 2009.

Dadas, Caroline, and Justin Jorry. "Toward an Economy of Activist Literacies in Composition Studies: Possibilities for Political Disruption." *Literacy in Composition Studies* 3, no. 1 (March 2015): 143–55.

DeLuca, Kevin Michael. "Unruly Arguments: The Body Rhetoric of Earth First! Act Up, and Queer Nation." *Argument and Advocacy* 36, no. 1 (1999): 9–21.

DeLuca, Kevin Michael, Sean Lawson, and Ye Sun. "Occupy Wall Street on the Public Screens of Social Media: The Many Framings of the Birth of a Social Movement." *Communication, Culture & Critique* 5, no. 4 (2012): 483–509.

Happe, Kelly E. "*Parrhēsia*, Biopolitics, and Occupy." *Philosophy and Rhetoric* 48, no. 2 (2015): 211–23.

Kahn, Seth, and Jong Hwa Lee, eds. *Activism and Rhetoric: Theories and Contexts for Political Engagement.* Routledge, 2011.

Lim, Merlyna. "Clicks, Cabs, and Coffee Houses: Social Media and Oppositional Movements in Egypt, 2004–2011." *Journal of Communication* 62, no. 2 (2012): 231–48.

Logan, Shirley Wilson. *Liberating Language: Sites of Rhetorical Education in Nineteenth-Century Black America.* Southern Illinois University Press, 2008.

Madrigal, Alexis C. "Egyptian Activists' Action Plan: Translated." *The Atlantic*, January 27, 2011.

Mahoney, Kevin. "You Can't Get There from Here: Higher Education, Labor Activism, and Challenges of Neoliberal Globalization." In Kahn and Lee, 147–58.

Markham, Tim. "Social Media, Protest Cultures and Political Subjectivities of the Arab Spring." *Media, Culture & Society* 36, no. 1 (January 2014): 89–104.

Moody, Kim. *U.S. Labor in Trouble and Transition: The Failure of Reform from Above, the Promise of Revival from Below.* Verso, 2007.

Panagia, Davide, and Jacques Rancière. "Dissenting Words: A Conversation with Jacques Rancière." *Diacritics* 39, no. 2 (2000): 113–26.

Rancière, Jacques. *Disagreement: Politics and Philosophy.* Translated by Julie Rose. University of Minnesota Press, 1999.

Rancière, Jacques. *The Politics of Aesthetics.* Bloomsbury Academic, 2013.

Scott, Tony, and Nancy Welch. "One Train Can Hide Another: Critical Materialism for Public Composition." *College English* 76, no. 6 (July 2014): 562–79.

Sharp, Gene. *The Politics of Nonviolent Action.* Porter Sargent, 1973.

Warner, Michael. *Publics and Counterpublics.* Zone Books, 2002.

Welch, Nancy. *Living Room: Teaching Public Writing in a Privatized World.* Boynton/Cook, 2008.

PART I

BRINGING BACK
THE BODY

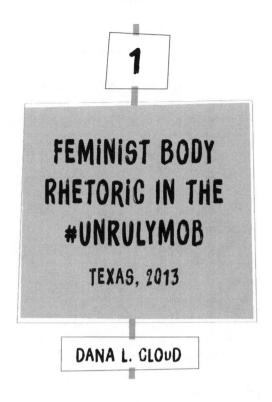

1

FEMINIST BODY RHETORIC IN THE #UNRULYMOB

TEXAS, 2013

DANA L. CLOUD

If we don't invent a language, if we don't find our body's language, it will have too few gestures to accompany our story. We shall tire of the same ones and leave our desires unexpressed, unrealized. Asleep again, unsatisfied, we shall fall back upon the words of men—who, for their part, have "known" for a long time. But *not our body*.

—Luce Irigaray (88)

R hetorical appeals to decorum and civility can perform functions of social discipline. This discipline can take the form of a condemnation of affect, the condemnation of crowds and mass protest, and the condemnation of controversial views as in and of themselves "hurtful" (Cloud, "Civility"). Such disciplining rhetorics are deployed when women (whose affect is suspect), queer persons, persons of color and other minorities (whose standpoints are suspect), and activist groups (whose bodies are feared but whose demands are suspect) rise up to challenge hegemonic power. Yet sometimes a movement rises to make its demands heard and, in the process, successfully protests both oppressive policy and the conventions of politeness and decorum that mask power. Kevin Michael DeLuca has made this argument with regard to the "body rhetoric" of the activist groups ACT UP, Queer Nation, and Earth First! He describes how the invasion of hetero-familial space by queer organizations formed "radically democratic disorganizations" (9; see also Haiman). DeLuca concludes that bodies are an unorthodox resource for advocacy that rejects formal modes of public argument. Similarly, Nathan Stormer examines how the naked body can "speak" in public through the violation of norms of decorum and morality.

More than extending the idea of the body as a rhetorical resource in general, however, my purpose is to offer a specifically gendered analysis that forefronts the urgency of the recognition of women's bodies in public discourse. Women's bodies are simultaneously the site of ideological and political contestation in public and the repository of everything private, dangerous, disgusting, and out of bounds in politics proper. When women, in Irigaray's terms, find "our bodies' language," we come up against what men in the context of hegemonic masculinity and the privatization of social responsibility (which requires women's containment) "have known for a long time": that women who can tell the stories of our bodies and our desires and demand their satisfaction are not just unruly but dangerous.

A case in point is the "people's filibuster," an uprising of thousands of Texans against a draconian omnibus antiabortion bill in the Texas legislature in 2013. Texas conservative politicians denigrated participants in the feminist uprising in Texas as an "unruly mob." The discourse of the Texas Republicans was obsessed with the bodies of protesters, and especially the scatological and reproductive regions of those bodies. They had entrants to the Capitol searched for non-existent "jars of poop" and banned tampons from entering the premises lest they be used as projectiles or to wick Molotov cocktails. The activists, emboldened by the absurdity of the politicians' apparent terror of women, appropriated the discourse of unruliness and the symbols of bodily leakage, wearing hats and garments made of tampons and using labels to coordinate action on Twitter around the hashtags #unrulymob and #feministarmy.[1] The shift from the former (mob) to the latter (army) rearticulated the force of organized numbers as a coherent intentional political vehicle.

In what follows, I will describe the interrelated rhetorical elements of unruly rhetorics as the feminist uprising at the Texas Capitol in 2013 embodied them: the comic frame, scatology, and the material force of bodies. Each of these elements is a violation of conventional rules of decorum, and the protests against the antiabortion bills also amounted to a protest of conventional governance in which rules of decorum literally policed the public's voices. These events generated among participants a profound sense of their bodily agency in the context of conservative political hegemony. The #unrulymob of women and men also triggered real fear on the part of conservative politicians set back on their heels by their own misogynistic terror of women and women's bodies, in Western culture automatically fearsome and disgusting threats to reason and order.

Another dimension of such stigmatization is the opprobrium against the non-reproductive female body. Antiabortion rhetoric typically foregrounds the fetus and its personhood over that of the mother/woman, who is reduced to the status of incubator (Condit; Luker; Petchesky; Saletan). As I have argued elsewhere, antiabortion rhetoric is a component of the larger conservative project (shared by neoliberals) of privatizing social responsibility. Assigning women to the maternal role justifies the private family as the site of all caretaking. Thus for women to interject their entire bodies and voices, foregrounding their agency, into the space of deliberation over abortion is especially disruptive and paradoxical. Ultimately, however, despite the creative and powerful interruption of the legislative proceedings on the part of thousands of Texas women and men, the setback to the antiabortion forces was only temporary, as Governor Rick Perry called a second special session during which the draconian legislation passed without challenge. In this light, I conclude the chapter with a discussion of the limits of rhetorical unruliness but also the potential of an awakened sense of our bodies' voices.

BACKGROUND: THE EMERGENCE OF THE #FEMINISTARMY

In June 2013, the Texas legislature held hearings on various versions of sweeping antiabortion legislation that ultimately would require clinics to meet standards for ambulatory surgery centers, doctors to have admitting privileges at a local hospital (resulting in the closing of all but four clinics in the state), and the state to prohibit abortion after twenty weeks' gestation. As word spread about the bills under consideration, hundreds of women signed up to testify largely against the legislation on June 21, 2013, four days before the filibuster (see Jones, "Extraordinary"; Jones, "People"; Stutz). Among those testifying was a young woman named Sarah Slamen. Called on late in the day, she challenged the legislators bluntly:

> I had some really eloquent remarks written out, but you guys have just worn me down all day. With all this terrible science, and glad-handing, and to be frank I get to move to New York next month, so I don't have to live in fear of you Texas legislators anymore and what you're going to do to my education system, or my healthcare system, 'cause I'm going to a state that doesn't kill its own inmates. That's how pro-life it is, up there.

I will thank you, though, first. It was destiny that you would discriminate against us and try to force your way inside the bodies of Texas women. Thank you! . . . You have radicalized hundreds of thousands of us, and no matter what you do for the next 22 days, women and their allies are coming for you. (Wing)

As she continued speaking, Slamen was carried out of the chamber by police. But she had summed up the moment quite aptly. Over the coming days, women and men of Texas would rise up against the legislation, inventing a body rhetoric that captured and deployed the paradoxical character of the entry of women's bodies into political spaces.

At the end of the first special session, on June 25, state senator Wendy Davis stood more than eleven hours to filibuster the final version of the legislation, Senate Bill 5. Inspired by and responding to a call by Planned Parenthood, the organization NARAL-Pro-Choice America, and their own consciences, a diversely gendered and multiracial group of Texans flowed into the Capitol building to watch and listen in the chamber and overflow rooms. The scene became a reunion of activists who had fought for *Roe v. Wade* in the 1970s alongside a burgeoning number of new young activists. When Republican leaders came up with three ostensible rules violations against Davis (Davis once leaned on her podium, was wearing a back brace, and at one point "changed the subject" to a discussion of intravaginal ultrasounds), her filibuster ended. That's when the *people's* filibuster ramped up.

With nearly two hundred thousand viewers glued to the live stream of events, protesters in the chamber, in the corridors, and in the rotunda "burst into claps, then cheers, and finally a nonstop roar" (Sinclair) that lasted more than fifteen minutes, past the midnight deadline, making it impossible to hear in the chamber and therefore to pass the bill. All night long, radicalized Texans chanted and sang about their victory. Lieutenant Governor David Dewhurst charged the protesters with being "an unruly mob, using Occupy Wall Street tactics." Protesters appropriated the label as images and updates circulated on Twitter under the hashtags #unrulymob and #feministarmy. New activist organizations emerged and rallies took place into early July, when a second special session of the legislature ultimately passed the legislation.

Throughout these events, the embodiment of protest in a specifically feminist body rhetoric was key to the victory of the insurgents. The specter of hundreds of women breaching legislative decorum was, to the leaders of the legislature, both grotesque and terrifying. For many of those protesting the legislation, the capacity of bodies to disrupt, interrupt, and exert instrumental control over the proceedings was a revelation of the agency of women. Images of the reproductive body also emerged in protest signage and public symbolism in ways that highlighted and mocked conservative fear of women's unruly physicality. To understand these features of the unruliness of the #feminist-army, I will connect feminist theory with the rhetorical study of decorum and theories of comic inversion of the bodily grotesque before turning to a more detailed discussion of the events of June and July 2013.

Feminism, Embodiment, and the Comic Frame

As a number of feminist theorists have pointed out, the hegemony of Enlightenment thought in modern society, while progressive in many respects, depends upon the denial and symbolic exclusion of the bodily necessities of social reproduction such as childbirth and rearing, caretaking, and labor, pain, and death. The invasion of civilized talk by matters of bodily necessity—filth, blood, and labor—appears as grotesque. All of these elements are, in the history of Western philosophy, aligned with a denigrated womanhood. Elizabeth Grosz explains, "Relying on essentialism, naturalism, and biologism, misogynist thought confines women to the biological requirements of reproduction on the assumption that because of particular biological, physiological, and endocrinological transformations, women are somehow *more* biological, *more* corporeal, and *more* natural than men. The coding of femininity with corporeality in effect leaves men free to inhabit what they (falsely) believe is a purely conceptual order" (14). When women's corporeality intrudes into the conceptual and material order of an oppressive society, politicians devoted to that order find their freedom challenged.

In perhaps a disorderly way of my own, I am articulating two feminist traditions in this chapter. The first is that of French radical feminism, with its insights that the feminine poses a threat to a Symbolic order naturalizing a material system that attempts to contain women in the realm of embodied intimacy and reproduction (Cavallaro). I am tying this insight to the socialist feminist theory of social reproduction (Battacharya; Laslett and Brenner). Capitalism, especially in its neoliberal incarnation, depends upon the privatization of social responsibility (Cloud, "Rhetoric of Family Values"). The private domain, understood as the realm of women, is where the reproduction—in biological and social senses—of generations of working people occurs. The assignment of women's identities and labor to this domain solves the problem of caretaking and socialization for nation-states and the capitalist interests they sustain. Concretely, this arrangement warrants the outright abuse of labor and inattention to education, housing, health care, and material infrastructure on the part of corporations and states. The transgressive eruption, heralded by French feminisms, into political intelligibility exposes the oppressively gendered—but also shockingly porous—division of society into political (decorous and abstracted from necessity) and personal (invisible and necessary) spheres. The French feminist Hélène Cixous wrote, "It is necessary that woman write herself; that woman write about woman and bring women to writing, from which they have been driven away as violently as from their bodies; for the same reasons . . . it is necessary that woman put herself into the text—as into the world and into history—by her own movement" (875; see also Biesecker). "Write yourself," she adds (880). "Your body must be heard."

While the bodies, identities, and demands of women, slaves, and the laboring classes more generally were always excluded from the privileges of citizenship in every ostensibly democratic society, it is women whose porous, bleeding bodies and historical tie to reproduction pose the greatest existential challenge to the artificiality of the abstractions of public political discourse. This challenge is heightened when political elites undertake deliberation *about* women's bodies (as in the case of abortion) while trying to sustain a civil façade that cannot admit knowledge of them. This tension became a deconstructive resource for the #unrulymob, as protesters foregrounded the biological, inverting Cartesian dualisms in a celebration of women's reproductive organs and combining symbols of femininity with the historically hyper-masculine. Such tactics risked reinforcing the reduction of women to their bodies; however, the particular ways in which women deployed body imagery and their own bodies exploited contradictions in the right's discourse.

Indeed, theorists Peter Stallybrass and Allon White have noted the enormous disruptive, transgressive inventional potential in the symbolic and practical inversion of the grotesque and the enlightened, the filthy and the refined, and the lower and the higher (in the Cartesian cartography of the body). They state, "Inversion, so dominant a feature of carnival and fairground acts, could be mobilized, then, as a way of remodeling social relations" (57). In a passage on Freudianism, they note, "It is above all the woman's body which becomes the battle-ground in the hysterical repression of the grotesque form" (184).

Some tendencies in feminist thought recognize this power of inversion. Judith Butler's work describing queer performativity as disruption of regulative ideals of sex and gender comes to mind. Melissa Deem, in an important article about feminist scatological rhetorics, describes how feminist manifestos afford a kind of agency for women not recognized in the political public sphere where feminism is relegated to a "minor discourse" (511). In contrast, feminist practices that render sexualized bodies—male and female—shockingly visible may have transgressive potential. Deem describes the literal castration of John Wayne Bobbit by his wife, Lorena, in 1993 alongside the manifesto of the Society for Cutting Up Men (known as the SCUM manifesto) as sites of recognizing the disavowed violations of women's bodies by men. The politics of these tendencies is "not nice, safe, or sexy" but, rather, marked by collective rage (521). Radical feminist Andrea Dworkin once described the feminist project as "the atrocity work"—the shit work, the rape work, the incest work, the trafficking work, the pornography work, the abuse work (133). This articulation of feminism insisted upon bringing bodily atrocities into public view (in keeping with the slogan, "the personal is political"), interrupting the stylized performance of mainstream politics (see Hariman).

While such violations of decorum might not seem good candidates for comedy, they do fit Kenneth Burke's concept of the comic frame: the expression of outrage without pretension to superiority, in the spirit of recognizing that the powerful, in their mistaken-ness, often act as fools (see Burke, *Attitudes toward History* 173; Simons). The comic frame is a dialectical modality tied to Burke's advocacy of the production of "perspective by incongruity," or a rhetorical tactic that shows how mistaken dominant ideas can be by putting them surprisingly up against another image or term that provokes awareness of complexity and contradiction (*Permanence and Change* 69–90). It is the insertion of the discomfiting into a situation whose decorum demands a fitting response. As architecture scholar Tim Anstey observes, decorum is an appeal to control over space, voice, and action (see also Rebhorn). We have witnessed attempts to control space and voice of women among Texas legislators; at the same time, we have seen those attempts mobilized in a practice of comic—and sometimes comedic—symbolic inversion among the #unrulymob.

"BUT NOT OUR BODY" AND THE RHETORIC OF UNRULINESS IN THE #FEMINISTARMY

The Body of Wendy Davis

Understood narrowly, it was one woman's body that triggered the feminist uprising in Texas: that of legislator Wendy Davis. She was praised as the epitome of a brave woman in a man's political world, standing without rest or nourishment for hours on end in her pink running shoes, talking without pause and with relentless focus on a single issue. The slogan "I Stand With Wendy" appeared on signs and T-shirts as pro-choice Texans mobbed the Capitol.

Mainstream media coverage of the filibuster focused tightly on Davis's body, with an almost obsessive attention to her pink running shoes. The *Washington Post* ran a story under the headline "Wendy Davis' Sneakers: These Shoes Were Made for Filibustering." The story focuses on her "rouge-red" pair of Mizuno "Wave Riders," contrasting Davis's choice against that of Senator Rand Paul during a filibuster in March 2013. Although he stood longer than Davis, he commented, "I didn't wear my most comfortable shoes or nothing" (Hell). The implication in this statement is that, unlike women, men in politics do not allow their bodies to intrude into the legislative process. Unlike women, men can achieve mind over matter. The *Daily Beast* noted the sexist double standard in the focus on what political women wear (Kohn). Yet the shoes became a kind of feminist talisman, a symbol of women's taking control over their bodies. In this way, Davis's stand attempted to enact a disembodied politics while her shoes and the media coverage of them became symbols of bodily, feminine intrusion into the proceedings.

Davis's stand was admirable to be sure. At the same time, the filibuster itself and the rules for its conduct represent the Cartesian demand to dissociate the political from the body. As if disembodied discourse without regard for bodily need or comfort is the pinnacle expression of political discipline, Davis attempted to fulfill the form of this demand. In the end, however, she was punished for her embodiment, for requiring a back brace, for leaning momentarily on the podium for support, both violations of the rules of the filibuster, like a marathon, a test of endurance without regard for pain or recognition of the massive, usually invisible, bodily investment in the maintenance of power. At the filibuster's end, State Senator Leticia van de Putte stood to challenge the president of the Senate and was ignored. Finally, she shouted, "At what point must a female senator raise her hand or her voice to be recognized by her male colleagues?" (Reilly).

Protesters inside and outside of the Senate chamber were about to demonstrate what it really takes for women to be heard. When the filibuster ended and the Senate threatened to pass the bill, they were met with the most unruly sounds of collective outrage that literally stalled the political process. Attempts at control in the legislative chambers also became targets of protest images pointing up contradictions in Texas leaders' political commitments and jarringly commingling the personal and the political, as Texas women deployed the comic frame to express outrage toward and solidarity against the leaders of the legislature. I take up each of these expressions in turn.

Slogans, Images, and the Comic Frame

Demonstrators at the Capitol mobilized a deep repertoire of body-based critique. Recalling protest signs of abortion rights protests across the last five decades, numbers of slogans invoke the body outright: "Republicans, get out of my uterus!" for example, or simply, "That's mine," referring to the uterus. "Think outside my Box!" read one sign; "Don't be a Dick, [Governor] Rick [Perry]," another. The classic symbol of the coathanger (symbolizing dangerous, self-induced abortions) with a line through it was common. However, one image in particular exemplifies the comic inversion identified by Stallybrass and White and Kenneth Burke. In fine feminist form, it violates political dis-

FIGURE 1

course with bodily references. This image, increasingly visible on signs and T-shirts, appropriates a classic Texas political image and slogan, a cannon with the words below: "Come and take it" (see figure 1).

According to Hlavty, this image and slogan became the flag of the Texas Revolution in 1835 at the Battle of Gonzales. Its slogan is one of defiance, daring an opposing foe to try to come and take one's weapons. Intriguingly, the flag "was created by Sarah Seely DeWitt and her daughter, Evaline, from Naomi DeWitt's wedding dress." Thus, even during the Texas Revolution the feminine intruded into martial space. During the feminist uprising of 2013, a new version of this image appropriated the masculine battle cry for the defense of women's reproductive choices (see figure 2). In this image, a uterus and ovaries replace the cannon, usurping the fetish of weaponry while echoing the dare and defiance of the original.

The image's meaning is compounded as revealed by other slogans of this event that call attention to how the state is more interested in regulating women's bodies than guns. One woman had written on her umbrella: "If Only My Uterus Could Shoot Bullets—Then It Would Not Need Regulation." This example of perspective by incongruity enacts the comic frame described by Burke: calling attention to the folly of one's antagonists through disjuncture rather than diatribe. In the context of such signs, the fear of women's bodies and attempts to regulate them appear as ridiculous, obsessive, and disproportionate —and seriously motivated by political alignment rather than by scientific concern for anyone's well-being.

FIGURE 2

Scatology, the Reproductive Grotesque, and "Tampongate"

The most compelling instance of the inversion of the biological and the political revealed how serious the legislature was about controlling women *as* women. Over the days of the hearings and filibuster, Capitol security, under instructions from the politicians, began confiscating tampons and sanitary napkins from women who wished to enter, at first the gallery, and eventually the building. (They also searched entrants for ostensible, but fictitious, jars of feces and urine; see Whittaker.) What was, in effect, the symbolic purgation of menstruating women was justified by the fear that women could use feminine hygiene items as projectiles from the gallery to the House floor. There is something telling in the idea of women's menstrual supplies as weapons: the very biological fact of womanhood is figured in this farcical attempt to control a threat to governance and order.

Given the exclusive emphasis in antiabortion rhetoric on the personhood of the fetus, menstruating women also symbolize a rejection of the maternal role necessary to a neoliberal order that relies on the private family and the domestication of women to raise and care for new generations of workers. This role is belied by both menstruation and the bodies of women in politics. Nevertheless, it is crucial to social reproduction, a feminist concept that understands gender essentialism and the regulation of women's bodies as part and parcel of the broader global capitalist imperative toward privatization of all social responsibility (see Bhattacharya; Laslett and Brenner).

Women's body parts and the formalities of neoliberal rule are thus at odds. A report in the *Huffington Post* said as much: "Officers clarified that the list of items not permitted in the gallery was not new and that the confiscations were an effort to maintain the 'rules of decorum.'" According to this report, Lieutenant Governor David Dewhurst stated, "We're going to have strict enforcement. If there are any demonstrations, we are going to clear the gallery. I hope that we don't get to that point, but if we do, we do. This is a democracy and we will not be interrupted by an unruly mob" (Lavender and Wing). In this statement, the prohibition of menstruating women is justified as the protection of democracy. Women's embodiment is a threat to democracy and the very presence of artifacts related to menstruation makes the protesters unruly. Dewhurst might as well have said, "This is a democracy and we will not be interrupted by women."

In response, protesters engaged in the politics and poetics of transgression as described by Stallybrass and White. They performed the literary trope of the scatological, references to the grotesque body and functions of excretion or excrement. Women and men arrived wearing wigs, jewelry, and articles of clothing made of tampons and sanitary pads. One man arrived wearing a bandolier of tampons and carrying a squirt gun. On the television network MSNBC, host Melissa Harris-Perry donned earrings made of tampons. Memes circulated on Twitter mocking the male legislators' fear. A new version of the "Come and Take It" flag appeared, made even more funny by the visual similarity between cannon and tampons (see figure 3).

The outright mockery of what came to be known as "tampongate" placed the serious efforts to control women in a comic frame that exposed such efforts for what they were (not responses to actual physical threats) and ridiculed the security officers who searched women's bags and pockets for what is usually unmentionable in polite company—or in political discourse. The confrontation revealed something quite serious, however: how the consignment of women, justified on the grounds of biology, to the realm of necessity works in the service of a neoliberal social order. Thus the control of womanhood and awareness of the fact of it appeared at the same time, rendering efforts at discipline unstable and the ideology of neoliberalism potentially unstable. The mass deployment of protesters' bodies amplified this challenge.

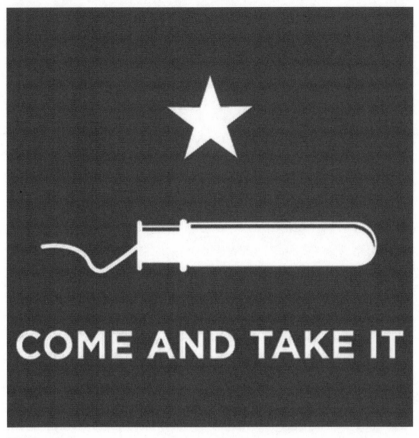

FIGURE 3

The Sound and the Fury

Sound is a physical thing, a wave that moves through space and exerts pressure at various wavelengths and volume on people and things. In daily life, one is used to the idea that sounds "carry," but collectively produced sounds in music and in protest illustrate the physicality of sound most profoundly. I was present at the hearings and rallies in the Capitol leading up to the attempted vote on the bill, and outside the chamber when we were called upon to make as much noise as possible to drown out the proceedings inside for more than fifteen minutes, past midnight, the official end of the session. It is difficult to describe the sheer physical pressure and pleasure of the sound we produced, its pressure on ears and skin, raising the hair on neck, arms, and legs. The sense of collective power through the physical unification of bodies was immensely pleasurable as well. What we produced was the opposite of controlled sound; it was *noise*, unintelligible, uncontrollable, unreasoning, and unruly (see Attali). The experience was de-individuating and revelatory of the power inherent in a mass of bodies, startling in its implications: We have agency—we have *power*—in our bodies, together. One telling headline the next day read, "Unruly Mob Shouts Abortion Bill to Death in Texas" (Webster). The journalist Brandi Grissom described it this way:

> The scene last night was unlike anything I have ever seen at the Texas Capitol, or experienced there, and I've been covering the Legislature since 2005. Protesters lined the halls of the Capitol, from the rotunda on the bottom floor all the way to the third floor, where the Senate was. And they really, as the debate came to a crescendo at midnight, created this deafening noise within the Senate chamber, which is such a *place of decorum, typically quiet and staid, sort of steady debate. And it just completely erupted.* You could hear nothing that was happening on the Senate floor, and the leaders in the Senate were really just at a complete loss for how to go forward. ("Texas Showdown," emphasis added)

In French feminist terms, the event enacted the project of the transgression of the Symbolic order that arranges and regulates sex, including in regimentation of the properly public denial of the body and the monstrously and erotic private domain. Perhaps it is the pleasure of such a transgression that awakened activists to the visceral power of body rhetoric. For my part, like Grissom, I have never experienced another moment so transformative of collective self-consciousness. It was an intense moment of inversion, in which interrupting bodies controlled the scene instead of being controlled by norms of decorum. When Rick Perry called the demonstrators an "unruly mob," he meant it as an epithet. But the protesters claimed it, defending the idea and practice of being unruly as disturbing and fearsome.

As incredible as those fifteen minutes were, however, the momentum of the #unrulymob was not sustained. If participants had settled in to occupy the Capitol (with all the attendant hardships and risks), the recalcitrant presence of interrupting bodies might have prevented the easy passage of the bill in the second special session. However, in the pre-dawn darkness after the victory, there were other factors that turned an instrument of mass power into something friable. As the *Austin Chronicle* noted, "And thus the anti-climax. That Hollywood moment—where, all other options exhausted, hundreds of ordinary Texans shouted down legislation that would have severely regulated their bodies—but the celebration never did. There was never a 'We beat 'em!' moment to cap everything off with the catharsis that we're conditioned to accept after weeks of struggle, culminating in a victory" (Solomon). The subsequent events afford scholars and activists alike a number of insights about the limits of unruliness.

THE LIMITS OF UNRULINESS AND THE PERSISTENCE OF CONSCIOUSNESS

I have argued that the actions of the #unrulymob/#feministarmy in the Texas State Capitol in 2013 illustrated three characteristics of what might be called a rhetoric of unruliness: scatology, comic inversion, and the mobilization of their actual, material bodies. Although Stallybrass and White describe high-low inversion as a characteristic of a number of discourses involving both men and women, the reification of woman-as-body suggests that women's body rhetorics of inversion are particularly heinous affronts to civility and decorum as disciplining norms. They are revelatory in an erotically powerful way of neoliberal capitalism's disciplining imperatives. The social denial of the body is the fantasy of a state and economic system in denial of the ethics and politics of care. The monstrosity of bleeding, fecund, yet uncontrollable women in the decorous setting of the Texas legislature fundamentally challenges that fantasy.

Even so, as Franklin Haiman noticed, the instrumental effectiveness of body rhetoric depends on its actual, material (in addition to symbolic, contra Grosz) capacity to obstruct and interrupt business as usual. Such bodily capacity is important because established elites control most other means of coercion, containment, and influence, including the police and funding. The bill that finally passed the Texas legislature was crafted by a national think-tank called the American Legislative Exchange Council (ALEC). With almost limitless resources, ALEC crafts model legislation and hires and tours doctors and lawyers to present this legislation to state legislatures across the country. The Texas bills were not a local effort but a calculated and heavily financed piece of a national strategy. The majority Republican legislators controlled public space and disciplined people who broke decorum. They controlled the rules and procedures that finally ended Davis's filibuster. Their efforts at control were at times ridiculous, but no slogan or image, no amount of civil testimony, could have stopped that bill from becoming law.

An extended occupation might have challenged it more effectively. Preserving the collective voice, knowledge, strength, resourcefulness, and insight of those gathered on June 25 might have become the basis for building numbers and public outrage. For a number of reasons, an extended occupation did not happen. One reason for the dissipation of the #unrulymob was, undoubtedly, the actions of the mainstream abortion rights organizations, Planned Parenthood and NARAL Pro-Choice America, and those of the leadership of the Texas Democratic Party.

In the ungodly hours of June 26, representatives of those organizations encouraged protesters to leave the Capitol to attend a Democratic Party rally at another site. Many protesters were confused and angry about these instructions, but the cohesion of the #feministarmy was broken. The leaders of mainstream electoral politics intentionally un-occupied the Capitol, taking the demonstrators away from the heart of their power into a domain controlled by others. Efforts to get out the vote replaced concerted mass action. All of the electoral bids, predictably, failed, including Wendy Davis's run for governor. Ironically, a movement defined by its unruliness was channeled into more decorous—and less effective—political processes.

The disassembly of the #unrulymob is important to understanding the rhetoric of unruliness in a materialist feminist frame. Symbolic work—filibustering, testifying, creating signs and T-shirts with compellingly critical images and slogans—builds numbers and unites large groups across differences of identity and political perspective. But it is the literal "body-rhetoric" that can compel establishment actors to change direction. Thus this case study points to the limits of symbolic carnivalesque inversion as described by Stallybrass and White and of a feminist model that extols symbolic disruption without a material counterpart.

Not every vestige of the #feministarmy disappeared. In the months after the uprising, two groups emerged to collect participants with ongoing interest in building an instrumental movement outside the mainstream electoral process: Rise Up and Feminists United (Boas). Presently both of these groups are inactive. At the same time, thousands of women across Texas—mostly rural and poor—have lost their access to preventative health care, contraceptive services, and abortion.

Perhaps, however, the consciousness-raising moment of "shouting a bill to death" will prove to have had more lasting effects on the consciousness of and willingness to struggle on the part of those who were there the night of June 25, 2013. I hope that Slamen was right when she said, "You have radicalized hundreds of thousands of us, and no matter what you do for the next 22 days, women and their allies are coming for you." Ultimately what is needed is a multi-racial, gender-diverse, solidaristic movement that can not only put women at the center of abortion discourse but also challenge a society that places all caretaking at the stoop of the private home. In Irigaray's formulation, we are unsatisfied but not asleep, not likely to fall back permanently on the words of men.

NOTES

1. Emerging scholarship is taking up the use of social media during these events; see Elyse Nicole Janish, *20 Weeks, 13 Hours, 140 Characters*; Lila Garcia, *The Revolution Might Be Tweeted*.

WORKS CITED

Anstey, Tim. "The Dangers of Decorum." *Architecture Research Quarterly* 10, no. 2 (2006): 131–39.

Attali, Jacques. *Noise: The Political Economy of Music.* University of Minnesota Press, 1977.

Batthacharya, Tithi. "Explaining Gender Violence in the Neoliberal Era." *International Socialist Review* 91 (2013). www.isreview.org/issue/91/explaining-gender-violence -neoliberal-era/.

Biesecker, Barbara A. "Towards a Transactional View of Rhetorical and Feminist Theory: Rereading Hélène Cixous's 'Laugh of the Medusa.'" *Southern Communication Journal* 57, no. 2 (1992): 86–96.

Boas, Hallie. "The People's History: The Birth of the New Feminist Army in Texas." *Austostraddle*, August 14, 2013. www.autostraddle.com/the-peoples-history-the-birth-of-the -new-feminist-army-in-texas-243282/.

Burke, Kenneth. *Attitudes toward History.* New Republic, 1937.

Burke, Kenneth. *Permanence and Change.* New Republic, 1935.

Butler, Judith. *Bodies That Matter: On the Discursive Limits of Sex.* Taylor and Francis, 2011.

Cavallaro, Dani. *French Feminist Theory.* Continuum, 2003.

Cixous, Hélène. "Laugh of the Medusa." *Signs* 1, no. 4 (1976): 875–93.

Cloud, Dana L. "Civility as a Threat to Academic Freedom." *First Amendment Studies* 49 (2015): 13–17.

Cloud, Dana L. "The Rhetoric of Family Values: Scapegoating and the Privatization of Social Responsibility." *Western Journal of Communication* 62, no. 4 (1998): 387–419.

Condit, Celeste. *Decoding Abortion Rhetoric.* University of Illinois Press, 1994.

Deem, Melissa. "From Bobbit to SCUM: Re-memberment, Scatological Rhetorics, and Feminist Strategies in the Contemporary United States." *Public Culture* 8, no. 3 (1996): 511–37.

DeLuca, Kevin Michael. "Unruly Arguments: The Body Rhetoric of Earth First!, ACT UP, and Queer Nation." *Argumentation and Advocacy* 36, no. 1 (1999): 9–21.

Dworkin, Andrea. *Letters from a War Zone.* Lawrence Hill Books, 1993.

Garcia, Lila. *The Revolution Might Be Tweeted: Digital Social Media, Contentious Politics and the Wendy Davis Filibuster.* Master's thesis, University of Washington, Seattle, 2014.

Grosz, Elizabeth. *Volatile Bodies: Toward a Corporeal Feminism.* Indiana University Press, 1994.

Haiman, Franklyn. "The Rhetoric of the Streets: Some Legal and Ethical Considerations." *Quarterly Journal of Speech* 8, no. 2 (1967): 100–14.

Hariman, Robert. "Decorum, Power, and the Courtly Style." *Quarterly Journal of Speech* 78, no. 2 (1992): 149–72.

Hell, Emily. "Wendy Davis' Sneakers: These Shoes Were Made for Filibustering." *Washington Post*, June 26, 2013.

Hlavaty, Craig. "The Story behind the Co-opting of 'Come and Take It.'" *Houston Chronicle*, October 2, 2015. www.chron.com/houston/article/Come-and-take-it-in-Texas-turns-179-5796732.php.

Irigaray, Luce. "When Our Lips Speak Together." In *Feminist Theory and the Body*, edited by Janet Price and Margrit Shildrick, 82–90. Edinburgh University Press, 1999.

Janish, Elyse Nicole. *20 Weeks, 13 Hours, 140 Characters: The Abortion Controversy in the Texas State Senate and Online*. Master's thesis, Syracuse University, NY, 2014.

Jones, Carolyn. "Extraordinary Turnout for Citizen's [*sic*] Filibuster of Anti-Abortion Bills." *Texas Observer*, June 21, 2013. www.texasobserver.org/extraordinary-turnout-last-night-for-the-citizens-filibuster-of-anti-abortion-bills/.

Jones, Carolyn. "The People behind the 'Unruly Mob.'" *Texas Observer*, July 1, 2013. www.texasobserver.org/the-people-behind-the-unruly-mob/.

Kohn, Sally. "Why Wendy Davis's Iconic Shoes Are Newsworthy." *Daily Beast*, July 6, 2013, and August 14, 2015. www.thedailybeast.com/why-wendy-daviss-iconic-shoes-are-newsworthy/.

Laslett, Barbara, and Johanna Brenner. "Gender and Social Reproduction: Historical Perspectives." *Annual Review of Sociology* 15 (1989): 381–404.

Lavender, Paige, and Nick Wing. "Tampons Confiscated, Guns Still Allowed at Texas Capitol." *Huffington Post*, July 12, 2013. www.huffingtonpost.com/2013/07/12/tampons-confiscated-texas_n_3588177.html.

Luker, Kristin. *Abortion and the Politics of Motherhood*. University of California Press, 1984.

Petchesky, Rosalind. *Abortion and Woman's Choice*. Verso, 1984.

Rebhorn, Wayne. "Outlandish Fears: Defining Decorum in Renaissance Rhetoric." *Intertexts* 4 (2000). www.highbeam.com/doc/1G1-80849923.html.

Reilly, Mollie. "Leticia Van de Putte, Texas Legislator, Slams Male Colleagues during Abortion Filibuster." *HuffingtonPost.com*, June 26, 2013. www.huffingtonpost.com/2013/06/26/leticia-van-de-putte_n_3500497.html.

Saletan, William. *Bearing Right: How Conservatives Won the Abortion War*. University of California Press, 2004.

Simons, Herbert W. "Burke's Comic Frame and the Problem of Warrantable Outrage." *KB Journal* 6, no. 1 (2009): 3–10.

Sinclair, Kelly. "Texas 'Women Power' Blocks Anti-abortion Bill." *PeoplesWorld.org*, June 28, 2013. www.peoplesworld.org/article/texas-women-power-blocks-anti-abortion-bill/.

Solomon, Dan. "A Victory by the People." *Austin Chronicle*, June 26, 2013. www.austinchronicle.com/daily/news/2013-06-26/a-victory-by-the-people/.

Stallybrass, Peter, and Allon White. *The Politics and Poetics of Transgression*. Cornell University Press, 1986.

Stormer, Nathan. *Naked Politics: Nudity, Political Action, and the Rhetoric of the Body*. Lexington Books, 2012.

Stutz, Terrence. "Hundreds Testify for, against Sweeping Abortion Bill as Sides Rally at Texas Capitol." *Dallas Morning News*, July 8, 2013. www.dallasnews.com/news/local-politics/2013/07/08/hundreds-testify-for-against-sweeping-abortion-bill-as-sides-rally-at-texas-capitol/.

"Texas Showdown: Anti-abortion Bill Fails after Protesters Fill Capitol to Cheer Marathon Filibuster." *Democracy Now*, June 26, 2013. www.democracynow.org/2013/6/26/texas_showdown_anti_abortion_bill_fails/.

Webster, Stephen C. "'Unruly Mob' Shouts Abortion Bill to Death in Texas." *Raw Story*, June 26, 2013. www.rawstory.com/2013/06/unruly-mob-shouts-abortion-bill-to-death-in-texas/.

Whittaker, Richard. "Shit or Shinola? Dewhurst Puts His Foot in It." *Austin Chronicle*, July 26, 2013. www.austinchronicle.com/news/2013-07-26/shit-or-shinola-dewhurst-puts-his-foot-in-it/.

Wing, Nick. "Sarah Slamen, Texas Woman Removed from Senate, Finishes Her Pro-choice Testimony." *Huffington Post*, July 12, 2013. www.huffingtonpost.com/2013/07/12/sarah-slamen-interview_n_3585739.html.

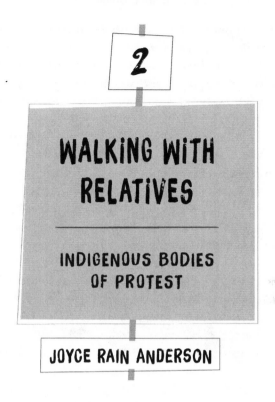

2

WALKING WITH RELATIVES

INDIGENOUS BODIES OF PROTEST

JOYCE RAIN ANDERSON

We are protectors, not protesters.

—Honor the Earth

One thing our people could not surrender was the meaning of land. In the settler mind, land was property, real estate, capital, or natural resources. But to our people, it was everything: identity, connection to our ancestors, our pharmacy, our library, the source of all that sustained us. Our lands were where our responsibility to the world was enacted, sacred ground.

—Robin Wall Kimmerer, *Braiding Sweetgrass*

Bodies carry stories; bodies tell stories. This is a story among the many stories we hold close.

I n spring 2016, there were about two hundred people; later the number camped along the Mnisose or Great Swirling River (known as the Missouri), on treaty lands of the Hunkpapa Oceti or Standing Rock Sioux, grew to more than ten thousand, becoming the tenth largest community in North Dakota. The water protectors came to the Red Warrior Camp, Sacred Stone

Camp, and other camps to stop the Black Snake or Dakota Access Pipeline (DAPL) from being constructed through their territory, under the riverbed. The pipeline threatens sacred sites and access to clean water. The protectors' tactics are nonviolent, taping their bodies to heavy machinery and standing strong in the way of authorities to hold a nation to its promises to its Indigenous peoples.

While the more well-known Keystone XL pipeline had been shut down by the federal government, until recently DAPL was "fast-tracked," as Standing Rock Chairman Archambault relates in a *New York Times* article. He explains that DAPL used "the Nationwide Permit No. 12 process, which grants exemptions from environmental reviews required by the Clean Water Act and Environmental Policy Act by treating the Pipeline as a series of small construction sites" (cited in LaDuke, "Winona LaDuke"). The now completed pipeline spans 1,172 miles through four states (North Dakota, South Dakota, Iowa, and Illinois), and the plans are for it to transport over 550,000 barrels daily (Heim). The potential for leaks and spills likely compromises the Missouri River and clean water for all those who get their water from the river. DAPL disregarded Native American rights from the start, and once the gathering grew, hired an out-of-state private security company to come in with dogs. More recently released documents reveal that Energy Transfer Partners worked with a private security firm, Tiger Swan, to portray the water protectors as "potential terrorists" (*Lakota Country Times*). According to the *Lakota Country Times* on June 1, 2017, recently leaked documents "provide a glimpse into the extreme measures that were taken by law enforcement, Big Oil, and state and federal enforcement agencies to undermine the efforts of water protectors who sought to stop construction of the Dakota Access Pipeline." North Dakota officials were not supportive of the "protest."[1] The governor declared a state of emergency, prompting the National Guard to be on call. Further, roadblocks were set up to discourage more people from joining. However, over 280 Native Nations and non-Native groups across the country and globally sent representatives, supplies, and support for Standing Rock.

The Stand at Standing Rock is by no means the first time Indigenous peoples, as protectors for Mother Earth and our relations, have risen up and protested against colonization. In discussing other recent protests, Jeremy Wood asserts, "It's important to dispel a misconception that's been too common in the media that this came out of nowhere. Settlers like to believe that colonialism, sad as it was, has ended, and that Indians are, at best, part of the great tapestry of America. We've resisted from the start. This is the continuation of a long history" (Sandalow-Ash). Indeed we have been resisting since 1492 and even before. We honor names like Metacom, Weetamoo, Little Turtle, Tecumsah, Red Cloud, Sitting Bull, Crazy Horse, Geronimo, and many more who laid their lives on the line to fight the onslaught of colonial terrorism. From the earliest treaty in 1613, the Guswanta or Two Row Wampum, Native peoples have made attempts to live alongside the settler colonials, but because the latter continually violate treaties, Native peoples have found themselves in situations where they are consistently forced to rise up. For example, in the late 1800s the Ghost Dance became a nonviolent protest, which ultimately resulted in a massacre by the US Army at Wounded Knee in 1890. A resurgence of Native resistance took place during the 1960s and 1970s. This "campaign of resistance" (Smith and Warrior) included the taking over of Alcatraz Island in 1969, the Trail of Broken Treaties march, the occupation of the Bureau of Indian Affairs (BIA) in Washington, DC, the second siege of Wounded Knee, covering Plymouth Rock in sand and boarding the *Mayflower* and throwing a replica pilgrim overboard, and many others, some enacted through the American Indian Movement (AIM) and some through individual nations protecting their lands and rights. Yet as Native American peoples continue to resist a historical legacy that threatens their sovereignty, few of these movements gain the attention of the world.

(IN)VISIBLE INDIGENOUS BODIES

In the Americas and elsewhere, Indigenous bodies have endured much. Knowing ourselves to be inextricably connected to the earth, we, as Native peoples, have resisted an ideology that would sever that connection. In this and other work, I align with Julie Nagan's research in (re)mapping the colonial body. Further, I consider the Indigenous body as deeply rooted to place. As an example, the Wampanoag word for land was "akeem," with an "m" indicating the inseparable connection of the land to the body. In speaking, people used "nutakeem" as in "I am the land." Following contact and particularly written into the religious tracts in the Wampanoag language, the "m" was dropped from the word (Baird). Disconnecting the body from the land is directly connected to the way maps of the "new world" were constructed showing vacant spaces. Julie Nagam points out, "Colonial maps describe the ['new world'] space as void or *terra nullis* by the lack of bodies and their focus on the vast 'empty' space. In these land surveys, the purported lack of bodies denies the embodied or living knowledge situated in the land and the indigenous bodies" (149). I argue this change in language is equal to a change in mindset: a conversion narrative. Equally, the idea of land as vacant still persists in colonial discourse and threatens Native territories today. Settler colonialism mentality has always been incongruous with an Indigenous worldview. Settler colonials in order to justify their lust for land and its resources 'claim Indigenous bodies to be inferior to their own; colonial texts often liken Indigenous bodies to beasts and heathens in a savage state. Zillah Einstein argues in *Hatreds* that "'Otherness' is constructed on bodies. Racism uses the physicality of bodies to punish, expunge, and isolate certain bodies and construct them as others" (210). Because settler colonialists view themselves as superior, Native bodies have endured forced conversion, imprisonment, theft, relocation, abuse, violence, and restrictions. From praying towns to residential boarding schools, Native peoples were taken from their homes, forced into servitude, imprisoned in institutions, and interred in camps. Historically, strikes against the Native body continued as the settlers deliberately removed bodies from their homelands through government policies. This removal was done through relocation, setting up reservations, breaking up their lands into allotments, placing them in boarding schools, relocating them to cities, and denying Native peoples their religious and spiritual practices. Further, government policies of the United States and Canada still determine who can be recognized as Indian and how Indigenous nations exist within these nations. In response, Native peoples then use their bodies as vehicles by which to speak back to the settler colonial regime. While most label these actions as protests, Native peoples call themselves protectors. In most Native nations, the people see themselves as caretakers of Mother Earth, enacting that inseparable link between land and body. In other words, we are relatives, and that relationship calls for responsibility. Winona LaDuke explains that for land-based peoples, "Teachings, ancient as the people who have lived on a land for five millennia, speak of a set of relationships to all that is around, predicated on respect, recognition of the interdependency of all beings, an understanding of humans' absolute need to be reverent and to manage our behavior, and an understanding that those relationships must be reaffirmed through lifeways and through acknowledgement of the sacred" (LaDuke, *Recovering the Sacred* 64). Indian peoples see a responsibility for those who came before, are here now, and are yet to live, and this means taking care of our mother who sustains us all. The continued digging of fossil fuels has already caused destruction and endangers the future. It is a responsibility to stand and protect.

This chapter is born from the recent resistance strategies of Indigenous peoples and in recognition and honor of the ancestors who also resisted. This is a story of embodied rhetorics—that is, rhetorics located within and in Indigenous bodies and generated for Indigenous bodies. Judith Butler has considered bodies in relationship to limitations set on them; she states, "not only [do] bodies tend to indicate a world beyond themselves, but this movement beyond their own boundaries, a movement of boundary in itself, appeared to be central

to what bodies 'are'" (viii). Indigenous bodies have been continually responding to limitations put on their sovereignty through, as de Certeau might argue,
"disquieting [the] familiarity" of colonial discourse. Through "tactics" of dance
protests, hunger strikes, and human blockades, a resurgence of Indian protests
"navigate[s] the strategies of institutions and power structures," bringing renewed attention to environmental concerns, treaty rights, and sovereignty (de
Certeau 96). Protest or protection is a way of disseminating embodied rhetoric.

JOINING THE ROUND DANCE

In November 2012, there were whispers of Indigenous uprisings, stories and
discussions of Indigenous peoples and environmental issues. By December,
drumbeats called us to malls and plazas and street corners. Simultaneously
hunger strikes, roadblocks, and marches were undertaken; at this moment
Indigenous bodies gathered to protest Canada's passage of Bill C-45, which
threatens Canadian environmental protection and violates treaties. And, as
Thomas King wrote in *The Inconvenient Indian*, "Now I don't want to give anyone the impression that I think treaties are a bad idea. Treaties aren't the problem. Keeping the promises made in the treaties is a different matter" (225). Like
our ancestors before us, Indigenous people turned to story, to dance, to the
body as a vehicle for protest and protection to let governments know that we
continue to be idle no more.

Started by four Canadian women—Jessica Gordon, Sheelah McLean, Sylvia
McAdams, and Nina Wilsonfeld—the most recent movement Idle No More
(INM) began as "a national [international] grassroots movement through its
first day of action" (Inman, Smis, and Cambou 254). Its platform was started
to discuss the issues surrounding Bill C-45 including the Indian Act and Nav-
igable Waters Act, which infringe on both environmental protections and Ab-
original and Treaty rights. The women used Facebook, Twitter, and a website to
disseminate information; other social media also spread the word. The website
provides the vision and story for the movement, along with a manifesto and
notices of events as they occur. The purpose is simple: to resist settler colonization as it still occurs today, "The impetus for the recent Idle No More events
lies in a centuries old resistance as Indigenous nations and their lands suffered
the impacts of exploration, invasion and colonization. Idle No More seeks to
assert Indigenous inherent rights to sovereignty and reinstitute traditional laws
and Nation to Nation Treaties by protecting the lands and waters from corporate destruction. Each day that Indigenous rights are not honored or fulfilled,
inequality between Indigenous peoples and the settler society grows" (INM
website).

Among other issues, Bill C-45 imperils streams and lakes and amends the

1867 Indian Act without having consulted First Nations peoples. According to Inman, Smis, and Cambou, Canada also may have violated its "duty to consult with indigenous populations prior to action that would, directly or indirectly, impact them on their lands" (254). Moreover, it violates articles 18, 19, and 20 of the UN Declaration of Rights of Indigenous Peoples (UNDRIP), which was passed in September 2007. The four countries initially opposed to the Declaration of Rights of Indigenous Peoples are (not surprisingly) Australia, Canada, New Zealand, and the United States. While these countries have since announced their support (the United States being the last in 2010), policies and actions continue to threaten lands of Indigenous peoples. In Canada, Bill C-45, which has been renamed as the Jobs and Growth Act 2012, is linked to other pieces of legislation that include S-6, the First Nations Education Act. In the United States, Congress voted in December 2014 on the National Defense Bill, which included a provision to sell twenty-four hundred acres of sacred Apache land to a copper mining company (McAuliff). These and other pieces of legislation have a massive impact on Indigenous sovereignty. The United States and Canada continue to promote policies and plans that directly violate rights found in UNDRIP. The Keystone XL Pipeline, the Northern Gate Pipeline, unlimited fracking, and changing regulations that protect waterways are merely a few examples. These issues have been exacerbated following the election of Donald Trump in 2016 because of his close ties to companies directly related to the fossil fuel industry. Not only did Trump sign an executive order on January 24, 2017, to restart Keystone and DAPL, he has selected cabinet members who deny climate change and promote dirty energy such as coal and oil.

New Year's Eve 2012 sparked many flash mob round dances. From the Mall of America in Minnesota to Boston's Faneuil Hall to places all over Canada and the United States, Indigenous peoples gathered in circles and invited supporters to join them. As one media pundit suggested, What can be more unsettling than a crowd of people dancing in the face of authority? (David). Yet for Indigenous peoples, dance has always been a tactic for protest and embodies who we are as Native peoples. In *The People Have Never Stopped Dancing*, Jaqueline Shea Murphy explains, "indigenous dance practices embodied ideologies counter to those the governments were corporeally enforcing. Dance practices and gatherings . . . affirmed the importance of history told not in writing or even words but bodily" (31). And globally, dancing as protest has indeed been a symbol of resistance to oppression. Take for example in Brazil where capoeira, a form of martial arts, was disguised as dance so that slaves could practice their skills without punishment. Or in Africa where the *toyi-toyi* was used—beginning with the MauMau in Kenya resisting English colonists to South Africa in the fight against apartheid. It is a marching foot movement, with hands held skyward motioning back and forth, and leaders call "awadla" (power) and are answered with "awethu" (to us; to the people). Crowds pour into the streets joining each other, rising up to impossible circumstances and confronting those who held the real guns (Nevit). Among Native peoples, resisting through dance is peaceful protest. Paiute Wo-vo-ka began to promote the Ghost Dance in the late 1880s to reinforce help and cultural survival for Indian peoples who were facing starvation, dislocation, and death from settlers and even agents of the US government. He encouraged people to bring back traditional knowledge that they needed to sustain themselves and to dance in prayer. It was the US government who turned violent and massacred the dancing people at Wounded Knee in 1890.

Round dancing is said to originate with the Cree people, and it is considered a healing dance. Although it is now commonly a pan tribal social dance, it is still used in ceremony. As a social dance, it encourages more people to join the dance while it fosters a sense of identity within Native communities. To dance, one clasps hands with the people on either side and engages in a counter-clockwise step then shifts the other way moving around the circle; a symbol of equality, kinship, harmony, the circle reconnects us with the earth. The dance creates relationships and helps us remember how we are all connected. It carries memories of our ancestors who have passed and those who are yet to come. Dance, too, is ceremony.

The Idle No More movement encouraged people to gather in public spaces and hold flash-mob round dances. The flash mob became a way to enact free assembly (Salmond 95). Howard Rheingold refers to these as Smart Mobs, as they have a definite cause as social protests while using contemporary media to organize (95). Messages are sent out via social media, and potential participants provide contact information; they go to an agreed-upon place at an agreed-upon time and wait for a text message. Drums start beating and dancers emerge joining hands. Some may carry signs to indicate the cause, and others in the watching crowd are invited to join in the round dance. Shea Murphy contends that "this relationship of dance and memory carries not only the physical sense of dance as something that is learned from others and held and remembered in one's body. It also carries a spiritual sense in which learning to dance, and the act of dancing, enact a spiritual physical connection to other beings, including those who passed on, as well as those who will come later" (220–21). Bodies enact these dances at malls, city plazas, and other places that have significant meaning; the drums and dancing bodies reinvent and reconstruct the meaning of the space, reclaiming it as Native space (Endres and Sendra-Cook 258–59). We can understand the significance of reclaiming space through thinking about how the Alcatraz takeover literally marked the island as Indian Land, a marking that still exists, or about Chief Spence marking her space by setting up a tipi in Ottawa challenging the position of Parliament Hill. Likewise, the round dances took place in public spaces like city plazas in Toronto, Sacramento, Boston, and many other major cities, or in shopping plazas. Over one thousand people participated in the 2012 New Year's Eve round dance in the Mall of America, a space that marks boundless consumerism. Interestingly on New Year's Eve 2013 (the following year), Patricia Shepard and Reyna Crow were arrested upon entering the Mall of America and were told that drums were not allowed in the mall. On New Year's Eve 2012 in Boston, we gathered at Faneuil Hall, which was built in 1742 and known as the Cradle of Liberty. Even briefly reconstructing the meaning of these places makes them Native space, and bodies dance to bring about justice.

STARVING INDIGENOUS BODIES

Coinciding with the actions of Idle No More, Teresa Spence, chief of the Attawapiskat Reserve in northern Ontario, began a hunger strike. She did so in direct response to C-45 when she and other First Nation Chiefs were barred from entering the House of Commons on December 4, 2012. Other elders also engaged in hunger strikes including Grand Elder Raymond Robinson. However, Chief Spence was also responding to "concerns she had raised in 2011" regarding substandard housing and health conditions on her reserve. Despite an officially declared state of emergency, the Canadian government issued no response (see Ornelas). Setting up a tipi on Victoria Island in Ottawa, Chief Spence began her hunger strike on December 11, 2012; she made it clear that she would end her strike when Prime Minister Harper and Governor General David Johnston convened a meeting with a First Nation chief and recommit to Canada's and the Crown's treaty obligations. She declared, "We need to reignite a nation to nation relationship based on our inherent and constitutionality protected rights as a sovereign nation. We are demanding our rightful place back here in our homeland that we call Canada" (McCarthy and Bradshaw). In her protest, Chief Spence used her own body by denying her own body and exercising sovereignty over her body.

Historically, many have used the hunger strike as a protest tactic. Scholars agree that the hunger strike is used as a method of nonviolent action where the powerless struggle to create political opportunities out of nothing to correct a perceived injustice (Scanlan et al. 276). We have heard of hunger strikes in prisons such as Guantanamo, yet Indigenous groups have seen this tactic, Macarena Gómez-Barris notes, as "bodily performances of self-starvation [which] enact what it means to live in a barely livable state of colonial difference" (Gómez-Barris 121). In another example, Jennifer Shirmer discusses the protests of women in Guatemala and Chile in the 1970s and 1980s who persisted in seeking answers about their missing family members. They took over public spaces and called on the government to investigate disappearances and murders. In 1978, one hundred of these women engaged in the Long Hunger Strike with the support of Chilean society. Likewise, in her study, Gómez-Barris shows the Mapuche in Chile have used hunger strikes since 2004 as "a dominant form of political expression and of embodied cultural politics" to demonstrate that "the starving body of the hunger striker has become the site of resistance against the modern nation state's continued practice of colonial subjugation" (120).

As a protest tactic, hunger strikes mean that the striker undertakes great risks and thus must be willing to die for a cause. This tactic involves potential self-destruction of the body. Hunger strikes become dangerous to the body in only a few days when the body begins to break down fat in order to produce energy and ends up consuming itself from within to survive (Scanlan et al. 277). And while the idea is to call attention to a cause, a striker must also endure the emotions of the public.

There was both support and outrage regarding Spence's decision to go on a hunger strike. These came from both sides. In the mainstream media, the fifty-year-old Spence was often ridiculed and attempts were made to undermine her leadership. In fact, Patrick Brazeau (Algonquin) in Harper's Conservative Party claimed that Spence's action set "a bad example for First Nation youth" (McCarthy and Bradshaw). One of the most telling aspects of the media attack came when it was revealed that Spence was drinking lemon water, medicinal teas, and fish broth. Fish broth was characterized as "the cheat." And in media accounts, the words "hunger strike" became "liquid diet," thus tempering the phrase. Anishinabe writer Leeanne Simpson replied, "it's as if a liquid diet doesn't take substantial physical, mental, and emotional toll or substantial physical, mental, and emotional strength to accomplish" (Simpson).

Fish broth can be what Norma Alacón calls tropography or the interanimating relationships between metaphor and places (Brady 138). Spence was embodying cultural tradition. Her fast incorporated her peoples' cultural traditions of eating fish broth, which would be used traditionally to sustain communities when there was no food. According to Simpson, "Spence is eating fish broth because metaphorically colonialism has Indian people on a fish broth diet for generation upon generation" (Simpson).

As Simpson reasons, Chief Spence was in ceremony, and fasting as a ceremony is difficult. Roxanne Ornela, who visited Chief Spence during her strike, wrote, "I can relay with certainty that I know what bravery looks like while standing on the edge of life. I saw unwavering determination and courage in

Chief Spence's face while she held to her conviction in calling for changes to the government's apparent arrogance and mistreatment of First Nations" (6). Chief Spence and Grand Elder Robinson ended their strikes after forty-four days when the government and the Assembly of First Nations developed a plan agreeing on intergovernmental cooperation over the next five years ("First Nations: Working for Fundamental Change").

DIS/EMBODIED INDIGENOUS BODIES

Among the recent events to bring attention to issues in Indian country are displays and physical actions. During The Longest Walk, which took place in 1978, Indigenous bodies marched from San Francisco to Washington, DC, to bring attention to Native rights. While the 1978 walk is called the last of the Red Power Movement's activities (see the National Library of Medicine's "Native Voices" timeline), there have been a few more gatherings over the years, and most recently in July 2016 (called The Longest Walk 5). Other walkers include women who, since 2003, take on Mother Earth Water Walks carrying water from one end of the river to the others. In 2016, the women walked the Mississippi River from the gulf to her beginnings to bring water to her source. Most who are elders stop at sacred places along the way to do ceremony and ask healing for the river (Rendon).

To raise awareness of the missing and murdered Indigenous women (MMIW), the Ahtahkakoop Cree Nation held a Walk a Mile in Her Shoes march. Men squeezed their feet into red high heels to walk and raise money for a domestic violence shelter in addition to raising awareness. This event and the other activities above are all done in prayer for the sacredness of life, demonstrating the use of Indigenous bodies to honor and connect to all our relations.

However, the domestic abuse and violence against Indigenous women is both visible and invisible due to the lack of attention brought to this crisis. Thus, a form of disembodied display and awareness has emerged. In 2000, Jaime Black, a Metís artist, asked people to donate red dresses and hang them outside to bring awareness to the missing and murdered Indigenous women (Rieger). In a similar disembodied installation, *Walking with Our Sisters* is a commemorative traveling display of moccasin vamps placed on created red cloth pathways to honor the unfinished lives of missing and murdered Indigenous women. Through social media Christi Belcourt invited artists to make and donate the vamps, which now total over seventeen hundred (*Walking with Our Sisters*). The first installment opened on September 20, 2013, and is booked through 2018. Visitors are asked to remove their shoes and "walk with these women" to honor them.

Thus, Indigenous protectors seek various ways to bring justice to their causes. The physicality of movements uses endurance as a tactic to raise aware-ness. We must not, however, see the disembodied displays as separate from the others. The *bodies* of these missing and murdered women are just as present in these displays. Red dresses move with the elements to help us remember the women. In the same way, the making of the moccasin vamps and the vamps themselves call back to our memory loved ones whose lives were unfinished. As Indigenous people, we know our relatives and ancestors still walk among us, and we are responsible to honor them.

PROTECTING INDIGENOUS BODIES

Occupying tactics have been used by Indigenous peoples in many situations, yet there is an argument to be made that these lands have always been In-dian lands, thus Indian peoples are reclaiming and maintaining rather than occupying them. In 1969 a small, quiet group reclaimed Alcatraz Island and were joined by others in their stay of nineteen months. During the American Indian Movement (AIM), Indigenous bodies took over Wounded Knee and the Bureau of Indian Affairs offices in Washington and, most recently, have been reclaiming and maintaining spaces to prevent endangering Mother Earth or to reassert their rights to hunt and fish. As Adam Barker clarifies, these In-digenous occupations differ from the recent Occupy Movement in that Native peoples "have sought to reclaim and reassert relationships to land and place submerged beneath the settler colonial world. Their occupations do not ques-tion simply the divisions of wealth and power . . . they question the very ex-istence of settler colonial states" (329). Unlike the 99 percent as those in the Occupy Movement called themselves, Indigenous peoples address decoloniza-tion from their relationships to land and their role as protectors.

Indigenous bodies continue to place themselves at the forefront of protect-ing Mother Earth from the onslaught of greedy developers who try to extract every resource from her body. These developers don't consider the conse-quences of their greed. For example, Oklahoma is experiencing daily earth-quakes attributed by experts to the disposal of wastewater from fracking. Oil spills from fracking are happening everywhere, contaminating water supplies and land. In 2006 the Alberta pipeline "broke and spilled one million litres of oil" (Laboucan-Massimo 116), contaminating waters in traditional territories. The Keystone XL, DAPL, and other pipelines still loom as threats to Indigenous nations in North and South Dakota and Canada. Laboucan-Massimo writes that multiple spills have occurred "in other parts of North America, from Ka-lamazoo, Michigan to the Kinder Morgan spill along the west coast as well as spills . . . along the Keystone XL pipeline" (116). Despite the environmental concerns, hundreds of millions of dollars are being poured into getting crude oil out of Alberta into pipelines. Tribes like the Miq' maq of Els-i-potg engaged in protests, holding a roadblock on October 13, 2013. The Royal Canadian Mounted Police responded with teargas and rubber bullets. Other tribes have joined to develop Moccasins on the Ground training by Owe Aku's Sacred Water Protection Project; many of these people have joined the Sacred Stone Camp. The organization Owe Aku's focus on skills, tactics, and techniques of nonviolent direct action in three-day training camps. They demonstrate how to blockade heavy equipment, and they hold workshops on strategic media, street medic training, and knowing legal rights with respect to civil disobedience (Owe Aku). Indigenous bodies continue to protect the future for generations to come.

Threats to the environment and land are directly connected to the health of the body. Indigenous peoples argue that these threats also assault their cultural and spiritual beliefs and practices and endanger future generations. As Schlosberg and Carruthers agree, "The emphasis is on the health of the environment, and the protection of local economies, and the preservation of local and traditional cultures and practices. Specific demands focus not only on religious, cultural, and traditional abilities, but also on the political freedoms and the self-determination and community functioning" (18). Thus it is imperative to have a rhetorical and historical understanding of the issues in Indian county. Gloria Anzaldúa notes, "for images, words, stories to have . . . transformative power, they must arise from the human body—flesh and bone" (97).

It is our responsibility as Native peoples to care for our lands and our peoples: to walk with our relatives who came before us and with those who will come in the future. We understand our interconnectedness to all our relations and hold them in reverence. While the protectors at Standing Rock and Idle No More have brought renewed attention to the issues, longtime activist and musician Buffy Sainte-Marie emphasizes, "We've had an indigenous peoples grassroots movement all long. It didn't show up because we didn't have anything to do that day" (Ostroff). While our issues and lives are often kept in the shadows, our peoples have never been idle; we have indeed laid our bodies on the line over and over again.

We will continue to do so.

ACKNOWLEDGMENTS

I wish to thank the editors of *Unruly Rhetorics* for asking me to participate in this conversation. As well, I wish to thank and honor all the Indigenous peoples who have participated in and supported these movements to bring rights to our peoples.

Kutâputamunuw.

NOTES

1. I use "protest" here to indicate the non–Native American view of the camp. People participating and Native Americans in general refer to themselves as protectors, not protestors.

WORKS CITED

Anzaldúa, Gloria. *Borderlands/La Frontera: The New Mestiza.* 3rd ed. Aunt Lute, 2007.

Baird, Jessie little doe. *We Still Live Here—Âs Nutayuneân.* Directed by Anne Makepeace, 2008.

Barker, Adam J. "Already Occupied: Indigenous Peoples, Settler Colonialism and the Occupy Movements in North America. *Social Movement Studies* 2, nos. 3–4 (August–November 2012): 327–34.

"BIA Aware of Mercenaries at Standing Rock." *Lakota Country Times* 13, no. 37, June 1–6, 2017. www.lakotacountrytimes.com/news/2017-06-01/Front_Page/BIA_Aware_Of _Mercenaries_At_Standing_Rock.html.

Butler, Judith. *Bodies That Matter.* New York: Routledge, 1993.

David, Dan. "In the Spirit of Crazy Dance: Why Rounddancing Is Revolutionary." *Media Indigena*, January 29, 2013. www.mediaindigena.com/dan-david/issues-and-politics /in-the-spirit-of-crazy-dance/.

de Certeau, Michel. *The Practice of Everyday Life.* University of California Press, 2011.

Einstein, Zillah. *Hatreds: Racialized and Sexualized Conflicts in the 21st Century.* Routledge, 1996.

Endres, Danielle, and Samantha Senda-Cook. "Location Matters: The Rhetoric of Place in Protest." *Quarterly Journal of Speech* 9, no. 3 (August 2011): 257–82.

"First Nations: Working for Fundamental Change." Assembly of First Nations Declaration of Commitment. www.afn.ca/2013/01/29/declaration-of-commitment-january-23-2013/.

Gómez-Barris, Macarena. "Mapuche Hunger Acts: Epistemology of the Decolonial." *Transmodernity: Journal of Peripheral Culture Production of the Lusa-Hispanic World* 1, no. 3 (2012): 102–31.

Heim, Joe. "Dakota Access Pipeline Foes Bring Their Fears to Capitol Hill" *Chicago Tribune*, December 10, 2016. www.chicagotribune.com/news/nationworld/ct-dakota -pipeline-protest-washington-20161210-story.html.

Honor the Earth. www.honorearth.org.

Inman, Derek, Stefaan Smis, and Dorothée Cambou. "'We Will Remain Idle No More': The Shortcomings of Canada's 'Duty to Consult' Indigenous Peoples." *Goettingen Journal of International Law* 5 (2013): 252–85.

Kimmerer, Robin Wall. *Braiding Sweetgrass: Indigenous Wisdom, Scientific Knowledge and the Teachings of Plants.* Milkweed Editions, 2014.

King, Thomas. *The Inconvenient Indian.* University of Minnesota Press, 2013.

Laboucan-Massimo, Melina. "Awaiting Justice: Indigenous Resistance in the Tar Sands of Canada." *Open Democracy*, April 22, 2015. www.opendemocracy.net/5050/melina-loubicanmassimo/awaiting-justice-%E2%80%93-indigenous-resistance-to-tar-sand-development-in-cana/.

LaDuke, Winona. "Winona LaDuke on the Dakota Access Pipeline: What Would Sitting Bull Do?" *Yes! Magazine*, August 29, 2016. www.yesmagazine.org/planet/an-oil-pipeline-and-a-river-what-would-sitting-bull-do-20160829/.

LaDuke, Winona. *Recovering the Sacred: The Power of Naming and Claiming*. Haymarket Books, 2016.

McAuliff, Michael. "Defense Bill Passes, Giving Sacred Native American Sites to Mining Company." *Huffington Post*, December 12, 2014. www.huffingtonpost.com/2014/12/12/defense-bill-passes-rio-tinto_n_6317946.html.

McCarthy, Shawn, and James Bradshaw. "Idle No More Protesters Block Main Toronto-Montreal Rail Line in Support of Chief Spence." *Globe and Mail*, December 30, 2012 updated March 26, 2017. www.theglobeandmail.com/news/national/idle-no-more-protesters-block-main-toronto-montreal-rail-line-in-support-of-chief-spence/article6802286/.

Nagam, Julie. "(Re)mapping the Colonized Body: The Creative Interventions of Rebecca Belmoe in the Cityscape." *American Indian Culture and Research Journal* 35, no. 4 (2011): 147–66.

National Library of Medicine. "Timeline." *Native Voices: Native Peoples' Concept of Health and Illness*. www.nlm.nih.gov/nativevoices/timeline/index.html.

Nevit, Lisa. "Toyi-toyi?" *Cape Town Magazine*. n.d. www.capetownmagazine.com/whats-the-deal-with/toyi-toyi/125_22_17384/.

Owe Aku: Bring Back the Way and International Justice Project. "Moccasins on the Ground." www.oweakuinternational.org/moccasins-on-the-ground.html.

Ornelas, Roxanne T. "Implementing the Policy of the U.N. Declaration on the Rights of Indigenous Peoples." *International Policy Journal* 5, no. 1 (February 2014).

Ostroff, Joshua. "Buffy Sainte-Marie on Idle No More, Stephen Harper and Residential Schools." *Huffington Post Canada*, June 3, 2015.

Rendon, Marcie. "Sacred Water, Water Women Feature: Recognizing the Interconnectedness of All Things." *Minnesota Women's Press*, July 15, 2017. www.womenspress.com/main.asp?Search=1&ArticleID=4848&SectionID=1&SubSectionID=233&S=1/.

Rheingold, Howard. *Smart Mobs: The Next Social Revolution*. Basic Books, 2003.

Rieger, Sarah. "Red Dresses Draw Attention to Canada's Missing and Murdered Indigenous Women." *Huffington Post Alberta*, September 30, 2015. www.huffingtonpost.ca/2015/09/29/red-dress-aboriginal-women-redress-project_n_8216104.html.

Salmond, Michael. "The Power of Momentary Communities: Locative Media and (In)Formal Protest." *Aether: The Journal of Media Geography* (March 2010): 90–100.

Sandalow-Ash, Rachel. "What It Takes to Fight for Indigenous Sovereignty and Environmental Justice." Interview with Jeremy Woods. *Generation Progress*, March 15, 2013. www.genprogress.org/voices/2013/03/15/18611/interview-with-an-idle-no-more -organizer/.

Scanlan, Steven J., Laurie Cooper Stroll, and Kimberly Lumen. "Starving for Change: The Hunger Strike and Non-Violent Action, 1906–2004." *Research in Social Movements, Conflicts and Changes* 28: 275–323.

Schlosberg, David, and David Carruthers. "Indigenous Struggles, Environmental Justice, and Community Capabilities." *Global Environmental Politics* 10, no. 4 (November 2010): 12–35.

Shea Murphy, Jacqueline. *The People Have Never Stopped Dancing: Native American Modern Dance Histories*. University of Minnesota Press, 2007.

Shirmer, Jennifer G. "'Those Who Died for Life Cannot Be Called Dead': Women and Human Rights in Latin America." *Feminist Review* (1998): 3–29.

Simpson, Leeanne. "Fish Broth and Fasting." *Opinion*, January 16, 2013. *Walking with Our Sisters*. www.walkingwithoursisters.ca/about/.

3

A GROOVE WE CAN MOVE TO

THE SOUND & SENSE OF QUEBEC'S *MANIFS CASSEROLES*, SPRING 2012

JONATHAN STERNE

Most of this chapter was originally written during the Quebec student strike of 2012.[1] That year, hundreds of thousands of Quebec university and college students went on strike to protest increases to what was then the lowest tuition in the United States or Canada. Quebec has always had its own political traditions, and free university education was one of the promises of the Quiet Revolution in the 1960s, right alongside free secondary education. While university tuition is not free, it has not skyrocketed as it has across the United States, and while students still sometimes take on debt for an education, it is nothing like the debts that students of US universities sometimes carry. In 2011, the Liberal provincial government proposed a significant tuition increase, and the students took to the streets. This was not a spontaneous protest: it reflected years of organizing on the part of several student unions. In comparison with #Occupy, which was happening at the same time, the strike was more an example of the power of union syndicalism than it was social media or other supposedly new political situations. The Quebec strike was also much bigger, with protests that—conservatively counted—went over one hundred thousand people. Not all students went on strike. While the Université du Québec à Montréal and the Université de Montréal lost a semester, students at my university (McGill University) were considerably more divided on whether—and how—to participate. The protests were eventually banned by the government, which had the effect of bringing even more people out into the streets, people who may not have supported the original student cause but who were offended by the ban on expression, or who simply were excited to participate in what became a carnivalesque atmosphere.

In the Anglo press, there was some debate over the use of the term "strike," which was clearly meant as a reference to the French practices of student strikes in the tradition that had developed since May 1968. It is true—in the narrow definitional sense—that students are not employees with a legal right to strike, though, of course, students who are employees have their own unions and can strike. Some more pedantic English-language commentators called the walkout a "boycott," though it should be noted that this was almost always in the context of condemning the students. The term "strike" was preferred by the activists, and as part of the history of student activism in the Francophone world it is a much better description of what actually transpired.

The texts I wrote were efforts to make sense of the strike, in the tradition of the left intellectuals I admired. They were also efforts to publicize the strike and notify international academic audiences that were not otherwise aware of what was happening in Quebec. The texts do not tell the whole story of the strike by any means, and they are not meant to (and cannot) represent a student perspective. If you read French, I recommend a book such as *On s'en câlisse* from the Collectif de débrayage.[2]

But since I wrote at a particular time for a particular purpose, my analysis should not be taken as complete. As with all political action, the *result* of the protests was contradictory. The students "won" in the sense that they toppled the Liberal government, and its proposed tuition increase did not go through. However, the Parti Québécois (PQ) government that was elected the following September turned out to be just as damaging to students but in other ways. After briefly flirting with a tax increase for the richest Quebeckers, they turned around and slashed budgets for health care and education (including a retroactive cut to university budgets in an effort to balance their own books). They also created a tuition increase that was indexed to inflation. In other spheres, the PQ was even worse, proposing a "Charter of Values" designed to drum up anti-Muslim sentiment and to rally ethnic nationalist votes. The student unions did not respond. In part this is because the 2012 strike was not spontaneous, and so it would be wrong to assume that they *could* spontaneously respond to the PQ's measures. In part, it had to do with the particulars of Quebec politics. Eighteen months after the Liberals were thrown out, the PQ lost an election they had called—and the Liberals came back into power. Now, as I write in August 2015, the largest unions in the province are organizing a general strike against the Liberals' wildly unpopular austerity measures. Student unions are working with organized labor so, if it comes off, this strike will look very different from the last one. What it will bring to the province is anyone's guess. But the lesson to take is that the work of social change is always unfinished. There is always more to do, and more is always possible.

BODIES-STREETS

The city provides the order and organization that automatically links otherwise unrelated bodies. . . . *The city orients and organizes family, sexual and social relations insofar as the city divides cultural life into public and private domains, geographically dividing and defining the* particular social positions and locations occupied by individuals and groups.

—Elizabeth Grosz, "Bodies-Cities"

Every night around eight o'clock, in neighborhoods across Montreal and Quebec, you can hear the din of clanging pots and pans in *manifs casseroles*. (*Manif* is short for *manifestation en cours*, a street protest.) About a block from our home in Montreal's Villeray neighborhood, at the intersection of Jarry and St-Denis, one of the major epicenters, our local *manif* begins with people crossing in the crosswalks, banging loudly and rhythmically. We see neighbors and people from local businesses, families with small children, elderly and retired people, working adults, and many students.

Sometimes a *manif casserole* sounds like random banging, but most I've experienced leave sheer raucous pounding for moments when one march meets up with another, or when someone on a balcony does something particularly cool to cheer on the marchers. A rhythm usually arises from the chaos, encircling the disorder and enveloping everyone. Sometimes the rhythms connect with chants like "*la loi spéciale, on s'en câlisse*," which roughly translates to "we don't give a fuck about your special law."

Eventually, the numbers grow, and then all of a sudden, as if by magic or intuition, we stand in the middle of the intersection, blocking traffic. The police have taken to simply routing traffic away from the protest. Eventually, we march south on St-Denis toward other neighborhoods (the exact route varies), often swelling into a giant parade of thousands, or as E. P. Thompson might suggest, a parody of a formal state procession, announcing the "total publicity of disgrace" for its subject (6, 8).

The numbers are part of the politics. For the last one hundred days or so, most Quebec students have been on strike against tuition increases of over 70 percent in five years.[3] Some protests have numbered in the hundreds of thousands. The Quebec government tried to suppress the student movement by passing Bill 78 on May 18, 2012. Among its many preposterous provisions, any spontaneous gathering of over fifty people is illegal without prior police approval—even a picnic. Protesters must disclose not only their planned route but also their means of transportation. According to Law 78, people are criminals the minute they join a protest, which is why so many people have taken to the streets.

Marching south on rue St-Denis in our nightly #casseroles protests, I am struck by how different my neighborhood looks from the middle of the street. Looking from an imaginary viewpoint directly above, the street says a lot about the organization of cities. Thin strips of sidewalk at either side are for pedestrians. The vast middle is for cars. That simple division of space speaks volumes about the order of things physically inscribed into city life.

PROTEST'S EXTENDED TOUCH

So much of the controversy over the tuition strike and Law 78 has been about the politics of possibility and the politics of space. The politics of possibility surround the fundamental questions of the tuition strike. Arguments around the strike rehearse controversies we have heard all over the world regarding neoliberalism: What, exactly, is the horizon of reasonable expectation for everyday people? What are the obligations of the state to their populations, and how do those obligations relate to the politics of high finance? The politics of possibility consist of struggles over what we are allowed to imagine as alternatives to the present social order, and which imagined social and economic relations are admissible to serious public political discussion. Proponents of the hike argue that the province cannot afford to keep funding education without raising tuition. They argue for a very restricted social imagination, one that hews closely to the current social order and keeps the large portfolio of provincial economic and policy priorities intact. Opponents of the increase point back to the promises of free tuition that came with the Quiet Revolution and ask us to reconsider who should pay for education, how and when. The call for free college and university tuition might sound outrageous to some, but this is precisely because of a limited imagination—whether intentionally or unintentionally. Germany has done just fine with such a system, and there was a time not so long ago when free education for primary and secondary students was also a radical proposition.

We can say the same thing about the protests. Law 78 resulted from the failure of the Liberals to persuade enough people to limit their imaginations to existing social relations. If people won't accede freely to limited politics of possibility, then perhaps they could be coerced. Law 78 decried and criminalized bodies out of place, fifty at a time, because they interfered with normal urban flows—flows of people and flows of money.

The *Montreal Gazette*'s daily sensational headlines also argue that the problem with the strike is that it disrupts normal flows of people and money, and in the process the editors implicitly argue that some economics are more important than others. On May 30 they ran a mostly fictional story about how the strike "could" hurt student enrollment and faculty recruitment, despite the fact that no reliable source would corroborate the proposition. On May 31 they ran a story about the "human cost" to service workers, and yet the sources quoted claiming there was a cost were not service workers or unions but, rather, business leaders. Of course, strikes and protests inconvenience people—that is the point, after all. Of course, they have economic ramifications, though if the concerns about the economy are paramount, we must question the lack of coverage of the effects of student debt, which is also a serious financial concern not just in Quebec but in many countries. My own university's injunction against striking clerical staff last fall followed a similar logic. The basis for the injunction was that the noise of the strike could be heard in offices and classrooms. The noise of university-sanctioned, corporate-sponsored parties during frosh week can be heard all over campus as well, yet these continue each year unabated. The point is clear: inconveniences for business purposes are fine. Inconveniences for meaningful politics are not.

Inside the *manifs casseroles* the percussion is overwhelming, beating a rhythm of phenomenal collectivity that is entirely immersive because it is so loud. At some distance, the noise tickles neighborhoods, enticing some neighbors to join in, while others such as Montreal's mayor cringe at the protesters' extended touch. Because they happen collectively and in the streets, the *casseroles* protests materialize and metonymize a critique of the horizons of possibility as set out by the provincial liberals. Many commentators have pointed out that the *manifs casseroles* have brought out groups that are otherwise unconnected politically: students, nationalists, anarchists, union activists, religious groups, the elderly, and so on. But this is to miss the point entirely. All politics are about connection, and any political movement or political party is made up of what Stuart Hall (following Ernesto Laclau and Chantal Mouffe) calls articulations: non-necessary connections among disparate elements to create a temporary "whole" (Hall; Laclau and Mouffe; Slack). We know this about political parties; they are all bundles of contradictions when you look under the blanket. But we forget and talk about the party as a unified thing. The same should be said for the movement. Sure, it contains contradictions, but the movement is united in refusing Law 78 and in reaching out to other possible social arrangements. As Natalie Zemon Davis and I argued in a coauthored piece for the *Globe and Mail*, it is an attempt to collectively redress a violation of the community.

TWENTY-FIRST-CENTURY CHARIVARI

In the *Globe and Mail* (Sterne and Davis), we connected the *casseroles* with a seven-hundred-year-old Francophone tradition of *charivari*. In English, the tradition is called "rough music"; there are also Italian, German, and Spanish versions, and the practice has spread from Europe throughout its former colonies. Groups of disguised young men would meet up at night and bang on pots and pans and make a grand din outside an offender's home. Usually the offense was against some heterosexual norm, but they sometimes took on a political character, and older people would join in. As Allan Greer has shown in *The Patriots and the People,* they played an important role in Lower Canada's failed rebellion of 1837–1838, where charivaris greeted British officials who would not surrender their commissions (252–57).

In the French tradition, charivaris were (usually) an alternative to violence on occasions where community reparation was possible. Charivaris were largely inclusive, as the subjects of harassment were usually allowed to return to good standing after paying some type of fine. This history may well have resounded in Jacques Attali's ears when he described music as a simulacrum of violence in *Noise*: "the game of music resembles the game of power: monopolize the right to violence; provoke anxiety and then provide a feeling of security; provoke disorder and then propose order; create a problem in order to solve it" (28). Of course, the broader multinational traditions of rough music have no guaranteed politics. Pots and pans were sometimes heard before lynchings in the American South but also as improvised instruments for black musicians in the public squares of New Orleans. John Mowitt has even suggested that rough music is one of the cultural roots of the drummer's trap kit, that backbone of rock and jazz music.

In the twentieth century, varieties of rough music largely moved from domestic concerns to political protest, though again without guarantees. Rough music has greeted bank failures in Latin America and, most recently, Iceland; it was the sound of Spanish citizens opposed to their government's involvement in the 2003 Iraq war. In Chile, protesters used pots and pans to protest Allende in the early 1970s and, later, to protest Pinochet in the mid-1980s. The *casseroles* thus have symbolic roots in charivari, but of course they are also creatures of social media and the particularities of Quebec culture and politics. A popular 2003 Loco Locass song "Libérez-nous des libéraux" (Liberate us from the liberals), written for the provincial election, mentions a charivari for Quebec's Liberal party. And, as the student movement has already demonstrated, the protest cultures here are extremely vital. While New York's May Day Parade was happy to attract tens of thousands in a metropolitan area of over ten million, participation here can be counted in the hundreds of thousands for a region with three million.

RHYTHM AND PARTICIPATION

We need to listen to the *casseroles* protests to understand them. They are, after all, embodied acts in the old-fashioned sense, performed loudly and defiantly by people in the streets. They have a politics of volume and frequency, as well as rhythm. In *Percussion,* John Mowitt wrote, "there is something extraordinary about the importance of beating, of creating a specifically percussive din . . . as though a distinctly sonoric response was called for when a breach in the community's self-perception was at issue" (98). Rhythmic participation in the *casseroles* is a kind of political involvement, and participation of various kinds plays a role in most of the positive political visions associated with music.

This utopian dimension of the *manifs* is most strongly manifested in the middle of the street, in disrupting the presumptive organization of the city. Bylaws that prohibit people from walking where cars are supposed to go obviously enforce a measure of safety, but they also enforce what Ivan Illich calls a radical monopoly: "Cars can thus monopolize traffic. They can shape a city into their image—practically ruling out locomotion on foot or by bicycle in Los Angeles. They can eliminate river traffic in Thailand. That motor traffic curtails the right to walk, not that more people drive Chevies than Fords, constitutes radical monopoly" (52).

The organization of movement is thus closely tied to political and social organization—just look at which neighborhoods on this continent have access to good public transport and which do not. So to take back the streets in the form of marching, especially in light of a law banning fifty people from gathering *anywhere* outdoors without prior notice to the police, is a way of interrogating that order of rights and mobilities. Writing of cars in the United States, Zack Furness argues that the automobile "functions as both the literal and symbolic centerpiece of a narrative equating individual mobility and personal freedom" (7).

Although the story is slightly different in Quebec, the *manifs casseroles* and larger street protests in Montreal function a lot like the critical mass protests chronicled by Furness. They "slow down the world" (Furness 88), creating opportunities for encounters between people. Although these encounters are not themselves particularly dialogic—it is hard to talk over the din—they show that local organization can happen, that the city can be taken over by the people who live in it. Walking with thousands of my neighbors down the middle of the street, in a space reserved by law for cars, in a procession banned by law because of its size, I greet the people I see night after night, we make music together, and I know an alternative social order is possible. I know it physically because of where my body—and the bodies of my neighbors—have been together.

"Participation is the opposite of alienation," wrote Charlie Keil in his essay "Participatory Discrepancies and the Power of Music," and his account of music as a social process in "Motion and Feeling through Music" helps us better understand the *casseroles*' particular combination of clangor and rhythm. Writing amid massive changes in the 1960s, Keil challenged prevailing theories of musical affect, like Leonard Meyer's, which assumed that musical meaning was lexical and syntactic, contained in melody and harmony. While Meyer attempted to draw universal conclusions about emotion from Western art music and its attendant values, Keil derived his theory of musical affect from African American traditions such as blues and jazz. Against the ideals of concert hall perfection and rational mastery, Keil—along with writers such as Christopher Small, Leroi Jones, and Steven Feld—argued that music should be understood as action. Thus, Small coined the term "musicking," describing music not as a collection of rarefied texts performed by experts and professionals but, rather, as a field of social action that includes all participants, from musicians to the people cleaning up after the event.

By the 1980s Keil specified the affective power of music through its "participatory discrepancies," the mixture of groove on one hand and timbre and texture on the other (96): "music, to be personally and socially valuable, must be 'out of time' and 'out of tune.'" Over the minutes and hours, the *casseroles* sway in and out of both, as people join and exit, and as the procession happens to each new block. Because of their unique musical character, the nightly *manifs casseroles* are profoundly inclusive. They are in many ways closer to the utopian ideals of collective musicking that one finds in Keil's and Small's work, and that of Attali's "composition," than the so-called digital revolution in musical instruments. They are also good fun, as any child will tell you.

Anglophone press caricatures recast the protests as the product of entitled, rabble-rousing students.[4] But the *casseroles* transcend differences that often structure local politics—like language, class, and race—as well as gender and age, which can present barriers in music-making (especially drumming) in addition to politics. Because the instruments are simple, cheap, and improvised, almost anyone can join in. Because the music is deliberately nonprofessional, the ideals of mastery and perfection and the weighty gendered and aged assumptions about who can be a "good musician" are inoperative. The beats are easy to pick up and play in time—and if you swing a little out there, all the better. I have heard skilled drummers syncopate catchy rhythms on single drums or cymbals, but most people are content to simply move in and out of time with everyone else. (My partner and I join with maracas and an otherwise rarely used buffalo drum—I am a bassist at heart—though we offer guests pots and pans.)

NOW PEOPLE GREET AND TALK

Taken together, volume and frequency work to immerse some in its proximal footprint, while hailing others at a distance. The sheer power and volume for someone inside a *casseroles* protest is hard to convey. My neighbor on a pot is a lot like my drummer hitting a cymbal. The transient (the sharp initial part of the hit) can be piercing at close range due to frequencies at the very top of the audible range traveling at a high sound pressure level (this is why drummers often lose their hearing faster than guitarists). Inside the *casseroles* march, our ears are percussed with every hit; many people show up wearing earplugs.

The frequencies dull a bit farther away, and the more pitched sounds of the *casseroles* tickle the ear's center of hearing in a gentler cacophony that is both declarative and invitational. Since the point of the protests is to audibly flout Law 78, the fact that they can be heard much further than they can be seen helps make this law-breaking an expressly public and political act. Montreal mayor Gerard Tremblay acknowledged as much: "They can stay on their balconies to make noise. I'm in Outremont [a wealthy enclave next to Mile End and the Plateau, another epicenter of the protests] and I can hear it. No need to go onto the street, to walk around and paralyse Montreal" (Corriveau).

The volume's territorial reach also works as an invitation for others to join in, either by banging along on one of Montreal's ubiquitous porches or by entering the procession itself. While at the other end of the frequency spectrum from Steve Goodman's "bass materialism," the volume of the *casseroles* affords some of the "collective construction of a vibrational ecology" he describes in *Sonic Warfare* (196), as the whole sound of the pots and pans becomes greater than the sum of its parts. Participants' overwhelming response to the *casseroles* has been a kind of weighty sentimentality, an outpouring of emotion and relief that one can see in letters like this one to the editors of *Le Devoir*:

> Now people greet and talk. Now neighborhood meetings, discussions, vigils start up casually among neighbours on the steps and balconies of Montreal. The neighborhood will be less and less alien. This is a true political victory!
>
> We should repeat this friendly beating [the evocation of *tapage* doesn't quite work as well in English] possibly in other forms, until the land is occupied by neighbours who recognize one another, encounter one another each day by chance, and have known one another over the years. That is how we live in a place, that is how we become citizens. My heart swells with joy. (Lutfi)

Because "the clashing of pots and pans . . . is so blatantly percussive, it is hard not to hear in the retributive structure of rough music something like a beating back—a backbeat, in short, or a response on the part of the community to what it perceives as a provocation, a call to act," Mowitt wrote (98). The connections to charivari matter: the *casseroles* protests are local, neighborhood, community movements asking for a simple redress—the repeal of a heinous law. Of course, there are many other resonances: signs can be seen challenging various aspects of neoliberalism alongside symbols of Quebec nationalism (which, I must remind Anglophone Canadians, is not automatically separatist). In my neighborhood, people collect food donations.

When we recently spoke about the differences between student activists in the 1960s and now, my former teacher Lawrence Grossberg pointed to the central role of music in the 1960s. Those movements had songs that everyone knew, and through which shared affect grew. Like many other observers, he doesn't see music playing the same role today (perhaps supplanted by a wider range of media practices, as the usual story goes). Apart from viral videos and the revivified Loco Locass tune, I'm not sure the current Quebec movement has unifying songs. But it certainly has a groove we can move to.

NOTES

1. This essay, in different form, appeared previously as "Bodies-Streets," in *wi: Journal of Mobile Media* (June 2012) and as "Quebec's #Casseroles: On Participation, Percussion, and Protest," in *Sounding Out* (June 4, 2012), both published under a Creative Commons 2.0 license and reprinted here with the author's permission and with the author's revisions and updates.

2. If you do not read French, some of the French writings from the time are now archived in translation online at www.translatingtheprintempserable.tumblr.com/.

3. See Léo Charbonneau, "Quebec Student Protests" for a primer on the student strikes.

4. See Margaret Wente, "Quebec's Tuition Protesters Are the Greeks of Canada" for an example of the typical press coverage.

WORKS CITED

Attali, Jacques. *Noise: The Political Economy of Music.* University of Minnesota Press, 1985.

Charbonneau, Léo. "Quebec Student Protests: An Explainer." *The Guardian*, July 9, 2012. www.theguardian.com/higher-education-network/blog/2012/jul/09/international -fees/.

Corriveau, Jeanne. "Tintamarre contre la Loi 78: Tremblay ne veut pas que les Casseroles descendent dans la rue." *Le Devoir*, May 24, 2012. www.ledevoir.com/politique /montreal/350793/prix-en-democratie-theatre-absurde-a-l-hotel-de-ville-de -montreal/.

Feld, Steven. *Sound and Sentiment: Birds, Weeping, Poetics, and Song in Kaluli Expression.* University of Pennsylvania Press, 1990.

Furness, Zack. *One Less Car: Bicycling and the Politics of Automobility.* Temple University Press, 2010.

Goodman, Steve. *Sonic Warfare: Sound, Affect, and the Ecology of Fear.* MIT Press, 2009.

Greer, Allan. *The Patriots and the People: The Rebellion of 1837 in Rural Lower Canada.* University of Toronto Press, 1993.

Grosz, Elizabeth. "Bodies-Cities." In *Sexuality and Space*, edited by Beatriz Colomina and Jennifer Bloomer, 241–54. Princeton Architectural Press, 1992.

Hall, Stuart. "On Postmodernism and Articulation: An Interview with Stuart Hall." *Journal of Communication Inquiry* 10, no. 2 (1986): 45–60.

Illich, Ivan. *Tools for Conviviality.* Harper and Row, 1973.

Jones, Leroi. *Blues People: Negro Music in White America.* Harper, 1999.

Keil, Charles. "Participatory Discrepancies and the Power of Music." In *Music Grooves*, by Charles Keil and Steven Feld, 96–108. University of Chicago Press, 1994.

Laclau, Ernesto, and Chantal Mouffe. *Hegemony and Socialist Strategy: Towards a Radical Democratic Politics.* 2nd ed. Verso, 2001.

Lutfi, Jaber. "Lettre—Victoire collatérale." *Le Devoir*, May 24, 2012. www.ledevoir.com /opinion/lettres/350721/victoire-collaterale/.

Meyer, Leonard. *Emotion and Meaning in Music.* University of Chicago Press, 1961.

Mowitt, John. *Percussion: Drumming, Beating, Striking.* Duke University Press, 1992.

Slack, Jennifer Daryl. "The Theory and Method of Articulation in Cultural Studies." In *Stuart Hall: Critical Dialogues*, edited by Kuan-Hsing Chen and David Morley, 113–29. Routledge, 1996.

Small, Christopher. *Musicking: The Meanings of Performing and Listening.* Wesleyan University Press, 1998.

Sterne, Jonathan, and Natalie Zemon Davis. "Quebec's Manifs Casseroles Are a Call for Order." *Globe and Mail,* May 31, 2012. www.theglobeandmail.com/opinion/quebecs-manifs-casseroles-are-a-call-for-order/article4217621/.

Thompson, E. P. "Rough Music Reconsidered." *Folklore* 103, no. 1 (1992): 3–96.

Wente, Margaret. "Quebec's Tuition Protesters Are the Greeks of Canada." *Globe and Mail,* May 19, 2012. www.theglobeandmail.com/opinion/quebecs-tuition-protesters-are-the-greeks-of-canada/article4186821/.

4

STEVEN SALAITA'S RHETORICAL REFUSAL

TAKING TO TWITTER AS A FORM OF POLITICAL RESISTANCE & PROTEST

MATTHEW ABRAHAM

> I want to suggest only that when bodies assemble on the street, in the square, or in other forms of public space (including virtual ones) they are exercising a plural and performative right to appear, one that asserts and instates the body in the midst of the political field, and which, in its expressive and signifying function, delivers a bodily demand for a more livable set of economic, social, and political conditions no longer afflicted by induced forms of precarity.
>
> —Judith Butler, *Notes toward a Performative Theory of Assembly*

In "Rhetorical Education and Student Activism," Jonathan Alexander and Susan C. Jarratt explore how five Muslim students (Taher, Osama, Assad, Yousef, and Mohamed) at the University of California, Irvine—as participants in "The Irvine 11"—responded to the Israeli ambassador to the United States, Michael Oren, when he spoke on campus in February 2010. Oren had served as a paratrooper in the Israeli Defense Forces (IDF) during Israel's 1982 invasion of Lebanon and was appointed ambassador to Israel in 2009 during Israel's Operation Cast Lead in Gaza. One of the students, Osama, reflected on the Irvine 11's rhetorical goals: "The direct goal was to send a message to Michael Oren. And it was to be rude." Osama then goes on to elaborate a strong and sophisticated critique of civility: "You have to be rude sometimes, especially if you're dealing with systems of injustice. . . . There is no room to be polite to injustice. . . . You can be polite if you feel someone can be convinced otherwise, then obviously you can take into consideration what is the best way to approach this person. But I think this is not that sort of situation" (Alexander and Jarratt 536). Osama rejects the concept of civil dialogue as an appropriate rhetorical approach in this context. Alexander and Jarratt observe, "Osama's search here for an adequate vocabulary reveals the *limitations of a discourse of middle-class behavioral norms*—politeness versus rudeness—often employed in a paternal way by university administrators faced with vigorous activism" (536, emphasis added).

Alexander and Jarratt invite us to consider how these students' protest against Oren's presence as an Israeli government official on UCI's campus can teach us much about the limitations of the liberal deliberative model of debate, within which dispassion and reasoned argument are highly valued. This liberal deliberative model frames expressions of anger and disgust against state violence as being irrational and uncivil and necessitating intervention against those who engage in such expressions. Alexander and Jarratt do not develop their argument in this article around the figure of the Palestinian body in protest, but one can see how the Muslim students (one of whom is Palestinian) represent the Palestinian body politic by confronting Ambassador Oren about Israel's military actions during the 2008–2009 Operation Cast Lead against Palestinian bodies in Gaza. The relationship between these Muslim students advocating on behalf of the Palestinian cause and the actual Palestinians on the ground in Gaza, the subjects of this advocacy, is a complex one. The very bodies of the protesting Muslim students at UCI act as stand-ins for the Gaza Palestinians—for whom these students seek to give voice. When the Irvine 11 were targeted for legal prosecution for disturbing a public gathering for their protest against Oren, they were targeted because they were representing Palestinian bodies that are continually excised and erased from public consciousness. Interrupting this excision and erasure—and attempting to advance the Palestinian permission to narrate—constitutes an unruly rhetoric because of the social-political and discursive constraints shaping the US public sphere.

By extending Alexander and Jarratt's insights to an examination of Steven Salaita's controversial tweets during the summer of 2014, just prior to when the University of Illinois rescinded his tenured position in response to the supposed incivility represented within the tweets, we might gain a better understanding of the intended and unintended rhetorical action informing those tweets. We might also obtain an appreciation for the larger context within which they emerged. Alexander and Jarratt explore how the students of the Muslim Student Association at the University of California, Irvine, in their deliberations about how best to protest Oren's visit, weighed how they would confront and highlight the issue of Israeli exceptionalism. In examining the tweets of Steven Salaita, I take a close look at the relevance of this discourse for activists seeking to promote what Edward Said called the Palestinian "permission to narrate."

Indeed, Salaita's tweets can be reframed as being part of the Palestinian quest to gain the permission to narrate and also as being part of a broader exploration into the conditions of possibility shaping the development of legitimate modes of protest within the public sphere. These modes of protest emerge alongside the struggles among bodies within public space fighting for acknowledgment and recognition. Such a reframing and exploration might reveal the very conditions of articulation separating "civil" from "unruly" expression.

The context for understanding the precariousness of Palestinian lives emerged long before the 2014 Gaza War, in the months leading up to the creation of Israel in 1948, when nearly seven hundred Palestinian villages were destroyed by the Haganah and the Stern Gang (precursors of the IDF) as part of the ethnic cleansing of Palestine at the time of Israel's founding.[1] In this context, Palestinian bodies were dislocated from the land of Palestine. Further dislocation occurred over time, with the accelerated building of Israeli settlements since 1967, along with the construction of the now ubiquitous separation wall snaking throughout the West Bank and around Jerusalem. These represent biotechnological interventions aiming to control and debilitate not only Palestinian bodies but also expressions of the Palestinian political will. Through the medium of Twitter during the fifty-one days of Operation Protective Edge, Salaita attempted to speak to this condition of the Palestinian body and political will, as this body and will sought to find sites of articulation and protest. Such sites for the articulation and protest of the Palestinian body and will are blocked by the Holocaust narrative, by the discourses of historical anti-Semitism and Israeli exceptionalism, and most recently, by the introduction of state legislation seeking to block the Palestinian permission to narrate by making participation in the Boycott, Divestment, Sanctions Movement a punishable offense (Edelman). The Holocaust narrative prioritizes historical Jewish suffering in the wake of what has been called the "Shoah," the Hebrew word for "calamity" or "catastrophe," positioning it as the ultimate example of human sacrifice to which no other genocide can possibly compare. The Arabic word for the 1948 dispossession of the Palestinians by Israel is called the "Nakba," which also translates into English as "catastrophe." However, for Zionists, the Palestinian Nakba—a precursor to the creation of Israel—constitutes a legitimate response to Jewish suffering experienced in Europe during the Holocaust.

In this sense, the Palestinians can be considered the "victims of the victims," in that they continue to pay for the European crime of the Holocaust by being forced to relinquish their homeland as the price that must be paid for Israel's creation and continued territorial annexation of the West Bank.[2]

Closely tied to the Holocaust narrative is the mindfulness about and fight against historical anti-Semitism, the Gentile hatred of Jews. Israel, as the proclaimed Jewish state, positions itself as a place of refuge for Jews fleeing anti-Semitism throughout the world. The Right of Return gives any Jew the option of the immediate Right of Return to Israel as the Jewish state. Many Jews choose to make "Aliyah" (the Hebrew word for "return") to Israel for religious and cultural reasons. Since Zionism posits that anti-Semitism is a perpetual part of the human condition and that Israel is the solution to this condition, the existence of anti-Semitism is ironically necessary to justify the main tenets of Zionism, tenets that include the push for the ethnic exclusivity of the state and the removal of its Arab citizens (20 percent of Israel's population). Zionism purposely conflates the discourse of anti-Semitism with Palestinian resistance to territorial dispossession so as to frame the Palestinian national liberation movement as part of the legacy of anti-Semitism. The ways of doing this are both subtle and overt: subtle, in that these Palestinians resisting Israel's territorial expansion become part of the drama to protect Jews against anti-Semitism in the wake of the Holocaust; overt, in that Palestinian lives are negligible in the context of Zionist expansionism.

Connected to this promotion of the discourse of historical anti-Semitism is the immunization of Israel through the discourse of Israeli exceptionalism, a reference to the special treatment that Israel receives in the international community because it is the Jewish State. Israeli exceptionalism allows Israel to do whatever is necessary militarily and diplomatically to defend itself and its interests. Israel is exceptional in this sense precisely because it is a safe haven for world Jewry. The Boycott, Divestment, Sanctions Movement challenges the prerogatives of Israeli exceptionalism by advocating an economic and academic boycott of those Israeli institutions that are complicit in legitimating and contributing to Israel's occupation.[3]

Salaita's tweets protesting the precariousness of Palestinian lives in Gaza during Israel's fifty-one-day Operation Protective Edge highlight the challenge of resisting these powerful, Palestinian voice- and life-denying discourses around the Holocaust, historical anti-Semitism, and Israeli exceptionalism. When Palestinians gather en masse to protest land confiscation, to object to the construction of an illegal settlement, or to mourn the killing of a Palestinian child by the IDF, then such mass protests constitute a possible security threat, since, for the Israelis, the wrong bodies have achieved a critical mass.

The threat inheres in the number and concentration of bodies coming together in a site of protest. Fists raised in unison, chants about freeing Palestine and ending the Nakba (the catastrophe) of 1948, calls for the enactment of the Palestinian Right of Return, as well as more overt acts of resistance such as rock throwing, all are met with tear gas, rubber bullets, and artillery fire from Israeli tanks and other combat vehicles. Protesting Palestinian bodies in the present—descendants of 1948 Palestinians—remind Israel that its ethnic cleansing of Palestine is still not complete.

These reminders of the Palestinian presence lurk within the realm of rhetoric and composition studies scholarship, despite efforts to completely erase that presence. It cannot be happenstance that these attempted erasures have coincided with the promotion of the global flows associated with digital and multilingual discourses. In a withering critique of Steven Fraiberg's "Composition 2.0," Tony Scott and Nancy Welch, in their "One Train Can Hide Another: Critical Materialism for Public Composition," interrogate composition's promotion of a seeming professional apartheid through its embrace of the global flows informing conceptions of multilingual discourse, pointing out that Fraiberg fails to recognize the irony that Israel shuts Palestinians out of its constituted society. In his focus on the emergence of Tel Aviv's high-tech culture and the ways in which English has been "woven into the fabric of everyday life of Israeli Society" (Fraiberg, "Composition 2.0," 100), along with his assertion that the "Israeli high-tech sector is a key site for studying the convergence(s) of semiotic, technological, cultural, national, and global forces" (107), Fraiberg refuses to look at the political-material forces structuring Israeli society in its ongoing struggle with the Palestinians. Buried in footnote 8 of the article, providing support for a statement that "In traditional stories of Israeli history, the trope of David and Goliath is commonly invoked, with a smaller, less-equipped Israeli army overcoming overwhelming force and odds" (108), Fraiberg notes that this is a viewpoint from within Israeli society (an emic perspective) and that Israeli revisionist historians, such as Benny Morris, "have argued that the Israeli army was in many ways superior and better organized than the Arab armies in the 1948 War of Independence" (120). Putting to one side that Fraiberg chooses to call the 1948 war "a war of independence," he makes no attempt to acknowledge Palestinian loss and dispossession, much less to even mention the word "Palestinian."

Scott and Welch interpret Fraiberg's silence on how Israeli society has constituted itself as indicating a refusal to address the precarious predicament of Palestinian bodies living under Israeli occupation. The fact that the Palestinian predicament lurks in the background of Fraiberg's article and is only obliquely addressed as "the ambiguity and uncertainty of the present political situation" is telling, an admission of a depoliticized argument unwilling to engage with material realities, specifically material bodies.[4] Scott and Welch emphasize that "Fraiberg's depopulating point-of-entry narrative clears the stage for celebrating linguistic multiplicity, multimodal creativity, and textual freedom of movement: the 'transcultural' and 'global flows' of discourse 'crossing' geographic boundaries that [Fraiberg] suggests have been made anachronistic and moot by twenty-first-century literacy practices (103–4)" (570).

In exposing Fraiberg's adoption of theoretical license in relation to the history of the Israel-Palestine conflict by promoting multilingual and multimodal discourses in his article, as well as rhetoric and composition's uncritical embrace of related theoretical efforts such as Actor Network Theory (ANT), object-oriented ontologies, affective ecologies, and the global flows associated with the rise of mobile technologies, Scott and Welch argue that the field has succumbed to a slide toward depoliticization, excluding a full consideration of the role of the body, labor, and protest in shaping current political landscapes. They note, "Such contemporary rhetorics sever the tools from human agents and turn them into commodity and technological fetishes" (568). For the field this is somewhat ironic and surprising given the usual emphasis within the field upon embodiment, affect, and situationality. As Scott and Welch argue, the emphasis on immaterial objects and actants isolates the discursive field from extradiscursive relations (struggling bodies).

Drawing upon the work of David McNally, Scott and Welch posit that postmodernism's new idealism "represses the regard for the physical body that labors within the global economy" (567), hiding the train of materiality from view in favor of focusing on the visible train of discursive and global flows. They argue, "The body is rendered nonhistorical, noncorporeal, independent of economic structures that fatigue, stoop, scar, and kill." In this new idealism, "Being is presented as discursive—and if Being is discursive, so too is agency, the act of discursive will" (567). By not realizing that the train of materiality has fallen away from our critical view, rhetoric and composition scholars may succumb to a fetishization of trendy discourses such as multilingualism and multimodality while the body, labor, and the struggles of oppressed communities—such as the Palestinians—fade from our disciplinary purview.

Perhaps Scott and Welch's analysis helps us to understand better why Salaita's tweets were so shocking: Salaita was bringing the Palestinian body back into view in the midst of an academy theorizing about discursive flows and effects. Palestinians living in the diaspora, such as Salaita, can be viewed as an extension of these resisting Palestinians in the West Bank and Gaza. Furthermore, Salaita's tweets enact a form of linguistic and rhetorical resistance against the discursive operations of Zionism that seek to deny Palestinian lives;

for this reason, they are considered uncivil, unruly, and necessitating containment, rejection, demonization, and ejection. Palestinian bodies resist in very real and visible material ways, but these acts of resistance can be restaged through the linguistic power and aggressivity of tweets such as Salaita's in the context of war. Obviously, Palestinian publics transcend the physical space of Palestine, whether that descriptor refers to the West Bank and Gaza or to all of historical Palestine—which would include present-day Israel, as well as Palestinians living in the diaspora.

Below are several of Salaita's tweets from the summer of 2014 during Israel's Operation Protective Edge. These capture the main themes animating Salaita's rhetorical interventions:

Steven Salaita @stevesalaita · July 8
Let's cut to the chase: If you're defending Israel right now you're an awful human being.

Steven Salaita @stevesalaita · July 18
By eagerly conflating Jewishness and Israel, Zionists are partly responsible when people say antisemitic shit in response to Israeli terror.

Steven Salaita @stevesalaita · July 27
I refuse to conceptualize #Israel/#Palestine as Jewish-Arab acrimony. I am in solidarity with many Jews and in disagreement with many Arabs.

Steven Salaita @stevesalaita · July 28
Thanks to Zionism, those opposed to child murder and ethnocracy have to defend themselves against charges of racism and insensitivity.

Steven Salaita @stevesalaita · July 28
#Israel's relentless bombing illuminates the human capacity for evil. The people of #Gaza illuminate our relentless capacity for courage.

Steven Salaita @stevesalaita · July 29
It's simple: either condemn #Israel's actions or embrace your identity as someone who's okay with the wholesale slaughter of children.

Steven Salaita @stevesalaita · July 29
I take my son to the playground with no expectation that he will be murdered by a warplane. The parents of #Gaza have no such security.

Steven Salaita @stevesalaita · July 31
Only #Israel can murder around 300 children in the span of a few weeks and insist that it is the victim.

Steven Salaita @stevesalaita · August 1
Supporters of #Israel should be forced—A Clockwork Orange style—
to view pics of smiling children who were killed on endless repeat.

Steven Salaita @stevesalaita · August 1
The first thing anyone sees in #Gaza are children: bounteous, beautiful,
boisterous, all eyes and curly hair. To harm them is unforgivable.

Steven Salaita @stevesalaita · February 23
Pro-Israel groups cannot win vis-a-vis ideas and evidence, so they
increasingly mobilize sites of authority to stifle debate altogether.

Steven Salaita @stevesalaita · January 27
When Zionists fret about free speech, they're usually less concerned
with universal rights than with defending Israel's reputation.

Steven Salaita @stevesalaita · January 21
In the new rules of academic freedom, you can't condemn:
-militarism
-Zionism
-colonization

But you can attack:

-Islam
-Natives
-the poor

Steven Salaita @stevesalaita · July 31
Nobody will ever convince the people of #Palestine to quit fighting for
freedom. You'll therefore never convince me to stop supporting them.

Steven Salaita @stevesalaita · July 28
It is impossible to remain unmoved by the images of Palestinian
suffering unless one firmly considers them to be subhuman.

Many of these tweets are undoubtedly painful to read, but they are also seeking—by marshaling linguistic aggressivity to match discursive and military aggressivity—to reject the framework provided by, and enforced by, the discourse of historical anti-Semitism. This discourse enables negative characterizations of Palestinian actions when Palestinians seek to affirm their humanity through acts of resistance against Israeli militarism and occupation. The successful integration of this discourse of historical anti-Semitism into mainstream media narratives about the conflict often places Palestinians in an untenable situation where the very presence of their bodies under occupation constitutes an anti-Semitic threat because the number and sheer materiality of these bodies clamoring for recognition serves to remind Israel of the lingering effects of its founding. Affective responses to ongoing and unfolding events, such as in Gaza, are shaped by how well Palestinian bodies cope with the demands of this discourse and the perceptions it produces. It is in this context that Salaita's counter discourse in these tweets aims to remind the world that Israel's militarism is destroying Palestinian lives in the effort to defend the concept of a "Jewish State." This counter discourse rejects claims that Israel, as "the Jewish State," cannot contribute to the precariousness of other people's lives, specifically Palestinian lives. In sum, Salaita's tweets attempt to expose and counter the logic of Israeli exceptionalism, an ideology (as I previously noted) that positions Israel as possessing unique rights to undertake military and political actions for the sake of its self-defense, and to respond to threats to the Jewish people even before such threats manifest themselves. According to M. Shahid Alam, Israeli exceptionalism advances the following arguments to justify Israel's extraordinary actions: Jewish chosenness, "the divine right of the Jewish people to nullify the historical and legal right of the Palestinians to their homeland" (6) necessitates Israel's existence; the creation of Israel against the heaviest of odds speaks to its special place in the world; Israeli achievements in technology, science, and the arts justify anything Israel may have done in the past to secure its existence; Israel, as the only democracy in the Middle East, is a beacon of moral clarity that deserves protection; the unique history of Jewish suffering necessitates Israel's special dispensations; Israel's vulnerability in the Middle East requires granting it immunity from criticism. As Alam notes, "Protected by the baleful language of exceptionalism, Israel claims the right to mangle millions of lives, to persist in violence, start new wars, and, more recently, to threaten its neighbors with nuclear holocaust" (6).

Beyond Israel's rights to pursue extraordinary actions in the service of its perceived defense needs, there is the expectation that the world powers will provide unqualified support for this exceptionalism, as Israel positions itself as the Jewish homeland in the wake of the Holocaust. Salaita's tweets counter and expose this discourse of exceptionalism by making Zionism's ideological commitments visible, especially with respect to the precariousness of Palestinian lives. These commitments include the belief that Palestinian lives are negligible and expendable when it comes to ensuring Israel's security. Salaita compresses his critiques of these commitments in the tweets above, leveraging them in the form of explosive polemics that track the unfolding situation in Gaza and suggesting that the world is giving Israel ideological cover for its actions.

The tonal pressure of the tweets seeks to push this recognition by forcing an outright admission: "Let's cut to the chase: If you're supporting Israel right now, you're an awful human being." Although he does not specify what he means by "support," one might infer that he is referring to both actual expressions of support (material or verbal) and the choice to not say anything about the deaths of Palestinians in Gaza at all—to remain silent. Salaita's attempt to push this "if-then" structure upon his audience and to have those who support Israel accept the consequences rubs up against the basic rhetorical principle that if one offends an audience it is impossible to achieve adherence with its psychology. Also, in these two tweets, Salaita suggests that Israel is engaged in a cover-up around the commission of war crimes and that its spokespeople are propaganda mouthpieces who have successfully duped those who are susceptible to accepting military explanations:

Steven Salaita @stevesalaita · August 1
Chew on this for a moment: people actually exist who listen to the @IDFSpokesperson and think, "Yes, that makes perfect sense."

Steven Salaita @stevesalaita · July 15
The @IDFSpokesperson is a lying motherfucker.

These tweets insist that it is morally outrageous to consider any interpretation other than that the IDF spokesperson is dissembling, but this stance is rhetorically purposeful: it forecloses nuanced and careful explanations as to why Israel is doing what it is doing, refuses elaborate evasions about how Israel cannot be held responsible for the disproportionate number of deaths of Palestinian civilians in Gaza, rejects hypertechnical explanations about the complexities of war, and refuses the attributions of Palestinian deaths to errors such as the Israeli Air Force's possessing the incorrect aerial coordinates for a Hamas installation and bombing a Gaza school or a UN compound instead. In other words, Salaita rhetorically refuses arguments advanced by Israel and its apologists as being part of a concerted clinical, corporate, and exterminationist discourse deployed against Palestinian bodies. These injured, maimed, or dead Palestinian bodies cannot speak for themselves but are, instead, spoken for by Israeli military officials and approved media voices. Salaita seeks to reverse this dynamic with his rhetorical refusal. His strong language and impatient tone reject the politesse of the news desk, the pundit, and the apologist for the state violence. His linguistic aggressivity corresponds to the groans and exertions of the Palestinian body seeking to resist the discursive and material constraints imposed upon it, a plea for recognition of the precariousness of Palestinian life on all levels. The late Israeli sociologist Baruch Kimmerling concluded that Israel sought to enact the "politicide" of the Palestinians, a reference to the destruction of the Palestinian political will through the destruction of Palestinian political institutions. By exerting control over the Palestinian body through repeated acts of dispossession, occupation, enclosure, and containment, Israel seeks to move closer to achieving the capitulation of the Palestinian political will. However, the groans and strivings of these Palestinian bodies and their collective political will can be heard in Salaita's rhetorical refusals.

In his *Rhetorical Refusals: Defying Audience Expectations*, John Schilb defines a rhetorical refusal as "an act of writing or speaking in which the rhetor pointedly refuses to do what the audience considers rhetorically normal." Although Salaita's audience cannot be precisely defined beyond those tuning into his Twitter feed during the summer of 2014, one can confidently state that this audience consisted of individuals with strong views on the conflict. Schilb further clarifies his definition of a rhetorical refusal by noting that the rhetorician appeals to higher principles than those expected within a genre: "By rejecting a procedure that the audience expects, the rhetor seeks the audience's assent to another principle, cast as a higher priority" (3). In the context of Salaita's tweets, the higher principle is the audience's recognition of the precariousness and suffering of Palestinian bodies. To secure this acknowledgment, Salaita embraced the production of an unruly rhetoric.

In describing his ideological opponents in the ways he does in his tweets, Salaita seems to presuppose that identities within the conflict are rigid and unchangeable, incapable of being transformed by rhetoric. While it might appear that there is little to no prospect for persuasion through the use of such tactics, representative of a seeming refusal to engage in dialogue, the defiance of rhetorical conventions establishes the clarity of one's position.[5] If Salaita were not interested in actually engaging with a public but only in interacting and engaging with a counterpublic that he knew already agreed with him, what then was the purpose of his tweets? Through his performance and stance, Salaita perhaps increased the likelihood that the issues around the precarity of Palestinian lives, for which he sought to clear public space and obtain public hearing, would be lost or ignored altogether. While this is certainly one reaction many had to Salaita's rhetorical performance and his seeming unwillingness to dialogue with those he described in such stark and unflattering terms, Salaita's refusal was central to his enactment of the Palestinian body in protest. Salaita positioned himself in relation to his Zionist interlocutors as ideologically pure, seemingly possessing a superior virtue to those he describes as "awful human beings." When he seemingly says, "I don't want to hear your arguments, they are apologetics for your nation state," he is engaging in a rhetorical refusal: he is rejecting the possibility that any information from or viewpoint expressed by

Zionists and Israel's supporters might change his mind or soften his positions. He solidifies the line between competing identities by insisting that Zionists have no arguments worth hearing or responding to. This marks a rejection of Zionism's perspective. As Schilb underscores, rhetorical refusals "require their audiences to take stands on issues of epistemology (how we know) and ontology (the nature of what exists)" (48).

Perhaps Salaita's rhetorical refusal is more strategic than it appears on first glance. In refusing to see the Israel-Palestine conflict as a conflict based on Jewish-Arab acrimony (tweet, July 27), for example, Salaita rejects the argument that Palestinian Arabs are anti-Semitic for refusing to accept the conditions imposed upon them by Israeli occupation. Furthermore, this tweet also rejects the view that Israeli Jews hate Arabs as a function of their Judaism; one can infer that this hatred, according to Salaita, is a consequence of an embrace of Zionism's ideological commitments. These refusals to think in terms of appeals to an audience psychology, the topoi provided by mainstream narratives about the conflict, and concerns about persuasion, all position Salaita's tweets within the parrhesiastic tradition. In this sense Salaita enacts a parrhesiastes's anti-rhetoric, a refusal to be rhetorical in speaking the truth as he sees it.[6] The compulsion to push his rhetoric in this forceful way is associated with a reduction and a simplification of an array of perspectives and views that all enable the issuing of a conviction-filled message.

This sort of single-mindedness resembles what Sharon Crowley in her *Toward a Civil Discourse* calls "fundamentalism," a psychological condition that rules out as irrelevant that which does not support one's worldview. According to Crowley, fundamentalists "invest their energy in protecting those ideals [the ideals that drive them] from assault by unbelievers" (14). Does Salaita's stance in his tweets foreclose dynamic rhetorical interaction capable of loosening entrenched positions? When the softening of one's ideological position is viewed as weakness, there is a definite tendency not even to entertain that the opposition has anything remotely truthful or useful to say in its defense. One might suspect this is particularly the case of historically oppressed peoples "dialoguing" with their perceived oppressors. To enter into dialogue is to humanize the Other, which would lead to the types of identifications so important to bridging ideological differences.

The tweets below, for example, refuse to engage with those who have offered alternative points of view, foreclosing arguments at odds with Salaita's. The tweets reveal an unwillingness to engage in rhetorical discourse, to cede that perhaps one's discursive certainty is misguided, or to find any redeeming value in speaking to an imaginary ideological Other who apparently endorses

Israel's military's actions. In his attempt to speak to broad ideological totalities in the social field, Salaita simplifies the range of views available to those he assigns an ideological valence associated with the killing of civilians and the defense of an ethnocratic state:

Steven Salaita @stevesalaita · August 1
Hit the block button, friends, it's pointless to argue with somebody who's okay with bombing schools, hospitals, and shelters.

Steven Salaita @stevesalaita · May 19
I don't want to hear another damn word about "nonviolence." Save it for Israel's child-killing soldiers.

Steven Salaita @stevesalaita · May 27
I stopped listening at "dialogue."

These tweets also constitute rhetorical refusals in that they posit that it is unproductive to engage with those who will defend Israel's military actions (the bombing of schools, hospitals, and shelters). This performance of claiming that one's ideological opponents do not deserve a hearing places these perspectives beyond the pale, as if holding them is a sign of one's inhumanity. Salaita reverses the frequent refrain that Palestinians should engage in tactics of nonviolence by suggesting that this advice should be given to Israeli soldiers. For Salaita, Israel's calls for dialogue represent an opportunity for Israel to make excuses and establish justifications for its continuing occupation—a forum that should be avoided since it is a strategy for containing Palestinian resistance and a delay tactic for avoiding compliance with international law. Salaita also places emphasis and tonal pressure on the Zionist commitment to controlling the number of Palestinian bodies residing within Israel as Israeli citizens. These Palestinian Israeli citizens—who number nearly 1.0 million, in addition to the 1.8 million Palestinians in Gaza and the 2.5 million Palestinians in the West Bank—represent an issue of deep concern for committed Zionists who seek to preserve the Jewish majority in Israel, while preventing Israel's absorption of West Bank and Gaza Palestinians through marriage to its citizens. On these concerns, Salaita's tweets seem on point:

Steven Salaita @stevesalaita · May 26
All of Israel's hand-wringing about demography leads one to only one reasonable conclusion: Zionists are ineffective lovers.

Steven Salaita @stevesalaita · May 20
All life is sacred. Unless you're a Zionist, for whom most life is a mere inconvenience to ethnographic supremacy.

When Palestinians seek out and assert their agency in resisting Zionism's placement of their bodies within a matrix of control, it troubles the chain of relationships of these bodies in relation to Israel and its demographic aspirations of a "Jewish" state without Palestinians bodies, or at least such a state with an adequately controlled percentage of those Palestinian bodies. The loss of a Jewish demographic majority in Israel constitutes an enormous threat to the Zionist project and is considered a ticking time bomb subject to intense biopolitical surveillance.[7]

Through the linguistic and tonal aggressivity of his numerous tweets, Salaita exposed the ideological commitments of Israeli exceptionalism by making Zionism's commitment to the precariousness of Palestinian lives visible, while also bringing the strivings and yearnings of the Palestinian body to the forefront of public consciousness. Salaita's tweets drew a relationship between the unruly and the political in the context of the Israel-Palestine conflict by demonstrating how the yearning of the Palestinian body is connected to the Palestinian body politic and its will. Salaita's tweets provide reminders of how Palestinian bodies refuse to abide by the demands of Israeli exceptionalism. This Palestinian political will flexes in and through acts of protest, reproduction, and presence. Salaita's tweets give salience and presence to the Palestinian political will, producing dis-ease among Zionists, as they deploy strategies of containment and exclusion against scholars seeking to humanize Palestinians.

We should take note of how Salaita's rhetorical refusal defied audience expectations on the way to appealing to the higher principle of embracing and articulating the positionality of the Palestinian body struggling to survive under occupation. Through Alexander and Jarratt's analysis, we understand that "when the deck of public discourse and opinion is heavily stacked in favor of one perspective, giving equal time is not ultimately equitable" (541). By joining with Scott and Welch in refusing to succumb to the lure of the discursive and its often reified jargon and by attending to the extra-discursive relations in which the body lives, dwells, works, and resists, rhetoricians will be better positioned to engage the material dimensions shaping human experience in the contexts of war and dispossession.

NOTES

1. See Hoffman; Suárez.

2. See Said and Hitchens.

3. See Barghouti; Dawson and Mullen; Lim; Wiles.

4. Fraiberg's latest attempt to extend discussion of multilingual and multimodal discourses can be seen in Fraiberg's *College Composition and Communication* article "Pretty Bullets: Tracing Transmedia/Translingual Literacies of an Israeli Soldier across

Regimes of Practice." In this article, where Fraiberg analyzes the literacy practices of an IDF soldier named "DaVe" through Actor Network Theory and other frameworks, Fraiberg once again leaves the Palestinian body out of view and misses an opportunity to complicate the conditions of possibility informing DaVe's literacy practices. The Palestinians are an absent presence in the article's understanding of DaVe's engagement with, and comprehension of, the world around him. One might be tempted to ask, Where do the Palestinians reside in DaVe's consciousness and how do they inform an IDF soldier's perception of himself and an Israeli society built on the exclusion of the Palestinian Other?

5. Interestingly enough, current efforts to push civility within universities, for example, try to portray those who are uncivil as being uninterested in dialogue. See Wise.

6. See Walzer and the Forum, "On Arthur Walzer's 'Parrēsia, Foucault, and the Classical Rhetorical Tradition'" in *Rhetoric Society Quarterly*.

7. See DellaPergola; Zimmerman, Seid, and Wise.

WORKS CITED

Alam, M. Shahid. *Israeli Exceptionalism: The Destabilizing Logic of Zionism*. Palgrave, 2009.

Alexander, Jonathan, and Susan C. Jarratt. "Rhetorical Education and Student Activism." *College English* 76, no. 6 (2014): 525–44.

Barghouti, Omar. *Boycott, Divestment, and Sanctions: The Global Struggle for Palestinian Rights*. Haymarket Books, 2011.

Butler, Judith. *Notes toward a Performative Theory of Assembly*. Harvard University Press, 2015.

Crowley, Sharon. *Toward a Civil Discourse: The Rhetoric of Fundamentalism*. University of Pittsburgh Press, 2006.

Dawson, Ashley, and Bill V. Mullen, eds. *Against Apartheid: The Case for Boycotting Israeli Universities*. Haymarket Books, 2015.

DellaPergola, Sergio. *Jewish Demographic Policies: Population Trends and Options in Israel and the Diaspora*. Jewish People Policy Institute. 2015. www.jppi.org.il/uploads/Jewish _Demographic_Policies.pdf.

Edelman, Gilad. "Cuomo and B.D.S.: Can New York State Boycott a Boycott?" *New Yorker*, June 16, 2016. www.newyorker.com/news/news-desk/cuomo-and-b-d-s-can-new-york -state-boycott-a-boycott/.

Forum. "On Arthur Walzer's 'Parrēsia, Foucault, and the Classical Rhetorical Tradition.'" *Rhetoric Society Quarterly* 43, no. 4 (2013): 361–81.

Fraiberg, Steven. "Composition 2.0." *College Composition and Communication* 62, no. 1 (September 2010): 100–126.

Fraiberg, Steven. "Pretty Bullets: Tracing Transmedia/Translingual Literacies of an Israeli Soldier across Regimes of Practice." *College Composition and Communication* 69, no. 1 (2017): 87–117.

Hoffman, Bruce. *Anonymous Soldiers: The Jewish Underground, the British Army and the Creation of Israel*. Vintage Books, 2015.

Lim, Andrea, ed. *The Case for Sanctions against Israel*. Verso, 2012.

Said, Edward. "The Permission to Narrate." *Journal of Palestine Studies* 13, no. 3 (1984): 27–48.

Said, Edward, and Christopher Hitchens, eds. *Blaming the Victims: Spurious Scholarship and the Palestinian Question*. Verso, 2001.

Salaita, Steven. Twitter feed. www.twitter.com/stevesalaita/.

Schilb, John. *Rhetorical Refusals: Defying Audience Expectations*. Southern Illinois University Press, 2007.

Scott, Tony and Nancy Welch. "One Train Can Hide Another: Critical Materialism for Public Composition." *College English* 76, no. 6 (2014): 562–79.

Suárez, Thomas. *State of Terror: How Terrorism Created Modern Israel*. Olive Branch Press, 2017.

Walzer, Arthur. "Parrēsia, Foucault, and the Classical Rhetorical Tradition." *Rhetoric Society Quarterly* 43, no. 1 (2013): 1–21.

Wiles, Rich, ed. *Generation Palestine: Voices from the Boycott, Divestment, Sanctions Movement*. Pluto Press, 2013.

Wise, Phyllis. "The Principles on Which We Stand." Chancellor's blog. August 22, 2014. www.illinois.edu/blog/view/1109/115906/.

Zimmerman, Bennett, Roberta Seid, and Michael Wise. *The Million Person Gap: The Arab Population in the West Bank and Gaza*. The Begin-Sadat Center for Strategic Studies, 2006. www.besacenter.org/wp-content/uploads/2006/02/MSPS65.pdf.

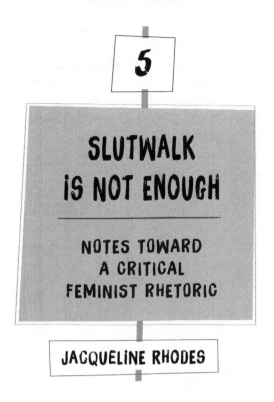

5

SLUTWALK IS NOT ENOUGH

NOTES TOWARD A CRITICAL FEMINIST RHETORIC

JACQUELINE RHODES

I'll be post-feminist in the post-patriarchy.

—Bumper sticker seen in Missoula, MT

L ate summer 2015 and I am inundated with the depressing and enraging news—almost daily—about violence (particularly police violence) against Black men and women. It is a killing summer, a snapshot of white patriarchy at its most damaging. Since the beginning of June, the news pounds like a drumbeat. Jonathan Sanders. Samuel DuBose. Sandra Bland. Kindra Chapman. Joyce Curnell. Ralkina Jones. Alexis McGovern. Raynetta Turner. From Charleston, we hear about Dylann Roof's murder of nine Black men and women in Emanuel African Methodist Episcopal Church. Sharonda Coleman-Singleton. Cynthia Hurd, Susie Jackson, Ethel Lance, Depayne Middleton-Doctor. Clementa Pinckney, Tywanza Sanders, Daniel Simmons Jr., and Myra Thompson. As of this writing, five trans women of color have been murdered just this summer. Mercedes Williamson. *India Clarke. KC Haggard. Amber Monroe. Shade Schuler. These five bring the total to 13 such murders this year. We've seen the August 9 anniversary of Michael Brown's murder and the peaceful Black protestors and not-as-peaceful armed white men who patrolled the streets of Ferguson on that day.*

REVISION: January 2016. Zella Ziona, Papi Edwards, Lamia Beard, Taja Gabrielle de Jesus, Penny Proud, Kristina Grant Infiniti, Mya Shawatza Hall, London Chanel. The names keep coming—trans women of color murdered last year. More Black men and women killed by the police; according to "The Counted," a database operated by the UK news site *The Guardian,* seventy-five unarmed Black men and women were killed by US police in 2015. At the very end of the year, an Ohio grand jury declined to indict police officers Timothy Loehmann and Frank Garmback for the 2014 killing of twelve-year-old Tamir Rice.

Don't go numb.

Don't look away.

#BlackLivesMatter.

#TransLivesMatter.

#SayHerName.

At the same time, #AllLivesMatter and the racist outrage about #BlackLives-Matter activists interrupting Bernie Sanders campaign events during the 2016 election laid bare white complicity, even liberal left complicity. White activists are called on our privilege, and rightfully so; we are urged to be more than *allies*. Rather, we should be *coconspirators* in the fight against the system we have created and by which we continue to benefit (Hackman). And so, as I—a white woman, a lesbian, born to the working poor and now middle-class because of education and income—write this chapter on SlutWalk and critical feminist consciousness, I am productively stymied about the place from which to speak, for I must both *speak* and be mindful *not* to speak for or speak over. Where is feminism today, in the face of such violence? How do we speak out in mindful, rhetorical, and antiracist ways? For mainstream US feminist movements—the ones that get the most media and coverage in history books, the ones that have "earned" the status of *waves*—have always been tainted by racism. Look at the first wave (late nineteenth century), in which a number of prominent suffragettes railed actively against Black men getting the right to vote. Look at the second wave (1960s–1970s), split open partially because of the white, middle-class, heterosexual focus of forebears such as Betty Friedan. The third wave (1980s and on) brought needed correctives to the second, and yet it is still not enough because until a radical upending happens, we can only *amend* the system, not challenge it at its base. And in fact, even talking about "waves" of feminism, to some sorry extent, points to a heritage of white privilege, a history of eliding the multifarious and often contradictory pulses of feminist movement, a history that brings us Gloria Steinem on speaking tours instead of Barbara Smith, that looks back more at *Ms.* magazine than the Combahee River Collective Statement. And so, I write, carefully, respectfully, full of rage, ready to conspire.

The white supremacist patriarchy is alive and well, dear readers, and I reject any *postfeminism* that tells us we've achieved equality. I also reject, however, any feminism that doesn't include systemic analysis as well as personal liberation—an analysis that must include discussions not just of gender but also of race, class, sexual orientation, ability, and how those things intersect. With this analysis comes new ways of thinking, acting, speaking—in short, engaging in a critical praxis of text and body: *rhetoric*. As Susan C. Jarratt writes in her introduction to *Feminism and Composition Studies*, "Rhetoric understood as a dual process of representation—as both a figurative and political act—gives names to language that articulates difference while exposing the power relations at work in acts of naming. . . . Rhetoric mobilizes an interaction between representation (political) and re-presentation (cultural), calling attention to where and by whom groups are described and with what effects. Examining rhetorical configurations keeps at bay any universal subject (man or woman), shifting the discursive grounds for authority" (9–10). It is this view of rhetoric—as the continuous act of examining the power relations behind seemingly individual movements toward "liberation"—that I wish to examine here. Such a rhetoric looks at how *and why* feminist movement happens today. Further, such a rhetoric is viral and performance based, emerging from the synergy of technology, persuasion, and performance, when performance is understood as "a creative act that occurs in specific times and places, and that promises to repeat, transform, contest, or transgress established cultural patterns" (Gencarella and Pezzullo 2). In transgressing those established patterns, such a rhetoric is necessarily unruly—it bumps repeatedly against and through expectations of "appropriate" political action.

I argue that what might most characterize an emerging antiracist, critical feminist consciousness in the early twenty-first century is (1) attention to performance, (2) use of viral technologies, and (3) serious attention to a constitutive intersectionality that takes theory into practice. Following in the footsteps of Jacqueline Jones Royster and Gesa Kirsch in their *Feminist Rhetorical Practice*, my hope is not to be prescriptive but, rather, descriptive. Specifically, I look at the rhetorically savvy blend of real bodies, sex, and social media in the SlutWalk protest, the Toronto-based feminist action gone viral (and global). I offer SlutWalk as a deeply flawed and yet useful example of a twenty-first-century critical feminism; I say "deeply flawed" because SlutWalk fits only jaggedly into my schema, and those mismatched corners point to deep fissures in any discussion of today's feminisms. That is, SlutWalk shows us the well-intentioned but also complicitous rhetoric of mainstream (read white) feminism at the same time as it engages in some of the unruliness needed to change US patriarchal culture.

#SLUTWALK

Your erection is not my consent.
—SlutWalk New York poster, 2011

In January 2011 Constable Michael Sanguinetti spoke at a safety forum at Osgoode Hall Law School in Toronto and told the ten people in attendance that "I'm not supposed to say this, however. . . . Women should avoid dressing like sluts in order not to be victimized" (O'Reilly 245). The story spread rapidly, from the campus to the *Toronto Star* and then further afield, thanks to activists on the University of Toronto campus and the viral spread over social media. And thus, SlutWalk was born. On SlutWalk Toronto's website, organizers write that "SlutWalk is a worldwide movement against victim-blaming, survivor-shaming, and rape culture. . . . The name [SlutWalk] resonated because of a particularly pervasive and insidious form of victim-blaming: shaming the survivor while making assumptions about their sexuality. The term 'slut-shaming' was coined to help name and discuss that issue, because of the way so many survivors have been bullied, blamed, and degraded for attacks against them by being called terms such as 'slut'" ("FAQ"). Andrea O'Reilly estimates that when the first "SlutWalk," designed to combat slut-shaming, took place about three months after Sanguinetti's comment, between three thousand and five thousand attended, "far greater in both numbers and enthusiasm than any feminist march or rally in the city of Toronto over the past two decades" (246). The movement went viral and global, emerging everywhere from Toronto to New York to Delhi, from London to Singapore to Riverside, CA. Although estimates vary, Katha Pollitt notes that SlutWalk events took place in "more than seventy-six cities in Canada, the United States, Europe, and beyond" in 2011 (9).

SlutWalk is one example of an emerging critical feminist activism, a viral in-your-face update of Take Back the Night marches and other street-theater protests of the last fifty years. SlutWalk harks back to older "waves" of feminism, not "finishing" them in some linear view of progress but drawing upon their tactics as a productive expansion of an activist toolkit. As Bonnie Dow and Julia Wood write, looking back at events such as the 1968 Atlantic City Miss America protest, the WITCH (Women's International Terrorist Conspiracy from Hell) hexing of Wall Street, Dyke Marches, and V-Day, "SlutWalks' use of provocative dress and actions continues a long-standing tactic of feminist protest" (27). Ironically, the success of the SlutWalks may be traced to the perception that they were somehow *different* from earlier feminist movement. Leora Tanenbaum writes that one reason the Walks were so successful "is that they were called, well, 'SlutWalks.' And contrary to the stereotype of the humorless, strident woman's libber . . . SlutWalk participants were playful, even zany" (284). SlutWalk participants made extensive use of social media, including websites, Facebook, and a Twitter campaign (#SlutWalk).

While the impetus for the SlutWalks may have been the same victim-blaming endemic in rape culture, the demonstrations themselves varied widely in terms of "playfulness," use of technology, and types of performance; in this sense, the protests can be seen as rhetorical in nature. In the original SlutWalk in Toronto, a sort of rhetorical starting point, protestors dressed in everything from lingerie to sweatpants to caution tape: "Women wrote messages on their arms, legs, chests, and faces. Others [carried] placards declaring: 'Stop Slut Shaming,' 'Don't Tell Us How to Dress,' 'This Is What a Slut Looks Like,' and 'I Am Not a Slut but I Like Having Consensual Sex.' . . . A quick search of news reportage of the various Walks reveals images of women marching in bras, mesh shirts, microshorts and miniskirts, dominatrix outfits, G-strings, pasties to cover nipples, and stilettos, as well as topless" (Nguyen 159–60). In contrast, marchers in Delhi were advised by organizers to "dress modestly" in order not to be seen as "sluts," but amidst the crowd, protestors also put forward messages about sexual violence and victim blaming with a "powerful street play, with actors dressed dramatically in black" (Borah and Nandi 416). In Hong Kong, marchers dressed in everything from their everyday attire to Power Rangers costumes and put on a performance in which protestors inscribed various cultural myths about sexual violence on sheets binding a group of performers (Garrett 100, 102). In all cases, as Pollitt writes in *The Nation*, the actions were "presented as media-savvy street theater that connects the personal and the political and is as fresh as the latest political scandal" (9).

At the same time as SlutWalk proved to be a popular and richly reported phenomenon, there have been powerful critiques of it. In "Feminism, Neoliberalism, and SlutWalk," for example, Kathy Miriam argues that SlutWalk is a "product placement ad for capitalist patriarchy itself" (266), and that with "SlutWalk, a smiley-face logo is slapped onto brute systems of exploitation" (265). She writes:

> SlutWalk, at its core, is an example of a kind of feminism that has effectively supplanted a collective world-changing project with individualized empowerment. Feminism here is converted from a term referring to a political movement to an identity term with no content save whatever empowers the individual woman

who chooses the identity. . . . The structural causes of how women dress and adorn ourselves *as a class* are obfuscated by the emphasis on *individual* self-determination. Thus a main slogan of SlutWalk—most often trumped by women dressed in Victoria's Secret lace and stilettos—is that women should be free to choose how they dress, and it's not an invitation to rape. While rape is of course never invited, this statement only makes sense from the most one-dimensional, flattened perspective—one that removes the individual woman from the matrices of social relations through which our choices are structured. (262–63)

In addition to charges of neoliberal (and patriarchal) complicity put forth by Miriam, Tram Nguyen, in "From SlutWalks to SuicideGirls," explores three additional critiques of the protests: "first, the problem of inversion or reclamation promoted by the Walks; second, the media and general public's reception and perception of these protests; and third, the reaction from women of color" (160). As to the first critique—reclamation—it's true that "slut" is not easily "reclaimed," even for parodic usage given the word's history as a pejorative marker of a woman's lack of "man-made ideals of female behaviour, namely chastity, obedience, piety, silence, and domesticity" (Wilson 58). Further, as Tanenbaum points out, "reclaiming 'slut' is a luxury that many women cannot afford" (289). Different bodies—namely, Black and Brown and poor bodies—are already hypersexualized in the language of capitalist patriarchy. It may indeed be a white Western capitalist prerogative to "slut" oneself. It may indeed be easier to claim (or reclaim) "slut" when you're a member of that transnational elite.

The issue of reclamation is tied closely to Nguyen's second and third critiques: reception/perception and the racism, real and perceived, of the movement. Pollitt notes that "the word—and the lingerie—are probably why SlutWalk has gone viral. The cheerful defiance, the in-your-faceness, the lack of hand-wringing and pleading—when was the last time feminism was this much fun?" (9). Point taken—parody and satire are a lot of fun. But "fun" is contextual and sexed, classed, raced. What happens when your intended audience—the very white patriarchal culture you're protesting—doesn't get the joke? As Nguyen points out, "The primary images of SlutWalk perpetuated by mainstream news media are of young women scantily dressed. . . . Left in the hands of photographers, editors, and news agencies, publicized images of the SlutWalks reinstall the very objectification the movements are invested in challenging" (161).

More important, who's left out of dangerous "fun" of this sort of protest? As Rituparna Borah and Subhalakshmi Nandi point out in "Reclaiming the Feminist Politics of 'SlutWalk,'" the Western origins of the SlutWalk protests caused deep concern for feminists internationally, since the protests point to a uniquely Western definition of liberation; as they write, the protests were "criticized for engaging with an issue that concerns the urban, English-educated, financially secure elite and for having no significance in India, where millions of poor women are struggling for daily survival" (417). In addition to critiques from feminists and other activists around the globe, important arguments against SlutWalk's usefulness emerged closer to home. One of the earliest critiques of the SlutWalk protests came from the Brooklyn-based Black Women's Blueprint collective, who in September 2011 published an open letter on their website, arguing that the protests reinforced white privilege. Black Women's Blueprint commends SlutWalk's organizers for "their bold and vast mobilization to end the shaming and blaming of sexual assault victims for violence committed against them by other members of society." At the same time, the collective writes:

> As Black women, we do not have the privilege or the space to call ourselves "slut" without validating the already historically entrenched ideology and recurring messages about what and who the Black woman is. We don't have the privilege to play on destructive representations burned in our collective minds, on our bodies and souls for generations. . . . For us the trivialization of rape and the absence of justice are viciously intertwined with narratives of sexual surveillance, legal access and availability to our personhood. It is tied to institutionalized ideology about our bodies as sexualized objects of property, as spectacles of sexuality and deviant sexual desire. . . .
>
> Although we vehemently support a woman's right to wear whatever she wants anytime, anywhere, within the context of a "SlutWalk," we don't have the privilege to walk through the streets of New York City, Detroit, D.C., Atlanta, Chicago, Miami, L.A. etc., either half-naked or fully clothed self-identifying as "sluts" and think that this will make women safer in our communities an hour later, a month later, or a year later. ("Open Letter")

I quote this letter at length because while the Black Women's Blueprint was not the only critique of the movement on the grounds of white privilege, it was the earliest and it pinpoints the structural racism of many US protest movements.

The critique of SlutWalk's racism continued in the blogosphere, with blogs such as *womanistmusings.com*, *crunkfeministcollective.com*, and *haifischgeweint* *.com* weighing in. On the blog *tothecurb.wordpress.com* (now defunct), the writer argues that SlutWalks not only marginalized and erased "black, poor, and transgender women," it in fact was a "maddening distraction" from real problems facing those women. Further, she writes of her concern about SlutWalk's global movement:

According to SlutWalk's website, the event is slated to be reproduced in Argentina sometime this year [2011]. It's the country I was born and raised in, among Spanish, Guaraní and Portuguese speakers—and I can assure you that the word "slut" is not used by anyone there. This is not what we need. I do not want white English-speaking Global North women telling Spanish-speaking Global South women to "reclaim" a word that is foreign to our own vocabulary. To do so would be hegemonic, and would illustrate the ways in which Global North "feminists" have become a tool of cultural imperialism. I will be going back home in about a month, and want to do so without feeling the power of white women bearing down on me from 6,000 miles away. We've got our own issues to deal with in South America; we do not need to become poster children to try to make you feel better about yours. ("SlutWalk")

At the same time as such critiques continued, rejoinders to those critiques emerged. Jacqueline Schiappa, for example, notes that Black Women's Blueprint's "Open Letter," while one of the first voices, is not "a definitive perspective of women of colour" (70). Further, she points out that not all SlutWalk organizers were white, as is often assumed. She includes statements from Global Women's Strike—"They [Black Women's Blueprint] say they 'do not recognize' themselves in it, while ignoring many thousands of us who do"—and the author Alice Walker (Schiappa 70–71) to point out a variety of responses to SlutWalk from women of color, in order to emphasize that the racialized history of "slut" should be acknowledged *at the same time* as we make space "for differing interpretations of how that history may be experienced" (71).

SlutWalk Toronto organizers in particular seem to have made a conscious attempt to reflect critically and work proactively on their white privilege. On the 2015 iteration of their website, they note, "In the original march, reappropriation [of 'slut'] was one of the goals. . . . After many conversations with folks from different communities that bear disproportionate levels of harm from these words, we now realize that we can better support survivors from across diverse communities by keeping our focus on challenging the language" ("FAQ"). Schiappa notes that in her conversations with SlutWalk Toronto organizers, cofounder Heather Jarvis said of the protest's name and the Black Women's Blueprint objection, "I fucked up, and I try to be accountable for that, I can't take it away. . . . If I could go back and change anything it would be to have a deeper analysis of the language we used" (70).

In SlutWalk, then, we have a snapshot of Western feminist movement today, performance-based direct action that makes use of viral technologies and that is in deep need of critical analysis of the discourses that inform it. I would argue that SlutWalk represents both the best and the worst feminist impulses today, coupling innovative and provocative protest with a blindness to the privilege that inheres in the very use of the term "slut." While SlutWalk's challenge to rape culture is welcome, critics have noted that the "personal empowerment" emphasis of the movement too easily moves away from Chela Sandoval's *tactical subjectivity* to an arhetorical individual subjectivity that can reinscribe white neoliberal patriarchy. If the movement—SlutWalk in particular and feminist action in general—is to mobilize the personal and political, it must, as Jarratt says, expose "the power relations at work in acts of naming" (9). And in fact, Heather Jarvis's statements point to self-awareness and self-critique, an acknowledgment of needed interventions to make the #SlutWalk actions more responsive, rhetorically speaking, to both the situated needs of activists inside and outside the movement *and* the systemic violence that shapes the very occasion for that movement.

TOWARD AND AGAINST THE WAVES

To what extent might we say that SlutWalk is indicative, albeit in a flawed way, of a nascent "fourth wave" of Western feminism? And what are the politics of using such a term, given the metaphor's troubled history? That is, to follow Jarratt, what are the power relations underneath such naming? By looking at the different irruptions of Western feminist activism in complex public spheres over the last century, it's possible to trace certain themes, challenges, problems, and complications that successive "waves" attempt to address. Abortion. Violence and rape culture. Equal pay. The pro-sex versus antiporn debate. Beauty standards. One theme in the revisiting of previous movement is looking at blind spots of earlier feminist activists; these blind spots usually have to do with race and/or sexuality, so the "waves" have justly been categorized as largely white, middle-class, heteronormative. Just as the metaphor of sisterhood, Jarratt notes, "began to obscure more than it revealed" (9), the metaphor of "waves" of feminism has tended to generalize large and fractious feminist movements into a more easily digestible shorthand. As Victoria L. Bromley writes in *Feminisms Matter*, the wave metaphor can give the illusion that feminist history has been "the calm and peaceful lapping of water on a beautiful beach," a linear process in which movement is "in a unified motion and in a singular direction" (132–33). More damningly, the metaphor "tends to emphasize mainstream feminist movement while eclipsing groups of feminist that don't fit comfortably into the imagined mainstream of white, middle-class, heterosexual, able-bodied women's movement" (Bromley 133).

Ednie Kaeh Garrison argues, however, that the wave metaphor need not be an empty one. In her view, recasting the metaphor as a radio wave can be useful, referring to the growing reach of feminist movement, "moving further away (in time and in sheer numbers)" with each generational iteration (Baumgardner 245). Additionally, metaphorical shorthand is useful, as long as we can see each wave as a general marker of historical context rather than as a "sign of generational descendence" (Garrison 145). In this sense, if we do continue the metaphor, it might be possible to stake out a fourth wave in feminism, referring less to a large-scale universalized shift in theory and activist practices and more to an emerging twenty-first-century concatenation of smaller movements that have some theories and strategies in common.

Arguing for the continued use of a problematic metaphor itself, however, does violence to any antiracist feminist future we might want to create; my use of the term "waves," then, is not a *naming* but a way of identifying prior discussions of where we are now in order to look toward where we might be. My vision—one that emphasizes performance, virality, and intersectionality—builds from one advanced by Jennifer Baumgardner in her *Fem! Goo Goo, Gaga, and Some Thoughts on Balls* (2011). Baumgardner dates what she sees as a "fourth wave" from approximately 2008 and writes that, at the same time as these feminists take up and transform the issues and strategies of prior activists, they are a "tech-savvy and gender-sophisticated" group of women and men who deploy social media for personal/political justice (250–51). Even more to the point is Garrison's discussion of "oppositional technologics," strategies derived from US Third World feminism. In 2000 Garrison pointed specifically to Sandoval's discussion of "oppositional consciousness" in that writer's 1991 "U.S. Third World Feminism." Garrison notes that the weaving together of "apparently disparate modes of consciousness, constituencies, ideologies, and practices" (146) by twenty-first-century feminists points to the postmodern nature of today's feminism, in which the movement culture is "disparate, unlikely, multiple, polymorphous. There are cohorts who remain indebted to their predecessors but who are simultaneously irreverent" (149). In her exploration of Sandoval's profoundly rhetorical idea of oppositional consciousness, Garrison writes, "According to Sandoval, differential oppositional consciousness is a mode of 'ideology-praxis' rooted in the experiences of U.S. Third World feminists. Modernist conceptions of oppositional politics center on mutually exclusive and essentialized identities. . . . In contrast, the differential mode of consciousness offers a strategic politics wherein modernist oppositional identities become tactical poses. . . . [A] differential oppositional ideology-praxis makes possible a 'tactical subjectivity' in which multiple oppressions can be confronted by shifting modes of consciousness as various forms of oppression are experienced" (147). In other words, I would argue, these feminists compose a critical twenty-first-century feminist rhetoric, employing a "tech-savvy"

(Baumgardner) "tactical subjectivity" (Sandoval) so as to engage in an examination of Jarratt's "dual process of representation" and to challenge (through text, theory, and direct action) the systemic configurations that keep white patriarchy in place.

This vision of a critical feminism is not incompatible with what mainstream pundits and academic writers have referred to as "postfeminism," if that term is explored carefully. In *Feminisms Matter*, Bromley notes that there are two understandings of what "postfeminism" means. First, there's the laughable idea that we're all equal now and therefore don't need feminism; according to Bromley, such an idea depends on the assumption that "women are . . . equal and social institutions are no longer steeped in sexism, racism, ableism, homophobia, or any other systemic inequities" (143). As Jess Butler points out, this view of postfeminism rests on "the conventional story[, which] goes something like this: women were tired of being obedient housewives, so they decided to get jobs and stop shaving their armpits. They thought that sex was really important, and they wanted to be able to do it without getting married or having babies. This was a pretty far-out idea. Some people were not too happy about it, but the feminists eventually got their way and—*voila!*—the problem of gender inequality was solved" (38). The "collective amnesia" about the women's movement (Butler 38) has led to a postfeminism that advances a "neoliberal discursive formation" that reproduces "inequalities of race, gender, and sexuality" (Butler 36). Such a representation of the "postfeminist generation" is also evident in Rory Dicker's *A History of U.S. Feminisms*, in which the author points out that "a popular refrain" in the US media in the 1980s was that feminism was not of interest to young women (107). This refrain, in tandem with a conservative backlash against feminism, created a self-perpetuating reluctance on the part of women to identify with the "f-word." Dicker notes that "feminist" had, in the 1980s, come to be seen as "something dangerous and profane, an explosive term angry, unfeminine women use to identify themselves" (137). Dicker uses what she sees as a generational skepticism toward feminism as a foundation from which to argue *against* generational divides and for "approaching feminism as a collective project aimed at eradicating sexism and domination [as] the most practical way to continue feminist work" (139).

Bromley's second representation of "postfeminism" is one I'd like to take up here, given that (1) structural inequality is still present and easily proven; (2) postfeminism understood as above both reproduces and reinforces that inequality (Butler 46); and (3) women continue to protest that inequality, through direct action, net activism, parody, and other means. Indeed, I would argue that critical feminist movement synthesizes the "performance politics and individual empowerment" of the third wave and the "rigorous theory" of

SLUTWALK IS NOT ENOUGH

the second (Coleman 10–11). Coleman notes that "in this postfeminist age of individualism, materialism and consumer culture, we need very robust analyses of agency and of resistance and subversion. Feminism is not simply about an individual woman choosing how she will live her life, and it is not sufficient to claim that an individual's *intention* to resist and subvert dominant power structures or societal conventions equates to feminist resistance and subversion" (11). A more critical view of US feminist movement today, then, foregrounds the idea that postfeminism, like postmodernism and postcolonialism, provides "space for engaging with and talking about . . . changing meanings and thinking [about feminism, in this case]. . . . [These] proponents call for an ongoing critical engagement with patriarchy and modernist thinking" (Bromley 144). Such engagement, again, needs to be rhetorical, in the sense that we need to understand both personal choice (to engage) and the power relations at work (who sets the terms of engagement?) in the act of choosing.

WHAT WE MIGHT LEARN FROM #SLUTWALK: INTERSECTIONAL VIRALITY

"This is still a violent, bigoted world, a world of neoliberal patriarchy that loves to make you hate yourself, especially if you're young, or poor, or weird, or a woman. To make you hurt yourself. To make you police the behaviour of others so they remain as cowed as you feel. To cope with the intimate terrorism of neoliberal patriarchy we've got to work on giving fewer fucks" (Penny 243). In my view of emerging feminist movement and a corresponding rhetoric, tactical subjectivity (a rhetorical response to systems of oppression) works with critical analysis through technological literacy and performance to disrupt those systems. A key part of that movement is the use of viral technologies, used critically, to effect change. #SlutWalk's Twitter campaign, for example, is one in an increasing line of activist uses of social media. And this line, too, isn't new but, rather, an adaptation and updating of prior feminist movements' interest in literacy and mobilizing through media. "Second-wave" activists relied on manifestos, newsletters, and the loose underground press movement. "Third-wave" activists had zines, which combined a DIY ethic with national and international distribution. The circulation (or virality) of prior movements had comparatively less velocity, because the technologies of literacy were slower—rhetoric inhabits technology inhabits rhetoric—but the goal was the same: to go viral, to pollinate, to spread the word. #SlutWalk, both as a Twitter campaign and a direct-action protest, went viral.

In *Still Life with Rhetoric*, Laurie Gries considers the logic beneath the phrase "going viral," part of everyday Internet-speak but not reserved exclusively for online actions and texts: "According to this logic, a thing is commonly said to be viral when it is perceived as being socially contagious due to its capacity to garner mass attention and spread via word of mouth and media. In common parlance, then, we say something like a video has gone viral based on the sheer speed at which the video has attracted a wide viewing, often, but not always, because it has circulated widely across media, been remixed, and inspired imitative spinoffs" (2). Surely the original SlutWalk protests have "circulated widely. . . . been remixed, and inspired imitative spinoffs" (2) not just as an online campaign but as a worldwide action of real, material bodies. Further, the viral nature of the protests also brings to mind Royster and Kirsch's discussion of social circulation within feminist rhetoric. Social circulation refers to the "connections among past, present, and futures in the sense that the overlapping social circles in which women travel, live, and work are carried on or modified and can lead to changed rhetorical practices" (Royster and Kirsch 23). The "carrying-on" and modification of those circles is a viral remix (Gries) of prior waves, of current feminist and postfeminist movements, of difference. It is a synergy of individual liberation, technology, and systemic critique. If we look at recent examples of tactical and viral protests, from street/online protests such as Occupy Wall Street and Arab Spring to (mostly online) movements such as #Kony2012 and #YesAllWomen (and #NotAllMen) and circling back to street/online protests such as #IdleNoMore and #BlackLivesMatter, we can see such synergy in action.

Much more important than virality for a critical antiracist feminist movement, however, is *intersectional* virality, which to date the SlutWalk movement has lacked. Intersectionality is an idea first advanced by Kimberlé Crenshaw in her 1989 "Demarginalizing the Intersection of Race and Sex: A Black Feminist Critique of Antidiscrimination Doctrine, Feminist Theory and Antiracist Politics." It's a seemingly simple concept that has been difficult for mainstream white feminism to grasp, if SlutWalk is our example. We must look not at discrete markers of identity, privileging one over another, but at the intersections— for it is at the intersections that we can see how the *interaction* of racism and sexism, for example, works specifically to enact violence (symbolic and real) on women of color. According to Crenshaw, "Black women are sometimes excluded from feminist theory and antiracist policy discourse because both are predicated on a discrete set of experiences that often does not accurately reflect the interaction of race and gender. These problems of exclusion cannot be solved simply by including Black women within an already established analytical structure. Because the intersectional experience is greater than the sum of racism and sexism, any analysis that does not take intersectionality into account cannot sufficiently address the particular manner in which Black women are subordinated" (140). While initial scholarship on intersectionality focused on intersections of race, gender, and class, the conversation has come to reference other social divisions, up to and including Helma Lutz's fourteen lines of difference: gender, sexuality, race, ethnicity, nationality, class, culture, ability, age, origin, wealth, North-South, religion, stage of social development (qtd. in Yuval-Davis 53). Expanded conversations are good, as long as they don't inspire us to back off, to let ourselves off the hook, to revert to single-sphere analysis because we're overwhelmed. For as Crenshaw reminds us, such single-sphere analysis enacts its own privilege: "it often overlooks the role of race. Feminists thus ignore how their own race functions to mitigate some aspects of sexism and, moreover, how it often privileges them over and contributes to the domination of other women" (154).

What is crucial to note is not just the number of divisions but the fact of those divisions' constitutive character. As Nira Yuval-Davis puts it in her "Intersectionality and Feminist Politics," *additive* intersectionality relies mostly on experiential analysis and a sense of intersectionality as the total of different forms of oppression. *Constitutive* views, on the other hand, see "each social division [as having] a different ontological basis, which is irreducible to other social divisions" (46). For Yuval-Davis, "Any attempt to essentialize 'blackness' or 'womanhood' or 'working classness' as specific forms of concrete oppression in additive ways inevitably conflates narratives of identity politics with descriptions of positionality. . . . Such narratives often reflect hegemonic discourses of identity politics that render invisible experiences of the more marginal members of that specific social category and construct an homogenized 'right way' to be its member" (46). Rather than relying purely on experiential evidence and analysis, constitutive intersectionality takes into account the connections between the organizational, intersubjective, experiential, and representational (Yuval-Davis 49). What this move allows is a richer view of intersectionality that might give us a clearer picture of how intersections not only *reflect* personal experience but also *constitute* the subject and that experience in a range of ways. In short, this sort of analytical frame is deeply rhetorical, demanding an attention to Jarratt's "dual process of representation" that looks at the interaction of personal and systemic vectors of identity and performance.

What might such intersectional virality mean for an emerging critical feminist movement? It might mean that we can indeed be a coalition of coconspirators, working sometimes alone and sometimes together to disrupt (and ultimately transform) a seemingly intransigent white system. It might mean that I shake off the safety of my white world, reflect on my own privilege, and then *act consciously* to mitigate its effects. This may sound utopian. Guilty as charged. But I take my sense of utopia from José Esteban Muñoz, who in *Cruising Utopia* argues for a rhetoric of potentiality: "Unlike a possibility, a thing that simply might happen, a potentiality is a certain mode of nonbeing that is eminent, a thing that is present but not actually existing in the present tense" (9). In a 2009 dialogue with Lisa Duggan, Muñoz writes, "Practicing educated hope, participating in a mode of revolutionary consciousness, is not simply conforming to one group's doxa at the expense of another's. Practicing educated hope is the enactment of a critique function. It is not about announcing the way things ought to be, but, instead, imagining what things could be. It is thinking beyond the narrative of what stands for the world today by seeing it as not enough" (278).

Educated hope, then, is a vision of the potential of critical reflection on the past in order to anticipate possible futures, related intimately to Royster and Kirsch's "critical imagination" or "a critical skill in questioning a viewpoint, an experience, an event, and so on, and in remaking interpretive frameworks based on that questioning" (19). Such notions of potentiality, of futurity, of critical imagination must be part of a vision of feminist rhetorics, and it is in this sense that SlutWalk offers us both an unruly example and a prompt for *more*. For if it succeeds—or attempts—to work the concepts of virality *and* constitutive intersectionality together, SlutWalk could offer us a change not just in feminist methods but in feminist goals. Our critical imagination might lead us to more than resignification. We might court not just the provocative protest but the provocative feminist subject-in-context(s)—incomplete, messy, but pushing toward critical and antiracist change of self and system. The raging tension between history and futurity—the always present "not enough"—might serve as the engine of critical feminist hope. And it is this hope I hold now.

Don't go numb.
Don't look away.
#BlackLivesMatter.
#TransLivesMatter.
#SayHerName.

WORKS CITED

Baumgardner, Jennifer. *F'em! Goo Goo, Gaga, and Some Thoughts on Balls*. Seal, 2011.

Borah, Rituparna, and Subhalakshmi Nandi. "Reclaiming the Feminist Politics of 'Slut-Walk.'" *International Feminist Journal of Politics* 14, no. 3 (September 2012): 415–32.

Bromley, Victoria L. *Feminisms Matter: Debates, Theories, Activism*. University of Toronto Press, 2012.

Butler, Jess. "For White Girls Only? Postfeminism and the Politics of Inclusion." *Feminist Formations* 25, no. 1 (Spring 2013): 35–58.

Coleman, Jenny. "An Introduction to Feminisms in a Postfeminist Age." *Women's Studies Journal* 23, no. 2 (2009): 3–13.

"The Counted: People Killed by the Police in the US, Recorded by *The Guardian*—with Your Help." *The Guardian*. www.theguardian.com/us-news/ng-interactive/2015/jun/01 /the-counted-police-killings-us-database/.

Crenshaw, Kimberlé. "Demarginalizing the Intersection of Race and Sex: A Black Feminist Critique of Antidiscrimination Doctrine, Feminist Theory and Antiracist Politics." *University of Chicago Legal Forum* (1989): 139–67.

Dicker, Rory. *A History of U.S. Feminisms*. Seal, 2008.

Dow, Bonnie J., and Julia T. Wood. "Repeating History and Learning from It: What Can SlutWalks Teach Us about Feminism?" *Women's Studies in Communication* 37 (2014): 22–43.

Duggan, Lisa, and José Esteban Muñoz. "Hope and Hopelessness: A Dialogue." *Women & Performance: A Journal of Feminist Theory* 29, no. 2 (2009): 275–83.

"FAQ." *SlutWalk Toronto*. www.slutwalktoronto.com/about/faqs/.

Garrett, Daniel. "Three Times a Lady: Images from SlutWalk Hong Kong." In Teekah, Scholz, Friedman, and O'Reilly, 92–106.

Garrison, Ednie Kaeh. "U.S. Feminism—Grrrl Style! Youth (Sub)Cultures and the Technologics of the Third Wave." *Feminist Studies* 26 (Spring 2000): 141–70.

Gencarella, Stephen Olbrys, and Phaedra C. Pezzullo, eds. *Readings on Rhetoric and Performance*. Strata, 2010.

Gries, Laurie E. *Still Life with Rhetoric: A New Materialist Approach for Visual Rhetorics*. Utah State University Press, 2015.

Hackman, Rose. "'We Need Co-conspirators, Not Allies': How White Americans Can Fight Racism." *The Guardian*, June 26, 2015. www.theguardian.com/world/2015/jun /26/how-white-americans-can-fight-racism/.

Jarratt, Susan C. "Introduction: As We Were Saying . . ." In *Feminism and Composition Studies: In Other Words*, edited by Susan C. Jarratt and Lynn Worsham, 1–18. Modern Language Association, 1998.

Miriam, Kathy. "Feminism, Neoliberalism, and SlutWalk." *Feminist Studies* 38, no. 1 (Spring 2012): 262–66.

Muñoz, José Esteban. *Cruising Utopias: The Then and There of Queer Futurity*. New York University Press, 2009.

Nguyen, Tram. "From SlutWalks to SuicideGirls: Feminist Resistance in the Third Wave and Postfeminist Era." *Women's Studies Quarterly* 41, nos. 3–4 (Fall/Winter 2013): 157–72.

"An Open Letter from Black Women to the SlutWalk." *Black Women's Blueprint*, September 23, 2011. Rpt. at huffingtonpost.com, September 27, 2011. www.huffingtonpost.com /susan-brison/slutwalk-black-women_b_980215.html.

O'Reilly, Andrea. "Slut Pride: A Tribute to SlutWalk Toronto." *Feminist Studies* 38, no. 1 (Spring 2012): 245–50.

Penny, Laurie. *Unspeakable Things: Sex, Lies, and Revolution.* Bloomsbury, 2014.

Pollitt, Katha. "Talk the Talk, Walk the SlutWalk." *The Nation,* July 18–25, 2011, 9.

Rhodes, Jacqueline. *Radical Feminism, Writing, and Critical Agency: From Manifesto to Modern.* State University of New York Press, 2005.

Royster, Jacqueline Jones, and Gesa E. Kirsch. *Feminist Rhetorical Practices: New Horizons for Rhetoric, Composition, and Literacy Studies.* Southern Illinois University Press, 2012.

Sandoval, Chela. "US Third-World Feminism: The Theory and Method of Oppositional Consciousness in the Postmodern World. *Genders* 10, 1991, 1–24.

Schiappa, Jacqueline. "Practising Intersectional Critiques: Re-examining 'Third-Wave' Perspectives on Exclusion and White Supremacy in SlutWalk." In Teekah, Scholz, Friedman, and O'Reilly, 63–76.

"SlutWalk: A Stroll through White Supremacy." *Tothecurb.wordpress.com,* 13 May 2011. www.tothecurb.wordpress.com/2011/05/13/slutwalk-a-stroll-through-white-supremacy/.

Tanenbaum, Leora. *I Am Not A Slut: Slut-Shaming in the Age of the Internet.* Harper Perennial, 2015.

Teekah, Alyssa, Erika Jane Scholz, May Friedman, and Andrea O'Reilly, eds. *This Is What a Feminist Slut Looks Like: Perspectives on the SlutWalk Movement.* Demeter, 2015.

Wilson, Nancy Effinger. "Dirty Talk: A History of 'Slut.'" In Teekah, Scholz, Friedman, and O'Reilly, 46–62.

Yuval-Davis, Nira. "Intersectionality and Feminist Politics." *European Journal of Women's Studies* 13, no. 3 (2006): 193–209. Rpt. in *The Intersectional Approach: Transforming the Academy through Race, Class, and Gender,* edited by Michele Tracy Berger and Kathleen Guidroz, 44–60. University of North Carolina Press, 2009.

PART II

CIVILITY WARS

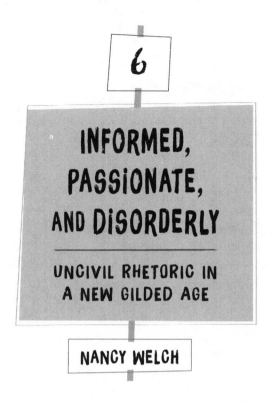

6

INFORMED, PASSIONATE, AND DISORDERLY

UNCIVIL RHETORIC IN A NEW GILDED AGE

NANCY WELCH

Civility may well be a virtue. But it is probably not a virtue that will be of much help in deciding the political questions that ultimately matter.

       —James Schmidt, "Is Civility a Virtue?"

It was the spirit of the workers that seemed dangerous. They were confident, gay, released, and they sang. . . . The gray tired crowds ebbing and flowing perpetually into the mills had waked and opened their mouths to sing, the different nationalities all speaking one language when they sang together.

'Revolution!' screamed the conservative press.

    —Mary Heaton Vorse, "The Lawrence Strike," in *A Footnote to Folly*

Nuclear Regulatory Commission (NRC) officials were in for a shock when, not three months after the Fukushima catastrophe, they arrived in Cortlandt Manor, New York, to give their annual safety debriefing on the Indian Point nuclear power plant.[1] The overflow crowd of more than four hundred—a startling turnout for the tiny town—carried signs imploring "Westchester Aglow—Where Do We Go?" They refused to sit still for the usual PowerPoint presentation. "Lap dogs!" and "Liars!" they shouted when officials claimed that the aging, accident-ridden plant had "operated in a manner that preserved public health and safety" (Clary; Chris Williams). Finally the NRC officials gave the crowd what they had politely requested at the meeting's start: two minutes of silence for Fukushima's victims and the suspension of the PowerPoint presentation (available online) so the meeting could proceed straight to Q&A. "Raucous" is how the local newspaper reporter summed up the open mic that followed. "Boisterous" and "confident" wrote environmental activist and Pace University professor Chris Williams. "One of the best public meetings I ever attended," declared local blogger Dawn Powell. The more than eighty people who stepped up to the microphone, she reported, were "informed, passionate, and empowering" ("No Fukushima-on-the-Hudson").

Less than three weeks later, however, this same meeting was roundly criticized by highly regarded antinuclear activist Raymond Shadis. In a public radio interview and on a Vermont news blog, Shadis decried the conduct of the Indian Point meeting attendees as "completely disorderly" (Dillon). Their rhetoric, he charged, had veered toward "irresponsible" incitement to "violence" (Shadis). Shadis's purpose in going public with this reprimand wasn't simply to find fault with the Indian Point protestors. Rather, he aimed to shape audience behavior at the NRC's next stop: Brattleboro, Vermont, in the shadow of the Vermont Yankee nuclear reactor. Coming on the eve of federal court hearings to determine whether to uphold or overturn the state's move to shutter the plant, the Vermont meeting promised to be fraught. Adding to the tension was the revelation that the NRC had sided with Entergy, the corporation that also owns Indian Point, in its bid to keep Vermont Yankee open. This was the context in which Shadis urged "civility" and "calm" among Vermonters lest "violent language . . . stimulate violent action" (Dillon). To be sure, Shadis acknowledged, the NRC should cease advancing unconvincing claims about reactor safety that only serve to "insult and infuriate" the public (Shadis). Infuriating, for instance, was the NRC's downplay of a Yankee cooling tower's partial collapse and tritium contamination from leaky pipes (Zeller). But "upset members of the public too," Shadis concluded, "need to find better means to communicate."

Shadis's counsel, especially as it came in the aftermath of the appalling shooting of Congresswoman Gabrielle Giffords, has strong persuasive appeal. That appeal is further bolstered by his reputation as an effective activist—he led the successful movement to end nuclear power in his home state, Maine—and by his practical wisdom in advocating keeping communication channels open. Through ethos alone, Shadis's statements have a resounding ring of truth, and his plea received wide broadcast, the story published under the headline "Nuclear Critic Urges Civility" on news sites nationwide.

Yet Ray Shadis did not attend the Indian Point hearing. Instead, he acknowledged, he was "contacted indirectly" by regulatory officials who were
concerned about "the safe and civil conduct of NRC public meetings" because
the "personal attacks" at the Indian Point meeting led "younger staffers" to fear
for their "physical safety" and a possible repeat of "the Representative Giffords
shooting" as a "mob mentality takes over" (Shadis). In his op-ed and radio
interview, Shadis did not mention contacting any of Indian Point's non-NRC
meeting participants. He seems also not to have consulted news stories about
the meeting and the local police blotter, none of which recorded violent language or threatening behavior. Compared with eye-witness accounts, Shadis's
single-source and apparently corporate-spun message starts to ring not with
truth but with what comedian Stephen Colbert dubs "truthiness."

But no matter. With the Indian Point hearing having received local coverage
while the Shadis interview enjoyed regional and even national circulation, the
NRC's version of the event took on its own reality. In place of Raging Grannies
belting out "Indian Point is a dangerous joint" ("Raging Grannies against Indian Point") and a state assemblywoman reminding the NRC, "It's your job to
protect the public, not the industry" (Clary), we have the frightening prospect
of "deranged individuals" overtaken by a "mob mentality" (Shaddis). "Shut it
down" becomes not the open demand of an informed and passionate public but
the concealed goal of a private industry and its quasi-governmental defenders
aiming to shut down audible protest—all in the name of civility.

WHAT'S WRONG WITH JUST BEING CIVIL?

"If you would civil your land, first you should civil speech": Auden's adage is
at the heart of Wayne Booth's influential "rhetoric of assent" or "listening rhetoric," first formulated from his dismay at the civil unrest of the late 1960s and
later offered as a remedy for a country that had just marched under false warrants into war (*Modern Dogma*; *Rhetoric*; "War Rhetoric"). Theresa Enos likewise turns to Auden as she recommends rhetorical restraint to create greater
space for deliberation and deeper respect between contending parties. If "we
can work toward more constructive, and civil, ways of expressing opposition,"
especially by "suspending urgency," Enos suggests, parties to a conflict can
open themselves to the "spaciousness of rhetoric" and create "greater comity"
between them (151). First-year composition courses, John Duffy writes in *Inside
Higher Ed*, are already engaged in the work of creating rhetorical spaciousness
and generosity, offering students Aristotelian lessons in argument and ethics
that can counteract the "corrosive language of figures such as Rush Limbaugh"
and move us toward "healthier, more productive, and more generous forms of

public argument." Especially given the toxicity of what passes for public discourse on corporate radio and cable-news broadcasts, not to mention President Donald Trump's Twitter feed, the projects of cultivating civility and opening rhetorical space appear interdependent, the latter only possible through the former. Hence the rekindled interest among compositionists in civic literacy and public rhetoric along with a pedagogical emphasis on rhetorical listening, balance, ethics, and civility (see also Ratcliffe).

The story of the Indian Point meeting, however, troubles the belief in civility's powers to create conditions and space needed for democratic deliberation; it calls into question the power of well-reasoned, proof-backed claims alone to advance effective arguments for the public good. The Indian Point attendees were equipped with meticulously researched arguments regarding the dangers of and alternatives to nuclear power. Yet needed too was the audience's ability to challenge the NRC's authority to relegate their arguments to the meeting's end. By refusing to await the designated Q&A period, these audience members were indeed "uncivil" in two conventional and conservative senses of the term: incivility as indecorous behavior and incivility as refusal to subordinate one's grievances to the presumed greater good of maintaining order (Shils, *The Virtue of Civility* 4, 345). In this case their incivility served to make rhetorical space in which more views could be heard. They sought to civil their land—or at least this meeting—by unciviling their speech.

Why uncivil, even rude speech was necessary, a precondition for a democratic discussion, is captured by David Lochbaum of the Union of Concerned Scientists: "Absent dead bodies," he told the *New York Times*, "nothing seems to deter the NRC from sustaining reactor operation" (Zeller). In these circumstances, civility toward spokespersons for the nuclear industry may be a virtue—but not one in service to democracy. Instead, civility functions to hold in check agitation against a social order that is undemocratic in access to decision-making voice and unequal in distribution of wealth. Indeed, a neoliberalized regulatory body such as the NRC—one that seeks not to regulate an industry to safeguard the public good but to influence public opinion to safeguard an industry (Associated Press; Gonzales and Goodman; Zeller)—depends on civility so as to curtail rhetorical spaciousness.[2] Faced with working- and middle-class individuals and groups, opposing a corporation's considerable political power and economic resources, NRC officials deployed the accusation of incivility and the specter of mob violence as a regulatory force to discredit meeting attendees and to discourage future audiences from pushing for a democratic agenda. Through its calls for calm, the NRC effectively shifted the topic and focus from Entergy's record to the audience's conduct and from public rights to social manners.

IS THIS WHAT DEMOCRACY LOOKS LIKE?

The use of civility as a bulwark against agitation for the expansion of democratic rights isn't unique to the neoliberal era. It was in the interest of polite peace, James Schmidt reminds us, that Congress adopted the infamous "gag rule" of 1836 against any discussion of slavery or abolition (36). In his classic *Civilities and Civil Rights*, William Chafe examines how the white progressives of 1960 Greensboro, North Carolina, prided themselves on "being hospitable to new ideas"—so long as no substantive move toward integration was required (7). Such civility was also the hallmark of the Obama presidency—a kind of hospitality for which we, as teachers of rhetoric, might feel nostalgic but which also served to emphasize manners over matter. Through his first term in office, for instance, President Barack Obama presented himself as hospitable to discussion about LGBT marriage while relying on the Jim Crow warrant of states' rights to justify federal inaction.[3] Amid the burgeoning Black Lives Matter movement, he joined a diverse chorus of both liberal and conservative commentators in chastising social justice movements on campuses such as the University of Missouri for their "unwillingness to hear other points of view" (Inskeep). Here, too, we find civility's sleight of hand as the problems raised by protestors—racism, rape culture and misogyny, student debt burden, and program defunding—are renamed as a problem of tone and tolerance. To be sure, civility, as hospitableness to other points of view, can smooth dialogue about contentious issues between people *already* meeting on a plane of equality and respect. Under conditions of de facto Jim Crow inequality, on the other hand, civility enables "timid acquiescence" to masquerade as "reasonable compromises" (Schmidt 37).

This history of civil accommodation to injustice, argues Ellen Meiksins Wood, isn't incidental to but constituitive of liberal democracy with its elevation of private rights, especially property rights, above public. The "liberal" in liberal democracy is specifically *economic* liberalism where individual "liberty"—the freedom of the market and the right of owners to exploit resources for maximum profit—trumps "rule by the *demos*" (Wood, chapter 7). Even as historically excluded groups have won juridical recognition and political enfranchisement, Wood points out, the institutions and ideas of a liberal or capitalist democracy ensure that "many varieties of oppression and indignity" are "left untouched by political equality" (224) and that "vast areas of our daily lives . . . are not subject to democratic accountability but governed by the powers of property and the 'laws' of the market, the imperatives of profit maximization" (234). Here the social norms and social discipline of civility (see Cloud, this volume) safeguard the private rights of property and profit from public encroachment and outcry.

Hence, while the celebrated tenets of liberal democracy—the civil-liberties brake on state absolutism, for instance—appear to enable expansive democratic participation, at liberalism's historic heart is fortification from democratic interference. Fortification of individual gun-ownership rights and free-market health care from democratic interference and public programs is what the gun-toting Tea Party members sought through their intimidating presence at August 2010 congressional town hall meetings. Freedom from critical perspectives on race, the Israeli state, and more is what the mounting campaigns, including but not limited to the Professor Watch List and Canary Mission, seek in their campaigns to discredit, intimidate, and even remove from their positions university faculty (see Abraham, Trimbur, this volume). These protests and campaigns don't aim to enlarge space for public debate, decision-making, and provision but, rather, to reprivatize the issues of the day as purely the concerns of the individual and the market. Such protests and campaigns can appear in manner to be uncivil, if incivility is defined as inhospitality to other viewpoints. In substance, however, the Tea Party town hall attendees shared at least one goal with the Obama administration (which had already partnered with industry insiders to remove any "public option" from healthcare reform) and with the NRC (partnering with Entergy to keep nuclear power plants running): the goal of curtailing "uncivil" public challenges—like that of the Indian Point residents—that could threaten the rights of profit. Likewise, faculty witch-hunting groups such as Turning Point USA and Campus Reform share with the US Congress (which, as I write, is considering bipartisan legislation to criminalize support for boycott campaigns against the Israeli state) the warrant of civility in squelching critical questioning and debate.

This participation-inhibiting civility is the "substantive civility"—beyond a set of hospitable manners—that the conservative Chicago School thinker Edward Shils championed as protecting liberal democracy from such threats as "collectivist liberalism," "emancipationism," "populism," and "egalitarianism" that would mobilize the demos to expand the realm of government beyond "enact[ing] laws which protect the market" (*The Virtue of Civility* 4–5, 345; "The Virtue of Civility" 297).[4] Such civility—in service to preserving an unjust social order, safeguarding as private and free-enterprise prerogative the treatment of labor, the environment, and so on—is also what more than two centuries of collectivist, populist, and emancipatory movements have indeed contested. These collectivist, populist, and emancipatory movements have brought measurable expansions of who is included in the political sphere and what democratic rights and social justice oversight can be exercised in the economic domain. But these collectivist, populist, and emancipatory movements were also widely denounced in their moments as uncivil and violent. In fact, such movements were widely denounced as uncivil and violent even though their major rhetorical legacies—for instance, soapboxing, sitdowns, boycotts, and the persuasive tactic of folding the arms or withholding labor—are ones we think of today as staples of nonviolent resistance.

Here I will turn to a chapter from one such movement for social and economic justice: the 1912 Bread and Roses strike. As a rhetorician concerned with how working-class and oppressed groups create space and means to exercise public voice, I'm drawn to the US Progressive Era because its conditions suggest how neoliberalism's diminished conception of democracy doesn't mark a brand-new development but, instead, a restoration, a return to the constricted conception of public rights and public good that likewise defined civil society in the first Gilded Age. For coming to terms with Indian Point's lessons for public rhetoric, a look back to Bread and Roses seems particularly instructive because unfettered corporate power and the civic institutions poised to protect that power were likewise what the immigrant workers of Lawrence, Massachusetts, were taking on. They did so with the scantest of means, making this strike a celebrated chapter in US social justice history. What few of us learn in school, however, is that the strike also drew sharp rebuke—not just from the robber barons whose dominion the strikers challenged but also from prominent reformers who accused the workers of using violence to press their argument. What was the danger to civil society posed by this strike? What makes the assertion "We Want Bread and Roses Too" violent? This strike illustrates the unruly rhetoric necessary to challenge civil boundaries that shield vast realms of injustice from democratic reckoning. Its ensuing controversies also reveal how a ruling class enlists middle-class sentiments to oppose social justice arguments and defend a civil order not for the good of democracy but against it.

A COLLEGE FOR THE WORKERS

"People who have never seen an industrial struggle think of a strike as a time of tumult, disorder and riot. Nothing could be less true. A good strike is a college for the workers" (*Footnote* 11–12). So wrote journalist Mary Heaton Vorse from the front lines of the Lawrence textile strike during the bitterly cold winter of 1912. Sparked by a thirty-cents-a-week pay cut to a workforce already living on starvation's edge, that now fabled strike was carried out by some twenty-five thousand workers, primarily women and girls, coming from more than two dozen ethnic groups speaking some fifty different languages—"all the peoples of the earth," Vorse told her *Harper's* readers, "of warring nations and warring creeds" ("Trouble" 32). The next nine weeks would demonstrate that the immigrant workers shunned by the American Federation of Labor (AFL) could unite against such daunting forces as the powerful Wool Trust monopoly and J. P. Morgan, whose American Woolen Company ran Lawrence's largest mills.

"Better to starve fighting than to starve working." This assertion by mill workers, whose average wage was less than six dollars a week and whose life expectancy at the time was half that for a Lawrence lawyer or minister, was no hyperbole (Vorse, "Trouble" 31; Tax 243). The strikers' desperate economic demands were also inseparable from a political demand for recognition by a society that regarded them, the mills where they worked, and the mill-owned tenements where they lived as the manufacturers' private property, shielded from public interference. It wasn't only mill owners who viewed Lawrence's workers as little more than extensions of the looms they operated. A Lawrence charity society official denied any difference between "ball playing and bobbin tending, school work and mill work, as long as the child was occupied" (Dubofsky 231). When Vorse interviewed "the principal men of the town and all the ministers and several prominent women," they insisted that the workers were "pigs" who "preferred to live as they did to save money" (*Footnote* 18).

Against such ruling sentiments the strikers asserted "We Want Bread and Roses Too." The nation would be made to "see that we are something more than mere textile workers, but are human beings," proclaimed Joseph Ettor of the Industrial Workers of the World (IWW), the radical new labor movement under whose banner the strike was waged (Palmer 1697). How the Lawrence workers with the IWW made a nation hear their arguments—making this strike a college for all who want to learn how social justice arguments are pressed and won—is the subject of numerous histories and memoirs (e.g., Dubofsky; Flynn; Foner; Kornbluh; Tax; Vorse, *Footnote*). Here I'll focus on the strikers' commitments to mass participation and strike democracy, which both created the conditions for comity—recognition of Lawrence's workers and regard for their arguments—and unleashed backlash arguments equating their mass democratic action with riotous behavior and mob violence.

The strike's earliest hours included window and machinery smashing by workers who were outraged to have been shorted "four loaves of bread" in their weekly pay (Palmer 1690). But as the city banned standing pickets and the state called in twenty-four infantry companies and cavalry troops (one filled with Harvard students who accepted strike-suppression duty in exchange for Cs in their courses ["Harvard Men"]), the strikers embraced the principle of "folded arms" or nonviolence. They did so not from a philosophical commitment to pacifism but, rather, from an understanding that mass organizing provided their most practical means to resist the state's repressive forces; their power to withhold labor rivaled the power of the bosses' bayonets and guns. For nonviolence to become a mass-participatory reckoning force, the strikers needed to foster unity across a multiethnic and multilingual workforce. They did so in part by setting up a strike committee with representatives from each of the ethnic groups; the biggest questions were decided through assemblies of all strikers. The commitment to full participation extended across gendered boundaries; women served on the general strike committee, led mass pickets, and confounded police who lamented that "there were no leaders in the streets. . . . The crowds on the street were usually led by women and children" (Tax 249).

As the strikers served together on committees and led mass pickets, they thus created rhetorical space to challenge the hegemony of market logic and also to shake off such "age-old tyrannies" as nativist and sexist chauvinism (Vorse, *Footnote* 15). In the great meetings and marches, Vorse observed, the Lawrence workers were "the antithesis of mob" as they "came together to create and build" and learned through the strike to "get up on platforms and speak with fire and with the eloquence of sincerity," "write articles and leaflets," and "invent new forms of demonstration" (*Footnote* 12–13). Those new forms included the mass moving picket line, a visual demonstration of workers' resolve that also deterred strikebreakers. As they marched, they sang, the joyous scene contrasting sharply with the lethal violence meted out by police and utterly at odds with propaganda painting the strikers as lawless dynamiters. "The public as a whole realized that the strikers are peacefully inclined although determined in their manner," the *Lawrence Evening Tribune*, no friend of the strikers, had to admit (Foner 332).

From strike democracy also came the struggle's turning point. When a Syrian boy was killed, bayoneted in the back by a soldier, Italian workers recommended a common European strike practice of sending the children away to sympathetic families. Photos of emaciated children arriving in New York City drew national sympathy; the scandal of Lawrence police clubbing children and tossing women into paddy wagons to stop the exodus drew national censure. In the *New York Times* incendiary headlines—"Fear Dynamite in Lawrence Strike," "Revolutionary Socialists Incited Workers"—gave way to "More Strike Waifs to Be Sent Here" and "Heads Broken over Order to Prevent Strikers Shipping Their Children Away."

Newspapers did not retreat from their antistrike editorializing. The *Times*, for instance, scolded the strikers as "selfish" because the "demand that something be done instantly for these poor children . . . ignores how much has already been done for their class" ("Children and Society"), while the *Boston Morning Journal* continued to represent the strikers as an "angry mob" waging vicious "battle" against the militia ("Cavalry Repulses Rioters' Attack"). But photographs of small children marching beneath banners proclaiming "They

Asked for Bread. They Received Bayonets" drew both public sympathy *and* investigation. Government inspectors, journalists, the wife of President William Howard Taft, and many scores of heretofore absent reformers and trade unionists poured into Lawrence. In Washington, Congress convened hearings. By mid-March the mills capitulated with an agreement that included progressive wage increases of up to 25 percent; as a strike wave spread across New England, manufacturers extended wage increases to some quarter million textile workers across the region (Tax 263–64).

What workers gained, Vorse reported in *Harper's*, went well beyond money for bread: "Young girls have had executive positions. Men and women who have known nothing but work in the home and mill have developed a larger social consciousness. A strike like this makes people think. Almost every day for weeks people of every one of these nations have gone to their crowded meetings and listened to the speakers and have discussed these questions afterward, and in the morning the women have resumed their duty on the picket lines and the working together for what they believed was a common good" (Vorse, "Trouble" 34–35). The strike also developed Vorse's social consciousness. Upon seeing the "six stores and seven soup kitchens" plus regular "mass demonstrations and mass amusements, huge picnics and concerts" that the workers had organized, she gave up the assumption that the working class required the middle class's moral shepherding. "*All* laws made for the betterment of workers' lives have their origin with the workers," she argued. "Hours are shortened, wages go up, conditions are better—*only* if the workers protest" (*Footnote* 14, emphasis added).

Unsurprisingly, Lawrence's social elites and textile barons did not share Vorse's enthusiasm. Their vociferous condemnation, wrote Vorse, was "the inevitable reaction of the owning group protecting itself instinctively against any vital workers' movement" (*Footnote* 18). But also upset by and outright hostile to the strike were some of the Progressive Era's most prominent reformers. In issues of *The Outlook* and *The Survey* devoted to disseminating the strike, the era's leading intellectuals and social reformers didn't join Vorse in praising the strike and applauding its advances; instead, as I'll detail below, they roundly condemned it.

It can be perplexing to imagine why middle-class social workers, journalists, educators, and labor organizers would join the textile barons in denouncing a movement that won some of the very reforms they had been advocating. Or it can be perplexing until we consider that the strikers' desperate economic demands were inseparable from a political demand for recognition by a society—the reformers included—that regarded them as outside the bounds of civil society and civil recognition. The "trial" of Bread and Roses held in leading progressive journals through the remainder of 1912 reveals how ruling ideas of civility can recruit middle-class reformers to reinforce the civil boundaries and social manners that allow injustice to flourish.

THE TRIAL OF BREAD AND ROSES

To read of Bread and Roses in *The Survey*, the journal of the social welfare settlement house movement, is to encounter an event almost entirely different from what Vorse described. Edward Devine set the tone for the April 1912 issue on "The Lawrence Strike from Various Angles" with an editorial explaining that, although no one should "seek to keep alive" the strike's "bitter controversies" and "tragic incidental blunders," *The Survey* "as a journal of constructive philanthropy" had an obligation to assess these recent events "in an atmosphere far removed from the angry tumult of the labor conflict" (1). In this issue can be found a very few strike champions: Women's Trade Union League founder Mary O'Sullivan, who declared the IWW "the best possible thing that could happen to the labor unions of America" (72–73), and Professor Vida Scudder, whose strike support nearly cost her job at Wellesley and became an early test of the idea of academic freedom. Many more of the issue's contributors focused on censure (of the strikers), guilt (of the IWW and also of reformers for allowing workers to fall prey to a radical union), and absolution (of the military and police). For example:

The strike, argued Walter Weyl (who later founded the *New Republic*), did not open up a promising direction for achieving the reformers' heretofore thwarted agenda of ending child labor and improving factory safety. Instead, it marked the middle class's failure to stand as guardians of the immigrant poor, leaving Lawrence's workers to trade "oceans of public sympathy" for "an ounce of working class revolt." (65)

The xenophobic Robert Woods—the head of Boston's South End House and a settlement movement founder who also called Lawrence's workers "the very clod of humanity" ("The Clod Stirs" 1932) and later turned toward promoting eugenics—declared that the strike victory "represents an amount of harm which only years of aggressive educational effort can overcome." ("The Breadth and Depth" 68)

Carl Carstens, head of the Massachusetts Society for the Prevention of Cruelty to Children, absolved the police who beat children and women at the Lawrence train station, arguing that the police were "entitled to the credit of having acted with sincere good intentions" to prevent the children from being shipped "to a place where they might be brought up as thieves or prostitutes." (71)

Their solutions varied: Weyl exhorted the middle class to greater vigilance; Harvard's James Ford favored workers' cooperatives as an evolutionary road to prepare mentally unfit immigrants for democratic participation; Devine and Woods recommended restricted immigration; a mill overseer advocated the restoration of patient petition by workers and benevolent patronage from employers. These contributors shared, however, the convictions that workers should not attempt to solve their own problems and that their mass-unity means were inherently violent.

The Survey's prominent characterization of the strikers and their union as violent is at first startling. After all, by now it had been widely acknowledged that Lawrence's workers—three dead, many hundreds wounded and beaten, at least one miscarriage resulting—were victims, not perpetrators. By now the nation knew that it was a Lawrence school board member who, apparently at the behest of the American Woolen Company's president, had planted dynamite caches to fuel headline hysteria (Dubofsky 247; Flynn 129–30). As for the pillorying of the IWW as "blood-stained Anarchists," it was the IWW, O'Sullivan reminded *Survey* readers, that brought to the strike a "policy of non-resistance to the aggressions of the police and the militia" (73). Yet from Devine's opening characterization of an "angry tumult" to sociologist John Graham Brooks's closing warning that the IWW aimed for "the immediate inclusion of the tramp and gutter bird" in respectable unions (Brooks 82), most contributors gravitated to the truthy appeal that strike violence had been promulgated by "imported leaders" (Devine 1) who led astray Lawrence's "poor ignorant fellows" ("A Mill Overseer" 75) whose "mistakes of threats and violence" were "inevitable . . . within a large population so alien and mentally impoverished" (Ford 70).

Influencing their responses were, of course, the settlement movement's currents of nativism and paternalism as well as the conservative drag of the AFL, which had aggressively opposed the strike. Also evident is the indignation of reformers at immigrant workers acting on their own authority. Perhaps, too, we might hear these responses as the expressions of what Barbara and John Ehrenreich would later term the "professional-managerial class" that joins together "salaried mental workers," such as social workers and teachers, in seeking the "reproduction of capitalist culture and capitalist class relations" for their own interests distinct from both labor and capital (45). But in the wide agreement among reformers that the strike had been dismayingly violent and that responsibility lay with the workers for striking in the first place, we find something quite different from a group acting in its own professional-managerial class interests. We find instead the enlistment of the middle class in the corporate class project to undo the strike victory and reassert a strict separation between the narrow sphere for practicing formal democracy, from which most mill workers were excluded, and the vast sphere of free-market liberty, into which democracy was never to encroach.

The enlistment of these reformers in defending an undemocratic order in the name of civil ideals becomes most evident when they try to explain what precisely made the workers' actions violent. The workers and the IWW, wrote Devine, were not "frankly breaking out into lawless riot which we know well enough how to deal with"; instead, they relied on such "strange" forms of "violence" as "direct action" and "the general strike," which threatened "the fundamental idea of law and order" and the "sacredness of property" (1–2). The IWW's method of "folding the hands," warned Brooks, was intended to create a "riot of confusion" and revealed their "inveterate hostility toward society as it now exists" (82). Devine and Brooks weren't wrong in surmising that the aspirations of Lawrence's laboring majority went beyond the economic demands of higher pay and fewer hours. They were not wrong in suspecting that the workers had scant faith in such institutions of civil society as the mill-aligned press, the parsimonious relief societies, and the courts that held strike leaders responsible for police bullets and militia bayonets. The strike demonstrated that those institutions do not serve as impartial mediators providing open deliberative spaces but, instead, as custodians for ruling interests. The workers—who vowed to continue seeking an "ever-increasing share of the value of the product of labor" and "increasing control of the machines that the workers operate" (Lawrence Textile Workers 79)—were indeed arguing for the rule by the demos that liberal democracy's foundational institutions oppose. Whereas Vorse celebrated that the new society workers were "coming together to build and create" (*Footnote* 13), Devine, Brooks, and others rallied to defend the social order these workers also sought to undo.

This isn't to say that these reformers were not deeply disturbed by the dire conditions the strike spotlighted. "If textile workers are earning less than a living wage," Devine argued, "we should pay them more, not because they will follow strange doctrines and smash machinery if we do not, but because it is right and decent that they should have a living income" (2). Posed, too, were troubling questions about the very nature of US democracy. "When we turn to the processes of industry, can we say that America is democratic?" asked the editors of the leading progressive journal *The Outlook*: "Is there not something wrong in our industrial system itself, when thousands upon thousands among those who make the clothes of the Nation and produce the food of the Nation and help to supply the other wealth of the Nation are ill clad and on the edge of starvation? There is justice in the law, 'Work or starve,' but what justice is there in conditions that virtually say to thousands of workers, 'Work and starve'?"

("Violence and Democracy" 352–53). Yet although *The Outlook* acknowledged that democracy should extend into the workplace, "substituting for industrial oligarchy a prevailing industrial democracy," its editors argued that this could not happen through workers withholding their labor and thus refusing to subordinate their grievances for the good of civil peace: "It is right that the people through their representatives should use the bayonets of the militia and the clubs of the policemen to restore order whenever disorder arises" (353). Economic justice would come instead, promised *Outlook* columnist Theodore Roosevelt, through management that is both "intelligent and sympathetic" and workers who "understand and sympathize with management" (354). With this assurance that comity between enlightened employers and patient workers will bring, eventually, recognition and rights, Roosevelt sets aside the "work and starve" facts of the mill workers' relationship to mill managers. The rhetorical ideals of moderation and mutuality are put to work to reprivatize the strike's public complaints as a matter best dealt with between employer and employee.

Echoing this counsel is Jane Addams's "A Modern Lear." *The Survey* printed Addams's essay, written in response to the 1894 Pullman strike, with the added headnote contextualizing it as "a message for today" (Addams 131), near the end of 1912 just as silk workers in Paterson, New Jersey, had started to stir. In casting the conflict between capital and labor as a family drama in which both father/owner and daughter/worker have forgotten their obligations to one another, Addams's parable can be read as a middle-class woman's sidelined helplessness in Pullman's pitched battle between the railroad magnates and US Army on one side and workers and their union on the other. Given how Bread and Roses had released women from the home as well as the mill, opening up new identities as organizers, speakers, writers, and leaders, "A Modern Lear" also needs to be placed within the campaign to reverse the Lawrence strike's gains and reprivatize, as a "family matter," the economic and political status of women.

By the time *The Survey*'s debate on Bread and Roses appeared in April 1912, the mill owners' "God and Country" campaign to re-divide workers and break their new union was well underway. By the start of the 1920s the Red Scare had not only decimated the IWW but witch-hunted progressives like Jane Addams as well (McGerr 306–8). The AFL's claim to moderate respectability provided no cover, as the corporate class unleashed its "open-shop" campaign, reducing its membership by half. When Vorse looked back on Bread and Roses twenty-three years later—amid the Depression decade's upsurge that would finally secure (until the rollbacks of our new Gilded Age) much of the Progressive Era's reform agenda—she saw "an indignation whose fire has never gone out" (*Footnote* 19, 21).

WHAT DEMOCRACY LOOKS LIKE

The pattern that emerges in Bread and Roses is one that repeats through the twentieth century's social justice flashpoints: big-idea arguments and actions of exploited and oppressed groups test society's boundaries and draw ruling-class reprisal. Within that polarized struggle, the middling middle class is pulled in one direction (Weyl warning that to revolt against the social order means forfeiting public sympathy) or another (Vorse discerning that through a strike's upheaval "Harmony, not disorder, was being established . . . a collective harmony" [*Footnote* 13]). For the journalists, labor organizers, women's suffrage advocates, and social reformers who stood in the middle of Lawrence's argument between the producers and appropriators of the region's wealth, social class was not a fixed position on a sociological scale. The ideas of Bread and Roses coupled with direct observation and experience drew strike witnesses like Vorse, O'Sullivan, and Scudder to the side of workers while Weyl, Devine, and the settlement movement's most visible leaders lined up with employers. "If we watch these men [and women] over an adequate period of social change," writes E. P. Thompson, we can "observe patterns in their relationships, their ideas, their institutions" (*The Making* 11).[5] The patterns we observe include that of the middle class not acting decisively and consistently for a uniform set of class interests but swayed toward supporting one side or the other in confrontations between labor and capital and between changing or maintaining a social order. This pattern—this class politics—is one that compositionists, especially those concerned with public rhetoric for social change, need to recognize, and also reassess, in the work of some of our field's most celebrated thinkers.

Like Weyl, for instance, Wayne Booth viewed radicalism and recognition, protest and sympathy, as mutually exclusive. Consider the opening to his 1974 *Modern Dogma and the Rhetoric of Assent* where he expresses puzzlement over "the inability of *most* protest groups to get themselves heard" (xi, emphasis added). His case in point: a sixteen-day sit-in by University of Chicago students protesting the tenure denial of a popular professor who had also spoken publicly against the Vietnam War. Here and throughout the book, Booth stresses his opposition to both the protest's method and substance, which he sums up as a "frantic and self-defeating multiplication and discarding of the issues" as the students advanced further demands such as voting rights on university committees, university-provided daycare centers, doubled salaries for service workers, and a democratic voice for Hyde Park residents in university appointments (8). Although it is for good reason that Booth's subsequent work of seeking a "revitalized rhetoric" to rival the "warfare" of "lying, trickery, blackmail, and physical persuasion" (149–50) has had such influence, we still need to trouble his founding premises: that the "protest groups" of the 1960s and early 1970s did not "get themselves heard"; that calls for university democratization are unreasonable; that such forms of "physical persuasion" as the sit-in are tantamount to blackmail, even warfare.

Just as we should place Addams's "A Modern Lear" in its historical and conservatized leave-it-to-the-family context, we should place Booth's appeals for a rhetoric of assent in its historical context: a harassed dean defending a university's limited participatory sphere against a burgeoning rule-by-the-demos argument. Doing so, we can bring into view, and into our teaching, the wider field of rhetorical practice and the history of the rhetorical means that have won social change. Through this history we and our students can consider, against the seemingly commonsense claim that audience unruliness always closes communicative channels, those instances where it has taken unruliness to create the conditions—"a rhetorical field," according to Booth, "what [John] Dewey called 'a public'" (*Modern Dogma* 149–50)—within which communication and respect can actually flourish.

But more, we need to place particular standout moments of social justice struggle in their historical context and in a longer historical timeline. Doing so, we can better appreciate the rich social ecology that favored a particular movement: for example, the political ideas and agitational experiences that immigrant workers carried from their home countries, the legacies of the late-nineteenth century's eight-hour day and Populist movements, and the Progressive Era's myriad reform campaigns that all contributed to the IWW's rise and the Bread and Roses moment. Doing so, we can also grasp why it is ever necessary, as Raymond Williams put it, to "go again to Hyde Park" (9)—to agitate for the rights and recognition that liberal democracy's free-market rights will always attempt to trump: for example, the continuing struggle for environmental justice as Entergy finally shuts down Vermont Yankee but delays for decades any cleanup; as activists reorient for a dual fight against fracked-gas and Tar Sands oil pipelines plus the deceptive rhetorical rehabilitation of nuclear energy as a "safe" alternative to these fossil fuels.

At stake in engaging our students in a fuller appreciation of the rhetorical assets required—and the rhetorical controversies and continuing struggles that ensue—in arguments for social change is the future of the very idea of a public good. The imperilment of the public good is what Shadis recognized when he called out the NRC for "infuriating" audiences with its nuclear-industry propaganda. In a revealing footnote near the end of *Modern Dogma and the Rhetoric of Assent*, Booth also anticipated the threat of the advancing neoliberal agenda to any rhetoric of mutual recognition and common ground. Despairing of the utter lack of comity at the core of capitalist democracy, he states:

It is . . . not just the advertising and political propaganda spawned by capitalism that must go: the whole "liberal" assumption that men are not accountable to their fellows for how they acquire and spend their private fortunes is unten-able. . . . [I]t seems clearer and clearer that if we do not find some way to move beyond our inhumane economic system, we will lose what is left of our humane political traditions . . . as our present economic system induces viciousness, de-ception, and privatization to the point of psychosis. "Weak" forces like tradition, the church, the university, or natural altruism, if any, cannot combat this sys-tematic destructiveness indefinitely. (201n32)

These words not only point ahead to today's neoliberalized democracy, where state governors push legislation to privatize public resources for the profit of corporate donors and where regulatory agencies are staffed by for-mer executives from the industries for which they are to serve as watchdogs. Booth's words also point back to the same problem of capitalist plutocracy that the IWW captured in an editorial cartoon for its journal *Solidarity* depicting a textile magnate standing on a map of the United States, wiping his feet on child labor laws and first-amendment protections while in the corner a cowering Uncle Sam bites his nails (Young). Before we lose what is left of "our humane political traditions," we should consider and teach that what is humane and what is democratic in those traditions is owed to people, from the workers of Lawrence to the residents near Indian Point, who have been informed, passion-ate, and when confronting an entrenched and unjust social order, frequently disorderly.

NOTES

1. An earlier version of this essay appeared in the *Community Literacy Journal*. I'm grateful to Shannon Carter and Deborah Mutnick for their insightful reading of early drafts. This expanded and revised version of the essay appears with the permission of the *Community Literacy Journal*.

2. This argument about neoliberalism's dependence on civility might seem coun-terintuitive since most often it is associated with shock-doctrine tactics and disaster opportunism. But corporate privatization has also depended on a fuzzy language of consensus, compromise, and "shared sacrifice" in service to privatizing goals (Lecercle 219–20; Welch).

3. At an LGBT fundraiser for Obama's reelection campaign, a few audience mem-bers heckled the president with shouts of "Marriage!" The fact that they also paid up to $35,800 a plate to be able to do so (Werner and Pace) illustrates the neoliberalization of protest itself—public voice purchased at a hefty price—to which the Madison capitol takeover, Occupy park encampments, and the Black Lives Matter protests have all pro-

vided a welcome counterpoint. Welcome too was Obama's 2012 acknowledgment that same-sex couples should be able to marry—though, by qualifying his position as personal and emphasizing that the question should be decided state by state, he effectively denied that at stake is a constitutional right to equal protection under the law.

4. For Shils's elite conception of the "civil citizen," see also Shils, "The Virtue of Civility," 304; for a survey of antidemocratic sentiment in Plato and Aristotle, see Wood, chapter 6.

5. The US Populist and Progressive Eras provide rich illustrations of social class not as a *thing* but as a *relationship* and class consciousness not as something *given* but as something *made* (Thompson, *The Making* 9–11; Wood, chapter 3). The exploitation and antagonism that workers experienced across diverse workplaces and ethnicities also made it possible for them to think in what E. P. Thompson terms "class ways" about the ruling ideas, including ruling ideas of racism and nativism, that would subjugate and divide them. The super-exploitative relations of production that marked the era did not automatically produce working-class solidarity and instigate mass action. Instead, as Thompson emphasizes, *experience* figured as a "necessary middle term between social being [of exploitation and oppression] and social consciousness [of one's means with others to intervene]" (Thompson, *The Poverty of Theory* 98; see also Wood, chapter 3).

WORKS CITED

Addams, Jane. "A Modern Lear." *The Survey: A Journal of Constructive Philanthropy* 29, no. 5 (November 2, 1912): 131–37.

Associated Press. "AP Impact: Federal Nuclear Regulators Repeatedly Weaken or Fail to Enforce Safety Standards." *Washington Post*, June 20, 2011.

Booth, Wayne C. *Modern Dogma and the Rhetoric of Assent*. University of Chicago Press, 1974.

Booth, Wayne C. *The Rhetoric of Rhetoric: The Quest for Effective Communication*. Blackwell, 2004.

Booth, Wayne C. "War Rhetoric, Defensible and Indefensible." *JAC: A Journal of Rhetoric, Culture, and Politics* 25, no. 2 (2005): 221–44.

Brooks, John Graham. "The Shadow of Anarchy." *The Survey: A Journal of Constructive Philanthropy* 28, no. 1 (April 6, 1912): 80–82.

Carstens, C. C. "The Children's Exodus from Lawrence." *The Survey: A Journal of Constructive Philanthropy* 28, no. 1 (April 6, 1912): 70–71.

"Cavalry Repulses Rioters' Attack in Brisk Battle." *Boston Morning Journal*, February 26, 1912. ProQuest Historical Newspapers.

Chafe, William H. *Civilities and Civil Rights: Greensboro, North Carolina, and the Black Struggle for Freedom*. Oxford University Press, 1980.

"Children and Society." *New York Times*, February 20, 1912. ProQuest Historical Newspapers.

Clary, Greg. "Indian Point Opponents Disrupt NRC Safety Forum." *Journal News* (White Plains, NY), June 3, 2011.

Devine, Edward. "Social Forces." *The Survey: A Journal of Constructive Philanthropy* 28, no. 1 (April 6, 1912): 1–2.

Dillon, John. "Nuclear Critic Urges Civility at Yankee Briefing." *Vermont Edition*. Vermont Public Radio, June 21, 2011. www.vprarchive.vpr.net/vpr-news/nuclear-critic-urges-civility -at-yankee-briefing/.

Dubofsky, Melvyn. *We Shall Be All: A History of the Industrial Workers of the World*. Quadrangle, 1969.

Duffy, John. "Virtuous Arguments." *Inside Higher Ed*, March 16, 2012. www.insidehighered .com/views/2012/03/16/essay-value-first-year-writing-courses/.

Ehrenreich, Barbara, and John Ehrenreich. "The Professional-Managerial Class." In *Between Labor and Capital*, edited by Pat Walker, 5–45. South End Press, 1979.

Enos, Theresa. "A Call for Comity." In *Beyond Postprocess and Postmodernism: Essays on the Spaciousness of Rhetoric*, edited by Theresa Enos and Keith D. Miller, 131–57. Lawrence Erlbaum Associates, 2003.

"Fear Dynamite in Lawrence Strike." *New York Times*, January 18, 1912. ProQuest Historical Newspapers.

Flynn, Elizabeth Gurley. *The Rebel Girl: My First Life (1906–1926)*. International Publishers, 1994.

Foner, Philip S. *The Industrial Workers of the World 1905–1917*. Vol. 4 of *History of the Labor Movement in the United States*. International Publishers, 1997.

Ford, James. "The Co-operative Franco-Belge of Lawrence." *The Survey: A Journal of Constructive Philanthropy* 28, no. 1 (April 6, 1912): 68–70.

Gonzales, Juan, and Amy Goodman. "New Exposé Reveals Nuclear Regulatory Commission Colluded with Industry to Weaken Safety Standards." *Democracy Now!* June 2011. www.democracynow.org/2011/6/24/new_expos_reveals_nuclear_regulatory _commission/.

"Harvard Men on Guard." *New York Times*, February 1, 1912. ProQuest Historical Newspapers.

"Heads Broken over an Order to Prevent Strikers Shipping Their Children Away." *New York Times*, February 25, 1912. ProQuest Historical Newspapers.

Inskeep, Skip. "Video and Transcript: NPR's Interview with President Obama." *All Things Considered*. National Public Radio. 21 December 2015. www.npr.org/2015 /12/21/460030344/video-and-transcript-nprs-interview-with-president-obama/.

Kornbluh, Joyce. *Rebel Voices: An IWW Anthology*. Charles Kerr, 1988.

Lawrence Textile Workers. "Lawrence and the Industrial Workers of the World." *The Survey: A Journal of Constructive Philanthropy* 28, no. 1 (April 6, 1912): 79–80.

Lecercle, Jean-Jacques. *A Marxist Philosophy of Language*. Translated by Gregory Elliott. Haymarket, 2009.

McGerr, Michael. *A Fierce Discontent: The Rise and Fall of the Progressive Movement in America, 1870–1920*. Free Press, 2003.

"A Mill Overseer's View." *The Survey: A Journal of Constructive Philanthropy* 28, no. 1 (April6, 1912): 75–76.

"More Strike Waifs to Be Sent Here." *New York Times*, February 13, 1912. ProQuest Historical Newspapers.

O'Sullivan, Mary K. "The Labor War at Lawrence." *The Survey: A Journal of Constructive Philanthropy* 28, no. 1 (April 6, 1912): 72–74.

Palmer, Lewis E. "A Strike for Four Loaves of Bread." *The Survey: A Journal of Constructive Philanthropy* 27, no. 18 (February 3, 1912): 1690–97.

Powell, Dawn. "Close Indian Point." *Points*, June 7, 2011. www.dawnpowell.wordpress .com/ 2011/06/07/close-indian-point/.

"Raging Grannies against Indian Point." *Indian Point Miscellany*, June 15, 2011. www .indianpointmiscellany.blogspot.com/2011/06/raging-grannies-against-indian-point .html. Last accessed June 16, 2015, but no longer available.

Ratcliffe, Krista. *Rhetorical Listening: Identification, Gender, Whiteness*. Southern Illinois University Press, 2006.

"Revolutionary Socialists Incited Workers." *New York Times*, February 8, 1912. ProQuest Historical Newspapers.

Roosevelt, Theodore. "A Phase of Industrial Justice." *The Outlook* 11, no. 7 (February 17,1912): 353–55.

Schmidt, James. "Is Civility a Virtue?" In *Civility*, edited by Leroy S. Rouner, 17–39. Notre Dame University Press, 2000.

Shadis, Raymond. "NRC: Manners, Methods, Messages." *VTDigger*, June 21, 2011. www .vtdigger.org/2011/06/21/shadis-nrc-manners-methods-messages/.

Shils, Edward. *The Virtue of Civility*. Liberty Fund, 1997.

Shils, Edward. "The Virtue of Civility." In *The Civil Society Reader*, edited by Virginia A. Hodgkinson and Michael W. Foley, 292–305. Tufts University Press/University Press of New England, 2003.

Tax, Meredith. *The Rising of the Women: Feminist Solidarity and Class Conflict, 1880–1917*. University of Illinois Press, 2001.

Thompson, E. P. *The Making of the English Working Class*. Penguin, 1968.

Thompson, E. P. *The Poverty of Theory and Other Essays*. Merlin Press, 1978.

"Violence and Democracy." *The Outlook* 11, no. 7 (February 17, 1912): 352–53.

Vorse, Mary Heaton. *A Footnote to Folly: Reminiscences of Mary Heaton Vorse*. Farrar and Rineheart, 1935.

Vorse, Mary Heaton. "The Trouble at Lawrence." 1912. In *Rebel Pen: The Writings of Mary Heaton Vorse*, edited by Dee Garrison, 29–35. Monthly Review Press, 1985.

Welch, Nancy. "La Langue de Coton: How Neoliberal Language Pulls the Wool over Faculty Governance." *Pedagogy* 11, no. 3 (Fall 2011): 571–79.

Werner, Erica and Julie Pace. "Obama at Gay Fundraiser as NY Weighs Marriage OK." *San Diego Tribune*, June 23, 2011. www.sandiegouniontribune.com/sdut-obama-at-gay -fundraiser-as-ny-weighs-marriage-ok-2011jun23-story.html.

Weyl, Walter E. "It Is Time to Know." *The Survey: A Journal of Constructive Philanthropy* 28, no. 1 (April 6, 1912): 65–67.

Williams, Chris. "No Fukushima-on-the-Hudson." *Indypendent*, June 6, 2011. www .indypendent.org/2011/06/no-fukushima-on-the-hudson/.

Williams, Raymond. *Culture and Materialism: Selected Essays.* London: Verso, 1980.

Wood, Ellen Meiksins. *Democracy against Capitalism: Renewing Historical Materialism.* Cambridge University Press, 1995.

Woods, Robert A. "The Breadth and Depth of the Lawrence Outcome." *The Survey: A Journal of Constructive Philanthropy* 28, no. 1 (April 6, 1912): 67–68.

Woods, Robert A. "The Clod Stirs." *The Survey: A Journal of Constructive Philanthropy* 27, no. 18 (March 16, 1912): 1929–32.

Young, Art. "Uncle Sam Ruled Out." *Solidarity*, June 7, 1913. Reprinted by Labor Arts. www.laborarts.org/collections/item.cfm?itemid=424/.

Zeller, Tom, Jr. "Nuclear Agency Is Criticized as Too Close to Its Industry." *New York Times*, May 7, 2011. www.nytimes.com/2011/05/08/business/energy-environment/08nrc.html.

7

CIRCULATING VOICES OF DISSENT

REWRITING THE LIFE OF JAMES EADS HOW AND *HOBO NEWS*

DIANA GEORGE AND PAULA MATHIEU

I will try not to overlook the cruelties victims inflict on one another as they are jammed together in the boxcars of the system. I don't want to romanticize them. But I do remember (in rough paraphrase) a statement I once read: "The cry of the poor is not always just, but if you don't listen to it, you will never know what justice is."

—Howard Zinn, on writing *A People's History*

Ⅰn July 1930 Staunton, Virginia, like much of the nation, was in the midst of a record-setting heat wave. For days, temperatures had reached above 100 degrees and as high as 109 degrees in the Staunton area alone. In some Virginia cities, those temperatures remain the hottest on record.¹ This was early in the Great Depression years, but for the millions of unemployed living in the streets all across the United States, 1930 was simply another in the round of depression cycles that had begun with the collapse of Jay Cooke and Company and the Wall Street Panic of 1873. By 1877, and in response to mass layoffs coupled with a rash of wage reductions across major industries, the Great Railroad Strike hit, threatening an already shaky economy. Thirty years later, the Panic of 1907, fueled by the Knickerbocker Trust Company failure, set the stage for yet another stock market crash.

It had to be a bad time to be homeless—few escapes from the oppressive heat and humidity, tramp laws that meant always being on the move, and meals that were rare and hard to come by. In that setting, on July 22 in Staunton's King's Daughters Hospital, James Eads How died at age sixty-one from pneumonia brought on, according to his death certificate, by severe malnutrition.[2] If someone hadn't recognized the dead man as the "millionaire hobo," How might have disappeared entirely, mistaken for a shabby itinerant, buried in the paupers' section of Staunton's local cemetery. Once he was identified, however, news of How's death spread quickly across the country, with an Associated Press story appearing, with few variations, in small town and major metropolitan newspapers nationwide. The *Kansas City Star* ran the same AP story with the subhead, "Member of a Wealthy St. Louis Family. He Spurned Society to Travel with 'The Knights of the Road.'" Perhaps in an attempt to account for this odd lifestyle, the *New York Times* report noted the "marked eccentricities" James How had displayed soon after entering theological college where he "sold his dress suit and gave the proceeds to the poor. Soon afterwards, he gave his banjo away to one he thought would be benefited by it" ("James Eads How Dies"). Like many of the mainstream press accounts that circulated both before and after his death, this one characterized How as an oddity—the Millionaire Hobo—whose hapless attempts at helping others left him living in inexplicable, self-imposed poverty and physical deprivation.

Born in 1868 into a wealthy and prominent St. Louis family, educated at Harvard and Oxford, trained as a physician and theologian, widely traveled, and the primary heir to the family fortune, James Eads How could have enjoyed easy luxury at a time when millions were out of work and living in abject poverty. Instead, he refused wealth that he had not earned. Instead, he chose to echo the opposition voiced by Eugene Debs and others to "a social order in which it is possible for one man who does absolutely nothing that is useful to amass a fortune of hundreds of millions of dollars, while millions of men and women who work all the days of their lives secure barely enough for a wretched existence" (Debs, "Statement to the Court").

Our readers may well ask why we even bother telling James Eads How's story now so far removed, as we are, from those events and that time. After all, unlike Debs or Emma Goldman or Mother Jones or any number of other much better known social and labor activists of the time, our subject is barely remembered. In terms of name recognition, at least, his legacy seems not to have lasted. Our purpose here, however, is not simply to recover a great story but, rather, through that story to demonstrate how very difficult—some might say unlikely—it is for dissenting voices to circulate even in the hands of a free press.

In a sense, then, we aim to rewrite James Eads How's obituary by telling the fuller story of the ways he lived his political choices among a class of the unemployed. Rather than painting him as the Angel of Fortune or the Crazy Rich Guy, we seek to broaden the story, to show how he both embodied and sponsored a collective, unruly rhetoric for a group of displaced and impoverished jobless workers. "This is the object of our brotherhood," he told a *New York Times* reporter in 1911. "We are attempting . . . to organize this vast floating element of labor which at present has no voice" ("Millionaire Hobo Seeks a Cure"). With our rewrite, we hope to illustrate in what ways James Eads How— together with the tramps, bums, and hoboes flooding the streets and rail yards at the time—circulated important counter public messages, rallying for justice and fair treatment as they carried *Hobo News* with them, distributing the paper wherever and whenever the trains stopped.[3] We open, then, with the man himself—with a tale that begins many years before his death.

"THIS STRANGE YOUNG MAN": AN EMBODIED RHETORIC

In 1899, after his father's will had been sorted out, James Eads How walked into the Saint Louis mayor's office to offer his entire inherited fortune to aid the poor of that city. This event was chronicled in one *New York Daily News* article with its headline describing How as one who "Scorns His Own Million": "The first thing he did was to walk into the office of the Mayor of Saint Louis, where the family is well-known, and hand him a check for all he possessed. . . . He asked the Mayor to spend the money for the poor. The Mayor, however, ordered that an investigation be made as to his sanity" ("Scorns"). Perhaps the best shorthand for the mayor's befuddlement appears in 1901 as the headline for a feature story in the now defunct *Saint Louis Republic*: "What Are the Purposes of This Strange Young Man?" It was common in such reports to wonder what religious or political or philosophical reason How might have had for his refusal to spend his inheritance on himself. In fact, when one pastor challenged him with, "You are not a Christian!," How's reported response was to say he wasn't a member of any church, though he might be closer to being a Buddhist than a Christian, and occasionally he thought he might be more of a Christian than a Buddhist ("Refuses a Million"). That story, as did so many before and after it, then quickly turned to How's appearance: "His ascetic, or at least, abstemious, habits have given him a somewhat gaunt look, but his face, with its beaminess and its strong humility, is more Christlike than half of Christ's heads painted by the masters" ("Refuses a Million"), thereby suggesting How had to be either a saint or a crazy man and perhaps both.

To read mainstream press accounts of James Eads How's life, death, and funeral is to read about a man who had everything handed to him but failed to take advantage of his good fortune. Some seem almost to delight in what must have looked like a sorry end to a misguided life. From a July 25, 1930, *New York Times* account of How's funeral, readers could easily have gotten the impression that, no matter in what way he had lived his life or spent his money to help the impoverished, How died alone and unappreciated—so alone that his pallbearers had to be hired: "No ragged 'knights of the road,' and but one representative of all those he befriended in his life, joined his brother and a few college mates in attending the funeral today for James Eads How, so-called 'millionaire hobo,' in All Souls Unitarian Church. . . . At the conclusion of the service, conducted by Dr. Robert B. Day, the body of How, who had devoted much of his life to the cause of the unfortunate, was borne by six paid pallbearers" ("Hoboes Fail to Attend").[4] This reporter, in what reads like a what-was-the-point-anyway sneer, concludes with a final dig: "The one man representing Mr. How's International Brotherhood Welfare Association [IBWA] was Harry W. Johannes, Jr. of Baltimore, who distributed copies of *The Hobo News* outside the church." It should come as little surprise that the mainstream press did not seem to know how to write about him, resorting instead to condescension with an air of puzzlement. To say, for example, that James Eads How "spurned society to travel with the 'Knights of the Road,'" is to engage in a kind of double deceit: that "society" is the moneyed class and that those forced to live on the tramp were romantic wanderers or outright bums who chose to move from place to place without a care in the world except for where to get the next handout.

As memorials to a man who devoted his life to educating others about inequality and injustice, these press stories stand as a kind of cruel irony through which the fiction of poverty as personal choice elides the reality of economic and political inequality, effectively pulling out of circulation the story James Eads How had been telling for years both in his sponsorship of *Hobo News* and in the way he chose to live his life. Reports of his collapse and subsequent death do not mention, for example, that only four months earlier, How had led a delegation of fifty-to-sixty jobless men to DC to testify before Congress on the plight of the unemployed ("Unemployed Appear"). Those reports fail, in other words, to do the work of the typical obit/story on the life of a man whose influence reached far beyond that Great Army of Tramps—yet another social and economic phenomenon the press had trouble explaining.

The truth, however, is that How was not at all forgotten by the people he served even if his name did effectively disappear from the press after 1932.[5] Not long after the fancy (though sparsely attended) Washington, DC, service arranged by his brother Louis, the hobo world held a memorial of its own at which hundreds gathered in honor of How's life. Even before the DC service, hobo leaders had declared a thirty-day period of mourning for his death. Franklin, Pennsylvania's *News-Herald* ran a brief but buried report on this alternative funeral, pointing out that hoboes were not welcome at the family funeral, held as it was in DC's "fashionable All Souls' Unitarian Church," providing How "in burial the luxury he had scorned in life" ("Tramp World Goes into Mourning"). Two years later, on the anniversary of How's death, leaders of the IBWA, the organization How founded, paid tribute to its leader, telling those gathered, "Let us echo the name of James Eads How from pillar to post and all say a good word for one who never forgot others" ("Hoboes in Tribute"). For the mainstream press, once How made his decision to embody the rhetoric he believed—to refuse to profit by the labor of others—he became a curiosity or, later, a bad caricature, someone who was likely crazy and surely playing at being poor.

A PATHOLOGY OF POVERTY

> But it is said that a very large proportion of the unemployed are men who are unwilling to produce—the unworthy and the lazy.
>
> —A *New York Times* reporter's question to James Eads How
> ("Millionaire Hobo Seeks a Cure" 1911)

One of the difficulties, even today, for activists seeking justice for the homeless or the economically impoverished in our society is the popular notion that there is something wrong with a person who cannot make a living. That same *New York Times* reporter quoted above, for example, describes How as "an extraordinary man" who has chosen to give all he has "to work among the unemployed and the *incompetent*" ("Millionaire Hobo Seeks a Cure," emphasis added). Like so many other reporters, this one opened his story with his shock at seeing the "really extraordinary spectacle" of the young millionaire standing in his mother's mansion (where, the reporter failed to mention, he did not live) "garbed in an old and shabby suit and a blue flannel shirt." For many, the very look of poverty points to the incompetence of the impoverished. Why *choose* that look?[6]

James Eads How's very lifestyle, as a form of embodied rhetoric, challenged others to take note. That challenge was surely a problem for reporters tasked with writing about him. After all, to tell the story of How's work would have meant taking him seriously. Moreover, to tell the story of How's work would have meant keeping his principles, in particular his opposition to capitalism, at the forefront. Instead, typical press reports moved very quickly from identifying How as heir to a wealthy and prominent family to the longer story of his odd practices and, of course, the shocking state of his appearance.[7]

Reporters' seeming obsession with How's physical body and social eccentricities is hardly isolated to that time, those writers, or to How's story. Instead, it echoes stories that continue to circulate about those living in poverty and homelessness. During How's time, it was an obsession that might be traced back to a pervading fear of out-of-work tramps, bums, and hoboes. Only a few years after the close of the Civil War, the public became increasingly and uncomfortably aware of a growing stream of migratory laborers soon to be known and feared as that "Great Army of Tramps." Historian Todd DePastino attributes this rise of the visibly homeless (primarily white men) to broad economic changes rather than to individual failings or an increasing number of "idle poor," as some had already been calling the tramping population for many years ("The Philadelphia Mills").[8] Instead, DePastino argues that the end of the Civil War had moved the country from a slavery-based agrarian economy to an industrial wage-based economy leaving hundreds of thousands of workers unemployed (9–17). This shift also increased the concentration of wealth among a few rich, leaving the jobless and their families in, or at the edge of, dire poverty.

Adding to that shift in the labor economy and long before the start of the Great Depression in 1929, the powerful banking firm Jay Cooke and Company collapsed, triggering the Wall Street Panic of 1873 followed by years of bankruptcies and, eventually, worldwide depression and labor unrest (DePastino 4). In the wake of these events, an unprecedented stream of unemployed and homeless workers scrambled to fit into a perilously unstable economic system, fueling, as historian Philip Katz demonstrates, a fear among elites that the wave of workers' uprisings stretching across Europe would soon reach the streets of US cities: "Out of work Americans were more conspicuous than ever and, together with numerous strikes and the growing militance of the labor unions, the unemployed throng made the working class seem like an ominous source of domestic disorder. By 1874 the *New York Times* was already worried that 'insane imitations of the miserable class warfare and jealousy of Europe' were beginning to afflict America. It was unprecedented, but not nearly as remarkable as the great strike wave of 1877, which burst upon the land 'like a thunderbolt out of a clear sky'" (*Appomattox to Montmartre* 161). Popular explanations for this sudden surge of out-of-work homeless wanderers point to any number of personal causes, most unrelated to economic realities. Some wrote of the masses of Civil War soldiers who had gotten so used to making do by moving around from place to place that, according to this overly simple analysis, men could no longer settle down to the responsibility of home, work, and family.

Even in that explanation we can see the roots of the romanticized tramp—the "Knights of the Road." Of course, as the numbers of unemployed continued to swell, politicians and academics offered a more substantial (though no less pathologizing or inadequate) explanation. Instead, mainstream journalists, charity workers, academics, and politicians responded in ways that were "not generous. Rather than offer charity, they called for mass arrests, workhouses and chain gangs," in effect dismissing these men as "lazy" and "shiftless" (De-Pastino 4). The highly esteemed charity reformer Professor Francis Wayland of Yale, for instance, charged that tramps constituted a "dangerous class" that was "at war with all social institutions" (DePastino 142). Such accounts increasingly obsessed over tramps' individual bodies as well as their perceived moral failings.

Early ethnographic and critical studies played a key role in characterizing tramps as lazy underachievers, responsible for their own economic plights. Such an assessment is the foundation of the 1893 critical biography of William W. Aspinwall, "a tramping worker," written by John James McCook, a minister and language professor at Trinity College. Even though Aspinwall could write well and corresponded for four years with the professor, McCook's work primarily focuses on Aspinwall's appearance, his grooming habits, and his choices of what to eat or drink. Not unaware of McCook's biases, Aspinwall unsuccessfully sought to steer the researcher's questions to the underlying causes of unemployment, leading him to "increasingly strident criticisms of the professor and his social class" (DePastino 54–55). Aspinwall's frustration is dismissed by McCook as the "melancholy that plagues all tramps" (DePastino 56). Despite being the focus of the work, Aspinwall does not control the narrative; we know him only through the descriptions McCook provides. In the end, the project is just one example of a much wider tide of negative public sentiment about the poor and traveling workers who created the rhetorical exigency for many dissident-press publications to arise. Such publications spoke to the need for impoverished individuals to express publicly and directly views excluded from mainstream publications.

Rather than representing a larger economic reality, then, homeless people tended to be—and still are today—scrutinized as failed *individuals*. Their bodies might be pathologized (as immoral, diseased, lazy) or turned into a comic farce. Such was also the case with James Eads How who, through the lens of history, is remembered first and foremost as an eccentric. By affiliating with the poor, he was treated like them, as more appearance than substance. News accounts never failed to mention his gaunt and haggard frame, his "stubborn adherence to a skimpy vegetable diet," or his thin and fraying clothing ("End of an Idealist"). They described him as someone who *looked like* a hobo, rather than someone genuinely trying to live on what he knew so many others had to live on. It was as if he were playing dress-up.

How's own motives were much more complicated than was acknowledged by those who reported on them. When he created the International Brotherhood Welfare Association (IBWA), the aim of which was to organize and educate hoboes and circulate their collective voices via the newspaper *Hobo News*, How was trying to change the very individualizing narrative that led reporters to focus so fully on his and others' appearances. He wanted to reclaim hoboes from those pathologizing stories. More than that, with both the IBWA and the *Hobo News*, he sought to organize the tramping population and to demand structural economic changes.

HOBO NEWS AS DISSIDENT COUNTERPUBLIC

In large part because of a popular notion that shifted responsibility for unemployment and homelessness onto the very individuals who were unemployed and homeless, How's strategy had to take as many forms as possible. Yearly IBWA Hobo Conventions where the politics and the direction of the organization were proposed, debated, and negotiated, for example, allowed hoboes to raise their own voices in a public forum. When these meetings were reported in major mainstream newspapers like the *New York Times*, those voices spread far beyond hobohemia. How's ultimate aim with the IBWA was to organize unemployed laborers (hoboes) in the same way workers were being organized by unions such as the IWW.

How then established (and, again, financed) Hobo Colleges along main stems in St. Louis, Chicago, Denver, and elsewhere.[9] These were free and open gatherings where the hobo population listened to radical and socialist politics from the likes of Margaret Sanger, Ben Reitman, Emma Goldman, Eugene Debs, and others. They debated each other and, on one occasion, debated students from the University of Chicago. Sociologist (and former hobo) Nels Anderson wrote that hoboes were "proud of the fact that the 'hoboes' literally 'tore 'em to pieces'" in winning the contest (92).

Hobo News, whose masthead proclaimed that it was written "Of the Hoboes, by the Hoboes, and for the Hoboes," circulated coast to coast from 1915 to 1929. It was distributed by the tramps who rode the rails, followed the harvest, and made what little living they could in bits and pieces on the streets, in the fields and forests, or down the mines. Its editors early on declared their intent to reveal to readers "the great truths of things as they are, by the men at the bottom of this system" (Editor's Statement 2). In effect, they had promised to become a collective voice of, as well as give individual voice to, the mass of out-of-work laborers that increased in number from the end of the Civil War through the Gilded Age and into the Great Depression.

Historian Lynne Adrian characterizes the content of *Hobo News* as functioning "primarily as a published version of a more oral format—meaning the campfire tale-telling and political discussion of the 'hobo jungle'" (Adrian 105). To some extent, her assessment holds. The paper did feature personal tramping stories, poems, and commentary that had the tenor of local talk. Still, the paper went far beyond that campfire tale-telling mode. *Hobo News* advocated for unorganized laborers and especially the unemployed. As the official publication of the IBWA, the paper published convention notes and organization news. It sought to revise the mainstream story about America's tramps, hoboes, homeless, out-of-work, and impoverished. As the editorial for the first issue says, "The writer admits that he doesn't like the word 'hobo,' but . . . We have got it and we are going to make it respectable" (*Hobo News* 1:1, 2).

In many ways, then, the paper challenged the mainstream press, accusing it of not doing the job of a free press. In 1920, for example, a *Hobo News* writer quotes Upton Sinclair's account of one journalist's remarks on "The Independent Press":

> There is no such thing in America as an independent press, unless it is in the country towns. You know it, and I know it. There is not one of you who dares to write his honest opinions, and if you did, you know beforehand that it would never appear in print. . . . The business of the New York journalist is to destroy the truth, to lie outright, to pervert, to vilify, to fawn at the feet of mammon and to sell his race and his country for his daily bread. . . . We are intellectual prostitutes. (*Hobo News* 5:3)

In its attempt to reach a broader readership, *Hobo News* tried at times to address a double audience—both those it was written for and about and those who were closer to centers of power who might be swayed to use that power to effect change. In 1917, for example, one writer directly addresses that second audience with a challenge: "We care not whether you be an aristocrat or a plebeian, a priest or millionaire, a professional man or worker—it is necessary for your welfare and all your fellow-citizens, that you should be in touch with the evils of the hobo life" (Adrian 111). The ample use of pathos, exclamation, and direct address, all of which *Hobo News* relied on to try to tell a truer story of poverty, are not strategies a mainstream press would typically use, at least not at this extreme. While the content of *Hobo News* certainly challenged and differed from that of the mainstream press, the trick of getting those "great truths out" relied heavily on getting the paper into the hands of readers. In other words, for this and other publications like it, *circulation* mattered as much as or more than invention, arrangement, or style.[10]

CIRCULATING UNRULY RHETORICS

A single wire story about How's death had a power that dissident-press papers lacked. That is, reprinted in mainstream presses across the country, a wire story traveled widely and found thousands of readers. Papers like *Hobo News* and its current counterparts—street newspapers, activist documentaries, and community publications—continually struggle to circulate beyond small, range-bound circles so as to find a responsive public. Even if a group has managed to get its newspapers into print (or its documentary online, or a radio show on the air), this doesn't assure that its message will get into the hands or heads of a larger public, especially the kind of public defined by Michael Warner—one that comes into being by virtue of texts and that circulates among strangers connected by nothing more than the ideas they embrace or reject. Circulation of counterpublic messages is key if we are to do as Howard Zinn once suggested: listen to the poor, the outcast, the voices on the margins. Moreover, just as Zinn warns, we know that those marginalized and dissenting voices can tell just as distorted a story as their mainstream counterparts, but to ignore or silence them entirely is a much more dangerous proposition. So it is the problem of circulation, what happens *after* the story is written, that How took seriously. When dissident or under-represented groups seek to be heard, issues of circulation become particularly tricky—and even dangerous.

The time of *Hobo News*'s run were the years leading up to and just following The First World War—a period during which Congress beefed up the eighteenth-century Sedition Acts by passing the Espionage Act. These were years when, empowered by that legislation, a minister in Iowa could be (and was) sentenced to five years in federal prison for preaching sermons that did not support the war; when radical labor leaders were jailed and murdered; when women like Margaret Sanger and Emma Goldman could be arrested for simply talking in public about birth control. During that time, opposition papers such as the IWW's *Industrial Worker*, Max Eastman's *Masses*, Ida B. Wells's *Memphis Free Speech*, the IBWA's *Hobo News*, and others like them were routinely suppressed. Some were vandalized by local police or shut down under the sedition acts, causing crises for the men and women associated with them. During that time, *The Masses* lost its second-class mailing privileges, and by 1918 several of its writers and editors were on trial accused of sedition. *The Masses* shut down. Editors and distributors of dissident publications were often arrested or beaten. As with *The Masses*, other papers lost their second-class mailing privileges, which made distribution through the mail too costly to continue. We are talking here about writing that must be produced and circulated cheaply, without corporate backing, and often with no guarantee that the publication will continue beyond its most current edition. Losing access to inexpensive means of circulation was no small matter. Government crackdowns on these organizations, it is important to note, nearly always included shutting down or severely limiting access to an audience that might constitute a vocal counter-public.

Hobo News was written and distributed first from St. Louis and later from Cincinnati. Some copies were sent through the mail (until the government pulled its second-class privileges), but, probably more important for actual circulation, *Hobo News* relied on men hopping trains in St. Louis (and, later, in Chicago, Cincinnati, and elsewhere) to carry bundles of papers to circulate on streets as far west as San Francisco and as far east as New York and Boston. James Eads How paid all expenses related to the newspaper, but distribution equally relied on the hoboes to carry the paper from city to city and share or sell them, person to person. These men were following the harvest in search of work and temporary pay. Some were already members of the IWW or they were Harvest Wobblies, members of the agricultural workers' union (AWIU). Others were members of the IBWA and carried *Hobo News* as the official voice of that organization.

These kinds of counterpublic activities were not isolated. They were, in fact, popping up throughout the country and forming around the IWW, around birth control movements, and through radical papers and magazines such as the *Industrial Worker*, *The Masses*, and *The Appeal*. As DePastino explains, publications like *Hobo News* and the *Industrial Worker* were at the center of revolutionary politics, for in them, "and other main stem papers, migratories saw *common concerns* and interests expressed *in an idiom that was distinctly their own*. While their primary task was to spread revolutionary propaganda, these papers also generated a sense of community through the stories, poems, illustrations, reports, and other commentaries they collected from migratories in the field" (111, emphasis added). In those papers, hoboes heard their own voices raised against what Dorothy Day would later call, "this filthy, rotten system" (qtd. in Gioseffi 103). While many readers may have at least a passing awareness of publications like the *Industrial Worker*, far fewer are likely to know that, as Michael Davis reports in his history of the labor press, "in 1885 this country could count at least 400 labor newspapers and even a national 'Associated Labor Press'" ("Forced to Tramp" 143).

That ongoing conflict—between the stories a nation might want to tell about itself and the lives many people actually experienced—propelled How's work as it continues to propel ours on the movement and power of dissenting voices.

News reports on How's death and the life he had led up until the moment he was discovered dying in a small town along the Virginia Central Railroad line offer one small look into just how easily a single wire story can largely shape how masses of readers view not only How's story but the story of a tramping underclass with its so-called hobo problem. That is the way such narratives typically become something like common knowledge. The question raised by *Hobo News* and publications like it, however, is how, then, is it at all possible for counter-narratives to form and circulate. How are they begun? More to the point, how are they sustained?

SPONSORING AN UNRULY RHETORIC

The labor and free speech movements of the mid-nineteenth and early twentieth centuries offer a rich opportunity to examine how dissenting voices circulate and help reshape mainstream narratives, even for a time. Circulation, neither easy nor cheap, thus becomes key. That certainly was the case with *Hobo News*. Like its counterparts, this paper and the people it represented needed money and a strong voice. One way of understanding the success of *Hobo News*, then, is to examine issues of sponsorship, and here we are indebted to Deborah Brandt's work on literacy sponsorship. We are suggesting that, in order to do more than publish, counterpublic media must seek out sponsors of circulation (to alter Brandt's metaphor). Such sponsors might be very local and makeshift, or they might involve making alliances with other organizations or entities that might alter or constrain their messages. Either way, they are at the core of dissent.

Raising Brandt here might seem like an odd digression from How's street work and the pages of *Hobo News*. And yet, her landmark article "Sponsors of Literacy"—offering as it does a powerful critique of our field's dearth of cogent and systemic economic arguments, our failure to "relate what we see, study, and do to these larger contexts of profit making and competition" (166)—has forced even scholars of rhetoric to examine more closely the economic and social conditions surrounding what we study. It is Brandt's challenge that pushes us to investigate the materiality of circulating the unruly, dissident rhetoric sent forth by a paper like *Hobo News*. So while How was indeed the sponsor of *Hobo News* financially, its circulation relied equally on a very real network of hoboes reading, carrying, and passing that paper along to others who would do the same. How and that Great Army of Tramps, together, sponsored the circulation of *Hobo News* in material and embodied ways.

In his effort to "educate the public mind to the rights of collective ownership in production and distribution" (IBWA manifesto), How's tactics included founding and financing an organization that focused more on the plight of migratories and the out-of-work than on those already employed. Clearly, *Hobo News* could not have existed without How's financial and ideological support. The paper, in fact, did not continue after his death. Still, *Hobo News* equally relied on the hoboes who carried the paper nationwide. It was lacking access to mail as a route of circulation, and the mobility of the nation's poor is what allowed *Hobo News* to move around and reach readers, both among the poor and beyond. Several of the paper's issues, for example, include short notices placed by families seeking to learn news about or make contact with a brother or son who took to the road in search of work. In other words, at some level, people beyond the hobo community knew of and were reading *Hobo News*. As the paper circulated its bold ideas about income inequality, the need for unemployment benefits, and other labor causes that eventually found their way into mainstream discussions, its ideas could and did reach a public that included, but was not exclusive to, the tramping poor. And although a full archive of *Hobo News* does not exist, a robust partial archive of thousands of pages of the paper are held in the special collections room of the St. Louis public library and can be read today.

To study the formation of unruly rhetorics is to pull back from a narrow focus on the persuasive discourse itself to explore the networks of association from which these discourses arise and those which they create. Such networks exist across space as well as time, invoking the need for researchers to understand circulation as a social process, in much the same way Gesa Kirsch and Jacquelyn Jones Royster explain in *Feminist Rhetorical Practices*. They choose the term "Social Circulation" as one of their four "critical terms of engagement," to evoke connections among past, present, and future as well as the "overlapping social circles in which women travel, live and work," which they argue are central in studying rhetorical movements from a feminist perspective (23). Circulation, in this context, must be about how people and texts interact and move and change each other.

Any notion of "circulating voices of dissent" must begin, then, with the understanding that, though they might occasionally reach out to a readership beyond their own sphere, papers like *Hobo News* are never really written for anything like a general public. They depend on ever-shifting pockets of support that often come together around one issue only to disperse after that issue has played itself out or another comes into prominence. Clearly, Susan Wells's challenge to our discipline—to think of public writing in light of Negt and Kluge's revision of public sphere theory, in effect to imagine a proletarian public sphere or, rather, multiple counterpublic spheres—has been significant for understanding the kind of circulation we are talking about here. Wells reminds us that counterpublic or (for our purposes) dissident voices must be opportunistic in order to develop tactics for building multiple public spheres that are, necessarily, temporary, partial, contradictory, and fragmented ("Rogue Cops"). Those are the voices central to this study.

Wells's work also raises important questions of circulation. How, for example, do voices of dissent circulate to form counterpublic spheres, to build communities of concern, and to push marginalized (or suppressed) politics into a larger public conversation? Moreover, what tactics must groups draw upon to circulate writing that is crucial to social movements and yet so ephemeral? This is writing so easily tossed out with the trash, that these publications often disappear entirely with no archives, no carefully catalogued repository to last through the ages.

More to the point, we would recall John Trimbur's redefinition of delivery "as ethical and political—a democratic aspiration to devise delivery systems that circulate ideas, information, opinions, and knowledge and thereby expand the public forums in which people can deliberate on the issues of the day" (190). The tactics that many dissident groups must draw upon to "devise systems of delivery and circulate ideas" are multiple and, of necessity, always shifting as power structures attempt to close down access to the public at large. Our point in all of this is that one way to look at how these papers and these pieces of public writing work in social movements is to understand that they never do that work alone. They can, however, become the place where counterpublic voices meet, where politics are discussed, and where people have a voice. Government crackdowns on these organizations, it is important to note, nearly always included (and continue to include) shutting down their means of public communication—that vehicle for circulating information and ideas.

Ultimately, the embodied individual is both key to the circulation of *Hobo News* and the locus of pathologized interpretations of homelessness because individuals make for compelling stories. Moreover, the public's preoccupation with the individual's *body* (whether that be Aspinwall's or How's or another tramping hobo's sorry appearance) expresses a larger human tendency to crave that comforting lesson of how one person ended up as he or she did and another in similar circumstances seemed to triumph. Such a notion is, of course, inherently problematic because it tacitly accepts the idea that any individual's story tells us enough of what we need to know about the nature of poverty and homelessness. Our point is that when we fetishize individual impoverished bodies (or the wealthy bodies of those who associate with the poor), we lose sight of the causes, the structural agents, of the economic picture or what Rene Jahiel calls the "homeless makers and homeless making processes" (269). Such stories typically build their reality merely *by looking at* or picturing homeless people, by what Robert Desjarlais calls "spectral means": "The homeless can . . .

be identified by how they look. To describe someone as 'homeless' announces a lasting identity. . . . Homelessness denotes a temporary lack of housing but connotes a lasting moral career. Because this 'identity' is deemed sufficient and interchangeable, the 'homeless' usually go unnamed. The identification is typically achieved through spectral means: one knows the homeless not by talking with them but by seeing them" (Desjarlais 2). We can see this fetishization of the visual nature of poverty in a variety of places, ranging from nonprofit appeals (see George, "Changing the Face of Poverty") to a contemporary fashion trend called homeless chic (see Mathieu, "Public Rhetorics").

A key motive of counterpublic circulation, especially as it is related to *Hobo News*, is a collective effort to change the narrative of impoverishment, to change the conversation from individual bodies/individual failures to structural issues of unemployment and inequality. For How, that kind of change meant finding ways of circumventing the normal or more easily available avenues of information exchange and distribution; his method adumbrates Susan Wells's argument that these voices must be opportunistic. Such an action as founding the IBWA was crucial to this goal. Just as crucial was the fact that annual conventions were covered by national papers like the *New York Times*. In this way, How used the mainstream media to actually help circulate a counterpublic message. *Hobo News* itself had to rely on what many would have called the most unreliable of citizenry to make sure it was distributed all across the nation—to "expand public forums," to use Trimbur's words (191). How's system of Hobo Colleges that brought in some of the most poignant and powerful voices of the time—voices like Emma Goldman's and Ben Reitman's—was a way to make sure that people in the streets also learned about counterpublic views and politics. His choice to live and die in the same way as those he spoke with and for lived and died was not simply one of the odd details his life. It was a crucial embodiment of the unruly rhetorics, the dissident voices he both sponsored and performed. He was a rhetorical activist who took seriously the importance of circulation.

The importance of paying attention to the embodied materiality of writing and its circulation and delivery cannot be underestimated. By this we mean that, no matter how badly or beautifully crafted, writing (especially dissident writing) has little power without some means of distribution. For *Hobo News* this meant that Great Army of Tramps riding the rails and carrying copies of the paper to sell, read, distribute, and talk about. In some ways, the story sounds almost too simple, but these are the kinds of relationships that become so important for distributing dissenting (or, even different) views. James Eads How and an army of the poor physically circulated this paper hand to hand or train car to train car, gathering people to debate and campaign for ideas such as unemployment insurance that prevailed slowly and painfully. Or, as How himself might have said, for the paper to have any force at all, some hobo had to hop on a train with a wad of papers under his arm and get the thing to the next town, risk getting beaten up or jailed, and maybe make a few cents. It wasn't elegant, but it certainly got the job done.

NOTES

1. Weather figures are available at "July 20, 1930: Half of the US States Were over 100 Degrees."

2. Death certificate, Virginia Death Records, 1917–2014. Online at www.Ancestry .com/.

3. The title *Hobo News* was initially written *"Hobo" News* on the paper's masthead, perhaps as a way of saying, "this is what they call us." Eventually, the quotes were removed. We have opted to use the later version and eliminate quotes from around the word *Hobo*.

4. The characterization of How's life as eccentric and misguided and his death as lonely and pointless is made repeatedly throughout many US and Canadian sources. See "James Eads How, 'Millionaire Hobo,' Dies for Denying Self Food to Aid 'Unfortunates'"; "Millionaire Funeral Is Lonesome"; "Millionaire Hobo Forms Brotherhood"; and "Millionaire Hobo Seeks a Cure for the Jobless Man."

5. It is difficult to find mention of James Eads How from after 1932, though the International Brotherhood Welfare Association (IBWA) did continue and was even revived in 2011. See online at www.ibwacharity.org/history-2/.

6. See also "Rich and Ragged." The term "incompetence" was also used at the time to indicate mental illness. Even so, the suggestion that the homeless were in some way just not suited to work for themselves carries through.

7. How's maternal grandfather was the famous engineer James Buchanan Eads. His father, Lieutenant-Colonel James Flintham How, was a Civil War officer and vice president of the Wabash Railroad. His paternal grandfather, John How, was twice elected mayor of Saint Louis. To cap it off, How was a distant cousin, through his mother's family, of former US president James Buchanan. In at least one story on his death, the reporter describes How as literally starving to death, noting (we suppose, in an attempt to find a cause for this strange business) that he was a vegetarian ("James Eads How Dies").

8. The fact that the population was composed primarily of white men does not mean that women or men of color were not also displaced; they just did not have the freedom of movement or the visibility that riding the rails led to. Their homelessness was often hidden from public view, as they feared for their safety. For more on this, see DePastino 13–14.

9. The "main stem" referred to major routes or streets where hoboes primarily gathered. For example, according to the Chicago Historical Society's online *Encyclopedia of Chicago*, "Chicago's main stem occupied a stretch of West Madison Street from the

Chicago River to Halsted Street, where inexpensive restaurants, saloons, flophouses, and employment agencies catered to hoboes' basic needs." See "Hoboes."

10. For more on the dissident rhetoric of *Hobo News*, see George and Mathieu, "A Place."

WORKS CITED

Adrian, Lynne M. "The World We Shall Win for Labor: Early 20th-Century Hobo Self-Publication." In *Print Culture in a Diverse America*, edited by James P. Danky and Wayne A. Wiegand, 100–127. University of Illinois Press, 1998.

Anderson, Nels. *The Hobo*. University of Chicago Press, 1923.

Brandt, Deborah. "Sponsors of Literacy." *College Composition and Communication* 49, no. 2 (1998): 165–85.

Davis, Michael. "Forced to Tramp: The Perspective of the Labor Press, 1870–1900." In *Walking to Work: Tramps in America, 1790–1935*, edited by Erik Monkkonen, 141–70. University of Nebraska Press, 1984.

Debs, Eugene. "Statement to the Court: Upon Being Convicted of Violating the Sedition Act, September 18, 1918." *Eugene V. Debs Internet Archive.* www.marxists.org/archive /debs/.

DePastino, Todd. *Citizen Hobo: How a Century of Homelessness Shaped America.* University of Chicago Press, 2003.

Desjarlais, Robert. *Shelter Blues: Sanity and Selfhood among the Homeless.* University of Pennsylvania Press, 1997.

Editor's Statement. *Hobo News* 1, no. 1 (1915): 2.

"End of An Idealist," *Time Magazine.* August 4, 1930. Vol. 16, no. 5. www.content.time .com/time/magazine/article/0,9171,740008,00.html.

George, Diana. "Changing the Face of Poverty: Nonprofits and the Problem of Representation." In *Popular Literacy: Studies in Cultural Practices and Poetics*, edited by John Trimbur, 235–52. Pittsburgh University Press, 2001.

George, Diana, and Paula Mathieu. "A Place for the Dissident Press in a Rhetorical Education: 'Sending Up a Signal Flare in the Darkness.'" In *The Public Work of Rhetoric*, edited by John Ackerman and David Coogan, 247–66. University of South Carolina, 2010.

Gioseffi, Daniella. *Women on War: Essential Voices for the Nuclear Age from a Brilliant International Assembly.* Touchstone Books, 1988.

"Hoboes." *Encyclopedia of Chicago.* Chicago Historical Society. www.encyclopedia.chicago history.org/pages/590.html.

"Hoboes Fail to Attend Funeral of J. E. How; His Brother, a Few College Mates and a Representative of His Organization at Services." *New York Times*, July 25, 1930, 11.

"Hoboes in Tribute to Late Chieftain." *The Post-Crescent* (Appleton, WI), July 22, 1932, 2.

Jahiel, René, ed. *Homelessness: A Prevention-Oriented Approach*. Johns Hopkins University Press, 1992.

"James Eads How, 'Millionaire Hobo,' Dies for Denying Self Food to Aid 'Unfortunates.'" *Winnipeg Tribune*, July 23, 1930, 1.

"James Eads How Dies, Friend of Hoboes. Giver of Fortune to the Homeless Succumbs to Pneumonia in Virginia at Age 56." *New York Times*, July 23, 1930, 23.

"James Eads How Is Dead. Member of a Wealthy St. Louis Family, He Spurned Wealth to Travel with 'The Knights of the Road.'" *Kansas City Star*, July 22, 1930.

"July 20, 1930: Half of the US States Were over 100 Degrees." *Real Science*. www.steven goddard.wordpress.com/2013/07/20/july-20-1930-31-of-the-us-was-over-100-degrees/.

Katz, Philip M. *From Appomattox to Montmartre: Americans and the Paris Commune*. Harvard University Press, 1998.

Mathieu, Paula. "Public Rhetorics and Homeless Chic." *Expositions: Interdisciplinary Studies in the Humanities* 5, no. 1 (2011): 44–54.

"Millionaire Funeral Is Lonesome. Few Attended Last Rites of James Eads How of St. Louis." *Amarillo Globe-Times*, July 25, 1930, 14.

"Millionaire Hobo Forms Brotherhood." *New York Times*, September 16, 1907, 9.

"Millionaire Hobo Seeks a Cure for the Jobless Man. Over 4,500,000 without Work in the United States Says James Eads How." *New York Times*, Sunday, May 14, 1911, 55.

"The Philadelphia Mills. Depression in the Iron and Coal Trade—Prices and Wages—The Idle Poor." *New York Times*, November 13, 1873, 1.

"Refuses a Million. Extraordinary Case of James Eads How." *Lead Daily Call* (Lead, SD), March 8, 1900, 7.

"Rich and Ragged: A Wealthy Young Man Who Is Attempting to Do Good." *New York Times*, June 7, 1899, 7.

"Scorns His Own Million." *New York Daily Tribune*, September 3, 1899, 22.

"Tramp World Goes into Mourning for Millionaire Hobo." *News-Herald* (Franklin, PA), July 25, 1930, 15.

Trimbur, John. "Composition and the Circulation of Writing." *College Composition and Communication* 52, no. 2 (2000): 188–219.

"Unemployed Appear before Senate Committee Today." *Santa Ana Register*, March 18, 1930, 1–2.

Warner, Michael. *Publics and Counterpublics*. Zone Books, 2002.

Wells, Susan. "Rogue Cops and Health Care: What Do We Want from Public Writing?" *College Composition and Communication* 47, no. 3 (1996): 241–325.

"What Are the Purposes of This Strange Man?" *St Louis Republic*, January 6, 1901, 37.

"Winter and the Working Classes." *New York Times*, November 11, 1873, 4.

Zinn, Howard, Mike Konopacki, and Paul Buhle. *A People's History of American Empire: A Graphic Adaptation*. Metropolitan Books, 2008.

8

WE ARE NOT ALL IN THIS TOGETHER

A CASE FOR ADVOCACY, FACTIONALISM, AND MAKING THE POLITICAL PERSONAL

KEVIN MAHONEY

> Today tolerance appears again as what it was at its origins, at the beginning
> of the modern period—a partisan goal, a subversive liberating notion and
> practice. Conversely, what is proclaimed and practiced as tolerance today, is
> in many of its most effective manifestations serving the cause of oppression.
>
> —Herbert Marcuse, 1968

For many commentators and political observers, the 2008 presidential election marked a kind of watershed in the level of incivility in American politics, and there is little doubt that our socially mediated world has reinforced that perception. To bolster the point, one need only call to mind the infamous Tea Party "town hall meetings" on Obama's Affordable Care Act (Obamacare) in the summer of 2009; the images of right-wing radicals strapped with AR-15s waving banners proclaiming that it is time to water the Tree of Liberty with blood; or the overtly racist attacks on the first African American president that were streamed daily on talk radio. Of course, the 2016 presidential election has made the incivility of the 2008 election look almost quaint by comparison. It is useful to recall, however, how much the 2008 presidential campaign signaled a break in political norms—a break that set the stage for 2016. As bad as the vitriol was during the 2008 campaign and the Obama administration, calls for a "return to civility" or narratives about the "decline of civility" in the United States quickly began to grate on my nerves, especially following the sweeping Tea Party victories in the 2010 election.

It was a strange feeling. I have long appealed to a notion of "civil discourse" as an important aspect of fostering a critically democratic classroom. Civility, as I've understood it, is not simply about being "polite" or "not offending anyone." Rather, civil discourse was part of an often contestatory democratic rhetorical practice that is integral to any deliberative process worth its name. I have often invoked Mary Louise Pratt's notion of the "contact zone" in which "no one was excluded and no one was safe" (36), or Kenneth Burke's parlor dominated by vigorous and heated discussion (110–11) as useful guiding metaphors for critical civil engagement. It felt odd to find myself increasingly agitated at hearing renewed calls for civility in print and online. Perhaps that nagging feeling was not so misplaced, though. As Nancy Welch argues in this collection, civility has been used as a tool to constrain public participation that might contest the privatization project of neoliberalism.

The appeal for "civility" or "civil discourse" seemed to be especially urgent for Democrats working closely with the Obama administration and liberals more generally, especially those working in education. In 2012 Obama's Department of Education funded a national dialogue about "strengthening students' civic learning and democratic engagement as a core component of college study" (National Task Force vii). The resulting report, *A Crucible Moment: College Learning and Democracy's Future*, echoed the warnings of David Matthews, president and CEO of the Kettering Foundation, that a number of forces that sideline citizens in the United States, including "everything from the gerrymandering of voting districts to ensure the reelection of incumbents to the recasting of people's role from producers of public goods to consumers . . . are moving us toward what we cannot be—a citizenless democracy" (Matthews iv). In *A Crucible Moment*, the authors called on colleges and universities to "embrace civic learning and democratic engagement as an undisputed educational priority for all of higher education, public and private, two-year and four-year" (National Task Force 2). The report urged the higher education community to "not only theorize about what education for democratic citizenship might require in a diverse society, but also to rehearse that citizenship daily in the fertile, rolling context of pedagogic inquiry and hands-on experiences" (2).

A Crucible Moment still stands, in my mind, as one of the best and most passionate arguments for a renewed investment in education for democracy. The passion expressed in the report is also coupled with very practical pathways to reinject higher education with a commitment to cultivating an engaged citizenry at a time when workforce training seems to be all that state policy-makers want to talk about. If the media was filled with liberal laments about the loss of civility, *A Crucible Moment* seemed to provide concrete answers—or, at least a practical starting point—to those armchair laments.

Despite the mounting evidence that the United States is at risk of falling into a spectator society, as *A Crucible Moment* warns, I still hold on to higher education as one of the few places in which we can practice a fading democratic ideal. It is what got me in this game to begin with. However, the work I have done in my faculty union for over a decade helps ground any creeping idealism. I served as our faculty union's local vice president at a time of deep budget cuts and "retrenchment" (aka layoffs), which put me on the front lines defending academic programs, faculty jobs, and the purported mission of my university. This work made it virtually impossible to see any hint of commitment on the part of our university administration, our elected officials, and frankly, much of the public to higher education's democratic ideals of civil discourse and citizenship participation.

A Crucible Moment was the kind of report that normally would reenergize my commitment to democratic education, civil discourse, and the mission of higher education. Normally, it would have provided my next goal post on the democratic horizon. Not this time around. What happened? One word: Wisconsin.

THE ATTACKS ON UNIONS, WORKING FAMILIES, AND CIVIL RIGHTS IN WISCONSIN

If a commitment to civil discourse and democracy is little more than veneer in my little corner of academe, Wisconsin governor Scott Walker's all-out assault on collective bargaining, the rights of working families, access to affordable health care, and the progressive democratic compact at the core of the state's progressive social history was the wrecking ball. At the beginning of 2011, Governor Walker introduced the now infamous "Budget Repair Bill," claiming that gutting union rights and public services was necessary to fix a significant budget crisis. Beginning in February 2011, in a kind of political version of *War of the Worlds*, Walker's initial attacks on public sector unions was like an "activate" signal sent to sleeper cells around the nation programmed to destroy unions and public institutions. In Ohio, Indiana, Michigan, Idaho, and right here in my home state of Pennsylvania the attacks came fast and they were unrelenting.

For anyone who hadn't been paying much attention to politics for a decade or so, Walker's raiders must have sent their heads spinning. However, for observers like Naomi Klein, this new assault on working families and the commons was the logical next step for what she calls "disaster capitalism": "orchestrated raids on the public sphere in the wake of catastrophic events, combined with the treatment of disasters as exciting market opportunities" (Klein 6). Klein's book, *The Shock Doctrine*, documents how the proponents of free markets, followers of the late University of Chicago economist Milton Friedman in particular, figured out how to make use of natural and manufactured crises to usher in undemocratic, radical free market policies.

Writing in the *New York Times* a little over a week after Walker introduced his "Budget Repair Bill," Nobel Prize–winning economist Paul Krugman drew upon Klein's analysis in his op-ed, "Shock Doctrine, U.S.A.": "In recent weeks, Madison has been the scene of large demonstrations against the governor's budget bill, which would deny collective bargaining rights to public-sector workers. Gov. Scott Walker claims that he needs to pass his bill to deal with the state's fiscal problems. But his attack on unions has nothing to do with the budget. . . . What's happening in Wisconsin is, instead, a power grab— an attempt to exploit the fiscal crisis to destroy the last major counterweight to the political power of corporations and the wealthy" (Krugman). Walker's bill to gut collective bargaining rights for public sector workers was met with mass uprisings by students, organized labor, community-based organizations, farmers, and individuals around the state. This large, broad coalition of Wisconsinites gathered in Madison and occupied the Capitol building around the clock for two weeks. The occupation also helped embolden the state's Democratic senators, who fled the state to neighboring Illinois in order to block the quorum necessary to pass Walker's proposed budget bill (Walker). Eventually, Wisconsin Republicans were able to pass Walker's budget using technical parliamentary maneuvers. Once the bill was passed, the occupation ended, but political activity continued. An effort was mounted to recall Gov. Walker (it failed), while other participants in the protests continued to organize in their communities and workplaces.

In the months that followed, journalists such as John Nichols—a Wisconsinite—retold the story of Wisconsin's role as the leading edge in progressive labor movements in the United States ("Introduction"). In an article published on the first anniversary of the Wisconsin Uprising, Nichols proclaimed that "The uprising of February 2011 made a single word, 'Wisconsin,' not just the name of a state but the reference point for a renewal of labor militancy, mass protest and radical politics. But, it did something else. It signaled that a new generation of young Americans would not just reject the lie of austerity. They would lead a fight-back that has extended from the Capitol in Madison to Zuccotti Park in Lower Manhattan and across the United States" ("America's Youth Uprising"). The Wisconsin Uprising answered a question that had been posed, often cynically, about whether a generation wedded to social media, cell phones, and digital activism would "show up" and would have the skills to mobilize people in the streets.

That question, "Will they show up?" is an important one and is as much a practical question as it is evidence that reveals how our cultural narratives understand activism. Just a few months before the Wisconsin Uprising and "Tahir Square" (the mass occupation of a key public square in Cairo that helped usher in the 2011 overthrow of Egyptian dictator Hosni Mubarak), Malcolm Gladwell, writing in the *New Yorker*, rightfully criticized the "outsized enthusiasm for social media" as the cause for mass uprisings such as those in Moldova and Iran in 2009 (Gladwell). Even more pointedly—and more correctly, I would argue—Kentaro Toyama nailed the dynamic in his 2013 article in *The Atlantic*, arguing that "there is nothing inherently democratizing about digital networks." Instead, "we have free speech online because we have free speech offline, not the other way around. The fact that technology can be used to buttress or erode democracy means that technology itself doesn't carry democratizing power—what it does instead is to amplify the underlying political forces already in play" (Toyama, "Twitter").

Toyama's argument makes more sense from the perspective of the activist. While there are certainly social media activists who see technology itself as the prime mover for twenty-first-century social change, most activists who do the daily work of organizing see technology as a tool. It would be more accurate to say that it is the corporate media and academics who are most enthralled by the narrative of the "Twitter Revolution." In his book *Geek Heresy*, Toyama makes the case that in the "Arab Spring" or any other major mass uprising, "social media is neither necessary nor sufficient for revolution. Claims of social media revolutions commit the classic conflation of correlation and cause. To say that the Arab Spring was a Facebook revolution is like calling the events of 1775 in America a lantern revolution thanks to Paul Revere: 'One, if by land, and two, if by sea'" (34). "Revolutionaries," Toyama explains, "are contingency planners who exploit every tool at their disposal" (35). If there are hyped-up narratives about the magic of the tool, then the fault lies more with those constructing that narrative than it does with the users of the tool.

The events in Wisconsin during those cold weeks in February and March were no more spontaneously caused by social media than was the Arab Spring or the Occupy movement. The Wisconsin Uprising benefited from being literally walking distance from the University of Wisconsin–Madison, which has one of the longest and strongest histories of labor-oriented student activism in the United States. UW-Madison students formed the first Student Labor Action Coalition (SLAC) in 1994 as part of their "support for 700 workers who were locked out at the A. E. Staley Company in Decatur, Illinois," which led to the formation of SLACs across the country in the 1990s (Featherstone 106). Shortly thereafter, the AFL-CIO established their famed "Union Summer" internship program, providing labor organizing experience to a new generation of activists and opportunities for student activists to research the use of sweatshop labor on their campuses (Featherstone 11). Within a few years, students from Madison were on the ground floor in helping build a national movement and organization—the United Students Against Sweatshops (USAS)—to end the use of sweatshop labor in the manufacture of university apparel. Writing in *The Nation* in 1999, Marc Cooper noted just how much traction USAS had gotten in a short period of time: "There's been a smattering of campus protests around the war in Kosovo, and, like a movement Old Faithful, UC Berkeley has recently erupted in a fight over ethnic studies programs. But the big man on campus today is the worker. Indeed, for the past several months a tsunami of sweatshop and labor-related protests, rallies and demonstrations has flooded campuses from coast to coast. Even the *New York Times* recently concluded that this is the biggest uptick of student activism in almost two decades—since the surge of antiapartheid activity in the early eighties" (Cooper).

In addition to student labor activism, Madison is also home to the Center for Media and Democracy, a "nonprofit watchdog organization that conducts powerful investigations and publishes news that transforms the national conversation," specifically investigations looking into "the undue influence of corporations, CEOs, and front groups" on public policy (Center for Media and Democracy). The Center for Media and Democracy has been notable most recently for exposing the work of the American Legislative Exchange Council (ALEC) as part of its PR Watch project, "ALEC Exposed." In short, while there was collective outrage in response to Gov. Scott Walker's "Budget Repair Bill," it is unlikely that Madison would have seen such a militant mobilization and occupation of the state Capitol had it not been for the long and continuous history of progressive politics and activism in the city and the state's flagship university.

Yes, "Wisconsin" became a "reference point for a renewal of labor militancy, mass protest and radical politics" (Nichols 3). However, we could also frame it as a moment in which the unsexy, daily business of organizing became visible, once again, as bodies in the street. The coalition of students, union activists, farmers, and citizens that took over the state Capitol for two weeks were the physical and historical embodiment of the stuff out of which political movements are made. And more, the disruptive occupation of the state Capitol helped open a space for rhetorical action.

LIBERALS DISCIPLINING BODIES

In the wake of the Wisconsin Uprising, liberals such as Roger Hodge writing in *Politico* urged fellow well-meaning folks to look to Federalist Papers cosigner and fourth US president James Madison. Hodge made the case that an American left "seemingly bereft of principles" should seek to reclaim Madison's notion of republican liberty and principle that "derives 'its energy from the will of the society' and thus acts in the larger public interest—not in the narrow interest of a particular faction, whether composed of planters or financiers" (Hodge). Well meaning, for sure, Hodge closes his case with the following: "Even in our unhappy political circumstances, most Americans retain a profound attachment to the Madisonian principles that were meant to animate our constitutional system. We may yet rediscover the common ground on which to build a coherent, public-spirited opposition to the narrow factionalism of our current two-party system" (Hodge). Hodge's critique of an American left "bereft of principles," his longing for that common ground, his characterization of our current political circumstances as "unhappy," his appeal to "most Americans," and his use of the conditional "may" to hedge on a future common ground are all elements of a popular liberal sentiment with a Founding Fathers twist. However, this kind of response to an open war against working families did more to discipline those bodies sleeping on the marble floors of the Capitol in Madison and similar mobilizations than it did—or does—help reinstate a political common ground. In my mind, the appeal to Madison's warning against factions in our current political environment is a philosophical luxury if the goal is to defend democracy. The Founding Father who seems more appropriate to our "unhappy times" is not James Madison, but Thomas Paine.

In "Epistle to Quakers," Paine forcefully responds to Quakers who were condemning colonists for taking up arms against England. Instead of taking up arms, the Quakers argued, the colonists should appeal to higher values and continue along the path of reason. "Our plan is peace forever," wrote the Quakers. Paine wrote that revolutionaries shared the Quakers' desire for peace; however, there was no possibility of such a peace while the colonies were still under British rule. And that meant direct confrontation: "We act consistently, because, for the sake of introducing an endless and uninterrupted peace, do we bear the evils and burdens of the present day. We are endeavoring, and will steadily continue to endeavor, to separate and dissolve a connection which has already filled our land with blood; and which, while the name of it remains, will be the fatal cause of future mischiefs to both countries" (Paine). Paine was recognizing, of course, that the English were not going to simply change their minds and suddenly see that peace was in their ultimate interest.

At the same time, Paine was also suggesting that once England was denied its rule, the goal was to establish "peace forever." Paine indicts the Quakers as helping England maintain its rule by choosing the people *and the people only* as the target of their scorn:

> Alas! It seems by the particular tendency of some part of your testimony, and other parts of your conduct, as if, all sin was reduced to, and comprehended in, *the act of bearing arms*, and that by *the people only*. Ye appear to us, to have mistaken party for conscience; because, the general tenor of your actions wants uniformity: And it is exceedingly difficult to give credit to many of your pretended scruples; because, we see them made by the same men, who, in the very instance that they are exclaiming against the mammon of this world, are nevertheless, hunting after it with a step as steady as Time, and an appetite as keen as Death. (Paine, italics in original)

The message we should take from Paine is that acting in response to injustice, especially injustice that denies what Paine and the Founding Fathers saw as inalienable rights, is never pure. Idealism is for better times. While Madison was warning against factionalism, Paine argued *for* factions—we are NOT all in this together. Paine saw the Quaker appeal to civil discourse and persuasion, to civility (and Christian morality), as aiding and abetting England's continued rule of the colonies and filling the land with yet more blood.

I am not arguing that the post-2008 (or post-2016) election period perfectly mirrors that of early America. But invoking the Founding Fathers in the midst of political upheaval is rhetorically charged and calls all of us to understand the moment through a particular lens. If we must play the Founding Fathers' game, so be it. Hodge's appeal to Madison asks us to act in a particular way by framing a moment in American politics—a moment marked by occupations of state Capitols, racist attacks upon the president, public attacks on workers' right to organize, the list goes on—as a kind of breakdown of civility, or at least the high-minded ideas of Madison. Paine does not necessarily disagree with Madison about the ends; however, Paine makes the case that getting to this end has to go through a struggle for power. This struggle requires, of course, a high-minded ideological battle, but for one set of ideas to triumph over another there has to be a material confrontation—a battle that involves people putting their bodies on the line.

There is an important point to make regarding a distinction between civility as a strategy and as a tactic. The democratic project relies upon civility as a strategy. It rests upon privileging civil discourse as the means through which governing takes place. Once the rules of the game are established, civility becomes part of the democratic *habitus* (Bourdieu 62). People then use civility tactically. However, the *tactic* of civility requires the normalization of civility *as a strategy*. Put another way, in order for civility and civil discourse to be effective for managing a democracy, the people need to agree to the rules as a precondition to playing the game of self-rule. Madison is authoring the strategy of civil discourse that will call citizens to be tactically civil. His warning against factions provides us with a heads-up for how a republican democracy can fall apart. His hopes were to institute checks to the ability of factions to destroy a young constitutional democracy. However, as Paine reminds us, "seeking compromise" or "respecting the other side's opinion," as tactics, *are ineffective as tactics* if the strategy of civility has broken down—or has yet to be established. We have been seeing this dynamic play out in real time during the first term of the Trump administration.

What does this have to do with post-Wisconsin politics? In my mind, everything. As Robert Draper first documented in his book *When the Tea Party Came to Town*, on the night of Obama's inauguration, conservative wordsmith Frank Luntz convened a small group of "the Republican Party's most energetic thinkers" to develop a plan to undermine Obama and take back Congress and the presidency (Draper xvi). It was there that the strategy of "no" was agreed upon—Republicans would be united in their opposition to *everything* proposed by the Obama administration. In *The New New Deal: The Hidden Story of Change in the Obama Era,* Michael Grunwald reported on a Republican House leadership retreat in January 2009. The retreat focused on how to take back power after deep losses in 2008: "House Republicans were now an insurgency—an 'entrepreneurial insurgency,' Minority Leader Boehner declared—and [new campaign chair, Pete] Sessions thought they could learn from the disruptive tactics of the Taliban. The key to success in this asymmetrical warfare, he argued, was to 'change the mindset of the [Republican] Conference to one of "offense,"' to take the fight to the enemy" (142).

If the purpose of the "Majority is to Govern," Sessions told the group, "the purpose of the Minority is to become the Majority" (Grunwald 142). If the official Republican politicians were crafting a strategy of "no," the right-wing base was even more committed to "NObama." The conservative donor class was lining up for a full-scale assault on Obama, throwing money at a state-by-state strategy of attacking unions and helping to usher in a full-scale Tea Party takeover of state legislatures in 2010. Their strategy was bolstered by the Supreme Court's infamous decision in *Citizens United v. the Federal Election Commission*, which gave the green light to unlimited corporate spending on political campaigns. From the activist base to the wealthiest political donors, the goal was to take back power—civility, democracy, reason, and facts be damned.

Reaffirmation of the importance of civil discourse—or appealing to the higher-ideals of republican democracy—was not, and is not, going to bring about "peace forever." The problem is that a faction has out-smarted, out-organized, and (importantly) out-spent Madison's constitutional protections. My point, then, is that calls for seeking common ground—as Hodge and many other liberals have made—in the face of a well-funded, systematic factional attack, is like showing up to a gun fight with thank-you cards. The post–Obama era requires Paine-like thinking.

THE 72 PERCENT MINORITY

Am I overstating the case here? Let's look at some evidence. On April 16, 2012, the day before income taxes were due, Republicans in the US Senate filibustered and eventually blocked the so-called Buffett Rule. According to a report released by the White House's National Economic Council, the Buffett Rule "is the basic principle that no household making over $1 million annually should pay a smaller share of their income in taxes than middle-class families pay. [The billionaire] Warren Buffett has famously stated that he pays a lower tax rate than his secretary, but . . . this situation is not uncommon. The situation is the result of decades of the tax system being tilted in favor of high-income households at the expense of the middle class" (1). The Republican filibuster effectively killed the law that would have applied a minimum tax rate of 30 percent on individuals making over a million dollars a year. The law would have affected 0.3 percent of all taxpayers, or 433,000 individuals (Dixon and Temple-West).

Chris Hayes, guest host of the *Rachel Maddow Show* on the night of April 16, 2012, suggested that the failure of that piece of legislation poses significant questions for the state of US politics. Hayes raised the question as to whether our current political institutions still retained the ability to raise taxes on the wealthy: "It is an open question whether they retain that ability or not, because it has now been twelve years—and we've had Republicans in office and we've had Democrats in office—and our institutions have been unable to do that. Despite rising income inequality, despite increasingly heated rhetoric about the need to cut the deficit, they still cannot do it" (Hayes). It would be one thing if the vast majority of Americans—or even the more narrow category of "likely voters"—were opposed to raising taxes on the rich. But the polls show that the exact opposite is true. Hayes laid out the case:

> And just so we're very clear here, the reason the system can't do it is not because it is unpopular. Taxing the Rich is one of the most reliably popular things in American polling. Gallup polled on the Buffett Rule last week and they found 60% support for it. Then today, on the day of the vote, a new poll from CNN re-

vealed an even more lopsided result. When asked if they would support a policy like the Buffett Rule, 72% of Americans said yes. 72%. Nothing polls at 72%. . . .

We were brainstorming today about what the last political issue to poll at 72% was and we remembered that back in June 2009 during the health reform debate, the Public Option—the Public Option, ah, yes, the dearly-departed Public Option—polled at 72%. The government-administered health care program that would compete with private health insurance companies. We obviously did not get a public option in the end. (Hayes)

Hayes continued to flesh out the serious problem this pattern poses for the very core of US democratic institutions and part of the problem at the heart of the case I am making here. His argument is both pointed and sobering.

Hayes reminds his viewers that, although American democracy does not perfectly reflect the majority of public opinion much of the time, "the basic idea is that in order for a democracy to be functioning and credible, there's got to be some rough correlation between what the majority in the country wants and what their government actually does." With such a yawning gap between what the polls suggest people want and the policies favored by politicos and their donors, Hayes questioned whether "that sort of correlation still exists in the USA of 2012."

We need to take Hayes's concern seriously if we have any real investment in the practice of democracy in this country. And Hayes is certainly not the first one to pick up on this. In his 2008 book, *Unequal Democracy: The Political Economy of the New Gilded Age*, the noted political scientist Larry Bartels determined empirically that economic power translates into political power. Analyzing the "relationship between senators' policy choices and the views of their constituents" between the late 1980s and the early 1990s, Bartels was able to prove what most Americans broadly suspect: our voices are not equal. Bartels found that on the issues of the minimum wage, civil rights, government spending, and abortion it was economic power that determined the way in which senators voted:

I find that senators in this period were vastly more responsive to affluent constituents than to constituents of modest means. Indeed, my analyses indicate that the views of constituents in the upper third of the income distribution received about 50 percent more weight than those in the middle third, with even larger disparities on specific salient roll call votes. Meanwhile, the views of constituents in the bottom third of the income distribution received no weight at all in the voting decisions of their senators. Far from being "considered as political equals," they were entirely *un*considered in the policy-making process. (253)

Bartels's book was published right before the massive Wall Street–induced economic collapse of 2008–2009.

The work of the economist Emmanuel Saez and his colleagues demonstrates that the Great Recession of 2008–2009 was merely a pause in the march toward a New Gilded Age. In their 2014 working paper for the Washington Center for Equitable Growth, Emmanuel Saez and Gabriel Zucman show that inequality has dramatically deepened over the past several decades. Their report shows that "The share of wealth held by the top 0.1 percent of families is now almost as high as in the late 1920s, when 'The Great Gatsby' defined an era that rested on the inherited fortunes of the robber barons of the Gilded Age" (2). This concentration of wealth was further exacerbated by the 2008 financial crisis. Following the crisis, Saez and Zucman show that the "average wealth of the bottom 90 percent of families is equal to $80,000 in 2012—the same level as in 1986. In contrast, the average wealth of the top 1 percent increased almost back to its peak in 2007" (4). The glaring evidence of growing inequality coupled with Bartels's demonstration of the links between economic power and political power leads in pretty dystopic directions. I do believe that Chris Hayes had it right by questioning whether the correlation still exists between what we as a national body want and what our government actually does.

BODIES ON THE GEARS

Mario Savio, one of the student leaders of the Berkeley Free Speech Movement in the 1960s, gave his most famous and impassioned speech on the steps of Sproul Hall in 1964 right before he and eight hundred other students were arrested for attempting to occupy the hall in an act of civil disobedience. In his speech to a crowd of about four thousand people, Savio spoke about a kind of civil disobedience that was necessary for the Civil Rights Movement and the Free Speech Movement: "There's a time when the operation of the machine becomes so odious, makes you so sick at heart, that you can't take part; you can't even passively take part. And you've got to put your bodies on the gears and upon the wheels, upon the levers, upon all the apparatus, and you've got to make it stop. And you've got to indicate to the people who run it, to the people who own it, that unless you're free, the machine will be prevented from working at all" (Cohen 188). Savio's speech and the massive arrests on that December day in 1964 didn't "just happen" any more than the occupation of the state Capitol building in Wisconsin "just happened" in early 2011. Savio arrived at Berkeley in the fall of 1963 as a political moderate who was attracted to Berkeley's reputation for student activism (41). He slowly became part of a well-established and militant student activist movement over the course of that first year in which he gradually learned the importance of civil disobedience in the Bay Area Civil Rights Movement (45). In the summer of 1964, he joined other Berkeley activists in heading south to Mississippi as part of the Student Nonviolent Coordinating Committee (SNCC) Freedom Summer project. In short, Savio learned the tactic of throwing your bodies upon "the gears" of the machine from seasoned civil rights organizers, organizers from SNCC in particular. The point here is that the practice of occupying physical space, of throwing one's body on the gears, is one of the core practices of social movements seeking significant social change or any deepening of the democratic franchise. American history is a virtual textbook of the ways that the strategy of civility as a means to manage democratic rule has to be constantly propped up by communities of resistance. That is, in order for civil discourse to function effectively as a means of self-rule, people have had to periodically embrace incivility and faction when the gap between what the people want and what the government does becomes too great. Those who call for a return to civil discourse in the aftermath of the 2008 election seem to forget that reason alone cannot and has not secured the promise of democracy when power is overwhelmingly concentrated in the hands of a few individuals or a particular political faction, despite our Madisonian protections.

In a climate of rapidly escalating economic—and, by extension, political—inequality, we just may need to pay more attention to political activists and what they have to teach about the everyday tactics of social change. The lessons gleaned from activists may help temper more "authorized" experts who would urge caution and civility. If there is any hope of returning to civil discourse as a strategy of governing, it will be necessary for us to relearn the tactics of incivility, of factionalism, and of refusal to comply with unjust authorities.

The Wisconsin uprising and the birth of the Occupy Movement in 2011 reclaimed mass occupation of public space as a tactic of resistance. The 2013 "Moral Monday" mass protests and acts of civil disobedience in North Carolina against discriminatory legislation and the massive Black Lives Matter uprisings in 2014 and 2015 against police killings of black men and women renewed an urgency and militancy to civil rights struggles. The return of student occupations of university buildings as part of a "Fossil Free" movement to pressure universities to divest from fossil fuels recall the lessons of the South Africa divestment movement from the 1980s. And the historic Women's March in DC the day after Donald Trump's inauguration coupled with the explosive growth of Indivisible groups engaged in direct action at legislators' home offices in every state in the country point to a resurgence of acts of civil disobedience, of incivility, and a militant defense of democracy. In many ways, we are beginning to remind ourselves of our capacity to act collectively and effectively.

Throughout American history we have faced these moments—the need to fight faction with faction. John Brown understood this. Lucy Parsons understood this. Elizabeth Gurley Flynn understood this. Mother Jones understood this. Myles Horton understood this. Martin Luther King understood this. Saul Alinsky understood this. They understood rhetorical action in terms of a confrontation with power, and this confrontation was decidedly *uncivil*. They understood that in order to be heard over the narrative machine of those in power, you first have to stop the machine. Laying our bodies on the gears of the machine, occupying buildings and spaces to reclaim or repurpose them, and refusing to participate in the perpetuation of injustice or oppression does not represent a breakdown of rhetoric or its antithesis. It is intimately bound up in John Poulakos's sense of the *kairos* of rhetorical action—the "opening up a seemingly settled account . . . by introducing new ways of reasoning . . . leading to the formation of new beliefs" (95). Or, to put it in terms of the Zapatistas' most famous writer, Subcomandate Marcos, it's to "open a crack in history" (212).

We need to reclaim and embrace rhetorics of direct action, of incivility, and of faction from historical obscurity if we hope to turn back the assault on the commons. Fortunately, we do not have to wait for the academy to authorize this rescue. From Wisconsin to the Women's March, these traditions are being reanimated and reembodied with Paine's ideals of "peace forever" and a willingness to "bear the evils and burdens of the present day."

WORKS CITED

Bartels, Larry. *Unequal Democracy: The Political Economy of the New Gilded Age*. Princeton University Press, 2008.

Bourdieu, Pierre. *The Logic of Practice*. Stanford University Press, 1990.

Burke, Kenneth. *The Philosophy of the Literary Form*. University of California Press, 1941.

Center for Media and Democracy. "About Us." *Center for Media and Democracy's PR Watch*, June 15, 2015. www.prwatch.org/cmd/.

Cohen, Robert. *The Essential Mario Savio: Speeches and Writings that Changed America*. University of California Press, 2014.

Cooper, Marc. "No Sweat." *The Nation*, June 7, 1999. www.thenation.com/article/no-sweat/.

Dixon, Kim, and Patrick Temple-West. "Q&A: The 'Buffett Rule,' a Minimum Tax on the Rich." *Reuters*, April 16, 2012. www.reuters.com/article/us-usa-tax-buffett/qa-the-buffett-rule-a-minimum-tax-on-the-rich-idUSBRE83F05H20120416/.

Draper, Robert. *When the Tea Party Came to Town*. Simon and Schuster, 2013.

Featherston, Liza. *Students Against Sweatshops: The Making of a Movement*. Verso, 2002.

Gladwell, Malcolm. "Small Change: Why the Revolution Will Not Be Tweeted." *New Yorker*, October 4, 2010. www.newyorker.com/magazine/2010/10/04/small-change -malcolm-gladwell/.

Grunwald, Michael. *The New New Deal: The Hidden Story of Change in the Obama Era*. Simon and Schuster, 2013.

Hayes, Chris. "Congress Ignores Public Opinion (Again)." *The Rachel Maddow Show*. Guest host, April 16, 2012. www.msnbc.com/rachel-maddow-show/watch/congress -ignores-public-opinion-again-44139075877/.

Hodge, Roger. "In the Name of James Madison." *Politico*, February 16, 2011. www.politico .com/story/2011/02/in-the-name-of-james-madison-049561/.

Klein, Naomi. *Shock Doctrine: The Rise of Disaster Capitalism*. Picador, 2008.

Krugman, Paul. "Shock Doctrine, U.S.A." *New York Times*, February 24, 2011. www.ny times.com/2011/02/25/opinion/25krugman.html.

Marcos, Subcomandante. *Our Word Is Our Weapon: Selected Writings*. Edited by Juana Ponce de León. Seven Stories Press, 2001.

Marcuse, Herbert. "Repressive Tolerance." In *A Critique of Pure Tolerance*, edited by Robert Paul Wolff, Barrington Moore, Jr., and Herbert Marcuse, 81–123. Beacon Press, 1968.

Matthews, David. "Preface." In *Doing Democracy: How a Network of Grassroots Organizations Is Strengthening Community, Building Capacity, and Shaping a New Kind of Civic Education*. London, Kettering Foundation, 2010.

National Economic Council, The. "The Buffett Rule: A Basic Principle of Tax Fairness." The White House, 2012. www.obamawhitehouse.archives.gov/sites/default/files/Buffett _Rule_Report_Final.pdf.

National Task Force on Civic Learning and Democratic Engagement. *A Crucible Moment: College Learning and Democracy's Future*. Association of American Colleges and Universities, 2012.

Nichols, John. "America's Youth Uprising." *The Nation*. February 15, 2012. www.thenation .com/article/americas-youth-uprising/.

Nichols, John. "Introduction: Why Wisconsin." In *It Started in Wisconsin: Dispatches from the Front Lines of the New Labor Protest*, edited by Mari Jo Buhle and Paul Buhle, 3–9. Verso, 2011.

Paine, Thomas. "Epistle to Quakers." *The Writings of Thomas Paine*. G. P. Putnam and Sons, 1906. Online edition. Bartleby.com, 2013. www.bartleby.com/184/.

Poulakos, John. "*Kairos* in Gorgias' Rhetorical Compositions." In *Rhetoric and Kairos: Essays in History, Theory, and Praxis*, edited by Phillip Sipiora and James Baumlin, 89–96. State University of New York Press, 2002.

Pratt, Mary Louise. "Arts of the Contact Zone." *Profession* (1991): 33–40.

Saez, Emmanuel, and Gabriel Zucman. "Exploding Wealth Inequality in the United States." *Washington Center for Equitable Growth*, October 20, 2014. www.equitablegrowth.org /human-capital/exploding-wealth-inequality-united-states/.

Toyama, Kentaro. *Geek Heresy: Rescuing Social Change from the Cult of Technology.* Public Affairs, 2015.

Toyama, Kentaro. "Twitter Isn't Spreading Democracy—Democracy Is Spreading Twitter." *The Atlantic*, November 11, 2013. www.theatlantic.com/technology/archive/2013/11/twitter-isnt-spreading-democracy-democracy-is-spreading-twitter/281368/.

Walker, Don. "Democratic Senator: 'We'll Be Back Eventually.'" All Politics Blog, *Milwaukee Journal Sentinel,* February 18, 2011. Accessed July 23, 2017, but no longer available.

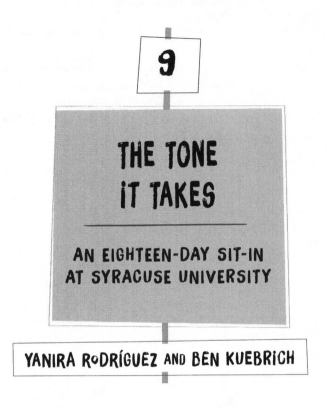

9

THE TONE IT TAKES

AN EIGHTEEN-DAY SIT-IN AT SYRACUSE UNIVERSITY

YANIRA RºDRÍGUEZ AND BEN KUEBRICH

THE General Body is a coalition of students, faculty, and staff at Syracuse University. . . . Our goals are to educate and inform other students and the administration about the grievances and problems that students of various socio-economic class, disability, ethnicity, nationality, gender, sexuality, and race experience on a day to day basis.

—"About"

We've attended listening meetings, participated in workgroups and spoken at forums with the administration. We've been committed to compromise while the administration has continued to override student and faculty government decisions with closed-door meetings. As Martin Luther King, Jr., wrote from Birmingham Jail in 1963, it is now necessary to "dramatize the issue so that it can no longer be ignored."

—"THE General Body Responds" editorial
from forty-seven members of TGB

An eighteen-day sit-in (November 3–20, 2014) at Syracuse University (SU) drew national media coverage. It resulted in graduate student organization and university senate resolutions supporting the movement and indicting the SU administration, putting participants under the constant surveillance of an armed "public safety" force, and deepening our understanding of unruly rhetoric. We argue for the importance, and at times necessity, of unruliness (in word and through bodies) to expose the very real divisions and inequalities in our society. We also specifically address the responsibilities of students, graduate students, faculty, and staff to upend the logic that "others" and criminalizes so-called unruly acts/bodies and to support social justice movements within the university.

As fellow participants and organizers of the sit-in and campus movement, we hope to demonstrate how proximity, rather than distance, allows for both clarity and a needed sense of urgency. Like holding an object close enough that one begins to see it both as a whole and for the fragments that constitute its makeup, proximity provides the necessary context and experiences that inform the knowledge- and decision-making processes of organized resistance. We therefore use narrative and personal experience in this account, alongside newspaper articles and public statements from movement participants, and we resist turning participants into objects of academic study. Consistent with feminist methodologies, our approach honors narrative and personal accounts. Through a decolonial approach, we hope to identify and problematize the logics of Western civilization at play in local and national struggles. Applying decolonial research methodologies (see Mora and Diaz; Smith), we rely heavily on the experiences of movement participants to frame our questions at the nexus of research, pedagogy, and organizing, but with organizing as the "leading activity" (Zavala 64). We do this to challenge the cold and abstract logic of writers who presume that scholarly or journalistic distance provides objectivity, for their distance is far from neutral—rather, it is often embedded in the very status quo that is challenged by unruly, embodied rhetorical acts.

For example, in an article following the first night of the sit-in, the editorial board of Syracuse University's student newspaper scolded protesters' "unruly behavior," characterizing us as "a mob incapable of compromise" and unwilling to listen to administration (*Daily Orange* Editorial Board). We are not here to critique student journalists, but this serves as a quick and representative example of the initial response to the sit-in, not unlike the reactions of many news articles or academic analyses of the early moments of social movements. As we learned, the editorial board and many other observers did not yet realize the full context and urgency of abuses at Syracuse University. From the fact that an Americans with Disabilities Act coordinator had not been hired in over a decade, to dismal mental health resources, to institutional and interpersonal racism faced daily by students of color, dissent had been brewing on campus for months and years. It took the sit-in to bring many of these issues into the public light, and the student editorial board and news coverage soon shifted along with widespread campus support. To put it within the language of the introduction to this collection, through the deliberate unruly rhetoric of student organizers, the disruptive actions of THE General Body turned from *noise* into *discourse* for the intended audience of the campus community—from incomprehensible chants and outrage to the legitimate grievances of students who had been striving for change for too long (Alexander and Jarratt, this volume). That it did not begin as discourse helps to demonstrate the necessary risk of such an action and the work of building and maintaining resistance against the perception of unruliness and unreasonableness.

THE GENERAL BODY, ACROSS SPACE AND TIME

It is important to place THE General Body's sit-in within its immediate context, as the tactics, attitudes, and issues reflect the particular national moment from the summer and fall of 2014. We are reminded of Jacqui Alexander's notion of "palimpsestic time," through which she argues that ideologies (and events) cannot be examined in isolation but are informed by contexts that move across time and space (246). This point is especially relevant to understanding how colonial oppression continues within the United States and the long history of resistance against it. Alexander's work helps us recognize that the university is not separate from the rest of the world or the rest of the nation, and so we must think deeply and critically about colonial oppression within academic spaces.[1] As much as the privatization and corporatization of higher education attempts to create a resort-like atmosphere on campus as an escape from daily realities (see Kannan, Kuebrich, and Rodríguez), the university both *produces* and is a *product of* society. Since movement participants continually discussed national events both on and off university campuses and drew inspiration from a deep tradition of social movements, this timeline provides some necessary and yet incomplete context.[2]

> March 3, 2014: Black students begin the "I, Too, Am Harvard" photo/video campaign on Tumblr as a "way of speaking back, of claiming this campus, of standing up to say: We are here. This place is ours" (*I, Too, Am Harvard*).

> May 30, 2014: SU's new chancellor, Kent Syverud, announces the closing of the Advocacy Center, a crucial center for survivors of sexual assault to heal and

advocate against rape culture. Buried in a four-page email to the faculty and student body, he mentions that the Advocacy Center will be shut down in one week, leaving a major gap in services for the entire summer session. Not a single faculty member or student was included in the decision-making.

June 24, 2014: Chancellor Syverud announces "Fast Forward Syracuse," a restructuring of the entire university from the mission statement to academic programs, to the physical layout of the campus.

Summer 2014: Syracuse University prematurely terminates contracts with the Posse Foundation—an organization that offered scholarships and programs to groups of public school students from Los Angeles, Atlanta, and Miami. The campus community was not informed of the decision.

August 9, 2014: The Ferguson uprising begins after the murder of Michael Brown. The killing of Michael Brown and others are moments when society's oppressions are unmasked, revealing the vile brutality necessary to maintain power and reminding us all of the equally vile colonial brutality that was required to gain that power in the first place.

September 2014: Emma Sulkowicz begins the "Carry That Weight" action at Columbia University in protest of the fact that the man who raped her (and who had been formally accused of sexual assault on three occasions by other students) was found not responsible by the university and allowed to continue attending school.

September 6, 2014: Hannah Strong, an SU soccer player, is caught on video yelling racist and homophobic slurs. This sparks the #itooamSU social media campaign in which students describe interpersonal and structural racism and homophobia on campus.

September 17, 2014: "Rally for Consent" at Syracuse University draws hundreds. Seventy-five attendees then march to Chancellor Syverud's office to protest the closing of the Advocacy Center and the persistence of rape culture at SU.

September 19, 2014: "Rally for a Difference" at Syracuse University. One hundred students and alumni protest the Posse Foundation scholarship cuts and demand more funding for students of color and programs.

September 24, 2014: Colgate University in Hamilton, NY (about an hour's drive from Syracuse) holds a five-day sit-in against racism on campus.

September 30, 2014: Divest SU rally argues for SU's divestment from fossil fuels as administration fails to respond to the growing movement.

September 30, 2014: Van Jones delivers a University Lecture Series talk on environmental and racial justice. After the talk, SU NAACP and Student African American Society leaders reach out to Divest SU to collaborate on campus. A dozen members of Divest SU attend a late-night meeting with the SU NAACP. Speaking to the connections, SU NAACP leader Danielle Reed said, "We don't have to just be about the environment, or just about racial equality, or just about gender equality. . . . We can be for all of those things" (Gorny).

October 2, 2014: Students, led by the SU NAACP, hold a silent protest of the "Express SU" event organized by university administration in response to the "Hannah Strong incident." This is the first student action to directly reject the university's "civil," institutionally sanctioned speak-out events.

October 7, 2014: THE General Body holds its first meeting, a coalition growing from campus protests associated with the Advocacy Center, Posse, SU NAACP, Student African American Society, and Divest SU. Over fifty official and unofficial student organizations and groups are represented. Regular weekly meetings continue and students meet in small groups around action planning, research, and media for the next month.

November 3, 2014: THE General Body holds "DAT Rally" for Diversity and Transparency. It links together several social movements around the university administration's irresponsibility, especially toward marginalized student populations.

November 3, 2014: Students march from DAT Rally to the university administration building and announce that they are not leaving until demands are met. They deliver a forty-three-page research and demands document.

As the above timeline demonstrates, THE General Body sit-in was the result of brewing social unrest on and beyond the campus as well as a broader history of student and national movements mediated by available rhetorical means/technologies. Its success can be measured as much by the immediate fulfillment of student demands as by the ongoing re-envisioning and creative use of the rhetorical power of unruliness.

CIVILITY AT SYRACUSE UNIVERSITY

We cannot condone the unruly and unprofessional behavior exhibited at the DAT Rally. . . . What could have been a chance for students to appear calm and willing to listen instead turned into a mob incapable of compromise. . . . Effective discussion requires compromise, respect and rationality. Regardless of personal issues students have with the administration, letting emotions drive discussion will only result in a group of angry students booing and chanting.

—*Daily Orange* Editorial Board,
"Unruly Behavior at DAT Rally Will Not Spur Change"

Civility is not a state of mind. It is a regime.

—Steven Salaita, *Uncivil Rites*

We quote again from the *Daily Orange* editorial board's initial reaction to the sit-in in order to demonstrate the commonplaces of civility trickling down to students as sound bites that police both individual and collective resistance. While these commonplaces of civility have multiple roots and expressions within so-called liberal democratic societies, we will look at one recent iteration that has spread through universities. With some background on the rhetoric of civility, we are better equipped to analyze and dismantle the regime of civility propped up with these commonplaces.

In 1997 Dr. P. M. Forni, a professor of Italian at Johns Hopkins University, cofounded the Johns Hopkins Civility Project. Forni's work has had widespread impact. A simple Google search yields more than fifty institutions that have founded their own civility projects, including Rutgers; George Mason; University of California; Davis; University of Missouri; and Miami University. His book *Choosing Civility* is common on campuswide summer reading lists. The uptake of Forni's concept of civility has varied from one institution to another, including civility as a response to the caustic and polarizing rhetoric of politicians and as a way of contending with hate speech (Bowman 6). Not every instance or aspect of these diverse civility projects works against the cause of social justice, but we do want to think critically about a few representative examples.

In his article "The Other Side of Civility" for *Johns Hopkins Magazine*, Forni describes a scenario in which two marketing executives enter a heated discussion, each offended because he feels undermined before authority figures. Forni describes in detail the biological changes and subsequent health risks caused by the stress of the encounter: "From dilation of the pupils to more of their blood being sent to their brains, hearts, and muscles, to glycogen being broken down to glucose in their bloodstreams for fuel, they are in full fight-or-flight alert." His recommendation to both men is "choosing congeniality as their default mode of relating to the world." Let us consider this example. Forni is conceiving of civility interpersonally and biologically between marketing executives (note the *Daily Orange* editorial board's use of "unprofessional" as a complementary adjective to "unruly"). Those executives are men (their names are Tom and Rob), and their boss is also a man. We also hear that their lack of civility is a simple matter of choice. Similar to the critiques of the *Daily Orange* editorial board who claimed that SU students were "letting emotions drive discussion," incivility is seen by Forni as a matter of uncontrolled personal feelings, and it is taken for granted that it is in everyone's interest that those feelings are suppressed. To summarize, Forni's example is written about a person of privilege who has no problems with the status quo. In the same article Forni describes civility with the metaphor of "letting someone merge into the flow of traffic." But what happens to the people who are not allowed to simply "merge" into the traffic of privileged life? What about the people who actually encounter fight-or-flight situations, both inside the university and elsewhere?

The shrewdest aspect of these civility projects is that the commonsense and simplified examples are meant to apply in all situations, including in political speech and student protest. One Forni-inspired publication titled "More Than Good Manners: Cultivating a Spirit of Open Dialogue and Civility on Campus" situates the civility project as a "conversation" and as an alternative to the protests in Wisconsin concerning Governor Scott Walker's decision to restrict collective bargaining (Bowman; see also Mahoney, this volume). In these cases, we understand how the regime of civility restrains those who strive for deep structural change. A case in point at Syracuse University is several events set up by SU's administration in the fall 2014 semester. After the university administration closed the Advocacy Center—a center that offered crucial services to survivors of sexual assault—a petition quickly gathered eight thousand signatures, and students began organizing meetings (Carter). In response, the university administration scheduled two "listening meetings"—meetings that the chancellor did not attend, instead sending his senior staff. At one meeting, agitated students were asked by a dean to quietly turn and acknowledge each other in the room, to sit together with administrators, and to begin seeing each other as having common cause. Meanwhile, Chancellor Syverud had yet to make a public statement regarding the petition, and administrators remained firm on the decision to keep the Advocacy Center closed, a decision that actively risked the safety of students. Within context, the "listening meetings" can easily be seen for what they were: attempts to placate angry students with superficial exercises, expressing themselves into passivity without any access to real decision-making power. This is the institutional expression of civility.

When a student group advocating for the center debated how to proceed, longtime student organizers encouraged everyone to remain active and demand that the center be reopened. A protest was planned, and seventy-five students showed up at Chancellor Syverud's office, where he finally made public comments on sexual assault and the Advocacy Center's closing. During the confrontation, students read anonymous comments about sexual assault on campus and the power of the Advocacy Center in helping them both to heal and to learn to fight rape culture (Merod and Iannetta). Student organizers brought the real listening meeting to the chancellor, and while it was powerful, it was just the beginning ("Chancellor Syverud Receives a Petition"). Soon after, the university held an "Express Yourself" forum in response to repeated incidents of racism on campus and protests over the administration's cuts to the Posse Foundation scholarships. Students of color led a silent protest outside the event, knowing that it was an attempt to appease them rather than make needed institutional changes. Both actions raised awareness about the strategies of the administration and built toward the sit-in, which demanded the Advocacy Center's reopening, the reinstatement of Posse Scholarships, and policy changes to support marginalized students.

Given the context of these administration-led meetings and speak-out events, one can discern that the true intention is what David Craig and Douglas Porter call an "inclusion delusion," the deployment of the "liberal language of empowerment and opportunity" in order for people in positions of institutional power to act as if they have the consent and collaboration of communities they exploit (15).[3] But to students and faculty not following each protest, news article, or meeting over the summer and first month of the fall 2014 semester, it may have seemed as if Chancellor Syverud and his upper administration were simply being responsive to student concerns. Listening meetings, expression, and dialogue—and other rhetorics put out by administrators during this period—sound good, but they mean nothing if only one side is empowered to make decisions. The impact of civility projects and civility rhetoric is the commonplace reduction of legitimate, historic social injustices into simple misunderstandings. To characterize the root cause of social problems as a lack of understanding masks real material difference and historic violence. In response, we must question who has created the parameters of acceptable exchange, and we must ask who benefits.

But not all are seduced by this call to "civility." Young activists and organizers around the country have become sharp analysts of civility rhetoric. Consider the protests that led to the resignation of the University of Missouri's president in November 2015. The same night that President Wolfe issued an apology to Concerned Student 1950 (an organization named after the year the first Black student was accepted to Mizzou), he told protesters outside that "systematic oppression is when you don't believe that you have the equal opportunity for success" (Zirin). The sound bite demonstrated a willful ignorance about the lives and experiences of his students as they confront daily interpersonal and institutional racism, and it exposed the public, surely well-vetted statement he had delivered that very night as disingenuous. Importantly, the quotation was recorded by Mizzou students who confronted Wolfe on a sidewalk, engaging him in an unofficial setting where he responded off the cuff. Three days and a football team strike later, Wolfe was forced to resign. This incident came on the heels of several other unruly confrontations, including when protesters blocked President Wolfe's car in a homecoming parade. The car attempted to move forward despite the protest, pushing into students, and police used excessive force to clear the road (Pearson). Without these protest tactics, Wolfe's personal and institutional biases and the violence and threats of violence necessary to protect his power at the university would not have been so swiftly exposed. Through these examples we can understand how so-called unruly actions and rhetorics do not divide but, instead, reveal the existing divides of structural oppression. This lesson isn't new, it has been a crucial component of nonviolent civil disobedience practices for decades, but it deserves repeating and updating in a society and university won over by the commonplaces of civility and the superficial rhetorics of diversity and dialogue.

TAPPING THE GLASS AND CRACKING CIVILITY

On November 5, 2014, Syracuse University's Chancellor Syverud and his executive team, including his lawyer, walked into the third night of the sit-in at the administration building, Crouse-Hinds Hall. The two-floor lobby with large windows was far from the highly controlled boardroom where he had urged us to meet him. We refused, recognizing the moment of our temporary power in the sit-in to set the conditions of exchange. He wanted us in private, with no press or electronic devices. We said that the movement and the students, faculty, and staff it represented would accept nothing less than a public negotiation. The lobby floor and the stairs that wrapped around it were packed, leaving little room to move. Banners hung down from the balcony above. They read, "Is This a School or a Corporation?" and "Power Concedes Nothing without a Demand." The wall was full of students' posters and pictures describing racism, sexism, homophobia, and ableism on campus. THE General Body set a table for Chancellor Syverud and his lawyer facing twelve student negotiators.

Throughout the meeting, students and faculty snapped their fingers in support of points raised by the negotiation team, an echoing flutter. By fire code, eighty people were allowed inside, including press. Those who could not fit in lined the windows outside, peering through the glass. A cell phone on speaker broadcasted the conversation from inside Crouse-Hinds. As THE General Body raised issues and argued, those on the outside tapped on the glass to complement the snapping.

Chancellor Syverud was in a public meeting where students determined the exchange, and he was held publicly accountable with direct questions about a history of program cuts and institutional abuses. The first demand, halting the passage of a new mission and vision statement at the center of a university-wide restructuring called "Fast Forward Syracuse," was accomplished immediately following this negotiation, proving that unlike the prediction of the *Daily Orange* editorial board who claimed that "unruly behavior" would "not spur change," unruliness worked. The proposed mission and vision was meant to be passed that week by the board of trustees, removing references to community, democracy, public intellectuals, and diverse students.[4] New language in the proposed mission and vision included "a culture of innovation and discovery," "entrepreneurial endeavors," and "professional studies" ("Vision and Mission Statements"), the banal language of a corporate university. Through subsequent meetings with administrators, students, and faculty, daily teach-ins, and actions around campus and inside the administration building, the movement continued to build and eventually made progress on several other issues during the eighteen-day sit-in, including an increase in teaching assistants' pay, an immediate and ultimately successful search for an ADA coordinator, and several policy changes that empowered student governance.

The movement succeeded well beyond the predictions of many, but it wasn't enough. The chancellor eventually apologized for the way he had closed the Advocacy Center and student activists built a task force to make recommendations about addressing sexual assault, but the center was never reopened. While we argued in meeting after meeting to recommit to the Posse program, the administration stood firm on limiting scholarships to racially and economically diverse students. The university made a weak commitment but a grand announcement about divestment from fossil fuels (Schwartz), using this and other small changes to create a narrative about its progressive actions. The complex outcomes of the sit-in and the day-to-day resistance of students, faculty, and staff are difficult to capture in the space allowed here, but what is clear is that without unruly action, none of the successes would have been possible. For more on the movement, curious readers may view THE General Body's website for an archive of over one hundred news articles and statements written by participants, professors, community organizations, local newspapers, and national publications such as *USA Today*, *Huffington Post*, *Democracy Now!*, *Inside Higher Ed*, and the *Chronicle of Higher Education* ("Press"). Several news articles address the movement's results and enduring impact (see Mattingly; Watson).

In our assessment, the real successes are less tangible: large groups of faculty (including entire departments and the university senate) endorsed and participated in the movement, community organizations gave their strategic and material support, and we connected with student activists from around the country. Perhaps the biggest victory was the hundreds of students, faculty, and staff who entered the space for daily teach-ins and the ongoing work of a revolving and committed group of activists who risked their safety, fought together, educated one another, and who continue in the struggle for social justice on and off campus. Since truly transformative victories are won by the collected weight of many discrete actions, we want to exchange a language that suggests finality for one that affirms the process of continued learning and resistance. As Paulo Freire asks, "What can we do now in order to be able to do tomorrow what we are unable to do today?" (115).

In *We Make the Road by Walking*, Myles Horton and Paulo Freire discuss the connection of education to organizing, with Freire claiming that educators "can take advantage of the process of organizing in order to develop a very special process of education" (121). This is why it is important that the teach-ins happened during the sit-in. What we learned together and shared in the evenings, we put into practice the next day. Education that empowers action and action that empowers education are found in the context of organizing spaces in ways that are often fundamentally different from university classrooms or administratively run speak-out events. This focus isn't meant to diminish those heroic teachers who raise consciousness and teach critical thinking in relation to social urgencies, but we want to emphasize the kind of education that, through collective action, makes demands on those in power and strategizes to recover rights and resources. Education in the sit-in, in many ways, reflects the sort of anti-imperialist university Ellen Cushman describes in an episode of *This Rhetorical Life*: "To me, a really interesting university would be one that is based on solving problems, almost exclusively . . . and [one in which scholars] work with multiple peoples to create knowledge" (Kuebrich and Soto).[5] The sit-in involved an interdisciplinary, intergenerational, multiracial, and multi-identity learning process put into the action of problem solving, through movement praxis and the development of policy, like the forty-three-page research and demands document. As Freire notes, "it's impossible to organize without educating and being educated by the very process of organizing" (Horton and Freire 121). It is with the particularly potent type of learning inside of movements that we sustain a long-term hopefulness and a disposition for continued struggle, and through these examples we begin to imagine new coeducational spaces of learning and resistance.

ALWAYS ALREADY UNRULY

After demonstrating the necessity of unruly rhetoric and action, now the task is to develop an attentiveness to and support for the bodies whose risk is disproportionate in the demand for change. As Linda Carty and Monisha Das Gupta argue, subjectivities that intersect at various geopolitical sites and have been acted upon by US imperialism and colonization acquire a broader perspective of justice and a sense of urgency that informs and interconnects organizing, research, and pedagogy. For some, this makes their participation in activist struggles "a matter of necessity, not choice" (Carty and Das Gupta 106). In contrast, those who benefit from the status quo may be more easily seduced by rhetorics of civility and the promise these rhetorics hold of shielding those who benefit from the pain of historical/ancestral complicity.

Civility and embodiment become significant here also in the context of the call for chapters to this collection, *Unruly Rhetorics*. While a call to analyze the forces that render certain rhetorics "unruly" is significant, the focus on social movements runs the risk of subsuming bodies that are always already unruly. Chandra Mohanty, via Michel Foucault, terms this potential a threshold of disappearance, "where one conceptual frame (systemic or intersectional) is quietly subsumed under and supplanted by another emerging frame, one that obscures crucial relations of power" (970). Our concern is how an examination of "unruly rhetorics" in the context of social movements might obscure the fact that the very presence of some bodies is treated as a disruption, both inside and outside of movement work. If we recognize social movements and protests as collections of individuals whose bodies may be very differently policed, restrained, dehumanized, and punished, it allows us to think about those who are unruly without even trying to be.

For example, administrators, press, and members of THE General Body treated us, Yanira and Ben (a woman of color and a white man), differently. In describing our specific experiences, then, we are not a "we." At the same time, we are not advancing a notion of individuality but thinking about the differential treatment of certain individuals within social structures. This analysis, aware of differential treatment but within a movement for collective action, helps us think about using difference in the service of structural change. How can collectives composed of people with varying access to resources and who are treated differently within systems of power use that difference deliberately in struggles for liberation and equality?

During the sit-in, members of the university administration sought to diffuse collective action through divisive tactics that often wrote people of color as unreasonable, irrational, emotional, or too unruly. For example, during a chaotic moment the first night of the sit-in, Yanira spoke firmly to administrators and the head of "Public Safety" about the number of people allowed to sleep in the building. Public Safety said we would be allowed to stay in the building, but only twenty of us. Seeing this limit as a way to slowly dwindle and delegitimize the group, Yanira told administrators, "This is a sit-in, a last resort action that is outside the parameters of regular rules. We have forty students staying over. You are in the business of safety—I am sure you have the resources to keep forty students safe, so I urge you to make it work." The dean of student affairs, in an attempt to undermine Yanira's comments and cause a rift between the reasonable and the unruly protesters, restated the administration's desire to engage in "productive" dialogue and said "the tone of the conversation has changed" in reference to Yanira's statement. As Yanira remained firm, other students joined to support the stance. Finally, after a perfunctory measurement of the lobby floor, Public Safety determined that we must cap our nighttime presence at forty. Risking unruliness in situations such as this was necessary throughout the entire movement, from summer organizing to the sit-in itself, and maintaining a steadfast group against commonplace rhetorics of civil and "productive dialogue" took vigilance and constant education within the movement.

In a contrasting example, administrators often attempted to pull Ben or several other white student movement leaders out of the crowd of organizers, asking them to make decisions and represent the entire group. Such treatment can feel good to those students who are sought after; they feel reinforced as being important and central to the movement. After some difficult conversations about these dynamics, we began to pull everyone available into conversations whenever administration came to speak with us. This tactic, along with insisting upon an evolving group of student negotiators, was cause for complaint by administration as they evoked a trope about leaderless movements.

In these moments, we witnessed how the administration attempted to use race as a dividing factor by more often categorizing white students as reasonable and students of color as unreasonable. They framed particular bodies and speakers as "unruly" for speaking outside normative, white modes of exchange, rules established specifically to avoid the contestation of power. Using race and various identities as a divisive tactic is not new, but the answer is not to blanket subjectivity or align under an all-encompassing flag ("we're all human" or "we all have struggles"). These answers can silence the different experiences and impacts of structural oppression that need to be voiced in order to create a just society. A similar silencing move is the tendency by some academically trained—often white—critics to characterize people of color's expressions and analysis of difference as "essentializing." There is an important distinction to be made between people in power essentializing characteristics to a specific marginalized group and marginalized people acting and resisting through a chosen political identity while invoking people who share in that identity. The invocation has the positive effect of foregrounding lineages of resistance as well as solidarity among oppressed people. It also calls forth future generations. This turning of critiques against the oppressor back on those they mean to oppress also happens when discussing systems of domination like white supremacy and cultural norms of whiteness: pointing out norms and systems of oppression is not the same as essentializing. We write this while also remaining attentive to the need for marginalized groups with different struggles to, as Dana Olwan argues, move "toward responsible, ethical, and mutual forms of solidarity that are historically situated and politically conscious" instead of "assumptive solidarities" that risk erasing unique struggles and histories (100). The work of understanding how systems of power differentially affect and condition us is often painful, but it is crucial in building the movements that our moment demands.

As Alexander and Jarratt's introduction to this collection suggests, the difference between acceptable protest and the unruliness that challenges the status quo comes down to competing definitions of "democracy." They cite Jacques Rancière's version of democracy as "ongoing disruption, as those subjects who had not even been capable of being seen breaking into the frame of vision, their voices once heard as noise making themselves heard in the conversation." With an understanding of "democracy as perpetually unruly" (Rancière qtd. in Alexander and Jarratt, this volume), we can reframe the always already unruly body as the democratic body—the body whose noise, tone, and disruption make a real democracy possible.

Understanding that the building of a true democracy requires constant disruption, we asked our audience for both organized collective struggle and daily solidarity. Collective struggle and daily solidarity isn't just showing up at a protest but also at those moments when the grievances of your fellow students are being dismissed and you're faced with the choice either to merge into the comfortable world of civility or to support an unruly disruption. Collective struggle and solidarity mean resisting when colleagues are being disrespected in meetings, when curriculums are slowly depoliticized, when students are forced out of graduate programs, and when departments are made unlivable for marginalized bodies. Collective struggle and solidarity mean resisting when movements are treated as academic objects and intellectuals "uncritically attribute political efficacy to textual critique" (Bourdieu qtd. in Smucker 40). The fight for material changes in the university cannot be separate from the daily fight to make the university more livable for the students whose very identities are deemed unruly, even though, as Alexis Pauline Gumbs states, "The university was not created to save [their] life. The university is not about the preservation of a bright brown body" ("The Shape of My Impact"). Daily struggle and risk with the many people whom the university was not meant to serve, save, or love is necessary alongside building grassroots organizations that create new possibilities and win the world we deserve.

RISK, STRUGGLE, AND REFUSAL

The risk and struggle of individual unruly bodies can be mitigated if we build a collective ethos, one of decolonial refusal. That is, through the refusal of the incorporation of our bodies, knowledges, and loyalties into the university's colonial legacy, we are refusing to sanction the very institutions who offer some of us awards while simultaneously policing others. An ethos of decolonial refusal would build on Quijano and Mignolo's concept of delinking. "Delinking doesn't mean . . . to abandon, but instead to invent decolonial visions and horizons, concepts and discourses," argues Mignolo (312). We have seen potent examples of this kind of refusal and invention in the scholarship, actions, and world-building projects of feminists such as Sara Ahmed and Alexis Pauline Gumbs, solidarity networks among women and nonbinary people of color in academia, and spaces such as the one created by the Crunk Feminist Collective, to name a few. In the sit-in we caught a glimpse of both a new space to learn and a new space in which to live—within the university, but with all our available tools sharpening against the university. Sam Blum, a student journalist who joined the sit-in for a night, observed that "the protesters have made a home out of a place that isn't one. And while they all stand by the fact that doing so was a last resort, it's become a haven for aligning beliefs and a representation for the change that they're demanding" ("Protesters At Sit-In").The alternative to engaging in resistance, risk, refusal, and building solidarity is incorporation into the university's project. As Gumbs points out, this incorporation leeches our genius, abuses our work, and exploits us after our death while simultaneously vilifying us ("The Shape of Our Impact").

We witnessed this incorporation and vilification in direct relation to the sit-in. The decisiveness we used to render operating logics as faulty and illegitimate was deemed unruly and, as we came to learn, even violent. In the semester following the sit-in, we were forwarded a memo sent from the chancellor's office to the staff, faculty, and administrators in Crouse-Hinds Hall about a safety training specific to the administration building. Occupants of the building would receive training on "protocols for shootings, protests, violent visitors, etc." We see here how disruption of the status quo through protest is lumped in with shootings and violent visitors, reminiscent of many historic and current social movements—from COINTELPRO, to Department of Homeland Security surveillance of Black Lives Matter, to the privately funded surveillance of the water protectors at Standing Rock—that have been treated as terroristic and violent (see, for instance, Brown, Parrish, and Speri; and Joseph). The fact that we had as many as ten armed "public safety" officers watching us in the building—cataloguing our entrances and exits and sometimes taking pictures of us as we slept—is consistent with this framing and the subsequent training for Crouse-Hinds occupants. But this characterization runs counter to the more public descriptions of the protesters by the administration, revealing the threat of incorporation and co-optation. In a message to the campus on night twelve of the sit-in, the chancellor wrote, "Like our students have done throughout the ages, they carried signs, chanted and encouraged passersby to join their cause. I cannot say enough how much I admire and respect the students' commitment to this University" (Syverud, "Message to the SU Community"). We treated all statements by administration during the sit-in as tactical rhetorical moves, but the chancellor's description of acceptable protest is telling. He lets the campus community know that carrying signs, chanting, and engaging passersby is acceptable. However, he does not name a history in which Syracuse University students formed the Coalition Against Racism and Apartheid and "hammered homemade wooden crosses into grounds surrounding the Administration Building . . . splattered [with] red paint" in an ultimately successful divestment campaign against South African apartheid (Greene). Nor does he mention the faculty and students who created a Syracuse chapter of the Congress Of Racial Equality and "locked themselves to construction equipment [and] climbed the rooftops of buildings" in downtown Syracuse to protest the bulldozing of a thriving Black neighborhood (Luther 7). And Chancellor Syverud doesn't mention the most critical feature of our protest: holding the university administration building for nearly three weeks. His statement begins the work of incorporating a sanitized version of events into the university's legacy.[6] Carrying signs is respectable and historic, an important component of the contemporary university where students are encouraged to speak their minds. The superficial elements of protest are cultural capital. But building resistance is deemed violent and terroristic, and the university is preparing to treat it as such.

THE AWFUL ROAR

If there is no struggle there is no progress. Those who profess to favor freedom and yet deprecate agitation are [folks] who want crops without plowing up the ground; they want rain without thunder and lightning. They want the ocean without the awful roar of its many waters. This struggle may be a moral one, or it may be a physical one, and it may be both moral and physical, but it must be a struggle. Power concedes nothing without a demand. It never did and it never will. Find out just what any people will quietly submit to and you have found out the exact measure of injustice and wrong which will be imposed upon them.

—Frederick Douglass,
"If There Is No Struggle There Is No Progress"

Leading up to the sit-in, we found it necessary to make a banner that read "Power Concedes Nothing without a Demand. It Never Did and It Never Will." These are lessons that organizers, activists, and others engaged in continual modes of resistance all know deeply. But we fear some scholars and students are coerced into civil modes of being and belonging that in fact police un-ruliness. Even as activists and organizers, we found the banner necessary to remind ourselves of what we were doing each day—plowing up the ground, making thunder and lightning, and demanding concessions. The language of demands itself was controversial, a contested word in our campaign. Skeptical students and faculty would question the right of students to make demands on a private university. We heard all the common reactions: love it or leave it, get a job, a generation that knows nothing of the real world, an employer wouldn't let you get away with this behavior, and so on.

Against the pressure to quietly submit, we fought and emerged from the sit-in at Syracuse University hopeful and determined. Our interactions with student activists shattered any notions that the emergent generation was apathetic, uncritical, or individualistic. We saw leaders coming to meetings after work in their SU dining uniforms, TAs juggling child care and organizing, and marginalized students of many identities fighting for an intersectional social justice that serves the collective.[7] We wrote this piece so as to think with readers about the necessity of unruliness, the dangerous shifts of meanings and logics that occur through the neoliberal uptake of dissent, the incorporation of certain bodies while criminalizing and demonizing others, the exclusion and seduction of rhetorics of civility, and finally, the danger of embracing fatalism. We hope the story of THE General Body encourages and inspires more unruliness.

NOTES

1. We realize that the world and the university are not distinct, unlike the suggestion made in a May 2015 letter to students written by Syracuse University Chancellor Syverud where he did address police brutality but assumed that such realities are outside of the university, describing how students "leave here and go out into the world" ("Message to Our Community").

2. The timeline was created by identifying the various threads of resistance, both local and national, that inspired and coalesced into THE General Body. See two Syracuse-based reporters for more on the local context leading up to the sit-in (Tobin; Watson).

3. See Kannan, Kuebrich, and Rodriguez, "Unmasking Corporate-Military Infrastructure," for the application of "inclusion delusion" to service learning and community engagement projects.

4. We recognize that these terms are compromised. "Democracy," "community," and "diversity" are flexible terms in a neoliberal society, used when they are convenient for corporate doublespeak. Still, the very nature of contested terms means that they can also be defined or redefined by faculty and students interested in social justice and critical thought, allowing at least a small window of possibility.

5. Cushman talks about this idea while discussing a way to counteract the imperialist legacy of universities. See Chatterjee and Maira, *The Imperial University*, on this point as well.

6. As another example of this tendency, pictures of the fall 2014 sit-in at nearby Colgate University adorned their university's homepage just weeks after the action ended.

7. See "The Combahee River Collective Statement" and Crenshaw, "Demarginalizing the Intersection of Race and Sex," for more on intersectionality.

WORKS CITED

"About." www.thegeneralbody.org/about/.

Alexander, Jacqui. *Pedagogies of Crossing: Meditations on Feminism, Sexual Politics, Memory, and the Sacred.* Duke University Press, 2005.

Alexander, Jonathan, and Susan C. Jarratt. "Introduction." In *Unruly Rhetorics: Protest, Persuasion, and Publics,* edited by Jonathan Alexander, Susan C. Jarratt, and Nancy Welch, 3–23. Pittsburgh University Press, 2018.

Blum, Sam. "Protesters at Sit-In Build Sense of Community in Crouse-Hinds." *Daily Orange,* November 18, 2014. www.dailyorange.com/2014/11/protesters-at-sit-in-build-sense-of-community-in-crouse-hinds/.

Bowman, Karen Doss. "More Than Good Manners: Cultivating a Spirit of Civility and Open Dialogue on Campus." *Public Purpose* (Summer 2011): 6–9.

Brown, Alleen, Will Parrish, and Alice Speri. "Leaked Documents Reveal Counterterrorism Tactics Used Standing Rock to 'Defeat Pipeline Insurgencies.'" *The Intercept*, May 27, 2017. www.theintercept.com/2017/05/27/leaked-documents-reveal-security -firms-counterterrorism-tactics-at-standing-rock-to-defeat-pipeline-insurgencies/.

Carter, Erin. "Reinstatement of the Advocacy Center to Provide Confidential Sexual Assault Support Services at Syracuse University." www.change.org/p/syracuse-university -reinstatement-of-the-advocacy-center-to-provide-confidential-sexual-assault-support -services-at-syracuse-university/.

Carty, Linda, and Monisha Das Gupta. "Solidarity Work in Transnational Feminism: The Question of Class and Location." In *Activist Scholarship, Antiracism, Feminism, and Social Change*, edited by Margo Okazawa-Rey and Julia Sudbury, 95–110. Paradigm Publisher, 2009.

"Chancellor Syverud Receives a Petition." *YouTube*, uploaded by Daniel Cheifer, September 18, 2014. www.youtube.com/watch?v=dqa1JbQIraQ/.

Chatterjee, Piya. "Transforming Pedagogies: Imagining Internationalist Feminist/Antiracists Literacies." In *Activist Scholarship, Antiracism, Feminism, and Social Change*, edited by Margo Okazawa-Rey and Julia Sudbury, 131–48. Paradigm Publisher, 2009.

Chatterjee, Piya, and Sunaina Maira, eds. *The Imperial University: Academic Repression and Scholarly Dissent*. University of Minnesota Press, 2014.

"The Combahee River Collective Statement." In *The Second Wave: A Reader in Feminist Theory*, edited by Linda Nicholson, 63–70. Routledge, 1997.

Craig, David, and Douglas Porter. *Development beyond Neoliberalism? Governance, Poverty Reduction, and Political Economy*. Routledge, 2006.

Crenshaw, Kimberle. "Demarginalizing the Intersection of Race and Sex: A Black Feminist Critique of Antidiscrimination Doctrine, Feminist Theory and Antiracist Politics." *University of Chicago Legal Forum* 140 (1989): 139–67.

Daily Orange Editorial Board. "Unruly Behavior at DAT Rally Will Not Spur Change." *Daily Orange*, November 4, 2014. www.dailyorange.com/2014/11/unruly-behavior-will -not-spur-change/.

Douglass, Frederick. "If There Is No Struggle, There Is No Progress." 1857. www.blackpast .org/1857-frederick-douglass-if-there-no-struggle-there-no-progress/.

Forni, P. M. *Choosing Civility: The Twenty-Five Rules of Considerate Conduct*. St. Martin's Griffin, 2003.

Forni, P. M. "The Other Side of Civility." *Johns Hopkins Magazine* 57.5 (2005). www.pages .jh.edu/jhumag/1105web/civility.html.

Freire, Paulo. *Pedagogy of Hope: Reliving Pedagogy of the Oppressed*. Bloomsbury Publishing, 2014.

"THE General Body Responds to Tuesday's Editorial." *Daily Orange*, November 5, 2014. www.dailyorange.com/2014/11/the-general-body-responds-to-tuesdays-editorial -board/.

Gorny, Nicki. "THE General Body: From General Interest Group to Social Movement in Two Months." *New House News*, November 20, 2014. www.thenewshouse.com/story /general-body-general-interest-campus-social-movement-less-two-months/.

Greene, John Robert. "The Eggers Years." *Syracuse University Magazine* (Summer 1999). www.sumagazine.syr.edu/archive/summer99/features/eggersyears/index.html.

Gumbs, Alexis Pauline. "The Shape of My Impact." *Feminist Wire*, October 29, 2012. www .thefeministwire.com/2012/10/the-shape-of-my-impact/.

Horton, Myles, and Paulo Freire. *We Make the Road by Walking: Conversation on Education and Social Change*. Temple University Press, 1990.

I, Too, Am Harvard. www.itooamharvard.tumblr.com/.

Joseph, George. "Exclusive: Feds Regularly Monitored Black Lives Matter since Ferguson." *The Intercept*, July 24, 2015. www.theintercept.com/2015/07/24/documents-show -department-homeland-security-monitoring-black-lives-matter-since-ferguson/.

Kannan, Vani, Ben Kuebrich, and Yanira Rodríguez. "Unmasking Corporate-Military Infrastructure: Four Theses." *Community Literacy Journal* 11, no. 1 (2016): 76–93.

King, Martin Luther, Jr. "Letter from Birmingham Jail." April 16, 1963. www.africa.upenn .edu/Articles_Gen/Letter_Birmingham.html.

Kuebrich, Ben, and Karrieann Soto. "This We Believe." *This Rhetorical Life*, September 5, 2013. www.thisrhetoricallife.syr.edu/episode-12-this-we-believe/.

Luther, Jason. "SPC and Student Activism: Two Cases from the Sixties." *Syracuse Peace Newsletter* (July–August 2014). www.peacecouncil.net/pnl/july-august-2014-pnl-836 /spc-and-student-activism-two-cases-from-the-sixties/.

Mattingly, Justin. "Faculty Discuss Continued Support of THE General Body 1 Year after Sit-In Began." *Daily Orange*, November 3, 2015. www.dailyorange.com/2015/11/faculty -discuss-continued-support-of-the-general-body-1-year-after-sit-in-began/.

Merod, Anna, and Jessica Iannetta. "Students, Staff, and Faculty March to Syverud's Office to Voice Concerns about Changes to Sexual Assault Services." *Daily Orange*, September 18, 2014. www.dailyorange.com/2014/09/students-staff-and-faculty-march-to -syveruds-office-to-voice-concerns-about-changes-to-sexual-assault-services/.

Mignolo, Walter. *The Darker Side of Western Modernity: Global Futures, Decolonial Options*. Duke University Press, 2011.

Mohanty, Chandra T. "Transnational Feminist Crossings: On Neoliberalism and Radical Critique." *Signs: Journal of Women in Culture and Society* 38, no. 4 (2013): 967–91.

Mora, Juana, and David Diaz, eds. *Latino Social Policy: A Participatory Research Model*. Routledge, 2014.

Olwan, Dana M. "On Assumptive Solidarities." *Feral Feminisms* 4 (Summer 2015): 89–102.

Pearson, Michael. "A Timeline of the University of Missouri Protests." CNN, November 10, 2015. www.cnn.com/2015/11/09/us/missouri-protest-timeline/index.html.

"Press." www.thegeneralbody.org/press/.

Quijano, Aníbal. "Coloniality of Power, Eurocentrism, and Latin America." *Nepantla: Views from South* 1, no. 3 (2000): 533–80.

Salaita, Steven. *Uncivil Rites: Palestine and the Limits of Academic Freedom.* Haymarket Books, 2015.

Schwartz, John. "Syracuse to Drop Fossil Fuel Stocks from Endowment." *New York Times,* March 31, 2015. www.nytimes.com/2015/04/01/science/syracuse-to-drop-fossil-fuel-stocks-from-endowment.html.

Smith, Linda Tuhiwai. *Decolonizing Methodologies: Research and Indigenous Peoples.* Palgrave, 1999.

Smucker, Jonathan M. *Hegemony How-To: A Roadmap for Radicals.* AK Press, 2017.

Syverud, Kent. "Message to Our Community." May 1, 2015. www.news.syr.edu/2015/05/message-to-our-community-68466/.

Syverud, Kent. "Message to the SU Community." November 13, 2014. www.news.syr.edu/2014/11/message-to-the-university-community-from-chancellor-syverud-89247/.

Tobin, Dave. "What Has SU's Chancellor Syverud Done to Prompt Four Protests in Two Months?" *Syracuse Post Standard,* November 5, 2014. www.syracuse.com/news/index.ssf/2014/11/what_has_sus_chancellor_syverud_done_to_prompt_four_protests_in_two_months.html.

Watson, Taylor. "Explaining THE General Body's History and Grievances." *Daily Orange,* July 10, 2016. www.dailyorange.com/2016/07/explaining-the-general-bodys-history-and-grievances/.

Zavala, Miguel. "What Do We Mean by Decolonizing Research Strategies? Lessons from Decolonizing, Indigenous Research Projects in New Zealand and Latin America." *Decolonization: Indigeneity, Education & Society* 2, no. 1 (2013): 55–71.

Zirin, Dave. "Three Lessons from University of Missouri President Tim Wolfe's Resignation." *The Nation,* November 9, 2015. Online at www.thenation.com/article/3-lessons-from-university-of-missouri-president-tim-wolfes-resignation/.

THE STEVEN SALAITA CASE

PUBLIC RHETORIC AND THE POLITICAL IMAGINATION IN US COLLEGE COMPOSITION AND ITS PROFESSIONAL ASSOCIATIONS

JOHN TRIMBUR

O n August 1, 2014, Chancellor Phyllis M. Wise of the University of Illinois at Urbana-Champaign (UIUC) informed Steven Salaita that his appointment as a tenured associate professor in the American Indian Studies program would not be submitted for final approval to the board of trustees.[1] Even though Salaita had been offered and had accepted the position nearly nine months earlier, resigned his post as a tenured faculty member at Virginia Tech, and was scheduled for fall semester classes at the University of Illinois—and despite the fact that Chancellor Wise had already approved tenure for Salaita—she now said it was "unlikely" the board would confirm his appointment. As later came to light, by the time she wrote Salaita on August 1, Wise had already met on July 21 with Illinois president Robert A. Easter concerning complaints from pro-Israel alumni, faculty, students, and donors about tweets Salaita posted protesting the mass destruction and civilian deaths caused by Israeli military operations launched against Gaza earlier that month. On July 24, Wise attended a board of trustees meeting, where it was decided in executive session to rescind the offer to Salaita.[2]

The Salaita case opened up a whole new dimension of stifling unruly political speech and especially heated criticism of Israel, such as Salaita's tweets, by labeling them "uncivil." As Chancellor Wise explained in "The Principles on Which We Stand," issued on August 22, 2014, in response to widespread objection at Illinois and elsewhere to Salaita's unhiring, the question was not Salaita's pro-Palestinian politics but the "tone" of his tweets. After reaffirming her commitment to academic freedom, Wise articulated a civility doctrine to govern faculty conduct: "What we cannot and will not tolerate at the University of Illinois are personal and disrespectful words or actions that demean and abuse either viewpoints themselves or those who express them." In an accompanying statement of support for Wise, President Easter and the board of trustees said they wanted to "ensure that faculty, students, and staff are comfortable in a place of scholarship and education." Their goal was to make the University of Illinois a "national model of leading-edge scholarship framed in respect and courtesy" (AAUP 8). In other words, what started as a pro-Israel witch hunt against Salaita turned into a full-blown rationale, discovered after the fact, for norms of academic civility that excluded "uncivil" political speech.

The Salaita case prompted extensive media coverage that framed the question of academic civility from different angles, including hand-wringing in the liberal free speech sector about "where the line is" for faculty and "what's going too far" (see, for example, Levine) as well as the shameful attack on Salaita's academic credentials and fitness for teaching by Cary Nelson, a former American Association of University Professors (AAUP) president and once upon a time a radical faculty member at Illinois (Flaherty). Very quickly, the AAUP, professional associations across a range of academic fields, and individual faculty quite properly recognized the threat that the Salaita case posed to academic freedom, shared governance, and well-established academic hiring practices. The Modern Language Association (MLA), Organization of American Historians, American Studies Association, National Women's Studies Association, and Native American and Indigenous Studies, among others, all issued statements condemning Salaita's firing. Over five thousand academics worldwide called for a boycott of the University of Illinois until Salaita's offer was reinstated, and prominent public figures such as Cornell West and Anita Hill canceled talks at the university. In April 2015, the AAUP issued a report on the Salaita case that censured Illinois, adding it to the AAUP's list of institutions sanctioned for violating principles of academic freedom and fair practice.

Given this widespread outcry, the question arises for those of us in US college composition about why the leading professional associations in our field—the National Council of Teachers of English (NCTE) and the Conference on College Composition and Communication (CCCC)—failed to say anything about the Salaita case. And it's not that they didn't have the chance. Between August and November 2014, Matthew Abraham corresponded with Adam Banks (CCCC chair at the time), the late Kent Williamson (NCTE executive director), and Ernest Morrell (then NCTE president) about making a statement on the Salaita case, as other professional associations were in the process of doing or had already done. The email exchange shows that CCCC and NCTE leadership were aware of the Salaita case, and that they felt some pressure to deal with it in some fashion. Abraham made the point persuasively that disciplines concerned with public rhetoric had a responsibility through their professional associations to address—and to clarify—the terms of controversy raised by Illinois's civility ruling and its broader consequences as a university policy. (See Abraham, this volume, on the erasure of Palestinian suffering from the public sphere.)

As Abraham suggests, there was a clear calling in fall 2014 to examine the Salaita case as a constraint of political speech at a particular moment of high contentiousness, marked in the American academy by mounting criticism of the Israeli occupation of the West Bank and Gaza and horror at the savagery of Israeli attacks on Gaza in July 2014. This opposition to Israeli policies was manifest most prominently in the Boycott-Divestment-Sanctions (BDS) movement but was also operating through channels of scholarship, literary work, theatrical productions, and fine arts on American campuses. For many people, Israel had come to resemble preliberation South Africa, with alarmingly similar apartheid policies of settlement, relocation, and population control that created a two-tier society and severely curtailed Palestinian lives. The impact of this alienation in the academic world from Israeli state actions (and the attendant loss of affection for the Israeli national project) led to a pro-Israel counterattack on student groups and faculty sympathetic to the Palestinian cause and a campaign to equate anti-Zionist politics and other criticisms of Israel with anti-Semitism as a principle of university policy.[3] At such a moment of conflict in 2014, as Gaza burned, an inquest into the concerns of public rhetoric in the Salaita case seemed like a fitting task for professional associations in rhetoric and writing studies.

In any case, this examination was not undertaken. The Salaita case slipped out of CCCC's sight and was handled by NCTE, which promised Abraham that its committee on academic freedom was preparing a statement to be presented to the NCTE executive committee at the November 2014 convention. After vague assurances to Abraham, NCTE ignored the Salaita case altogether, issuing the *NCTE Position Statement on Academic Freedom*, which consisted of a series of bulleted points drawn from David Moshman's *Liberty and Learning: Academic Freedom for Teachers and Students*, with a brief NCTE introduction affirming academic freedom serves the "common good." Moshman's points are mainly concerned with K–12 teachers and students, calling for freedom from censorship and indoctrination but also limiting student and teacher freedom of expression to "academic contexts" and matters "relevant to the curriculum." There is no mention of Salaita, public rhetoric, or freedom of expression outside the classroom, where the "academic contexts" that students and faculty inhabit overlap with other domains of human experience, including the political realities of the Israeli occupation and the newly available social media Salaita used to tweet his opposition to Israel's attack on Gaza. Instead, perhaps in an unintentional gesture to NCTE's next-door neighbors at the University of Illinois, the NCTE introduction to the position statement notes prominently that "inherent" to academic freedom is a "moral and educational obligation to uphold the ethos of respect"—a perfectly normal sentence given new meaning and consequence by Illinois's civility doctrine and the firing of Salaita. (The *NCTE Position Statement on Academic Freedom* appears in Appendix A below.)

Abraham never heard again from NCTE after the *Position Statement on Academic Freedom* was issued. No one at national headquarters or at CCCC responded to his emails asking what happened to the Salaita case.

# # #

Now, the fact is that, although NCTE said nothing about the Salaita case, the organization did, in effect, take a position that deflected uncomfortable political pressures by issuing an inadequate and problematic position statement on academic freedom. NCTE posed itself noncontentiously as a responsible professional association and honest broker of the public good: declining mention of Salaita was a productive rhetorical act, enabling NCTE—and by extension CCCC—to avow it got into the mix about the civility controversy in a timely fashion while dodging the question of the constraints on political speech in Illinois's civility doctrine and the unhiring of Salaita. Staying out of the Salaita case, as the professional associations in composition did, amounted to a blockage, a refusal to extend the bonds of professional collegiality and social solidarity to Salaita so as to buffer NCTE and CCCC from the turmoil of political controversy, the suffering of the Palestinians, and the risk of expending organizational capital on what must have seemed a losing cause.

The response from the rank and file of composition was hardly better. After Matthew Abraham, Lisa Rebekah Arnold, Seth Kahn, William Thelin, and Nancy Welch posted a "Call for Action in Salaita Case" on the WPA listserv on August 25, 2014, only sixty-five people signed the boycott endorsement, drastically underrepresenting faculty in US college composition compared to other fields.[4]

I have been trying ever since to make sense of why CCCC and NCTE, unlike professional associations in other fields, failed to protest Salaita's unhiring. It makes me wonder what held people back, given the ostensibly progressive sentiments of so many compositionists and the apparent commitment to public rhetoric. Is there something field specific to US college composition that made it feel easier and more prudent to assume a distance from Salaita's impassioned tweets, substituting an abstract sense of civility for an understanding of the underlying reasons for Salaita's heated denunciations of Israel or what was at stake professionally and politically in retracting his appointment?[5] I will take up these questions in a moment. But first, I need to complete the story of the Salaita case and composition's professional associations.

#　　#　　#

As you probably have gathered by now, I consider NCTE and CCCC's failure to address the Salaita case a dereliction of professional duty. This dereliction made me realize that composition's professional associations were not speaking for any kind of "we" I wanted to belong to and were hopeless in dealing with highly charged political issues such as the Israeli-Palestinian conflict, which inescapably formed the backdrop to the Salaita case. This caused me in 2015 not to renew my NCTE/CCCC membership.

At first I thought this was just a personal decision, and I didn't feel like making a big deal of it. But on further reflection, I began to think—jeez!—I'd been a member for over forty years, served on the CCCC's executive committee and on the editorial boards of *College Composition and Communication* (*CCC*) and the Studies in Writing and Rhetoric series, and won the book of the year and article of the year awards. Maybe I shouldn't just slink away.

So I sent a letter explaining why I wasn't renewing my NCTE/CCCC membership to *College English* and *CCC*, asking for it to be published. I didn't exactly expect it would, but I felt that the lack of concern about public rhetoric in the Salaita case was a compelling enough reason to ask that the letter be considered at the leading journals. I also sent the letter to the online list Matthew

Abraham had set up in 2014 to provide information about the case to Salaita supporters because I wanted colleagues to know what I had done—I thought it might cheer them up—and because I knew the people on the list were concerned about issues of public rhetoric and the stifling of political speech, especially in the case of criticism by American academics of the Israeli occupation.

Immediately, a number of people wrote back saying they had not renewed their membership on the same grounds and that they wanted to sign the letter too. Others wrote they felt politically aligned with the letter but, for various very good reasons, were not in a position to non-renew. One group wanted to have a more general letter that didn't take non-renewing to sign—or an additional letter. We went around and around on all this for a week or so.

What resulted was an open letter signed by eleven non-renewers, addressed to NCTE and CCCC but designed for wider circulation. The letter explained that the reason we weren't renewing our membership was quite simple— namely, that "neither NCTE nor CCCC issued a statement protesting the fact that the University of Illinois Urbana-Champaign revoked Steven Salaita's tenured appointment at the very last minute, right before the academic year was to begin in 2014." Instead, NCTE had issued a position statement on academic freedom that made no "mention of the Salaita case or the fact that his hiring was revoked due to his critique of Israel and the ongoing oppression of Palestinians." We closed by saying, "We believe this failure is so grave we can no longer count ourselves as members or trust NCTE/CCCC to represent our interests." I asked the editors at *College English* and *CCC* to substitute the open letter for the one I sent earlier (they are very similar). We knew by the time of the 2016 CCCC convention in Houston that *CCC* editor Jonathan Alexander had agreed to take the letter to the editorial board meeting. (The open letter appears in Appendix B below.)

Both *College English* and *CCC* declined to publish our letter, though both editors, Kelly Ritter and Jonathan Alexander, acknowledged the seriousness of the issues it raised. Alexander and the *CCC* editorial board particularly regretted the absence of a public forum where issues like the Salaita case could be addressed. But the decision hinged finally, both editors said, on space for peer-reviewed articles. This made me wonder how I would have voted if I had been on the editorial board. I know you can't just throw academic journals open to everybody with a beef. But I also know the neutralizing effects that standard academic operating procedures can have on the political imagination.

At the same time, largely through the efforts of Paula Mathieu and Les Perelman, we succeeded in getting the letter put on the agenda of the CCCC executive committee meeting in Houston. I sent information on the handling of the Salaita case, including Abraham's email correspondence with NCTE and

CCCC officers, to CCCC chair Joyce Locke Carter and members of the executive committee. On April 22, 2016, Carter wrote to the eleven non-renewers to report on the executive committee meeting. She said, first of all, she was sorry to see us go and that our letter "received a thorough and lively discussion." By Carter's account it sounds like the main theme of the discussion was whether general principles, such as the *NCTE Position Statement on Academic Freedom*, have more "force" than taking up specific cases, such as Salaita's—whether, that is, alignment with controversial cases somehow "limits" the organization (by cheapening its brand?) or whether there are cases so "egregious" that they deserve comment. No one could agree, however, on what such a "threshold of egregiousness" might be. At any rate, Carter said, the executive committee "agreed completely we do not want to be in the business of issuing daily condemnations" (Carter's letter appears in Appendix C below).

Carter conceded, based on the email thread I sent, that communication between Abraham and NCTE/CCCC "may have gotten dropped." Finally, she "reached out" to the eleven open-letter signatories asking, "if there are any steps we could take that you feel would represent your concerns about academic freedom." After some deliberation within the group, Nancy Welch wrote a second open letter from the eleven non-renewers, addressed to Carter on April 29, 2016. To my mind, this letter presents as clear and forthright a short briefing for US college composition as you can find on the issues of public rhetoric raised by the Salaita case (the letter to Carter appears in Appendix D below).

The letter to Carter pinpoints the weaknesses of the *NCTE Position Statement on Academic Freedom*—in particular its failure to "reflect our field's understanding of public rhetoric (including the ways in which rhetorical action on urgent issues has, historically and today, tested and transgressed the boundaries of civility and social manners) and because it is silent about the rights of faculty to speak and act on issues beyond their academic fields. It is silent too about a robust conception of public discourse rights and participation that includes social media channels." The open letter also held it was not too late, that the CCCC executive committee could still "show leadership" on the Salaita case and on "the broader issues of faculty rights of participation in public controversies." We urged the executive committee to issue a statement on the dangers to academic freedom of "equating criticism of Israel and anti-Semitism" and of "using the notion of 'civility' as a restraint on political speech."

We did not heard back from Joyce Locke Carter or anybody else at CCCC until a year later, when Carter wrote Nancy Welch on March 19, 2017, that she had apparently lost the letter in a move from Texas Tech to University of Arkansas–Little Rock. She was sorry if this looked like "willful silence."

\# \# \#

The silence of composition's professional associations on the Salaita case is not an organizational aberration. Rather, this reticence to speak out continues in the Trump era on urgent public issues that involve higher education, such as the Canary Mission and Professor Watch surveillance lists of liberal and leftist faculty and Trump's Executive Order on Immigration. While AAUP, MLA, and other professional associations have issued public protests, neither NCTE nor CCCC has said anything, though it is heartening to note that the Rhetoric Society of America, through its president Gregory Clark, made a strong statement against Trump's travel ban. Many compositionists have been involved as individuals in protests against the Trump agenda, as well as in ongoing community and political projects. US college composition has a powerful legacy of *Students' Right to Their Own Language*, Mina Shaughnessy's call for a literate democracy, the politicization of composition in the 1990s, and what Paula Mathieu more recently has called the "public turn." All these currents, in updated versions, continue to energize individual composition theorists, researchers, teachers, and program administrators. The question that remains, however, is why there appears to be such a disconnect between this understanding of composition as work that participates in public life and the near invisibility of composition's professional associations in the public sphere.[6]

There are no doubt a number of possible explanations. One is that the professional insecurities of an emergent academic discipline have left US college composition's professional associations worried about the field's respectability and leery of going public on controversial issues such as the Salaita case. I wonder if there is still a residual feeling that CCCC does not belong in the same league as more high-powered professional associations such as MLA or the Organization of American Historians, which feel no qualms about addressing contentious issues in higher education and public life.

Another—and related—explanation is that there are residual traces here of an older clash of sensibility between NCTE's midwestern values of social usefulness and MLA's edgier East Coast sophistication, between work and aesthetics, public servants and gentlemen amateurs. The unwritten folk history of composition has made it all too easy for compositionists to think of MLA's position statements as the posturing of a trendy leftist intelligentsia detached from the "real work" that composition does preparing students for academic success, careers, and citizenship.[7]

A third explanation, coming from within the radical ranks of composition, is that CCCC has left behind the political intensity of composition's cultural left in the 1990s to become a self-perpetuating mechanism dedicated to reproducing a round of annual conferences, the leading journal in the field, and the career-building elections of officers and executive committee members. From this perspective, CCCC is concerned for the most part with threats to the organization that Joyce Locke Carter identifies as "declining memberships over the years, increasing costs of conventions, dwindling first-year comp in the face of dual-credit, pressures of electronic access to our journals and other materials, and attracting and retaining new members" ("Re: Response for the CCCC Executive Committee").

These explanations may hold some truth, but they do not, to my mind, capture the full complexity of US college composition's current position in the academy and in public life. A more fruitful line of inquiry can be found, I think, in Donna Strickland's revisionist history of composition *The Managerial Unconscious in the History of Composition Studies*. Strickland notes that standard accounts of composition—such as James Berlin's landmark two volumes *Writing Instruction in Nineteenth-Century American Colleges* and *Rhetoric and Reality*, Robert J. Connor's *Composition-Rhetoric*, and Sharon Crowley's *Composition in the University*—have been largely intellectual histories focused on pedagogical theories and practices. Strickland's point is to add a greater attention to how writing program administration has shaped US college composition as a profession as much as an intellectual field. Indebted to Bruce Horner's materialist analysis in *Terms of Work for Composition*, Strickland examines the often unacknowledged managerial structures in composition—what she calls the "managerial unconscious"—that have given rise to the founding of CCCC and the Council of Writing Program Administrators and the professionalization of composition in the postwar "multiversity" as the management of a stratified workplace of contingent faculty and tenure-track administrators. For Strickland, even the "social turn" of composition in the 1990s, with its emphasis on collaboration and cultural critique in participatory classrooms, mirrors "new age" managerial demands for flexible, self-starting, critically minded, and emotionally invested team players in the post-Fordist workplace.

If Strickland is concerned for the most part with managerial control by "boss compositionists" of rank-and-file composition teachers, her analysis offers clues to understanding how the structural position of composition's managerial strata plays out in the professional association's reluctance to take on controversial political issues such as the Salaita case. What she hints at is that, although the managerial roles of compositionists who form the leadership of CCCC and WPA are not fixed class identities, compositionists are nonetheless, by virtue of their structural position, caught in the middle between the higher-ups in academic administration and the workers they manage and students they serve. The work of mid-level managers accordingly is a balancing act to cope with the competing pressures that inflect professional work more generally: on the one hand, the desire to produce the use value of providing high-quality service to students, clients, and patients and, on the other, the institutional imperative to produce the exchange value of measurable outcomes, retention, impact factors, and other productivity metrics, or billable hours.[8]

As Strickland argues, writing programs are not automatically vehicles of class reproduction so much as "sites of class struggle" (15), where the results, whether exploitative or emancipatory, cannot be determined in advance but, rather, emerge from the intersection of specific practices and interests at particular historical moments. It may be that the intermediate position of composition managers has had a constraining effect on taking sides in controversies such as the Salaita case that seem remote from the necessary and often overwhelming daily activities of trying to run a decent program that meets institutional goals of cost efficiency, evidence-based assessment, accreditation, student satisfaction, career readiness, diversity and inclusion, and civic engagement. The costs of getting identified with political controversies off campus—and particularly ones such as the Israeli occupation—may simply seem too steep compared with the benefits of preserving an important tactical alliance with a dean or of making sure a writing program's reputation remains intact.

There is also, Strickland suggests, another level that must be taken into account in understanding the managerial unconscious in composition, a deeply engrained common sense in composition work that can help explain in particular why the unruliness of Salaita's tweets may seem like no more than visceral responses and over-the-top rants to rhetorically trained compositionists who are committed to the norms and procedures of deliberative democracy. In an important rereading of James Berlin's now canonical works, Strickland argues that the "practices that Berlin and others in composition identify as 'democratic' tend to overlook inequities" that silence or otherwise disqualify voices that have been marginalized as an unruly clamor outside the mainstream of deliberative discourse. Moreover, according to Strickland, this "tendency for the subject of democracy to be conceived of as homogeneous" rests on the foundation of rational argument—"the expression of positions and reasons"—as "the traditional basis of democratic process." "Perhaps," Strickland continues, "this articulation between 'democracy' and 'rational argument' is part of the problem" (116).

I think this is indeed the case in Salaita's tweets, where his rhetoric of invective against Israel and his affective identification with the plight of Palestinians appear unruly and uncontrolled, in a clash with the favored practices of rational argument (though it is hardly irrational to want to protest the devastation caused by Israel's attacks on Gaza in 2014). To extrapolate from Strickland, the problem, at least in part, may lie not with Salaita and the ferocity of his tweets but with two conceptual separations common to US college composition that are given particularly sharp expression in Berlin's work. For one thing, as just noted, Berlin privileges deliberative rhetoric, understood according to his social-epistemic taxonomy as the rational analysis and knowledge production of cultural critique, compared to epideictic rhetoric, with its mission of praising and blaming and its appeals to emotion, the register of Salaita's tweets. In this regard, by assigning deliberative rhetoric to a preferred position in the discourses of democracy, Berlin at the same time restricts the range of rhetorical activity by undermining the legitimacy of epideictic rhetoric and thereby making unruly political speech such as Salaita's an unreasoned practice or at best a subject of reasoned classroom analysis. In a second conceptual separation, the central "binary" between rhetoric and poetics in Berlin's final work *Rhetorics, Poetics, and Culture* puts a related limit into place, this time between the rational argument of deliberative rhetoric and what might be called the unruly poetics of the political imagination.[9]

As is well known, Berlin employed the rhetoric/poetics binary to explain the relation of forces in English departments and the devaluation of rhetoric and the production of discourse for the public sphere—the center of oratorical culture in the classical curriculum—by an emergent literary studies that professionalized English studies through an emphasis on the reception of literary texts, aesthetics, and the formation of taste as a privileged sensibility. Berlin's project was to dissolve this binary by refiguring English studies under the aegis of a rhetorically informed cultural studies as the means of educating students as citizen-workers for participation in public life and for the requirements of the flexible workplace.

The problem, as I see it, is that despite the nobility of Berlin's undertaking to overturn the composition/literature split in English departments and to restore rhetoric to its proper place in the academy, his vision of poetics is restricted by its focus on the institutionalized poetics of literary studies in the modern research university. Berlin draws on Raymond Williams's account of the change in the meaning of "literature" from learning in general to the cultivation of a proper "felt sense"—a Leavisite discrimination—on the part of the newly educated middle-class "reading public." Following Williams, Berlin presents poetics as a response to the dehumanizing effects of industrial capitalism in the nineteenth century, marked by the Romantic turn inward toward the "imagination" and "creativity" and away from the realm of practical affairs. As a result, the worldly domain of "rational" and "informative" discourse was assigned to rhetoric, while the canonical formation of national literatures supposedly demarcated the realm where the highest universal and spiritual values in human experience were preserved and could be passed on to new generations of students.

Berlin's analysis, to be sure, goes a long way in explaining how the literary text, isolated from rhetorical texts, became the depoliticized object of inquiry in English departments. But that hardly exhausts the possibilities of poetics. The problem, rather, is that focusing on the dominant view of poetics in literary studies as a spiritualized and ahistorical domain makes it very difficult to find a place for the unruly poetics of the political imagination found in, say, Dada, surrealism, Brecht, the Situationists, and the Black Arts movement; in punk, reggae, graffiti, and hip hop; in Occupy and Black Lives Matter; or in the fury of Salaita's tweets.

The non-institutionalized poetics of the political imagination certainly includes works coded as "literary," but, in the expanded sense I believe it deserves, such a poetics, in its root meaning, refers to the *making* of memorable messages that throw sparks into the tinderbox of contradictions that beset but have not yet found expression in popular consciousness. Occupy's "99%" and "Resist Hate" in the Trump era—or the slogan derived from the *Communist Manifesto*: "Workers of the world, unite. You have nothing to lose but your chains"—are as much examples of such a poetics as the famous opening line in Allen Ginsburg's "Howl": "I saw the best minds of my generation destroyed by madness." The unruly poetics of the political imagination are allied to the praise and blame of epideictic rhetoric but go beyond Aristotle's rhetorical categories and functions to signal, as the emotional valence of the utterance, a deep feeling of unaccountability to the powers that be, righteous indignation, and disgust.

Such a structure of feeling is evident in the imagery of Salaita's August 19, 2014 tweet: "At this point, if Netanyahu appeared on TV with a necklace made from the teeth of Palestinian children, would anybody be surprised?" The unruly poetics of Salaita's tweet is meant to shock readers into a recognition of the barbarity of Israeli state violence, much in the same way as Robert Bly's poem "Counting Small-Boned Bodies" exposed the bureaucratic violence of the daily body counts of dead enemy soldiers during the Vietnam War:

> Let's count the bodies over again.
>
> If we could only make the bodies smaller,
> The size of skulls,
> We could make a whole plain white with skulls in the moonlight.
>
> If we could only make the bodies smaller,
> Maybe we could get
> A whole year's kill in front of us on a desk! (32)

Unruly poetics are transgressive, not for the thrill of transgression but as the rigors—and the sorrow—exacted in reckoning with the ruins of the present in order to imagine alternative social futures and new social solidarities. This is why unruly poetics such as Salaita's tweets can sound so disruptive and uncivil, like the soundtrack to a state of emergency: it is meant to be boisterous, obstreperous, wayward, and disobedient, signifying a disaffiliation from the way things are. Unruly poetics makes demands that are necessary to sustaining human life but that cannot be met by the present state of affairs. It brings in the noise. The unruly poetics of the political imagination make the integrated— at the University of Illinois and elsewhere—want to turn it off, to stop hearing the shouts of the unreconciled.

The problem, as we saw Strickland pose it earlier, is that the equation of democracy and rational argument cannot grasp how the sheer intolerance of unruly poetics—the refusal to tolerate the suffering and devastation of the existing order—is the work of the political imagination in preparing what Sharon Crowley calls the "emotional climates" that make change possible (58). If anything, the unruly poetics of the political imagination begins with an intolerance toward the very idea that the so-called marketplace of ideas promoted by university administrators and the mainstream respectable media like the *New York Times* or *Washington Post* is in fact free and open, the site of reasoned and civil exchange in an actually existing deliberative democracy. The unruly poetics of the political imagination understands the allure of deliberative rhetoric and how its iconic representation in the polis or the town hall meeting was capable of seducing Berlin, even though he knew instinctively that the game was rigged. What makes the political imagination appear so unruly is in part the poetic force of will required to figure, against powerful mainstream influences, the practice of deliberative democracy as counterfactual, a political horizon of democratic participation that has not been reached, the forms and purposes of which can only be determined by the relentless exposé of the limits and hypocrisy of the existing order and the visionary imagination of a new social future. This, in effect, is the struggle to overcome the separation of rhetoric and poetics that preoccupied Berlin, though the terms and the political dynamic are different.

\#   \#   \#

In closing, I want to note that although NCTE/CCCC never took a position on the Salaita case, the case has not exactly gone away either. At the CCCC 2017 annual convention, largely through the efforts of Bruce Horner, a Think Tank on Public Policy and CCCC took place, inspired in part by the Salaita case and in part by the looming threats of the Trump agenda (Horner's report on the

Think Tank appears below in Appendix E). I am a positive person, and despite the fact that I am no longer a member of NCTE/CCCC, I think it is not out of place, given my continuing, now unaffiliated commitment to the study and teaching of writing, to end with a suggestion in line with the work of the Think Tank on Public Policy about what US college composition's professional associations could do concerning unruly political speech such as Salaita's tweets.

The suggestion (which I'll come to in a minute) is based on the acknowledgment that CCCC does not at present have the organizational capacity to respond quickly to breaking issues such as the University of Illinois's violation of academic freedom and fair hiring practices—or Professor Watch or Trump's Executive Order on Immigration. CCCC remains a satellite operation of NCTE, without an executive director or the professional staff that enables other professional associations such as MLA to issue position statements in a timely fashion. This is a long-term issue that has been raised before about whether CCCC should break ties with NCTE and become an independent professional association. To my mind, that remains an interesting question.

Still, even in the current state of affairs, as the think tank made clear, there are things CCCC could do. To the suggestions offered at the think tank, I want to add an approach suggested by Matthew Abraham in his correspondence with NCTE/CCCC—that is, CCCC could draw on the professional expertise of its members to produce a report or white paper that clarifies what is at stake in the Salaita case for the concerns of public rhetoric. It could explain the genre of tweets and the limits and uses of the conventions of social media. It could evaluate the shaky claim that opposition to Israeli policies and actions amounts to anti-Semitism—and bring to light the interests behind this claim. And it could look very closely at the University of Illinois's civility doctrine as a restraint on rhetorical activity, even in its unruliest forms. CCCC, in other words, could contribute to a wider and more informed public understanding of public rhetoric and the unruly poetics of the political imagination.[10]

The big question, of course, is whether CCCC has the political will to do so, to connect the now flourishing scholarship on public rhetoric to the troubles and political possibilities of unruly poetics in public life. Most of all, the intellectual and political challenge is whether CCCC can resist the mainstream discourse that a deliberative democracy actually exists in the United States and effectively defines a credible rhetorical center of rational inquiry and argument. The task, rather, in my view is to reveal how a supposedly free market of ideas operates to patrol the boundaries of the status quo by casting the unruly poetics of the political imagination as the moral equivalent to the fear and bigotry spread through the demagoguery of Trump and his white supremacist America First supporters. What remains to be explained is how the civility doctrine of the rhetorical center pushes desires for human liberation, social justice, and a sustainable future to the margins—and how, like the return of the repressed, these longings reappear in the unruly poetics of the political imagination.

APPENDIX A. NATIONAL COUNCIL OF TEACHERS OF ENGLISH, POSITION STATEMENT ON ACADEMIC FREEDOM

NCTE Position Statement on Academic Freedom

Approved by the NCTE Executive Committee, November 2014

In its support of intellectual freedom, NCTE maintains that students have the right to materials and educational experiences that promote open inquiry, diversity in thought and expression, and respect for others (*NCTE Position Statement on Intellectual Freedom*, 2014). Academic freedom is intellectual freedom in academic contexts, though it may encompass a wider spectrum of rights, freedoms, interests, and responsibilities. The protection of academic freedom, required at all levels of education, not only serves the common good but also enhances academic integrity and the overall quality of education while protecting students from indoctrination.

Inherent in academic freedom is both a moral and an educational obligation to uphold the ethics of respect and protect the values of inquiry necessary for teaching and learning. Because situations involving academic freedom differ according to circumstances and grade level, NCTE encourages the discussion of the principles of academic freedom listed below, within faculties and institutions for the purpose of developing policies and procedures that will protect such freedoms.

Freedom of Belief and Identity

- Educational institutions may present alternative views and values but may not impose or require belief or commitment.

Freedom of Expression and Discussion

- In academic contexts, students and teachers have the right to express their views on any matter relevant to the curriculum.

Freedom of Inquiry

- Inquiry must not be suppressed by restricting access to particular authors, topics, or viewpoints or by hindering the formulation of objectionable conclusions.

Freedom from Indoctrination

- Educators and educational institutions must not require or coerce students to modify their beliefs or values. Efforts to convince students to modify their beliefs or values must be academically justifiable.

- Curriculum must be determined by teachers and other professionals on the basis of academic considerations. Suggested modifications of curriculum should go through a process in place by the school or district.

Equality, Privacy, and Due Process

- All students and faculty have an equal right to academic freedom.
- Educators and educational institutions must refrain from academically unjustified inquiries into beliefs, values, interests, or affiliations of students and faculty.
- Academic institutions must ensure that their formal and informal procedures provide sufficient due process to protect academic freedom.
- These principles are adapted from *Liberty and Learning: Academic Freedom for Teachers and Students* (Heinemann, 2009) by David Moshman

APPENDIX B. OPEN LETTER OF ELEVEN NON-RENEWERS

April 1, 2016
Open Letter to NCTE and CCCC Officials, Colleagues, and Friends:

We are not renewing our memberships in NCTE/CCCC, and we want to explain why. The reason is actually quite simple: unlike other major professional associations, neither NCTE nor CCCC issued a statement protesting the fact that the University of Illinois Urbana-Champaign revoked Steven Salaita's tenured appointment at the very last minute, right before the academic year was to begin in 2014.

The details of the case—and how they are tied up in wider controversies about Israel and Palestine—are public knowledge and do not need further exposition on our part. What concerns us is the moral and professional failure of NCTE/CCCC to address the unhiring issue in a forthright and principled manner. By June 2015, when AAUP censured the University of Illinois Urbana-Champaign for this violation of normal hiring procedures, free speech, and academic freedom, a number of professional associations—including the Modern Languages Association, Organization of American Historians, American Studies Association, National Association of Women's Studies, and Native American and Indigenous Studies—had already issued statements of protest. In contrast, all that NCTE/CCCC was able to do was issue the very general non-objectionable *Position Statement on Academic Freedom* in November 2014, without any mention of the Salaita case or the fact that his hiring was revoked due to his critique of Israel and the ongoing oppression of Palestinians.

We believe this failure is so grave that we can no longer count ourselves as members or trust NCTE/CCCC to represent our interests.

Sincerely,

Matthew Abraham Marc Bousquet Diana George Tom Huckin Harriet Malinowitz
Ken S. McAllister Jaime A. Mejia Aneil Rallin Luisa Rodriguez John Trimbur
Nancy Welch

APPENDIX C. CCCC CHAIR JOYCE LOCKE CARTER'S LETTER TO THE ELEVEN NON-RENEWERS

Matthew Abraham, Marc Bousquet, Diana George, Tom Huckin, Harriet Malinowitz, Ken S. McAllister, Jaime A. Mejia, Aneil Rallin, Luisa Rodriguez, John Trimbur, and Nancy Welch

22 April 2016

Dear signatories,

I received the letter detailing your resignation from the CCCC over the Salaita matter on April 1 before our Houston convention. I immediately reached out to Les Perelman and Paula Mathieu, who had forwarded me the letter, which led me to an email exchange with John Trimbur later that day. John provided me with some helpful context.

First, let me say I'm sorry to see you go. Looking through our Houston program, as well as previous convention programs, it's evident just how deep your participation in the C's has been, and it's clear that your absence will be our organization's loss going forward. I suspect you have also sent resignation letters to RSA, ATTW, CWPA, and other organizations representing our writing discipline, as they also did not respond forcefully to the Salaita matter. Our entire field's quality is certainly going to be lessened by your departure.

Although your letter did not request that the CCCC take any specific action, we did put it on the agenda of the Executive Committee, where it received a thorough and lively discussion on the Wednesday of our convention in Houston. Several members argued that the NCTE has a firm position statement on academic freedom (http://www2 .ncte.org/statement/academic-freedom), and that such a statement has more force than individual letters about specific cases. Other members disagreed, and argued that egregious cases like Steven Salaita's might require a response beyond such a position statement. Those members did, however, express concern over how an organization could discern the threshold of egregiousness, as it were, so that the organization could respond forcefully to some issues, but not to the majority of smaller offenses that take place all the time in higher education. We agreed completely that we do not want to be in the business of issuing daily condemnations.

Looking at the email thread that John provided me, it does appear that communications in 2014 between you and NCTE/CCCC may have gotten dropped. I don't think the intent is knowable in 2016. As you realize, the key figures in those email exchanges are no longer involved: Adam Banks resigned from NCTE, Kent Williamson died, and Ernest Morrell rotated off the NCTE Presidential Team. With so much time elapsed and personnel changed, there's not much for me, the new Executive Committee, or the new Executive Director to do regarding events of Fall 2014.

That said, since you ended your letter with the charge that our failure was so grave that you can no longer trust NCTE/CCCC to represent your interests, I wanted to reach out and ask if there are any steps we could take that you feel would represent your concerns about academic freedom. I know we cannot repair the events of 2014, but we *can* strive for excellence in the present and the future. We would certainly welcome you back and would be interested in working with you so that we could regain your trust going forward.

Sincerely yours,

Joyce Carter

Chair, CCCC

APPENDIX D. LETTER OF THE ELEVEN NON-RENEWERS TO JOYCE CARTER LOCKE

April 29, 2016

Dear Joyce,

Thank you for your note outlining the circumstances surrounding the CCCC Executive Board's inaction in the days and months following Steven Salaita's firing from the University of Illinois and requesting input on meaningful steps that can still be taken.

It is not at all too late for the CCCC Executive Board to show leadership on Dr. Salaita's case and the broader issue of faculty rights of participation in public controversies, including via social media and including on issues both within and beyond their academic fields. As you may know, Dr. Salaita once again faces an administration—this time the president of the American University of Beirut—seeking to cancel his appointment.

What we ask is for a statement or letter from the CCCC Executive Board that focuses on the Salaita case and the dangers to academic freedom it reveals

(1) of equating criticism of Israel and anti-Semitism, and

(2) of using the notion of "civility" as a restraint on political speech (whether unruly or not), including on social media.

A statement or letter from the CCCC Executive Board highlighting Dr. Salaita's case does not show disregard for other cases of faculty subjected to discipline and dismissal for their political speech and participation. Indeed, it seems appropriate for a statement to put Dr. Salaita's case in the broader picture of imperiled academic freedom and the deep chill on professorial speech across all ranks when even tenure is no longer any safeguard for faculty who contribute to campus and public debates.

A statement or letter is also needed because the NCTE statement on academic free-dom does not reflect our field's understanding of public rhetoric (including the ways in which rhetorical action on urgent issues has, historically and today, tested and trans-gressed the boundaries of civility and social manners) and because it is silent about the rights of faculty to speak and act on issues beyond their academic fields. It is silent too about a robust conception of public discourse rights and participation that includes social media channels.

Such a statement and show of leadership from the CCCC Executive Board, widely distributed through publication in one of our flagship journals, would do much to re-store us to the organization and, more importantly, break the board's silence on attacks that go to the heart of our discipline and our livelihoods.

Sincerely,

Matthew Abraham Marc Bousquet Diana George Tom Huckin Ken S. McAllister Jaime Armin Mejia Harriet Malinowitz Aneil Rallin Luisa Rodriguez John Trim-bur Nancy Welch

APPENDIX E. REPORT ON THE THINK TANK ON PUBLIC POLICY AND CCCC AT CCCC 2017 CONVENTION

TO: Carolyn Calhoon-Dillahunt

FROM: Bruce Horner

RE: Think Tank on Public Policy and CCCC at CCCC 2017 convention

In response to your call for reports on the 2017 Think Tanks, I present below my report on the 2017 CCCC Think Tank on Public Policy. This report is based on prelimi-nary draft reports from Nancy Welch and myself that were circulated by email to those who had attended the think tank who provided us with contact information. The report itself was circulated for comments prior to my sending it to you.

The Public Policy think tank was proposed in response to growing concerns about the apparent lack of involvement by CCCC as an organization in addressing matters of public policy relevant to the interests of the organization's members. Those concerns were illustrated by the decision by several prominent members of CCCC to resign from the organization to protest the organization's silence regarding the decision by the Uni-versity of Illinois to withdraw its offer to Steven Salaita.

The Think Tank met on Thursday, March 16, 2017, from 11:00 to 12:15. Approxi-mately twenty individuals participated. Those present first broke into small groups that then reconvened to share ideas. A handout distributed at the beginning of the session was used as a heuristic to guide the work of the participants.

Think Tank participants agreed that CCCC has to play a more public intellectual role, particularly in light of the current sociopolitical climate, nationally and globally, characterized by

- growing anti-intellectualism
- legislation, policies, and broader currents impacting CCCC members' ability to teach and students' ability to be present in and participate in academic realms through erosion of protections for rhetorical participation and ability to take part in public discourse beyond as well as within the academy erosion of the established nature of higher education as a site for the pursuit of truth through research, debate, and critique

At the very least, these seem to call for a public defense of the rights of writing faculty as public intellectuals to address this climate and its effects.

We rejected the concern that involvement by CCCC in making public statements on such matters would risk the professional status of the organization and alienate members. Instead, we believe such involvement might raise the public profile of the organization and lead to more, rather than less, involvement by members and prospective members.

Participants came up with various criteria by which an event or issue would merit an official response by CCCC as an organization, and we proposed possible means by which such responses and pro-active statements might be produced and amplified in terms of changes and charges to structural elements of the organization and in terms of specific projects that might be commissioned.

Proposed Criteria for Identifying Matters Meriting Official Statements from CCCC

Participants suggested that official statements by the CCCC might be called for in response to events that surface in national and international news media affecting the professional work of CCCC members as teachers and scholars of composition. In addition to events (e.g., legislation, university actions, statements by public figures) threatening or otherwise affecting the members' immediate work teaching and studying composition (and the teaching and learning of composition), these might also include events affecting the work of students and prospective students (e.g., K–12 students); matters of academic freedom; and matters of working conditions. It was also suggested that CCCC can respond to matters that have not received national/international media attention but about which CCCC members have professional expertise as teachers and scholars.

Proposed Means for Identifying, Formulating, and Publicizing Official CCCC Statements on Matters of Public Concern

We suggested the following means by which CCCC as a large and diverse organization might produce, and learn how to produce, such statements:

Solicit "planks" from standing groups and SIGs to provide CCCC direction for the delineation of matters like the above, and charge them to formulate and propose action statements;

Reinstate a public policy committee, to be charged with putting together a platform with input ("planks") from standing groups and SIGs and make recommendations when people should take action and in what form;

Learn, and learn from, the processes by which MLA and other similar organizations identify matters on which to issue public statements and formulate and publicize these in timely fashion (we can learn from others rather than reinventing the wheel);

Endorse other organizations' statements and reach out for joint statements: We don't have to do it all ourselves, and it's better if we don't try to do it all ourselves;

Engage and amplify and revise previous statements in light of emerging conditions and issues;

Have a forum at CCCC to understand how existing statements can be used;

Leverage the policy network that's already in place (and knowing more about it so that members beyond the leadership in NCTE and CCCC know what work is being done and can engage with and inform that work).

NOTES

1. I wish to acknowledge the editors and reviewers of this chapter for their helpful comments. Thanks especially to Bruce Horner for a careful reading, useful information, and comradely suggestions.

2. A good source of background information on the Salaita case can be found in the AAUP report *Academic Freedom and Tenure: The University of Illinois at Urbana-Champaign*. An appendix to the report includes a selection of tweets supplied by UIUC legal counsel and by Salaita.

3. Background on pro-Israel efforts in academia can be found in Jewish Voice for Peace, *Stifling Dissent: How Israel's Defenders Use False Charges of Anti-Semitism to Limit the Debate over Israel on Campus*. Also see Joe Catron, "On U.S. Campuses, Pro-Israel Groups Target Supporters of Palestinian Rights"; David Palumbo-Liu, "New Attack on Free Speech: Pro-Israel Groups Wage War on Campus Freedom."

4. See www.thepetitionsite.com/995/171/092/rhetoric-composition-and-communi cationscholars-statement-on-salaita-case/.

5. I take this point about the field-specific character of composition's silence in the Salaita case from Joyce Locke Carter, who asked (Carter, "Re: Email Chain") if any of the other professional associations in composition (Rhetoric Society, WPA, and the various technical writing associations) had issued statements and whether CCCC was an "outlier" or "if it's possible this situation might be rooted in disciplinarity somehow." Carter, of course, is not responsible for (and would probably not agree with) the direction I have taken in this inquiry, but I am indebted nonetheless.

6. Bruce Horner reminded me that there used to be a joint NCTE/CCCC committee on public policy but it was discontinued. The NCTE Doublespeak Committee has persisted since 1974 as an "ironic tribute to public speakers who have perpetuated language that is grossly deceptive, evasive, euphemistic, confusing, or self-centered"—people such as Trump and Rahm Emanuel or the American Petroleum Institute. Interestingly, no award was given in 2014.

7. Joyce Locke Carter's reflections on a round table at the 2017 CCCC convention, organized by Bruce Horner, to consider how CCCC might respond to public issues such as the Salaita case captures this sentiment cogently: "The MLA was held out on Thursday as a model for engagement—I disagree completely, as I find the MLA clownish in its bandwagon proclamations" (Carter, "Re: Response for the CCCC Executive Committee").

8. For more on the contradiction between use value and exchange value, see John Trimbur, *Solidarity or Service: Composition and the Problem of Expertise*, 76–80, 163–64.

9. Bruce Horner noted in an email that there may also be a third conceptual separation at work, this time between composition and rhetoric, whereby those who identify with composition as research-based pedagogical work may rule out rhetorical matters such as the Salaita case as being simply theoretical and detached from classrooms and programs. For more on this split, see Bruce Horner and Min-Zhan Lu, "Working Rhetoric and Composition."

10. For an example of such a report, see PEN America's *And Campus for All: Diversity, Inclusion, and Freedom of Speech at U.S. Universities*.

WORKS CITED

American Association of University Professors (AAUP). *Academic Freedom and Tenure: The University of Illinois at Urbana- Champaign*. April 2015. www.aaup.org/report/UIUC/.

Berlin, James. *Rhetoric and Reality: Writing Instruction in American Colleges, 1900–1985*. Southern Illinois University Press, 1987.

Berlin, James. *Rhetorics, Poetics, and Culture: Refiguring College English Studies*. National Council of Teachers of English, 1996.

Berlin, James. *Writing Instruction in Nineteenth-Century American Colleges*. Southern Illinois University Press, 1984.

Bly, Robert. *The Light around the Body*. Harper and Row, 1967.

Carter, Joyce Locke. "Re: Email Chain." E-mail received by John Trimbur, Les Perlman, and Paula Mathieu, April 2, 2016.

Carter, Joyce Locke. "Re: Response for the CCCC Executive Committee." E-mail received by Nancy Welch et al., March 19, 2017.

Catron, Joe. "On U.S. Campuses, Pro-Israel Groups Target Supporters of Palestinian Rights." *Truthout*, December 13, 2015. www.truth-out.org/news/item/34007-on-us -campuses-pro-israel-groups-target-supporters-of-palestinian-rights/.

Connors, Robert J. *Composition-Rhetoric: Backgrounds, Theory, and Pedagogy.* University of Pittsburgh Press, 1997.

Crowley, Sharon. *Composition in the University: Historical and Polemical Essays.* University of Pittsburgh Press, 1998.

Crowley, Sharon. *Toward a Civil Discourse: Rhetoric and Fundamentalism.* University of Pittsburgh Press, 2006.

Flaherty, Colleen. "In a Hurricane." *Inside Higher Ed,* August 14, 2014. www.insidehigher ed.com/news/2014/08/15/cary-nelson-faces-backlash-over-his-views-controversial -scholar/.

Horner, Bruce. *Terms of Work for Composition: A Materialist Critique.* State University of New York Press, 2000.

Horner, Bruce, and Min-Zhan Lu. "Working Rhetoric and Composition." *College English* 72, no. 5 (2010): 470–94.

Jewish Voice for Peace. *Stifling Dissent: How Israel's Defenders Use False Charges of Anti-Semitism to Limit the Debate over Israel on Campus.* 2015. www.jewishvoiceforpeace.org /stifling-dissent/.

Levine, Joseph. "Did Salaita Cross the Line of 'Civility'?" *New York Times,* December 14, 2014. www.opinionator.blogs.nytimes.com/2014/12/14/did-salaita-cross-the-line-of -civility/.

Moshman, David. *Liberty and Learning: Academic Freedom for Teachers.* Heinemann, 2009.

Palumbo-Liu, David. "New Attack on Free Speech: Pro-Israel Groups Wage War on Campus Freedom." *Salon,* September 24, 2016. www.salon.com/2016/09/24/new-attack-on -free-speech-pro-israel-groups-wage-war-on-campus-freedom/.

PEN America. *And Campus for All: Diversity, Inclusion, and Freedom of Speech at U.S. Universities.* October 16, 2016. www.pen.org/sites/default/files/PEN_ campus_report_final _online_2.pdf.

Strickland, Donna. *The Managerial Unconscious in the History of Composition Studies.* Southern Illinois University Press, 2011.

Trimbur, John. *Solidarity or Service: Composition and the Problem of Expertise.* Heinemann-Boynton/Cook, 2011.

Williams, Raymond. *Marxism and Literature.* Oxford University Press, 1978.

Wise, Phyllis M. "The Principles on Which We Stand." *Chicago Tonight,* August 22, 2014. www.chicagotonight.wttw.com/sites/default/files/article/file-attachments/PhyllisWise Statement.pdf.

PART III

LIMITS AND HORIZONS

11

ANSWERING THE WORLD'S ANTICIPATION

THE RELEVANCE OF *NATIVE SON* TO TWENTY-FIRST-CENTURY PROTEST MOVEMENTS

DEBORAH MUTNICK

> When black people get free, everybody gets free.
>
> —Alicia Garza, "Herstory"

> Life had made the plot over and over again, to the extent that I knew it by heart.
>
> —Richard Wright, *Native Son*

Famously called "everybody's protest novel" (Baldwin 13), Richard Wright's *Native Son* was initially hailed by reviewers as a literary breakthrough for African American fiction, a masterpiece, "the Negro 'American Tragedy'" (Jack 86). Critics compared Wright not only to Dreiser but also to Dostoevsky, Steinbeck, and Dickens (Fabre 178). Yet even Peter Monro Jack's favorable review of the novel in the *New York Times* claimed that Bigger Thomas, trapped in slums, his family on relief, "represents an *impasse* rather than a complex, and his tragedy is to be born into a black and immutable minority race" (86). On the first night of his new job as a chauffeur for the wealthy Daltons, Bigger kills their wayward communist daughter, Mary, by smothering her to death with a pillow, afraid of being detected and accused of rape by blind Mrs. Dalton. He then burns her remains in the furnace and later murders his black girlfriend, Bessie. Wright meant Bigger's grisly crimes to shock his readers into awareness of the horrifying dialectic of social and psychological consequences of American racism. It is just this dialectic that Frantz Fanon stresses in *Black Skin, White Masks*, observing, "In the end, Bigger Thomas acts. To put an end to his tension, he acts, he answers the world's anticipation" (139).

Bigger is answering a world—Chicago's South Side in 1930s America, fraught by global economic depression, catapulting toward World War II—in which millions of black Southerners fled Jim Crow terror for northern urban centers in search of "the warmth of other suns" (Wright, *Black Boy* 414). Their hopes were punctured by new social realities—different but ultimately as debilitating as the long nightmare of slavery and peonage they had left behind in the South—realities they did not so much discover as help create as six million black people migrated north from 1910 to 1970. Seventy-five years after *Native Son's* publication, a series of highly publicized police killings of black people from July 2014 to April 2015 brought renewed attention to the problem of racism in the United States, recalling the Kerner Commission's 1968 warning that America was "moving toward two societies, one black, one white, separate and unequal." I argue that the black, radical, Marxist critique of capitalism that informed Wright's portrait of Bigger Thomas in early twentieth-century Jim Crow America offers a critical lens for contemporary social justice movements such as Black Lives Matter (BLM) as they confront the rise of the "new Jim Crow" (Alexander). For composition scholars familiar with Edward P. J. Corbett's discomfort with the rhetoric of the "closed fist" embodied by the Black Power salute, this same analysis helps explain how liberal ideology—what Ta-Nehisi Coates calls "the Dream"—perpetuates racism in all its myriad, inhumane, violent manifestations.[1] For teachers across disciplines, this analysis suggests a critical pedagogy capable of uncovering the underlying patterns and structures of surface forms of reality and illuminating the "unruly rhetoric" that is the subject of this book.

In response to the current wave of violence against black people, widely broadcast through cell phone videos and social media, the Black Lives Matter movement rose up across the United States and the world. Founders Alicia Garza, Patrice Cullors, and Opal Tometi call it a "herstory," in which Cullors tweeted the hashtag #blacklivesmatter after George Zimmerman was acquitted of murdering seventeen-year-old Trayvon Martin (Garza, "Herstory"). Described by its founders as an affirmation of the humanity, resilience, and social contributions of black people, the hashtag, posted by Garza on Facebook, took hold as a grassroots movement after Michael Brown was shot dead in Ferguson,

Missouri, by Police Officer Darren Wilson on August 9, 2014. Just a few weeks previously, Eric Garner had died in a Staten Island police officer's illegal choke-hold. Over the next ten months—July 2014 to April 2015—US police also killed, among other black people, Tanisha Anderson, Akai Gurley, Tamir Rice, Walter Scott, and Freddie Gray. Of the five hundred US police fatalities reported by the *Guardian* in the first six months of 2015, unarmed blacks were killed at twice the rate as whites (Swaine), whose deaths Garza refers to as "collateral damage" in state-sponsored repression of black Americans ("Indicting").[2]

My focus here is on twenty-first-century Bigger Thomases, but there are several points I want to clarify from the outset. First, together with the litany of black men killed by police, many women of color from Eleanor Bumpers to Tarika Wilson and Tanisha Anderson, as well as transgender and queer black people like Tiffany Edwards and Cemia Dove, have been victims of police vi-olence. Second, though outside the scope of this essay, it is important to note that it is specifically Bigger Thomas's crimes against women that have led sev-eral critics to describe him as "monstrous" and his creator as "misogynistic." The novel is, according to early reviewer David L. Cohn, a "corrosive study in hate" (659; also Baldwin; Ellison; Mootry; Rascoe).[3] Third, rather than simply acknowledge my own identity (as a white, middle-class, female), I wish more meaningfully to locate my point of view in relation to Wright's perspective on race as always historically situated and dialectical. Anthony Dawahare argues that *Native Son* "both affirms and negates the very notion of black experience and presents a challenge for those who want to affirm black experience as somehow self-contained and others who want to liquidate it in some univer-sal category" (66). At the same time, to avoid the muddled thinking of lib-eral white guilt, white allies need to understand Garza's point that "when black people get free, everybody gets free" ("Herstory").

With these provisos, I offer an analysis of recent twenty-first-century ac-tivist responses to structural racism and related problems—the plot Wright knew by heart—in light of *Native Son*. Viewed through the conceptual lens of Marx's *Erscheinungsformen* (translated into English as the "phenomenal forms" or "forms of manifestation"), Bigger is the manifestation in *Native Son* of the underlying social structures of 1930s America, a racist, industrializing society founded on slavery and hit hard by the Great Depression.[4] This idea of phenomenal forms is evident, too, in Mikhail Bakhtin's chronotope—"an optic for reading texts as x-rays of the forces at work in the culture system from which they spring" (425–26). I will return to the question of the phenomenal forms presently; as for the chronotope, I invoke it here because it resonates with Wright's attribution of his "x-ray vision" in *Native Son* to his discovery in Chicago that "Bigger Thomas was not black all the time; he was white, too, and there were literally millions of him, everywhere. . . . It was as though I had put on a pair of spectacles whose power was that of an x-ray enabling me to see deeper into the lives of men" (*Native Son* 441).

What Wright saw in the 1930s was this: "a complex struggle for life going on in my country, a struggle in which I was involved . . . [and in which] the Southern scheme of oppression was but an appendage of a far vaster and in many respects more ruthless and impersonal commodity-profit machine" (*Native Son* 441). Wright exposed the hypocrisy of the wealthy, liberal Daltons who "gave millions of dollars for Negro education" yet rented rat-infested kitchenettes to Bigger's family and other "Negroes only in this prescribed area, this corner of the city tumbling down from rot" (174). It was a time of international revolutionary fervor, inspired by the Russian Revolution, sparking a "sullen" consciousness in Bigger (174) and convincing masses worldwide that socialism was inevitable. As a young, Mississippi-born, black migrant with an eighth-grade education, Wright arrived in Chicago in 1927 in the midst of swift urban change and radical political rhetoric. By 1934, he had joined the John Reed Club and the Communist Party USA (CPUSA); in 1935, he joined the Federal Writers' Project (FWP). Indelibly shaped by these experiences, as he was by his personal knowledge of black life and the white power structure, Wright forged a dialectical understanding of himself and his world.[5] With this "x-ray vision," I argue, we can more clearly see how the rhetoric of liberal democracy—the "open hand"—masks the violent means by which the dominant white capitalist power structure controls and destroys not only the Bigger Thomases of the world but also, ultimately, the very idea of "the Dream."

RICHARD WRIGHT'S X-RAY VISION

The Black Lives Matter movement is a response to contemporary structural racism and state violence, which systematically devalue, exploit, and destroy black lives. Part of a worldwide revolt against economic austerity and political oppression that spread from the Arab Spring and the 15-M Movement to Occupy Wall Street (OWS) and other uprisings, BLM is defined, as was OWS, by horizontal, consensus-based leadership—or leaderlessness—in a period of tenuous political direction with little unity or ideological agreement on how to turn the tide of the destructive forces unleashed by late capitalism. While conditions have improved for middle-class African Americans benefiting from the victories of the twentieth-century civil rights movement, they remain materially unchanged or worse for masses of black people whose bleak experiences of poverty, inequality, and terror are not unlike those that Wright encountered growing up in Mississippi in the early 1900s. As Garza puts it, "Black folks have been murdered since we were brought here" ("Indicting"). Despite these comparable contemporary exigencies, there is no parallel today to the powerful international socialist movements that forged Wright's worldview.

Through his experiences in the John Reed Club and the CPUSA, Wright discovered revolutionary ideas that excited his imagination and enabled him to envision the "possibilities of *alliances* between the American Negro and other people possessing a kindred consciousness" (*Native Son* 441). Similarly, twenty-first-century social movements have awakened hundreds of thousands of activists who express solidarity with protests worldwide across national, racial, and gender boundaries. Some tangible gains were made by the US anti–police brutality movement, such as the indictments of six Baltimore police officers for the murder of Freddie Gray (a case, however, that ultimately concluded in 2016 with zero convictions). Likewise, left-wing electoral victories, including Syriza in Greece, Podemos in Madrid and Barcelona, and an Occupy activist to the Seattle city council, make clear the potentially transformative power of new movements. Such achievements suggest that some of the grassroots uprisings since 2011 have begun to solidify and mature, inspired by one another and the contagion of social media that have helped expand traditional means of outreach to broader publics. However, in contrast to Wright's embrace by Chicago's well-organized left-wing milieu of workers, socialists, and communists, activists in today's new movements must rebuild a fractured left and clarify an ideological framework to guide, support, and unify their work. The left's current disarray can be explained by many factors, including persistent government surveillance and repression, the failures of twentieth-century socialism, especially the Soviet Union as the only counterforce to US imperialism, a weak labor movement, and an aggressive anticommunism campaign that only recently seems to have lost some influence after remaining remarkably effective decades after the Cold War ended.[6]

In addition to fierce political repression in the United States at the height of the Cold War, covert operations under the FBI's Counter Intelligence Program (COINTELPRO) from 1956 to 1971 sought to destroy left-wing movements, especially civil rights and black liberation organizations, sowing division and suspicion among them and forging a reality that preoccupied Wright toward the end of his life, as recorded in his unpublished last novel *Island of Hallucination* written in the late 1950s (Maxwell 30–31). Today it can be difficult to separate the impact of state repression from the internal contradictions of the left, whose authoritarian style and reproduction of racist and sexist ideologies alienated people of color and women in particular, creating political divisions that continue to haunt us. Such political divisions persist despite efforts by activists like Alicia Garza to link antiracist and working-class struggles. Garza points to the need for unity across racial lines, viewing repression in terms of not only state-sponsored violence but also economic austerity, attacks on labor, unequal access to housing, education, and jobs, and increasingly, deprivation of basic needs such as water ("Indicted").

At the same time, Garza and other BLM activists situate antiracist protests squarely in the tradition of the black liberation movement that repudiated a predominantly white and frequently racist left. Wright's experience with the CPUSA—which eventually led him to embrace first "third way" socialism, with European leftists such as Jean-Paul Sartre, and then anticolonial, Pan-African struggles worldwide—is mirrored by current left formations grappling with the tension between the need for international working-class solidarity and the demands of national liberation movements (see, e.g., Maxwell 30).[7] The complexity of Wright's commitments is significant. Despite recent scholarship reevaluating his relevance today, his consistently anti-imperialist, anticapitalist, antiracist stance is not widely understood by casual readers of *Native Son* or *Black Boy* who are unfamiliar with his biography or the history of radical movements in the United States and abroad.[8] Unlike some other former party members, he never betrayed comrades or repudiated left politics. He was also painfully aware throughout his career that he was a target of CIA and FBI surveillance.

What makes Wright's Marxist worldview and lifelong commitment to black liberation relevant today is his grasp of the contradictions of modern industrial society. He understood that the savage exploitation and exclusion of the Biggers of this world—black, white, American, Russian—from its dazzling array of material and cultural goods had also produced conditions that called this multiracial working class into existence, thrusting workers together in urban centers and generating the capacity for alliances among them.[9] Wright thus perceived the underlying structures of what Marx termed *Erscheinungsformen* or "phenomenal forms"—categories that arise from "the relations of production" and "often represent themselves in inverted form" (Marx, *Capital*).[10] Marx goes on to explain the effect of this inversion: "The final pattern of economic relations as seen on the surface, in their real existence and consequently in the conceptions by which the bearers and agents of these relations seek to understand them, is very different from, and indeed quite the reverse of, their inner but concealed essential pattern, and the conception corresponding to it" ("Supplementary"). The phenomenal forms are the perceptible, surface manifestations of "real existence" that conceal the inner workings or underlying structures of reality and may create ideological misconceptions—for example, the belief that certain behaviors and conditions are the cause of poverty rather than the effects of systemic social injustice. This understanding of the material basis not only for today's outrageous polarization of wealth but also its deepening racial divisions is especially important to recover in the United States, where for more than fifty years "Marx has been a taboo" (Wolff).

The word and the world are closely interwoven, Paulo Freire tells us, and reading them with "x-ray vision" can be thought of as an educational project. Wright's novel is especially illuminating with respect to the *Erscheinungsformen* because it names the underlying structures—the relations of production—that explain Bigger's rage and reveal his dreams and frustrations. For Wright, Bigger represents the black Southern migrant, what Marx called the *lumpenproletariat*, one of "those millions whom capitalism has crushed and maimed" (qtd. in Fabre 186); he is "resentful toward whites, sullen, angry, ignorant, emotionally unstable . . . unable even, because of his own lack of inner organization which American oppression has fostered in him, to unite with the members of his own race" (*Native Son* 448). It was precisely this characterization of Bigger to which critics—black and white alike—objected: as hateful (Cohn) and "sub-human . . . constrained, therefore, to battle for his humanity according to those brutal criteria bequeathed him at his birth" (Baldwin 22–23).

A similar misconception that the "problem" is blackness or black rebellion rather than the oppressive conditions that produce it can be seen throughout American history. After civil unrest erupted in Baltimore in response to Freddie Gray's death, Baltimore mayor Stephanie Rowlings-Blake, who is black, denounced "thugs" for "destroying the city" in spontaneous violent protest—language for which she subsequently apologized—reinscribing Baldwin's critique of Bigger Thomas and the dominant culture's condemnation of black people. Also commenting on the Freddie Gray case, Orlando Patterson invokes the phrase "problem minority" in a *New York Times* op-editorial about the Baltimore uprising. Reviving the sociological tradition of the widely discredited Moynihan report, which located the problems caused by systemic racism within black communities' values and behaviors, Patterson echoes Wright's critics, maintaining that within Baltimore's inner city, the "great majority of residents are law-abiding, God-fearing, and socially conservative." He concludes that, with respect to events in Baltimore and other cities torn apart by racial unrest, "it is thus a clear mistake to focus only on police brutality, and it is fatuous to attribute it all to white racism."

For Wright, such problems always resided in the white capitalist power structure, including the black bourgeoisie, whom he detested for being "more than others ashamed of Bigger and what he meant" (*Native Son* 449). Wright's genius was to understand that Bigger was symptomatic of the problem and his numbers were legion. His sympathies lay with the Biggers of the world—indeed, he admits that he might have "longed secretly to be like [Bigger] and was afraid" (435). In relation to recent antiblack violence, Bigger underscores the violability of today's young black men incarcerated at six times the rate of whites ("Criminal Justice Fact Sheet") and expelled from public schools at three times the rate of whites ("Data Snapshot"). While many charges against black youth are petty, if not entirely fabricated, systemic racial oppression to-day—as it has historically—fosters alienation and "outlaw" behavior that in turn reinforce racist beliefs, stereotypes, and state repression.

UNRULY RHETORICS AND HIDDEN REALITIES OF THE RELATIONS OF PRODUCTION

In connection to twenty-first-century radical movements such as Black Lives Matter, a key question raised by Wright's characterization of Bigger Thomas is whether the social stratum he represents—the *lumpenproletariat*—can be politically mobilized. Wright deeply sympathized with Bigger but did not nec-essarily believe he would turn to movements for social justice and freedom. Rather, Wright offers a cautionary tale in which "Bigger, an American product, a native son of this land, carried within him the potentialities of either Com-munism or Fascism" (*Native Son* 446). Wright poses the question in the follow-ing terms: "Whether he'll follow some gaudy, hysterical leader who'll promise rashly to fill the void in him, or whether he'll come to an understanding with the millions of his kindred fellow workers under trade-union or revolutionary guidance depends upon the future drift of events in America" (447).[11] To return to my linkage of "x-ray" vision with education, one answer to the dilemma posed by Wright may reside in Bigger's educability, elucidated by his transfor-mation from "dumb, cold, inarticulate hate" (67) in Book One to his shock-ing declaration at the end of Book Three to his left-wing lawyer Boris Max: "I didn't want to kill! . . . But what I killed for, I *am*! . . . When a man kills, it's for something. . . . I didn't know I was really alive in this world until I felt things hard enough to kill for 'em" (429). In relation to the "phenomenal forms" or *Erscheinungsformen*, the question of educability suggests a key to developing a multifaceted, liberatory pedagogy in and out of the classroom capable of build-ing a global, anticapitalist movement and proving "another world is possible."[12]

What, if anything, has Bigger learned? Does his transformation, however raw, suggest that he has begun to understand the causes of his oppression? What more "instruction" does he need in order to "realize the potentialities" of political resistance? To join forces, if he could, with those who reject fascism and fight for global social and economic justice? In the opening pages of the novel, after he kills a rat in their kitchenette, Bigger's mother scolds him for his cavalier attitude toward his sister Vera's fearfulness: "All you care about is your own pleasure . . . Bigger, honest, you the most no-countest man I ever seen in all my life." He replies, "You done told me that a thousand times. . . . Stop prophesying about me," to which she retorts, "I prophesy much as I please" (*Native Son* 9). This same prophecy can be seen unfolding in events in Ferguson, Baltimore, and elsewhere in the dialectic between intensifying oppressive conditions and cadres of alienated youth, especially young black men widely viewed as a "problem minority." As several scholars have noted, we have gone from Bigger Thomas to rapper Biggie Smalls in a social imaginary created by a socioeconomic system that perpetuates racism through both state apparatuses, including education, and the internalization and enactment of the very stereotype that so disconcerted Wright's critics in his portrayal of Bigger Thomas (see Ellis; Peterson).

Bigger's story can be seen today in interlocking manifestations of systemic racism in the "cool pose" and the mass incarceration of young black men. According to Richard Majors and Janet Mancini Billson, "The black male is socialized to view every white man as a potential enemy, every symbol of the dominant system as a potential threat. . . . Playing it cool becomes the mask of choice" (27). This cool pose "is a signature of true masculinity" (28). Having explained how Bigger was born based on a lifetime of observations, Wright notes, "the plot fell out, so to speak" insofar as rape charges against "some Negro boy being picked up on the streets and carted off to jail . . . had become a representative symbol of the Negro's uncertain position in America" (*Native Son* 455). This precariousness, as Majors and Billson explain, is deeply rooted: "Historically, the black mask of roles, façades, shields, fronts, and gaming helped to ensure survival. . . . Regardless of class, blacks knew that donning the masked role was the safest course. They played to the expectations of the powerful white audience" (60).

In particular, James Braxton Peterson traces Bigger Thomas's legacy to four rap artists: Biggie Smalls, DMX, Eminem, and Tupac Shakur. Especially relevant to my argument here is Peterson's discussion of Tupac Shakur's THUGLIFE, an acronym for "The Hate yoU Gave Little Infants Fucks Everyone" (220). Like the other rappers Peterson compares to Richard Wright as "oratorical authors," and to Bigger Thomas as characters in their own narratives, Shakur embodies the agony of growing up black in America in a post-1960s era of desegregation, resegregation, economic despair, and metaphorical and literal imprisonment. The son of Black Panthers, Shakur experienced a radical milieu of Panthers and members of the Black Liberation Army that is reflected in the political critique infusing his song "Trapped":

> Cause they never talk peace in tha black community
> All we know is violence, do tha job in silence
> Walk tha city streets like a rat pack of tyrants

Too many brothers daily heading for tha big penn
Niggas commin' out worse off than when they went in. (qtd. in Peterson 220)

In speaking "directly to thugs" in his music, Shakur demonstrates how "The alienated figure or the THUG, may be reached through narratives such as *Native Son* or 'Trapped,'" channeling "his/her alienation and angst . . . toward political consciousness and socio-economic progress" (Peterson 220–21).

Similarly, Annette J. Saddik notes in her analysis of rap music's "unruly body" that artists like Public Enemy "display their 'unruly bodies'—the threatening, half-naked, screaming, and sweating muscular body of the gangsta rapper . . . [and thus] threaten[s] the mainstream white authority that seeks to keep the 'savage' in its (his) place" (121). This double play of young black males parodying dominant white society with the very behavior the white world expects and fears is precisely the dynamic that Bigger embodies, starting in "Book One: Fear," as he stands outside the poolroom with his friend Gus: "They leaned their backs against the red brick wall of a building, smoking, their cigarettes slanting white across their black chins" (*Native Son* 15). They see a plane that is skywriting "a tiny ribbon of unfolding vapor" and wistfully observe to one another, "Them white boys sure can fly. . . . They get a chance to do everything" (16). It is the unmitigated denial of a chance to fly—"to do everything"—that turns Bigger to petty crimes like robbing stores and that redefines his acts of violence as his only way to assert free will and resist the oppression that prevents him and his family from doing "anything right or wrong that mattered much" (105). This inversion of values in which Bigger's crimes become an act of freedom puzzles even sympathetic Boris Max, whose eyes fill with terror at his client's admission that "what I killed for, I am" (429).

In his oft-quoted 1969 essay "The Rhetoric of the Open Hand and the Rhetoric of the Closed Fist," Edward P. J. Corbett tries to come to terms with 1960s protest rhetoric, which he defines as a form of persuasion that is closefisted, provocatively nonverbal, and coercive—"a group rhetoric, a gregarious rhetoric" (292). Lamenting what seems to him a loss of the well-reasoned rhetoric of the open hand, rooted in Renaissance sensibilities, Corbett acknowledges that the "younger generation . . . may see the civility, decorum, and orderliness of the old mode of discourse as a façade behind which the establishment in all ages has perpetrated injustices on have-nots" (296). Yet even in his effort to reconcile his reservations about the closed fist with the possibility that a liberal society's dominant discourses might conceal rather than redress injustice, he describes the problem as universal, natural, occurring throughout the ages, rather than historically specific, humanly created, and therefore susceptible to fundamental change. In other words, he cannot imagine a society without "have-nots," which was exactly what drove Marx and other political economists to theorize alternatives to capitalism.

A telling professional counterpoint to Corbett's nostalgia for a mythical, decorous, orderly past came at the 1968 Conference on College Composition and Communication in Minneapolis, during which participants learned that Martin Luther King, Jr., had been assassinated. In her impromptu eulogy, later published in *College Composition and Communication* as "Murder of the American Dream," Ernece B. Kelly bitterly criticized the institutional racism she experienced at the conference with its overwhelming whiteness, chauvinistic patronizing attitudes, and uncritical discussions about how to "upgrade" or "just plain *replace*" black students' dialects (107). Corbett and his colleagues would have been as shocked by her fierce declaration that King's death meant to her "that white men will listen only to gunfire and to the explosion of Molotov cocktails" (106) as readers of *Native Son* were shocked by Bigger Thomas. Kelly concluded, "I am pushed further into a blackness which approaches violence" (108). Like Wright, she understood such violence as responsive to assaults on African Americans since the slave trade began. The same dynamic holds true, often in overlapping contexts, for striking workers, women, LGBTQ people, and other oppressed groups.

The idea then of "unruly" or "body" rhetoric as a form of protest must first be understood in relation to exploitation, state and other violence, and the denial of civil, economic, and human rights.[13] Second, the modern nation-state typically prefers to exercise what Gramsci called "cultural hegemony" to win popular ideological support—the rhetoric of the open hand—but resorts to direct military or police force as needed to maintain control. In 1969 J. Edgar Hoover declared the Black Panther Party "the greatest threat to internal security of the country" and vowed to eradicate the organization within the year. Today, numerous reports indicate that the Department of Homeland Security contributed to shutting down OWS encampments and conducts heavy surveillance of BLM (Joseph). Third, the unruliness of individuals like Bigger Thomas, caught up in systems of oppression as social pariahs, signifies resistance that defies and parodies even as it confirms cultural stereotypes. Last, the "unruly rhetoric" of protest movements typically arises when other rhetorical means of persuasion have failed, leading in some cases to seizure of power and social justice victories and in others to periods of retreat or even extinction.[14]

RESISTANCE AND REBELLION IN THE AGE OF TWITTER

Absent an understanding of the underlying structures of society and the asymmetrical power dynamic of class conflict, the rhetoric of social protest can lead to support for authoritarian or fascist tendencies—as Wright made clear in *Na-*

tive Son and as the 2016 US presidential election reminds us. To liberal critics such as Corbett, such rhetoric reflects a breakdown in democratic discourse, when in fact it is the only means of response to a ruling elite invested in maintaining a deeply inequitable status quo. Although twenty-first-century social justice movements may be hampered by the lack of the sort of unifying ideological framework and vision that guided, however problematically, Richard Wright's radical political milieu in Chicago in the 1930s, their effectiveness has been enhanced by the wide reach of social media and citizen journalist videos. These new technologies contributed to—in many ways, created—the contagion of global uprisings from the Arab Spring to Black Lives Matter, which have mobilized large numbers of people in solidarity across national borders and expressed their own sense of linkage to one another (but see Alexander and Jarratt's introduction and Parks et al., this volume, for alternative views on the relationship between technologies and activism). The campaigns launched by these movements have often had astonishing success; both the OWS slogan "We are the 99%" and the hashtag #blacklivesmatter inspired popular support, captured media headlines, and helped change political discourse in ways that significantly influenced perceptions, policies, and election outcomes.

The two catchphrases of Black Lives Matter, "Hands Up, Don't Shoot" and "I Can't Breathe"—the one the iconic, if disputed, image of Michael Brown with his hands in the air and the other the dying words of Eric Garner—were mimed, tweeted, posted, chanted, and plastered on mass-produced and home-made posters and banners. They express the fear, frustration, and desperation of communities of color whose bodies are violated and whose lives are routinely devalued and destroyed in the name of order and democracy, by means ranging from militarized drug raids and mass incarceration to voting restrictions. BLM calls for justice were accompanied by "die-ins" in cities and college campuses nationwide as hundreds of thousands of demonstrators blocked traffic and lay down in buildings, on courthouse steps, and in the street, their bodies outlined by chalk. This rhetoric of bodily identification with police assault victims not only expresses solidarity in a show of collective resistance to state-sponsored violence but also reveals the poignant focus of the movement thus far, captured by a *New York Times Magazine* cover story headlined, "Our Demand Is Simple: Stop Killing Us" (Kang).

Like Twitter and Facebook, handheld bystander videos have influenced the course of history. Since George Holliday's videotape of the Los Angeles police officers' brutal beating of Rodney King in 1992, citizen journalism has become a powerful tool for confronting police brutality. With rapid advances in cellphone and Internet technology, the viral circulation of videos of police shootings and other abuses of black bodies has galvanized protest and pressured the criminal justice system to discipline police departments. Such hard evidence of police brutality has affected movement building and public perceptions—if not, in most cases, the prosecution of officers who cite *Graham v. Connor* and claim that reasonable fear for their safety justified the use of lethal force in the moment. Only in the clearest incidents of extrajudicial police killings have officers been found guilty, such as in the North Charleston case in which a bystander used his cell phone to record police officer Michael Slager shooting Walter Scott six times in the back during a routine traffic stop. Nevertheless, together with mass protests, the circulation of videos, alternative news, and information via YouTube videos, Facebook posts, tweets, and other social media helped interrupt the narrative of a postracial America to remind us of the horrors of racism.[15]

But social media and handheld cell-phone videos cannot replace face-to-face street protests, strikes, or political strategies. DeRay McKesson, who emerged as a leader in Ferguson, puts it this way: "When I tweet, I'm preaching mostly to the choir. . . . But the heart of the movement is in the actions. It's in shutting down streets, shutting down Walmarts" (Kang). According to one study, OWS's primary uses of Facebook—the most heavily utilized social networking site—were for recruitment, compiling and sharing news stories, distributing resources, telling personal stories, communicating quickly across geographical distances, and enabling multiple users to post their own ideas (Caren and Gaby). While the encampments were in place, the emphasis on participatory democracy fostered dialogue and face-to-face contact. But the online communication was not widely sustained once the encampments were shut down. As Christian Christensen notes, one danger of social media in the new movements is that blog posts and tweets can seem to substitute for "real political action" (156). Even more dangerously, he points out, sophisticated technology can serve "to simplify surveillance, disinformation, and repression" and lead to "techno-dystopianism" (156).

As we head toward the third decade of the twenty-first century, we must look forward and backward in order to address the interrelated systemic issues that have given rise to "Twitter revolutions" worldwide. There is a sense of terrible urgency to respond both to new threats to our survival like climate change and to ones we know by heart—so often repressed or forgotten—like extrajudicial killings of black people. To understand the causes and interrelationships of these annihilating threats will require a new pedagogy both in and out of the classroom, side-by-side with activists, students, scholars, theorists, and multiple publics, one that is dialogic, respectful, and critically conscious. As Jackie DiSalvo points out in her analysis of OWS, "the anti-capitalism of these young anarchists . . . obliges Marxists to work with formations like Occupy

Wall Street" (284). Marxists can contribute the sort of knowledge that Wright acquired in his formative years in Chicago, enabling him to tell Bigger's story. Other narratives by rappers such as Biggie Smalls and Tupac Shakur of life in poor black communities, alongside *Native Son*, can provide bridges to connect with youth and critical insights into local crises and their systemic causes. In order to build the capacity to stand outside and critique the discourses that shape our worlds and ourselves, and to perceive the concealed pattern of economic forms below the surface, we will also need to overcome the obstacles of racism, sexism, homophobia, and other antidemocratic practices that contribute to the demise of socialist states and continue to derail efforts to organize a global mass movement capable of "lasting change"—change that cannot occur "without overcoming the power of capital and confronting and reconstructing the state" (DiSalvo 282).

Without the x-ray vision—which Marxism helps illuminate—to explain capitalism's relentless drive for surplus profits and the accompanying ruthless extraction of wealth from the 99 percent, the leaderless (or leader-full), horizontal, fragmented movements that have sprung so bravely into existence will be difficult to sustain, unify, or mobilize in the fight for alternatives. Employing Corbett's open-handed rhetoric in his 1941 review of *Native Son*, Theophilus Lewis argued that "all oppressed races . . . make adjustments to their condition, adopt substitutions and compensations, and if their lot is not too harsh they may make gradual progress and finally escape their oppression." Such universalizing assurances of assimilation and accommodation have proved especially false for the masses of black people in the United States, whose racial identity continues to exclude them from the promises of American democracy and to make them tragically vulnerable to its most heartrending failures. It is this breach in our society that Ta-Nehisi Coates sees when he tells his son not to "struggle for the Dreamers. Hope for them. Pray for them, if you are so moved. But do not pin your struggle on their conversion," for they will "have to learn to struggle for themselves, to understand that the field for their Dream, the stage where they have painted themselves white, is the deathbed for us all" (151). As this precariousness is increasingly felt across racial, class, and national boundaries, it may yet give full voice to the "unruly rhetorics" of revolutionary protest movements in a collective answer to the world's anticipation.

NOTES

1. Coates pays homage to Baldwin's 1962 "Letter to My Nephew" in addressing his own son and to Wright's 1935 poem "Between the World and Me" in his book by the same title.

2. This trend continued throughout 2015 with a total of 1,134 young black men killed

by police, according to the ongoing *Guardian* study, including the highly visible cases of Lamar Clark in Minneapolis and Laquan McDonald in Chicago (Swaine et al.). Written in early 2015, the first draft of this chapter was completed on June 22, 2015, necessitating an artificial limit on references to racially triggered tragedies occurring with horrifying regularity, including the June 17 massacre by Nazi-sympathizer Dylann Roof of nine black churchgoers in Charleston, SC, at the Emanuel African Methodist Episcopal Church, whose cofounder Demark Vesey was among thirty-five congregation members executed in 1822 for plotting a rebellion against slaveholders.

3. Based on the unpublished novel Wright drafted after *Native Son* and later abandoned, Barbara Foley contests the view of him as misogynistic, concluding, "*Black Hope* reveals a radical appreciation of women's positioning in the struggle for a better world" (122).

4. Often unfavorably compared to Baldwin's ethos of "love," Wright's rage underscores his understanding of the humanly influenced—if not totally controlled—sociohistorical processes that gave rise to capitalism. See Anastas.

5. See Wald for an interesting account of Wright's generation as a cultural vanguard that gravitated toward the CPUSA and was committed to the social vision of the 1930s.

6. Even as American youth are reported to be increasingly pro-socialist (see, e.g., McGreal), and as a new wave of resistance emerged in the wake of Trump's election, left and liberal forces continue to wrestle with coherence, clarity, and unity, particularly with respect to electoral politics, the viability of the Democratic Party, and ultimately, that of neoliberal capitalism.

7. Patrick Manning contrasts Wright's *Native Son* to Lloyd Brown's *Iron City*, a 1951 novel set in the 1940s in which the black protagonist remains loyal to the CPUSA. Manning notes, "Brown recognizes the hurdles impeding the goals of the communist project; [but] . . . [d]espite the obstacles, Brown articulates the revolution's urgent necessity. For Brown, accomplishing the goal of the communist project will be difficult, but nothing short of survival . . . is at stake."

8. See, for example, Ayana Mathis and Pankaj Mishra, "James Baldwin Denounced Richard Wright's 'Native Son' as a 'Protest Novel.' Was He Right?" It is also important to note that in "I Tried to Be a Communist," later included in the anticommunist anthology *The God that Failed*, Wright criticized the CPUSA but remained deeply committed to liberatory struggles.

9. In "How 'Bigger' Was Born," initially published on June 1, 1940, in *The Saturday Review of Literature* and included in the edition cited herein of *Native Son*, Wright recalls reading a pamphlet with a scene of Lenin pointing out to Gorky, "'Here is *their* Big Ben,' 'There is *their* Westminster Abbey'" (443). Wright comes to understand that Lenin's expression of a "deep sense of exclusion . . . transcended national and racial boundaries" (443); that this was identical to Bigger's experience as a black man in Chicago; and that such denials of "the right to live with dignity" (444) would create revolutionaries

not only in "far away Russia" (444) but also in America in men such as Bigger: "That's Bigger. That's the Bigger Thomas reaction" (443).

10. I am indebted to Luis S. Villacañas de Castro for his excellent analysis of this concept in his essay on Vygotsky and Marx.

11. Here, it is interesting to note how this potential for the world's Bigger Thomases to turn to fascism was underscored by the electoral victories and near victories of populist leaders such as Trump and Marine La Pen who openly exploited racial differences to win over the white working class.

12. The slogan is the World Social Forum's answer to British prime minister Margaret Thatcher's notorious claim that "there is no alternative" (aka TINA) to the neoliberal globalization of capitalism.

13. Although the point may be obvious, state-sponsored violence by police or military forces is commonly understood as legitimate, while class struggle in myriad forms is routinely characterized and criticized by the state as "uncivil" and "violent" (Welch).

14. See Welch, "'We're Here, and We're Not Going Anywhere': Why Working-Class Rhetorical Traditions 'Still' Matter," for a fuller description of successful political struggles in which "the working class has proved a decisive force" (227).

15. It is worth noting that none of the officers involved in the highly publicized cases of Eric Garner, Michael Brown, and Tamir Rice, which gave rise to the BLM movement, were indicted. The Garner family was awarded $5.5 million in an out-of-court settlement, the Rice family was awarded $6 million in April 2016, and the Brown family's wrongful death civil suit was settled in June 2017 for an undisclosed amount. The prosecution of the first officer indicted in the case of Freddie Gray ended in a mistrial, and charges against all the other officers were dropped.

WORKS CITED

Alexander, Michelle. *The New Jim Crow: Mass Incarceration in the Age of Colorblindness.* The New Press, 2010.

Anastas, Benjamin. "Teaching the Controversy: James Baldwin and Richard Wright in the Ferguson Era." *New Republic*, May 25, 2015. www.newrepublic.com/article/121844 /teaching-james-baldwin-and-richard-wright-ferguson-era/.

Bakhtin, Mikhail. *The Dialogic Imagination.* Edited by Michael Holquist, translated by Caryl Emerson. University of Texas Press, 1982.

Baldwin, James. *Notes of a Native Son.* 1955. Beacon Press, 2012.

Caren, Neal, and Sarah Gaby. "Occupy Online: Facebook and the Spread of Occupy Wall Street." *Social Science Research Network* 24 (October 24, 2011). www.papers.ssrn.com /sol3/papers.cfm?abstract_id=1943168/.

Christensen, Christian. "Twitter Revolutions? Addressing Social Media and Dissent." *Communication Review* 14, no. 3 (2011): 155–57. doi.org/10.1080/10714421.2011.597235/.

Coates, Ta-Nehisi. *Between the World and Me.* Spiegel and Grau, 2015.

Cohn, David L. "The Negro Novel: Richard Wright." Review of *Native Son*, by Richard Wright. *Atlantic Monthly* (May 1940): 659–61.

Corbett, Edward P. J. "The Rhetoric of the Open Hand and the Rhetoric of the Closed Fist." *College Composition and Communication* 20, no. 5 (December 1969): 288–96.

"Criminal Justice Fact Sheet." National Association for the Advancement of Colored People. www.naacp.org/criminal-justice-fact-sheet/.

"Data Snapshot: School Discipline." *Civil Rights Data Collection*. US Department of Education Office for Civil Rights, issue brief no. 1, March 2014. www.ocrdata.ed.gov/.

Dawahare, Anthony. "Richard Wright's *Native Son* and the Dialectics of Black Experience." In *Richard Wright in a Post-racial Imaginary*, edited by A. M. Craven and W. E. Dow, 65–80. Bloomsbury Academic, 2014.

DiSalvo, Jackie. "Occupy Wall Street: Creating a Strategy for a Spontaneous Movement." *Science & Society* 79, no. 2 (April 2015): 264–87.

Ellis, Aimé J. *If We Must Die: From Bigger Thomas to Biggie Smalls*. Wayne State University Press, 2011.

Ellison, Ralph. "Richard Wright's Blues." *Antioch Review* 5, no. 2 (Summer 1945): 198–211.

Fabre, Michel. *The Unfinished Quest of Richard Wright*. 2nd ed. University of Illinois Press, 1993.

Fanon, Frantz. *Black Skin, White Masks*. Grove Press, 1967.

Foley, Barbara. "'A Dramatic Picture . . . of Woman from Feudalism to Fascism': Richard Wright's *Black Hope*." In *Richard Wright in a Post-racial Imaginary*, edited by A. M. Craven and W. E. Dow, 113–26. Bloomsbury Academic, 2014.

Garza, Alicia. "A Herstory of the #BlackLivesMatter Movement." *Feminist Wire* 7 (October 2014). www.thefeministwire.com/2014/10/blacklivesmatter-2/.

Garza, Alicia. "Indicting and Transforming the Systems of State and Capitalism: From Ferguson to Baltimore and Beyond." Feature event, Left Forum, John Jay College, May 30, 2015. www.youtube.com/watch?v=Dx2YVUT1Zug/, uploaded by Left Forum on August 7, 2015.

Jack, Peter Monro. "A Tragic Novel of Negro Life in America; Richard Wright's Powerful Novel 'Native Son' Brings to Mind Theodore Dreiser's 'American Tragedy.'" Review of *Native Son*, by Richard Wright. *New York Times Book Review*, March 3, 1940, 86, 95.

Joseph, George. "Exclusive: Feds Regularly Monitored Black Lives Matter since Ferguson." *The Intercept*, July 24, 2015. www.theintercept.com/2015/07/24/documents-show -department-homeland-security-monitoring-black-lives-matter-since-ferguson/.

Kang, Jay Caspian. "Our Demand Is Simple: Stop Killing Us." *New York Times Magazine*, May 4, 2015. www.nytimes.com/2015/05/10/magazine/our-demand-is-simple-stop -killing-us.html.

Kelly, Ernece B. "Murder of the American Dream." *College Composition and Communication* 19, no. 2 (May 1968): 106–8.

Lewis, Theophilus. "The Saga of Bigger Thomas." Review of *Native Son*, by Richard Wright,

Catholic World 153 (May 1941). *ChickenBones: A Journal for Literary and Artistic African American Themes.* www.nathanielturner.com/sagaofbiggerthomas.htm.

Majors, Richard, and Janet Mancini Billson. *Cool Pose: The Dilemmas of Black Manhood in America.* 1992. Reprint, Touchstone, 1993.

Manning, Patrick. "The Communist Party, the Popular Front and Reimagining 'America' in Lloyd Brown's Iron City." *Pennsylvania Literary Journal* (December 2009). www .sites.google.com/site/pennsylvaniajournal/Home/winter-2009-issue/the-communist -party-the-popular-front-and-reimagining-america-in-lloyd-browns-iron-city/.

Marx, Karl. 1867. *Capital.* Vol. 56. In *Great Books of the Western World*, edited by Mortimer J. Adler. Britannica, 1991.

Marx, Karl. "Supplementary Remarks." *Capital*, vol. 3, part 2, ch. 12. Marxists Internet Archive, Marx Engels Archives, 1867. www.marxists.org/archive/marx/works/1894-c3 /ch12.htm.

Mathis, Ayana, and Pankaj Mishra. "James Baldwin Denounced Richard Wright's 'Native Son' as a 'Protest Novel.' Was He Right?" Bookends, *New York Times Book Review*, February 24, 2015. www.nytimes.com/2015/03/01/books/review/james-baldwin -denounced-richard-wrights-native-son-as-a-protest-novel-was-he-right.html.

Maxwell, William J. "Wright among the 'G-Men': How the FBI Framed Paris Noir." In *Richard Wright: New Readings in the 21st Century*, edited by A. M. Craven and W. E. Dow, 27–38. Palgrave Macmillan, 2011.

McGreal, Chris. "'The S-Word': How Young Americans Fell in Love with Socialism." *The Guardian*, September 2, 2017. www.theguardian.com/us-news/2017/sep/02/socialism -young-americans-bernie-sanders?CMP=Share_iOSApp_Other/.

Mootry, Maria K. "Bitches, Whores, and Woman Haters: Archetypes and Typologies in the Art of Richard Wright." In *Richard Wright: A Collection of Critical Essays*, edited by R. Macksey and F. E. Moorer, 117–27. Prentice Hall, 1984.

Patterson, Orlando. "The Real Problem with America's Inner Cities." Op-editorial. *New York Times*, May 9, 2015. www.nytimes.com/2015/05/10/opinion/sunday/the-real -problem-with-americas-inner-cities.html.

Peterson, James Braxton. "The Hate U Gave (T.H.U.G): Reflections on the Bigger Figures in Present Day Hip Hop Culture." In *Richard Wright's Native Son*, edited by A. M. Fraile, 203–24. Rodopi, 2007.

Rascoe, Burton. "Negro Novel and White Reviewers." Review of *Native Son*, by Richard Wright. *American Mercury* (May 1940): 113. www.unz.org/Pub/AmMercury-1940 may-00113/.

Saddik, Annette J. "Rap's Unruly Body: The Postmodern Performance of Black Male Identity on the American Stage." *Drama Review* 47, no. 4 (Winter 2003): 110–27. www.muse .jhu.edu/article/48988/.

Swaine, Jon, "The Counted: Number of People Killed by Police This Year Reaches 500."

The Guardian, June 10, 2015. www.theguardian.com/us-news/2015/jun/10/the-counted
-500-people-killed-by-police-2015/.

Swaine, Jon, Oliver Laughland, Jamiles Lartey, and Ciara McCarthy. "Young Black Men
Killed by U.S. Police Reaches Highest Rate in Year of 1,134 Deaths." *The Guardian*,
December 31, 2015. www.theguardian.com/us-news/2015/dec/31/the-counted-police
-killings-2015-young-black-men/.

Villacañas de Castro, Luis S. "A Critique of Vygotsky's Misapprehension of Marx's 'Phenomenal Forms.'" *Science & Society* 79, no. 1 (2015): 90–113.

Wald, Alan. "On Richard Wright's Centennial: The Great Outsider." *Against the Current:
A Socialist Journal* 138 (January/February 2009). www.solidarity-us.org/node/2031/.

Welch, Nancy. "'We're Here, and We're Not Going Anywhere': Why Working-Class Rhetorical Traditions 'Still' Matter." *College English* 73, no. 3 (January 2011): 221–42.

Wolff, Richard D. "Marx: The System Is the Problem." Panel, Left Forum, John Jay College,
May 30, 2015.

Wright, Richard. *Black Boy*. 1944. Harper Perennial Modern Classics, 2006.

Wright, Richard. "I Tried to Be a Communist." In *The God that Failed*, edited by Richard
M. Crossman, 115–162. Columbia University Press, 2001.

Wright, Richard. *Native Son*. 1940. Harper Perennial Modern Classics, 2005.

12

DIGNITAS AND "SHIT SHOVELS"

CORPORATE BODIES AND UNRULY LANGUAGE

JASON PETERS

What is the relationship between corporeal bodies and the figure of the body as deployed in rhetorical resistance? In this essay I take the approach that this relationship is constituted by language, understood to be at once a bodily utterance and a discursive performance. My motivation in asking this question stems from a dissatisfaction with what happens to language when interactions between the body and discourse are studied in rhetoric and composition. While such studies advance our understanding of the relationship between discourse and the body in important ways, they leave out direct attention to language as an ideological field in which the relationship between discourse and the body gets constructed and negotiated, even while such studies claim to be attending to issues of language. In "Speaking

Matters," for example, Carl G. Herndl and Danny A. Bauer develop a model of "performative rhetoric and material articulation" to "[explain] how subject positions get created and legitimized by the speech of the subaltern" (560). In seeking to identify the potential for speech to "confront and ultimately alter the social order" (564), however, they trace out a relationship between discursive performance and material articulation but neglect to consider how issues of language standardization, language difference, local language attitudes, and the status-marking functions of those differences within local economies all might impinge on the value of a given discursive performance.

Similarly, feminist historiographers in rhetoric and composition have sought to articulate how the body is socially constructed in reference to discursive regimes and how modes of discursive performance can strategically respond to those constructions. In "Telling Evidence," for example, Carol Mattingly seeks to rehabilitate women's rhetorical history in part by attending to the way women strategically responded to discursive constructions of feminine and masculine bodies (106). In "Feminist Historiography," Christine Mason Sutherland describes the practice of reading her essays aloud to Robert Burchfield, editor of the *Oxford English Dictionary*. Drawing a gendered distinction between the masculine eye and feminine ear, Sutherland argues that reading her writing aloud constituted a feminist practice capable of opening "freer discursive spaces" in her thinking and writing than would have been possible for her through "impersonal forms of address" such as writing (111, citing Lorraine Code). In order to isolate the discursive functions of gender differences and gendered performances, projects such as Mattingly's and Sutherland's are forced to turn away from attending to what happens to language itself.

Although the interest in discourse arose after the linguistic turn across all of the social sciences, attention to discourse ends up neglecting language as language. As Alastair Pennycook reminds us, the linguistic turn was rather a cultural turn that bypassed language (*Language* 123). My particular focus, then, is neither on corporeal bodies nor on the discursive regimentations that shape and regulate them; rather, I investigate language itself as an ideological field—a field populated not just by the significations and representations of discourse but by the attitudes, improvisational utterances, and material practices of socially situated language users in everyday communicative contexts. In short, I argue that language itself is unruly, always uttered within and against ideological structures that attempt to regiment it yet always eluding those regimentations, less a performance of some fixed identity and more a trafficking and mobilization of identities.

In the global spread of English, the protection of minority language rights and the granting of access to dominant linguistic codes are conceived of as particular kinds of power relations in twenty-first-century global capitalist economies, conceptualizations that delimit the range of possible attitudes and practices that can be taken toward language difference within these economies. At one economic extreme, those attitudes and practices result in actual bodily alteration. For example, in "Living-English Work," Min-Zhan Lu cites a disturbing elective surgery growing in popularity in China and South Korea, in which a child's tongue is surgically altered in an attempt to help the child speak an accent-free English (606). Lu cites these surgeries as reminders that "people from all strata of the world are living under exponential pressure to use English and use it only with the kind of 'demeanors'—accent, lexicon, grammar, rhythms, pitch—that appeal to the few with the cultural, political, and economic capital" to provide or withhold access to socioeconomic opportunity (607). The anatomy of the body is altered, ordered, arranged, and suppressed according to the "rulings" (605) of monolingual ideologies, and these same rulings enable a range of possible responses to the pressures to self-alter, self-order, self-arrange, and self-suppress language practices that deviate from the expected demeanors. At this extreme, surgical alteration of the body is an attempt to outmaneuver the discursive regimentation of languages—and language users—within global capitalist economies.

What other attitudes and demeanors might be taken toward "the pressure to maintain the 'purity'—exclusivity and dominance—of U.S. English" in global contexts (Lu, "An Essay" 27)? As Lu asks us, is tongue surgery the only viable solution ("Living-English Work" 607)? The twenty-first century has already borne witness to a bewildering array of language protests around the world on behalf of minority language rights, as the global spread of English is met with various forms of resistance. This resistance is often enacted in the name of preserving minoritized cultural identities and traditions in the midst of Western political and economic hegemony. A number of seemingly unrelated examples over the past fifteen years demonstrate this point. In October 2000, several hundred Native Americans gathered at the Arizona State House to protest Proposition 203, English for the Children, which sought to eliminate bilingual education in the state's public schools (Gonzalez). In January 2014, two hundred Welsh protestors stood outside a Morrison's supermarket wearing "Welsh Not" gags "as a reminder of the nineteenth century practice banning children from speaking Welsh," after the store refused to fill an antibiotics prescription for a fifteen-month-old child because the prescription was written in Welsh and English (Trewyn). In March 2014, Sinn Fein treasurer Diarmuid Mac Dubhghlais was arrested and charged under antiterrorist legislation after responding to police in Irish rather than in English ("RSF"). Mac Dubhghlais concluded his statements to *Irish Republican News* deploring his arrest "with the words of 1916 rebel leader Padraig Mac Piarais: 'Tir gan teanga, tir gan anam' [A country that has lost its language is a country that has lost its soul]."

In contrast to the incidence of tongue surgery, these protests are a resistant use of the body to respond to the pressures of English purity in a way that seeks protections for minority language rights. These protests all make disruptive use of the body in public spaces in an attempt to make visible a counternarrative to the apparently enthusiastic uptake of English as an official language-of-state in locales all around the world. All of these protests target a civil discourse and a public sphere that is accused of excluding minority languages from state and corporate organizational structures. At least in the United States, the very existence of a public sphere and the maintenance of a civil discourse have historically depended on such exclusions, where English achieves hegemonic status as a "public" language while other languages are suppressed and excluded as "private." Language protests call attention to this arrangement, arguing that language suppression is equivalent to forms of racism and discrimination, and that bilingual and multilingual speakers should be accorded a representative share of public resources, protection of rights, and access to opportunity.

However, these protests end up reproducing the very same ideologies that legitimate the exclusionary state and corporate structures being protested. Language policies and language protests both reflect a conceptualization of languages as relatively fixed and discretely bounded entities that index a group's racial, ethnic, sociocultural, and national identities. What gets suppressed on both counts are alternate conceptualizations of languages as fluid, inherently unstable, and hybridized, simultaneously connected to global economies but constituted by local practices for local needs, in ways that outrun the ability of states and economies to manage them or account for them (Horner and Lu 141–45; Canagarajah 76, 129; Lu, "An Essay" 19–25; Pennycook, *Global Englishes* 60–77). I want to emphasize that these alternate conceptualizations are always already present in language practices but that they are suppressed in order to use language as an instrument of identification for the purposes of collective protest, political action, and economic transaction.

Contemporary language conflicts rely on a specific set of modernist assumptions about language that are shared by both resistance and dominance alike. Those assumptions, though effective in isolated local contexts of resistance and in the articulation of a minority identity politics in reference to language, continue to reinforce the incorporation of two distinct bodies: a purified body politic composed of modernized, native-speaking English subjects and a hybridized and minoritized body politic composed of multilingual language users perceived to be in need of modernization. Yet at the same time that these bodies are being made distinct from each other, they are also being mingled and shuttled via an alternate set of language practices that is present but unacknowledged and unaccounted for by those enmeshed in conflicting ideologies of language—which is to say all of us.

LINGUISTIC REGIMENTATION AND THE CORPOREAL/CORPORATE BODY

In the United States, the dominance of the ideology of monolingualism dates to the late nineteenth and early twentieth centuries. The view that language could be used to purify the body politic only emerged in response to the period of second-wave immigration that brought millions of multilingual Catholics to Ellis Island. Prior to the 1920s, the Catholic Church had operated as a transnational and multilingual institution, allowing different language enclaves to establish their own parishes operating in their mother tongues. The conflict between language purification and resistant identity politics can be traced back to the 1920s, when the Catholic Church (as well as many states) began passing language laws to suppress transnationalism and multilingualism in favor of "one hundred percent Americanism" ("No Racial Lines").

On a Sunday afternoon in July 1927, following Sunday Mass, almost one thousand French Americans gathered at Cass Park in Woonsocket, the center of Rhode Island's textile industry, to listen to a local attorney and newspaper publisher, Elphège Daignault, address them from the back of a flatbed pickup truck in protest of a newly established English-only language policy in the Catholic Church. Daignault had become a local celebrity after suing twelve French-speaking parishes for taking money from their treasuries—money contributed by French-speaking Catholics to maintain their French-language parochial schools—and giving it to the bishop, who was raising funds to build three English-language high schools in his diocese. Daignault's lawsuit sought to block the funding of the English-language high schools by clarifying the administrative relationship between the local parish church corporation—the only legal entity authorized to administer money from the parish treasury—and the larger Roman Catholic Church.

Daignault argued that the members of each parish themselves constituted the parish's corporation and that they alone had the right to administer the parish property that they had helped build. He argued, in effect, that when members of a congregation contribute funds to the parish, they have a vested interest in the administration of those funds. He sought to reduce the symbolic and transcendental "Church"—the body of Christ in perpetuity—into a material and tangible "church" consisting of the bodies and dollars of its parishioners. In the bill of complaint filed with the Rhode Island Supreme Court in 1928, for example, he argued that each parish corporation was bounded "within a defined area" of Woonsocket, the city in which the parishes were located (Curran

7). His claim that a corporation was a geographically bounded entity was an attempt to constrain the flow of money to within the parish itself and to prevent it from flowing from the parish into the larger diocese.

Further, he argued, the language of the state's church incorporation law implied a distinction between an individual parish church and the larger Roman Catholic Church. The law read that each parish corporation was "for the purpose of maintaining religious worship according to the doctrine, discipline, and ritual of the Roman Catholic Church, and for the support of the educational and charitable institutions of that church" (Jalbert 2–3). Daignault tried to argue that there is a material difference intended between the "Church" and the "church," signified by the use of a capital letter and a lowercase letter (*Mederic J. Masse et al. v. Church of Our Lady of Consolation*). The Rhode Island Supreme Court decided against Daignault, finding in Rhode Island's laws of church incorporation that each parish corporation consisted only of the bishop, his vicar, the parish pastor, and two appointed laypeople, that this corporation alone decided how to administer each parish's funds, and that this administration was not geographically bounded by the (small "c") parish church (*Mederic*). For my purposes, the point of representing these arguments is not to decide who was right and who was wrong but, rather, to understand that Daignault was trying to divert the materiality of the Church away from perpetuating the symbolic body of Christ and back toward supporting the multilingual bodies of the parishioners.

Flash back to the 1927 Cass Park demonstration, where one thousand demonstrators gathered to hear Daignault advocate for the rights of French-language users in their parishes. These demonstrators had not yet been found to lack legal standing to protect their interests in the corporations of their parishes. The Cass Park gathering was a collection of corporeal bodies disruptively occupying a public space at a strategic time, a Sunday afternoon following Mass, in order to make visible a dissenting position on the language policies of the Church. But the gathering was also a collection of private persons who had voluntarily subjected themselves and their language practices to a corporate administration in which they would eventually be found to have no legal standing. Their status in their own church was found to be more akin to the status of a consumer in relation to a corporate brand than to a shareholder in relation to a publicly traded company.

The corporeal and the corporate are two conflicting but interdependent relations at work in this protest scene, each of which depends upon the same conceptualization of language. First is the Church's position, which advocated for English as a centralized language of state. Its national council of bishops passed an English-only language policy that sought to purify the corporate body of the

Catholic Church in the United States through English. It's worth noting that these purifying functions of the Church were being accomplished not through the ceremonial aspect of the Mass (which would continue to be delivered in Latin until the Second Vatican Council in 1962) but through the administrative structures and policies of the global Church beyond the Vatican. An entire rhetorical tradition of canonist writings since St. Augustine has sought to clarify the transcendental functions of the Church's administrative structure. In many ways that tradition of thought also gave rise to the juridical practices of state administration in constituting and purifying the body politic. In the United States in the late nineteenth and early twentieth centuries, language became an important issue in Church administration outside Rome, while the use of Latin in the Vatican and for the Mass would remain largely untroubled until the Second Vatican Council. For the Church in the United States, purification depended upon setting a language policy in the administration of its parishes and schools so that monolingual English was legitimated, while other languages were excluded as not belonging to its institutional and corporate body.

In contrast to the Church's position is the disruptive presence of the congregation speaking on behalf of its own interests. This presence threatened the purity of the Church, which seemed no longer capable of speaking in a unified chorus but instead revealed itself to be an unruly body that could speak in tongues. This disruptive presence was being organized by a Franco-American élite, often first- or second-generation emigrants from Québec, who were well-educated and successful businessmen, journalists, or other professionals actively engaged in their communities. The élite were regarded as the political, economic, and clerical leaders of the French-speaking population in the United States. They were uniquely positioned to connect French people and communities to each other and to protect the French presence in North America. They had long sought to protect and promote French as a minority language representative of their identity. Their position argued for greater representation within the corporate structures of the Church in order to protect language rights and provide access to resources. In the Anglophone public sphere—state legislatures, English-language newspapers, and the courts—the élite officially endorsed French-English bilingualism as evidence of the French people's simultaneous distinction as an ethnic minority and of their allegiance to and willingness to participate in American political institutions. But within an alternate francophone public sphere (exclusively French political, cultural, and economic institutions that had formed throughout New England and Québec), they endorsed the cultural purification of the French people through their use of French only. Where the Church sought the purification of its corporate body in English, the French élite sought the purification of their body politic in French.

Both the positions of the Church episcopate and the French élite sought to enlist the corporeal multilingual bodies of French language users in New England into a representational political framework that attempted to suppress linguistic fluidity in order to constitute corporeal bodies into corporate bodies. The scene of the Cass Park language protest dramatizes a compelling problem between discourse and the body in this regard, because it leaves the discourse/body relation dependent upon the assumption of a shared language ideology between the hegemonic and the subaltern. How, then, can we understand bodies to be constituted differently, not by discourse but by an alternate conceptualization of language? How can we understand languages to be embodied by their users, and how can we understand bodies to be embodiments of certain representations and suppressions of language?

LINGUISTIC FLUIDITY AND BODILY DISRUPTION

When we examine the material rhetorics of bodily protest, we have already moved away from studying actual bodies, what Kantorowicz calls the substitutable "mortal components" of "the immortal body politic" (312). And we have moved toward studying the figure of the body as a rhetorical tool that unifies corporeal bodies and mobilizes them for collective action. As we saw in the previous section, one way the figurative body is constituted is through linguistic regimentation—the drawing of boundary lines between languages and the subsequent purification of linguistic identities in relation to those boundaries. When examining the political meanings of the body, we have to attend not only to its capacity for disruptive action but also to the context of that action within a body politic that is, in the end, linguistically constituted.

The binary positions produced by linguistic regimentation suppress the fluidity and hybrid practices of actual language users. Again, I want to emphasize that conceptualizations of language as fluid and unstable are always already present in language attitudes and practices but are suppressed in the interests of both incorporation and political resistance. To illustrate the suppressed presence of these alternate language practices, we can turn to Daignault's own writing style in the articles he published in his newspaper, *La Sentinelle*.[1] Daignault's style represents an array of language practices that do not conform to modernist conceptualizations of language regimentation and purification espoused both by the French American élite and the Catholic Church at the time. Instead, Daignault uses "la langage du carrefour," the language of the street corner, writing the way people might speak to each other at the intersection when one driver has cut the other driver off (Daignault, "Plaidoyer"). Although he seems to be aware of his own style as a rhetorically strategic response to the linguistic and material economy in which he was writing (he was trying to reach the masses), Daignault seems not to have considered the way his style was constituted by linguistic fluidity and local language practices of the French American working class. At the same time that he used the language of the street to offend and provoke in some of his writings, he defended his advocacy of French by valorizing Parisian French language and culture as the carrier and pinnacle of Western civilization.

Daignault's position was paradoxical. On one hand, he was a member of the Franco-American élite attempting to advance French identity in North America by aligning his political activism with a long tradition of French resistance to Anglo domination on the continent tied to the protection of the French language. His interest in French-language rights was attached to a belief in protecting the linguistic, cultural, and racial purity of the French people. On the other hand, he was basing his argument on the very same ideologies of linguistic modernity that valorized English over French in the North American linguistic economy. These arguments assumed languages to be discretely bounded and distinct from one another, capable of being purified, standardized, and enlisted in nationalist politics. Daignault relied on the validity of these assumptions when arguing before the Rhode Island courts that the funds for French parishes should be kept distinct from the funds for the majority English diocese. While he wanted to protect the French from subjection to the English in politics and education, he simultaneously sought to justify and explain his own social position by representing the position of the common people (*les nôtres*) as inextricably connected to a premodern past—there had to be people in need of this modernizing French education that he was arguing for. In arguing thus, he distanced himself from the very people he was representing. Daignault's philosophy of education held that education was an instrument of modernization, a way to bridge the temporal gap between the modern and the premodern by bridging the social gap between the élite and *les nôtres*. The problem he attempted to resolve in his writings was that the progress of a modernized French American élite depended on the maintenance of *les nôtres* as an unassimilable French-speaking minority from which the élite could continue to distinguish themselves.

Daignault attempted to resolve the paradoxes of his social position by deploying in his public writing a set of stylistic choices designed to incorporate his non-elite audience, and these stylistic moves were considered among his most offensive and abusive writings. In one article, for example, he suggests that the best way to respond to the Church's language policy is "with a shit shovel"

(Daignault, "La Supérieure"). In the same article, he wrote that the bishop was engaged in "criminal work" and was trying to "strangle" the French. In a 1926 article, he wrote that a rival newspaper, *La Tribune*, which was sympathetic to the Irish bishop of the diocese, "has finally reached a point, that old thing, where it vomits upon the Franco-Americans all the filth that the dirty Irish have placed in its mouth" ("Daignault's Campaign"). In a 1927 article, he wrote in response to an anonymous article in *La Tribune* that, if the author of that article would make himself known, "we could then make this hack, hiding in his own rubbish, swallow the drool emerging from his stinking mouth" (Daignault, "Les Grands"). By December 1927, prominent Franco-American community leaders were marginalizing Daignault, warning that his attack on ecclesiastical authority "only drags respect for authority through the mud and sows the kind of disdain and hate that leads to schism" (Chartier 152). Indeed, Daignault was a well-known Franco-American community leader, presiding over one of the region's French cultural associations; however, his writings led the church to sanction that association, citing Daignault's "total disrespect of ecclesiastical authority" (Chartier 152).

Daignault's writings seem to have been upsetting in part because of their preoccupation with the grotesque bodies of the bishop and his supporters—bodily functions, toilets, and vomit. His writings were accused of being schismatic and heretical, though they do not address Church doctrine directly. In the writings in which Daignault does address Church doctrine, he only attempts to hold the Church accountable to its own canonical laws and the recommendations of its own councils, such as the Council of Baltimore. Instead, the anxiety over the schismatic and heretical potential of his work derives from his insistence that the Church consisted of mortal bodies that could die—which was exactly his contention in the lawsuits, in which he claimed that the church corporation consisted of the actual parishioners. Calling attention to the mortal body of the Church threatened to subvert its immortal corporate body, as manifested in the dignity of the bishop's office.

In early 1927 the bishop's office indirectly responded to Daignault in its own official newspaper, the *Providence Visitor*. An anonymous writer in that paper defended the bishop who, "mindful of the dignity of his office, and charged with the high responsibility of maintaining the peace and welfare of his diocese has, during the past three years, chosen to suffer contumelies from an irresponsible layman" ("Daignault's Offence"). The move from the mortal body to the dignity of an office was a defense against the grotesque mortality of the church, a defense summed up by the medieval Church teaching: *Dignitas nunquam perit, individua vero quotidie pereunt* ("The Dignity never perishes, although individuals die every day" [Kantorowicz 385]). In *The King's Two Bodies*, Ernst

Kantorowicz investigates in the writings of early modern English jurists the genealogy of the legal understanding of *Dignitas*. That understanding began with writings in canon law that established the immortal aspect of the pope or bishop, and it ended with the establishment of secular corporations such as English duchies. In order to execute the demands of their offices, the pope, bishop, king, and duke all depended on the attachment to their natural bodies of "something supra-individual and perpetual . . . namely the *Dignitas quae non moritur*" (395). Daignault's style, then, profaned the body of the church in the office of its bishop, and the bishop responded with a dignity that constrained his ability to retaliate, a constraint designed to maintain the church's bodily coherence.

There is a second layer of supra-individuation, here, that must be considered before we can fully understand the complicated relationship between language and corporeal/corporate bodies. Just as with the language protests (Welsh, northern Irish, and American Indigenous) described earlier, Daignault's representation of minority-language rights depends on the construction and maintenance of a traditional folk people who are excluded from civil discourse and the public sphere because of language and culture, and who must rely on a modernized élite capable of representing them. Daignault's offensive writings, then, sought to make cohere a second corporate body, separate from the Church: the body politic of the Franco-American people themselves (*les nôtres*). Daignault's writing style could have been motivated not by a desire to profane the episcopal *Dignitas* but, rather, by an anxiety over the distance between the French American élite and the people whom they claimed to represent, specifically as that distance was measured by language difference.

The maintenance of these two bodies—the body politic of the French people and the corporate body of the Catholic Church—both depended on the same ideologies of linguistic modernity that set English against French and that set standardized metropolitan varieties of these languages against vernacular varieties. The subversive style of his writings has the potential to undermine these ideologies, based as they are on an alternate set of assumptions about language as mobile, fluid, and unruly. But they ultimately undermine Daignault's own position as one who was authorized to speak on behalf of all Franco-Americans, because they reveal his own privileged socioeconomic status in relation to the people he was trying to represent. As I have explained elsewhere, the French language in New England was stratified into *un mauvais français* spoken by the working class and *le bon usage* of the metropolitan centers of Montréal and Québec City (Peters 573). Daignault—educated in Québec and holding graduate degrees from Boston College and Columbia University—

attempted to write in a conversational style that indulges in what were surely the racial stereotypes and coarse speech that one would have heard at *les carre-fours du petits Canadas* of Rhode Island.

In linguistic terms, when resorting to vulgarities in his writing, he occasion-ally uses a Canadian French basilect known as *joual*. In one article, for example, he irreverently argues that the head of school in Manchester, New Hampshire, was more concerned with the cleanliness of the bathrooms than with pedagog-ical questions. The word he uses for "bathroom" is *la bécosse* (Perreault 10). *La bécosse* is a *joual* term derived from the English word "backhouse," meaning "outhouse" (Colpron 103). It is not considered standard Canadian French. We might interpret *la bécosse*/backhouse as accented speech, neither French nor English yet both at the same time. Daignault's use of *joual* marks a telling sty-listic move, for it shows him trying to position himself rhetorically alongside *les nôtres* by representing in writing a particular way of speaking that ideologies of linguistic modernity suppress as illegitimate, hybridized, nonstandard, and corrupted versions of purified, distinct national languages.

Reading Daignault's offensive style in this way reveals *la bécosse*/backhouse as a strategic language practice in which a dispossessed people—the working-class populations of les nôtres—subvert the structures of local material and language economies for their own purposes. The Catholic Church valorized standard English in its language politics and in its economic arrangements. The Franco-American leadership valorized standard metropolitan varieties of French—such as those spoken in Montréal and Paris—in its language poli-tics and in its economic arrangements. The use of *joual* in everyday life was a marker of a devalued racial and class identity within these local economies— it was the language of the French immigrant working class—and its tactical use had the capacity to resist the legitimacy of these dominant economies. We might think of Daignault's use of *la bécosse*/backhouse as a linguistic equiva-lent to Québec's later efforts to "francicize" (Fishman 295) Anglo political and financial institutions in the 1970s' nationalist movement. Just as Québec's Parti Québecois leadership strategically infiltrated Anglo institutions in order to make them representative of francophone interests, so do the language mixings of *joual* infiltrate dominant linguistic codes in order to represent marginalized identities. The popularity of Daignault's newspaper among the French in New England must be attributed at least to the satisfaction that many felt in seeing these suppressed language practices represented in writing.

The politics of Daignault's style was limited in its effectiveness, however, because he styled his French in this way in service of his own position. He wanted to mobilize the broad popular support that the élite rhetoric of more moderate Franco-American cultural institutions failed to elicit in the face of Americanization pressures in the state legislature and English-only pressures in the Church. As a producer of French nationalist discourse, Daignault's newspaper aimed to emulate the work of *Le Droit* in Ottawa: the creation of a transnational francophone identity that could organize against attacks on French-language schooling across New England, Ontario, and the western Canadian provinces.[2] The vision for this transnational identity, however, cohered around an imagined sense of French nationalism, geographically dispersed across North America but still a traditional European nationalism nonetheless. This vision did not represent the real cultural and linguistic experiences of francophone North America, which were dispersed into various cross-cultural and cross-linguistic hybrid variations, from the French-Cree Métis of Manitoba province, to the black American French Acadian mixings of New Orleans, to the Anglo-French mixings of New England.

All of these creolizations rely—as does the effectiveness of Daignault's argument—on an alternate conceptualization of language as mobile, unruly, and unstable, simultaneously connected to global economies but constituted by local practices for local needs. Daignault enlists linguistic mobility, but in service of an argument for protecting the status of French as a national language, an argument that diminishes the potential for linguistic mobility to create transnational relations in everyday life. He shows himself to be anxious to identify with les nôtres when, for example, he asks in 1925, "How can we protect ourselves against those who sell our rights while pretending to defend them?" (Daignault, "La Superieure"). This question captures exactly the kind of paradoxical position occupied by the élite—their privilege was predicated on the construction of a folk tradition embodied by people who remained subservient to them. The élite claimed to be serving the people, yet the people's subservience was required.

AN ARGUMENT FOR UNRULY LANGUAGE

Like the body, language is wild, unruly, and unrepresentable. Nevertheless, it is figured into political and economic arrangements, just as the body is taken up into corporate arrangements and bodies politic. At least in the context of the United States, contemporary language policies in favor of linguistic purity are resisted by language protests that deploy a rhetoric of rights. However, both of these arguments—for purity and for minority rights—stem from twentieth-century political struggles of linguistic minority groups as they sought greater political representation in American politics through the institutions available to them, in this case the Roman Catholic Church. The framework of purification and hybridization constrains our ability to see everyday language practices and to account for the unruly nature of language. On each side is a set of modernist conceptualizations of linguistic purity that draw a political border through cross-language relations. This same conceptualization seems to inform language conflicts outside the United States, such as the work of the Welsh Language Society in protesting the exclusion of Welsh from Morrison's supermarkets in the United Kingdom, or the Sinn Fein's use of Irish as a nationalist language to dramatize Northern Ireland's subjection to England.

An alternate approach is to subvert ideologies of linguistic modernity through the strategic use and study of unruly language practices such as Daignault's use of French Canadian *joual*. To study Daignault's protest movement only as bodily resistance to an oppressive discursive regime is to ignore what, to my mind, is the central role of language itself in his protests—how it is conceptualized as a social relation, and how that conceptualization operates as a framework that constrains alternate approaches to language in the controversy that left him and dozens of others excommunicated. Further, the politics of Daignault's style cannot be fully accounted for by the framework that he himself used to advocate for minority-language rights. Taking account of the unruliness of subversive linguistic stylings such as Daignault's can complicate our understanding of the movement between discursive regimentation and bodily resistance. Daignault's French created an opening, an incoherency, in the arrangement of the Church's corporate body. Unfortunately for Daignault (because his style did not suit his purpose), it also created an incoherency in the arrangement of a transnational francophone body politic led by the élite. We should not take the failure of Daignault's project as evidence of the illegitimacy of his tactics. Unruly language affords social actors the rhetorical agency necessary to confront, subvert, and alter discursive structures, disrupting and outmaneuvering the corporate body by rendering it incoherent and making it speak in tongues.

NOTES

1. I am indebted to the work of Robert Perreault, who first identified the offensive style in many of the *La Sentinelle* articles used in this essay.

2. Daignault attributed the idea for the newspaper to "a Canadian prelate" who saw similarities between the language politics of New England and the language politics of the Anglophone provinces of Canada (Daignault, *Le Vrai Mouvement sentinelliste* 227–28). The prelate suggested to Daignault that Rhode Island lacked a newspaper like *Le Droit* in Ottawa, which was advocating for French-language rights in the public sphere.

WORKS CITED

Canagarajah, A. Suresh. *Resisting Linguistic Imperialism in English Teaching.* Oxford University Press, 1999.

Chartier, Armand. *The Franco-Americans of New England: A History.* L'Institut Français and ACA Assurance, 1999.

Colpron, Gilles. *Dictionnaire des anglicismes.* Beauchemin, 1982.

Curran, Patrick P. "Respondent's Brief: *Adolphe E. Simard, et al. v. The Church of the Precious Blood of Woonsocket, et al. Eq. No. 802.*" Superior Court of the State of Rhode Island, Union St. Jean Baptiste Archives, Emmanuel d'Alzon Library, Assumption College, Worcester.

Daignault, Elphège J. "Les Grands 'Spasmes' patriotiques de Vézina." *L'Indépendant* (Fall River), March 29, 1927. Union St. Jean Baptiste Archives, Emmanuel d'Alzon Library, Assumption College, Worcester.

Daignault, Elphège J. "Plaidoyer 'pro domo' de M. le Curé Devoy." *La Sentinelle* (Woonsocket), September 3, 1925, 1. Union St. Jean Baptiste Archives, Emmanuel d'Alzon Library, Assumption College, Worcester.

Daignault, Elphège J. "La Supérieure devra toujours être irlandaise!" *La Sentinelle*, August 20, 1925, 1. Union St. Jean Baptiste Archives, Emmanuel d'Alzon Library, Assumption College, Worcester.

Daignault, Elphège J. *Le Vrai Mouvement sentinelliste en Nouvelle Angleterre, 1923–1929 et l'affaire du Rhode Island.* Les Éditions du Zodiaque, 1936.

"Daignault's Campaign Based on Anti-Irish Prejudice." *Catholic Messenger* (Worcester), March 24, 1927. Union St. Jean Baptiste Archives, Emmanuel d'Alzon Library, Assumption College, Worcester.

"Daignault's Offence." *The Providence Visitor*, February 18, 1927. Union St. Jean Baptiste Archives, Emmanuel d'Alzon Library, Assumption College, Worcester.

Fishman, Joshua A. *Reversing Language Shift: Theoretical and Empirical Foundations of Assistance to Threatened Languages.* Multilingual Matters, 1991.

Gonzalez, Daniel. "Tribes Protest Prop. 203." *English for the Children*, October 14, 2000. www.onenation.org/article/tribes-protest-prop-203/.

Herndl, Carl G., and Danny A. Bauer. "Speaking Matters: Liberation Theology, Rhetorical Performance, and Social Action." *College Composition and Communication* 54, no. 4 (June 2003): 558–85.

Horner, Bruce, and Min-Zhan Lu. "Resisting Monolingualism in 'English': Reading and Writing the Politics of Language." In *Rethinking English in Schools: A New and Constructive Stage*, edited by Viv Ellis, Carol Fox, and Brian Street, 141–57. Continuum, 2007.

Jalbert, Eugene. "Supplemental Brief for Respondents on Demurrer: *Mederic J. Masse et al. v. Church of Our Lady of Consolation et al. Eq. No. 8328.*" Superior Court of the State of

Rhode Island, Union St. Jean Baptiste Archives, Emmanuel d'Alzon Library, Assumption College, Worcester.

Kantorowicz, Ernst. *The King's Two Bodies: A Study in Medieval Political Theology*. Princeton University Press, 1952.

Lu, Min-Zhan. "An Essay on the Work of Composition: Composing English against the Order of Fast Capitalism." *College Composition and Communication* 56, no. 1 (September 2004): 16–50.

Lu, Min-Zhan. "Living-English Work." *College English* 68, no. 6 (July 2006): 605–18.

Mattingly, Carol. "Telling Evidence: Rethinking What Counts in Rhetoric." *Rhetoric Society Quarterly* 32, no. 1 (Winter 2002): 99–108.

Mederic J. Masse et al. v. Church of Our Lady of Consolation. Eq. No. 8328. Superior Court of the State of Rhode Island. Union St. Jean Baptiste Archives, Emmanuel d'Alzon Library, Assumption College, Worcester.

"No Racial Lines in Politics." *Providence Journal*, May 21, 1922. Union St. Jean Baptiste Archives, Emmanuel d'Alzon Library, Assumption College, Worcester.

Pennycook, Alastair. *Global Englishes and Transcultural Flows*. Routledge, 2007.

Pennycook, Alastair. *Language as a Local Practice*. Routledge, 2010.

Perreault, Robert B. *Elphège J. Daignault et le mouvement sentinelliste à Manchester, New Hampshire*. National Materials Development Center, 1981.

Peters, Jason. "Speak White: Language Policy, Immigration Discourse, and Tactical Authenticity in a French Enclave in New England." *College English* 75, no. 6 (July 2013): 563–81.

"RSF Man Arrested and Charged for Using Irish." *Irish Republican News*, March 8, 2014. www.republican-news.org/current/news/2014/03/rsf_man_arrested_and_charged_f.html.

Sutherland, Christine Mason. "Feminist Historiography: Research Methods in Rhetoric." *Rhetoric Society Quarterly* 32, no. 1 (Winter 2002): 109–22.

Trewyn, Hywel. "Protest outside Morrisons in Bangor after Welsh Prescription Row." *Daily Post*, January 13, 2014. www.dailypost.co.uk/news/north-wales-news/protest-outside-morrisons-bangor-after-6500403/.

13

REMIX AS UNRULY PLAY AND PARTICIPATORY METHOD FOR IM/POSSIBLE QUEER WORLD-MAKING

LONDIE T. MARTIN AND ADELA C. LICONA

For Lowlaa

T hrough our collaborations, in our individual inquiries, and in our community-engaged work with local youth as coresearchers for the Crossroads Collaborative, we have come to appreciate the place of play in our work as a source of possible joy and as a method for queer world–making.¹ We want to develop play as a creative, critical, and relational component of action-oriented, desire-based research with and for youth, and we turn to the queer as a crucial element of "hope's methodology" and as "a restorative herme-neutic" (see Muñoz 5; Warner xv). We note the rich world-making possibilities for youth-led participatory media productions to illuminate the value of a crit-ically utopic perspective and of a commitment to radical play—two modes of orientation to the everyday from which queer theory, in its current formations and iterations, could benefit. Scholars, including Avery Gordon, José Muñoz, Eve Tuck, and Sara Warner, are calling on academics to risk engaging and re-animating notions of the utopic.[2] When those of us who desire and work toward a queerer world embrace the riskiness of a utopic perspective (one that insists on a playful present and performs a more radically open and always uncertain, if not impossible, future), we do so against an uncritical conflation of radical hope with naïveté, of playfulness with childishness. The impulse to dream, de-sire, and pursue a queerer world is too often cast aside based on a rhetorical geography that locates play exclusively in the terrain of childhood—the only appropriate place for silliness and the unruliness it implies. Yet we are called in our participatory research to risk pursuing the pleasure and transformative potential of a playful orientation because it provides us with a way to imag-ine coalitions that resist hetero/normative logics and neoliberal imperatives. Such pursuits rely on an understanding of participants as coalitional subjects engaged in participatory endeavors and exchanging relational knowledges that emerge from formal and experiential literacies (Jenkins et al.; Licona and Chávez; Licona and Gonzales).

In this chapter we analyze two digital videos produced by youth during the 2011 Nuestra Voz social justice summer camp in Tucson, Arizona, that we both participated in as teacher-researchers. In our analyses of these videos—one confronting the violence of abstinence-only sex education and the other speaking back to the violence of the school-to-prison pipeline (STTP)—we heeded the call to engage in hopeful methodologies. We do so not only for the joy of such an endeavor but because our work and play with local Tucson youth comes at a time of what Donna Haraway might characterize as truly "monstrous" politics ("The Promises of Monsters"). Following Sara Warner, we argue that the playful methods and coalitions that emerged in these youth-produced, queer/ed digital videos can be understood as "acts of gaiety" or "play-ful methods of social activism and mirthful modes of political performance that inspire and sustain deadly serious struggles for revolutionary change" (xi). We adopt Brian Sutton-Smith's notion of play as neither necessarily opposed to work nor the derogatory purview of children (19), but as a more capacious and queer world–making practice "characterized by its own distinct performances and stylizations" (218–19).

With this understanding of play as both queer joy and vulnerable critique, we ask how we might inhabit a both/and perspective to conceive of youth-produced participatory media as queer world–making play that surpasses the adult/youth binary and can—at once—*both* reproduce normative aspirations *and* critically intervene in the tyranny of norms around gender, sex, sexuality, anatomy, and desire through disarticulations and reassemblages. This remixing emerges in a southern Arizona context as a life-sustaining response to state forces engaged in constraining and containing bodies—especially queer youth, youth of color, queer youth of color, and immigrant youth. As a response to increasing state control and surveillance (outlined in the following section) and in its displacement of an imposed heterosexual matrix as well as in its efforts toward disarticulating the body, sex, gender, and desire, this playful tactic of remixed and relational literacies intervenes in the delegitimation of particular bodies and its material consequences. Through the remixed literacies we outline here, we identify those moments when youth are playing/working to expand the very meaning of a valued and valuable body that at once desires and produces knowledge in the world and, in so doing, asserts other ways of knowing and other knowledges. The radical, unruly, and utopic edge of this play rests on its messiness, uncertainty, vulnerability, and even on its contradictions. As a form of resistance, this play is imperfect. It stumbles, takes risks, and even contradicts itself on its way toward a queer/er future that may never arrive but becomes "visible only in the horizon" through playfully performative dreams of the future (Muñoz 11).

MONSTROUS POLITICS AT PLAY IN A STATE OF PANIC/PANICKED STATE

The contemporary Arizona context can be defined by monstrous politics and practices. Within the womb of this monster, as Haraway describes it, a politics of unrestrained market flows buttresses a need for bodies whose mobility and visibility can be surveilled and constrained, particularly at the intersections of citizenship status, race, gender, disability, sex, and sexuality (319). Legislation produced by (and productive of) states of social and sexual panic in such monstrous contexts fuels xenophobia, homophobia, and transphobia and defines im/possibilities for being and belonging as well as conditions for mobility, visibility, and learning (see Gutiérrez et al.; Licona and Chávez; Licona and Maldonado). Such an actively cultivated, fear-inflected climate of panic has particularly detrimental consequences for youth, which moves us to ask, What are the re/generative possibilities youth, as unruly subjects, might seize when they speak up and out about such oppressive practices?

Recognizing youthful queer world–making practices is a particularly pressing project given the monstrous borders erected and patrolled through Arizona's assemblage of neoliberal, heteropatriarchal, settler colonial, and white supremacist legislation undertaken simultaneously with the privatization of detention centers and prisons. Introduced in 2010, Arizona's "Papers, Please" law (SB 1070) empowers law enforcement officials to question anyone based on suspicion of undocumented status, thereby emboldening racial profiling.

At the time, Arizona led the way with such anti-immigrant legislation; since then, other states—including Alabama, Florida, Nevada, and Texas—have introduced similar legislation (Fausset). Since 2010, the American Civil Liberties Union (ACLU) and the administration of former President Barack Obama have challenged the constitutionality of parts of SB 1070 (Santos), and a United Nations panel of experts on migration cited SB 1070 and HB 2281 together as constituting "a disturbing pattern of legislative activity hostile to ethnic minorities and immigrants" ("Arizona"). Keeping in mind that SB 1070 was authored in cooperation with—and some reports suggest in tacit collaboration with—representative groups from the for-profit prison industry, we understand Arizona's legislative context as a constellation of materially implicated attempts to discipline, contain, and control those bodies the state has deemed unruly (Sullivan)—to compel identification, triangulate locations, and restrict movement and the ability of communities to claim histories and space.

Introduced during the same session, HB 2281 targeted and dismantled Tucson Unified School District's (TUSD) Mexican American Studies (MAS) program, which had been linked positively to graduation rates and test performances. Where SB 1070 does not prevent law enforcement officials from questioning someone's citizenship status based on presumed racial identity, HB 2281 dismisses race as a necessary site of inquiry by prohibiting ethnic studies courses based on the following mischaracterizations of their goals:

1. Promote the overthrow of the United States Government.
2. Promote resentment toward a race or class of people.
3. Are designed primarily for pupils of a particular ethnic group.
4. Advocate ethnic solidarity instead of the treatment of pupils as individuals. (1)

When HB 2281 prohibits courses "designed primarily for pupils of a particular ethnic group," it upholds the racial chauvinism of Eurocentric curricula as the standard and erases the critical interventions of ethnic studies courses and of the contributions of people of color as historic, living, and thriving actors in the southwest borderlands.[3]

It is important to understand the emergence of HB 2281 as a specific attempt to contain unruly youth who dare to question the whitewashing constraints of Eurocentric curricula. In response to an earlier school event where noted labor activist Dolores Huerta gave a speech in which she reportedly declared that "Republicans hate Latinos," then superintendent Tom Horne (serving as Arizona attorney general until 2015) sent Margaret Garcia Dugan to counter Huerta's public testimony. In 2006, students at Tucson High Magnet School stood up in silent protest during a school assembly led by Garcia Dugan (then deputy superintendent of public instruction), and some students wore tape across their mouths as they collectively walked out of the assembly.

In 2007 Horne addressed the students' act of civil disobedience and called for the end of TUSD's MAS program in his "Open Letter to the Citizens of Tucson."[4] Horne argues that it is "wrong to divide students up according to their racial group, and teach them separately" (1), a statement that disregards how Eurocentric curricula assume and construct the classroom as a space of white, cisgender, heterosexual privilege—a space where dominant stories of colonization are re/produced toward hegemonic ends. Horne's failure to note the production of these privileges in classrooms colors his view of the students' act of civil disobedience and leads him to characterize their silent protest as rude: "In hundreds of visits to schools, I've never seen students act rudely and in defiance of authority, except in this one unhappy case. I believe the students did not learn this rudeness at home, but from their Raza teachers. The students are being ill served. Success as adults requires the ability to deal with disagreements in a civil manner. Also, they are creating a hostile atmosphere in the school for the other students, who were not born into their 'race'" (2). When school spaces are perceived and produced according to normative standards of whiteness (and heterosexuality), student resistance appears unruly, out of place, rude, disrespectful. However, the students who stood up and walked out during Garcia Dugan's speech demonstrated an astute awareness of the politics of space and of resistance: when adults panic and attempt to hold you in place, resistance can look like mouths covered in silence and sound like feet collectively shuffling across a linoleum floor. Here, the political acoustics of space as an unruly act of civil disobedience resound.

In a state where heteropatriarchal, white supremacist, and settler colonial panics spring from and foment widespread fear and anxiety over bodies marked as other, we bear witness to the uneven and still undeniable ill effects on youth of the removal of state-identified undesirables by attrition and the banning of ethnic studies. Further, queer youth of color are identified for erasure by abstinence-only-until-marriage sex education policies that affirm heterosexuality and marriage as the only pathways to sex and sexuality, effectively denying the existence of sexualities and gender expressions that exist and even succeed wildly outside of a heteronormative matrix.[5] In this Arizona context of growing fears and rising anxieties—what some might call a state of panic—and inspired by the young people we worked with, we ask, where does the possibility for another world reside?

THE UNRULY AND THE QUEER UTOPIC

Against dismissals of utopia as being imperfect, naïve, or impractical, José Esteban Muñoz, in *Cruising Utopia: The Then and There of Queer Futurity*, argues not only for the radical potential of utopia as a hermeneutic for performance and activism but also for the specific alignment of queerness with the utopian. "We are not yet queer," he argues, and we may never achieve queerness if we imagine it as a final destination, a resting in a perfected present (1). Rather, for Muñoz, queerness is "essentially about the rejection of a here and now and an insistence on potentiality or concrete possibility for another world" (1). This view of the utopic as hopeful possibility connects us to Lauren Berlant's concept of "aspirational normativity" as the kind of hope for a better life that makes sense even as it emerges from seemingly senseless spaces of abjection (167). Aspirational normativity indexes an affective both/and space where subjects simultaneously gesture toward and hope for the im/possibility of a better future that never quite comes into view and find pleasure in the present where "having a friend, or making a date, or looking longingly at someone who might, after all, show compassion for our struggles, is really where living takes place" (Berlant 189). This queer, utopic longing that shapes the experience of the present is performance of a queer futurity that imagines and makes possible a way out from what J. Jack Halberstam identifies as the heteronormativity of the here and now (*In a Queer Time and Place*). Queer political action, Muñoz argues, could benefit from queer futurity theorized as capacious social invention, because it opens the imagination to social action and possibilities outside of queer lives circumscribed by discursive moral panics and heteronormativities.

Against logics that fuel pathologizing representations of queer lives and desires, Jonathan Alexander and Jacqueline Rhodes offer an understanding of queer new media practices that seek out and thrive in an illegibility that not only resists reduction but does so playfully. They evoke multimodal queerness as a space through which subjects communicate and perform "community or a desire for play, but also a gesture of critique—a critique of the normalizing categorizations of people into gay and straight. It is a critique, in short, of the heteronormative, of the proliferation of sexual subjectivities coupled with regimes of power that reproduce certain kinds of families, certain kinds of acceptable intimacies, certain kinds of authorized lives" (Alexander and Rhodes 196). Moreover, they position multimodality as a way to "break the spell of static, flat (and flattening) tropes of identity" (200). A multimodal approach to youth activist play that informs and is informed by remixes of bodies and narratives works against partial perspectives and de/colonized knowledges.

This approach is produced and circulated through multimodality practiced as a disembodied and then reembodied way of re/making spaces and remixing literacies as interventions into normative re-productions of the exceptional with coalitional potential. Invigorated by these cross-disciplinary frameworks, we proceed against ideas that the utopic has no place in serious academic endeavors or that a queer politics should proceed without playful, unruly, utopic, or normative aspirations.

Now we turn to practices of desire-based research and participatory media and to the role of play in youth participatory media productions that emerged at the Third Annual Nuestra Voz summer camp in June 2011. As a former racial justice project of YWCA Tucson, the "Youth. Art. Activism." summer camp brought together youth, education, and activism through art. With adult allies and a youth advisory council, camp director and community educator Sarah Gonzales organized three annual summer camps—weeklong visual and writing arts day camps where youth learned about and shared knowledge of historic traumas at the intersections of race, class, gender, sexuality, and citizenship status. During these summer camps Gonzales emphasized art as inquiry, activism, and healing practice. Following the principles of youth action research that inform us as teacher-researchers, we were inspired by Gonzales's innovative pedagogy, which now guides our own inquiry. Throughout the spring of 2011, we worked with Gonzales and youth participants to codesign a research agenda that was especially committed to intervening in deficit-driven assumptions and approaches to inquiry. Such an approach, in the words of Eve Tuck, "appreciates that all of us possess a complex and oftentimes contradictory humanity and subjectivity that is never adequately glimpsed by viewing [one another] as victims or, on the other hand, as superhuman agents" (20).

Summer camp participants came from a broad range of local youth-serving organizations. Many young people arrived already identifying as activists with particular concerns that informed their intersectional, coalitional approach to participation. Youth from Kore Press's Grrls Literary Activism workshops had practice in using their writings and their individual and collective voices to speak up and out in the public realm about injustices including gender oppressions and exclusions.[6] Youth participants from Eon Youth Lounge arrived well versed in sexual health and justice to "strengthen the gay, lesbian, bisexual, two spirit, transgender, queer, questioning, intersexed, and straight ally youth communities."[7] Returning camp participants arrived with a keen understanding of race, racism, racial trauma, and racial healing. As teacher-researchers at the camp, we followed youth as leaders of their own media productions meant to frame their needs, interests, and desires as expressed from the bottom up and outside in.[8]

To better understand how remix strategies might contribute to a methodology of hope through utopic and wild reimaginings, we examine the subversion of norms enacted through everyday unruly rhetorics and performances that work in and through these youth-led participatory media productions. Such an understanding holds the possibility for ongoing and emergent social movements that secure the right to knowledges and to belonging by dismantling policies and ways of thinking that produce and mark some bodies as exceptional or only recognizable as marginalized subjects (see Licona and Martin). From these wild reimaginings, we consider ongoing possibilities for queer remixes to inform other participatory projects and movements for social change.

REMIXED LITERACIES AS QUEERING PRACTICES, PRODUCTIONS, AND WORLD-MAKING IM/POSSIBILITIES

In the preproduction phase for the video titled "Let's Talk about Sex Ed," youth first interviewed one another about their histories and their home and school communities to learn more specifically about their distinct and shared experiences with sex education and with being sexed and gendered students in their schools. They cut up the stories that emerged through their interviews and agreed to mix the parts up so that participants might read narratives on camera that they did not author. In this way, their calls for particular knowledges were made not necessarily by the writer of the narrative, but by an allied youth. Approaching their own bodies as palimpsest—embodied story-texts and layered, living textualities—they used bold black marker to write statistics that they found most troubling about youth and sexuality directly on their bodies. The strong lines of black marker would eventually fade away, yet their ephemerally marked bodies resisted the reductions that numbers alone might accomplish and performed a recognition of what numbers and stories, together, might instead accomplish.

The video opens with a group of youth laughing and playing with condoms and dental dams in defiance of Arizona's de facto abstinence-only curricular—actions that explicitly question both their effectiveness and their value as a harm reduction practice or as appropriate for play and pleasure. As the video introduction unfolds, one young person tries to fit a dental dam over their shoe as raucous laughter erupts and echoes in the hallway, which calls to mind a cardinal elementary school rule: there shall be no talking, and certainly no playing, in the hallway! But the laughing, unruly youth are eclipsed by the somewhat dramatic entrance and performed authority of a trans youth of color who looks directly into the camera, intent eyes outlined in a fiery red, and playfully invites viewers to "talk about sex ed." In this direct address, play is a both/and space where cheeky, irreverent, and spontaneous fun works collaboratively with a vulnerable, deadly serious insistence on a queer presence. This insistence plays out against the fallout of a heteronormative sex ed curriculum that centers whiteness, pathologizes teen pregnancy, damns queerness, understands STIs as a failure of morality, and fails to imagine pleasure as a possibility to perform a desire for knowledges—the absence of which continues to mark only some youth lives as worth living. Accompanied by foreboding music, the youth continue the video by speaking back to state power through remixed narratives that collectively address what they see and experience as the limitations of abstinence-only sex ed. As an apparent coalitional gesture, they relocate their remixed stories in the embodied voice of another. This coalitional strategy is accomplished by having straight-identified youth proclaim their desire for queer knowledge, and queer youth speak the desire for pregnancy prevention. We are interested, following Muñoz, in the world-making possibilities contained in these creative productions that remix, reproduce, and contest the majoritarian public sphere (Muñoz 5). In considering the video through a third-space framework, we are called to its contradictions and to its generative potential as well as to a different optic (for more on third-space frameworks see Licona 2012). As Muñoz points out, a queer optic "permits us to take in the queerness that is embedded in the gesture" (72) and, in this instance, written explicitly on the bodies-as-palimpsests through remixed narratives and relational literacies, that insist on bodies and beings as unfinished and unruly productions effecting a kind of still-becoming, bodies-so-far understanding of *these* particular bodies at play in this participatory and queer world–making production.

Youth in this video collectively perform the unruly act of taking themselves, their desires, their lived experiences, and even their play seriously. Through their remixed and unruly rhetorical performances, these youth insist on interrupting the viewing of these reassembled if still unruly bodies and narratives as indicating something other than "developmental failures, local impossibilities," or otherwise pathologized subjects (Butler, *Gender Trouble* 24). Their message also addresses what Butler calls the "mundane violence performed by certain kinds of [normative] gender ideals" (*Gender Trouble* xx). This produced remix accomplishes an intervention into a concealing logic that conceives of only certain youth as rightfully inquiring bodies. These desiring bodies—often figured in the mainstream as either exceptional or deviant—intervene in such normativizing logics. Their performances reveal the absurdity of restricting access to knowledge, information, and resources and then stigmatizing youth for un(der)informed choices with pathologized outcomes. Youth have insisted that all bodies count as bodies, and that desired and produced knowledges— particularly those considered transgressive at this historic juncture—count as knowledge they want to have collective access to. Yet we understand this youth production as also unruly in its attempt to achieve a kind of legibility—an aspirational normativity—through what is being produced as the illicit in Arizona at this time (Muñoz 46). As an appeal to viewers to do something about an abstinence-only approach to sex ed, the video ends with a neoliberal refrain; looking directly at the viewer and speaking in earnest and urgent tones, the youth say "it saved me," which suggests that each individual performer has been and can be "saved" by state-sanctioned comprehensive sex ed. This concluding strategy highlights the normative aspirations that have been in a productive tension with the queer world–making tactics throughout the video.

In the second untitled video, youth expressed a lived awareness of the need to be attentive to race, class, gender, sex, sexuality, immigration status, and disability in their considerations of the school-to-prison pipeline. Produced using stop-motion photography, the video is an everyday narrative that opens with images of youth using black marker and handwritten words on strips of white paper to create blindfolds that limit their vision of themselves along lines of sight established by the surveilling eyes of a school system that too often opts for punishment and pushing out: "no chance," "rebel," "trapped," "lazy," "failure," "criminal," "delinquent," "prisoner." Throughout the video, we see youth get up, get ready for the day, walk through halls, sit in classes, play outside, and visit the bathroom. The scenes share a similar structure: viewers see a few seconds of youth participating in school activities, and at the end of the scene, viewers experience a quick zoom to a critical message secreted away in the space. For example, at the end of the scene where youth are getting ready for school and playfully striking poses, the camera zooms in on a sheet of paper tacked to the mirror: "For every lesbian, gay and bisexual youth who is bullied, 4 straight students who are perceived to be gay or lesbian are bullied." Here, the youth express their lived understandings that to even be suspected of boundary transgression—of possibly being something outside of the heteronormative matrix—is enough to be identified as one who can be harassed, bullied, pushed out. It is not their reflection that seems to matter most but, rather, what surveilling eyes see, interpret, and produce as the youth move through their school and the broader location of the STPP institutionalized and maintained through systems of formal education.[9] For these youth, complicating experiences and perceptions of diverse sexualities will help create a more inclusive and secure environment, a transformation they perform when they preface this scene about perceived queerness with "What we see isn't what we want" and close it with "We want to see positive changes in our hallways." Through the reassembling of photographic story, bodies in motion, and quantitative data, they rewrite the space as one of lived meaning, open to the simultaneity of diverse identities.

Toward the end of the video, the youth highlight the social multiplicity of space as simultaneously experienced by a diversity of individuals. They invite various adults into the school space as allies, a strategy that addresses the youth's desire to reimagine the school environment as a more explicitly communal space, one where all are called to participate. They depict this expansion of audience and purpose as happening not just in the physical space of the school but also in the pedagogical, psychic space of the textbook, a site that Dolores Delgado Bernal, in "Critical Race Theory," and other LatCrit theorists identify as one of colonization through curriculum. Thus, in a scene that opens with them goofing off around a cafeteria lunch table, the youth directly respond to HB 2281 and the removal of MAS books from TUSD classrooms by zooming in on a message hastily stuck in the pages of a textbook: "We want support from teachers, parents, and our community."[10]

As Crossroads scholars have elsewhere pointed out, "LGBTQ youth of color in particular face persistent and frequent harassment and bias-based bullying from peers and school staff as well as increased surveillance and policing, relatively greater incidents of harsh school discipline, and consistent blame for their own victimization" (Burdge, Licona, and Hyemingway 3). Informed by their research on the STPP, youth identified space as their organizing concept and remixed their own common experiences of school life to create a collage narrative of a fictionalized day. For them, the STPP signals an oppressive control of space and movement that determines how they are differently treated and constrained in these spaces. Thus, when youth script their video critiques of the STPP as taking place in the very locations where they perceive the pipeline to be most insidious (the hallways, classrooms, and even hidden spaces of formal educational contexts), they perform a refusal and rejection of what they see in the present and a simultaneous desire for the pleasures of a better future—*right now*. Similarly, the youth who challenge abstinence-only education in their video push at the boundaries of heteronormative logics and any politics of respectability as they remix assumptions about narrative linearity and the uncontainable bodies who desire knowledge and pleasure that they are not supposed to seek. This production of alternative narratives also produces alternative temporalities and spaces of queer possibility and hope that do not follow a linear trajectory of normative progress toward a distant and inevitable (and seemingly always desired) point on the straight horizon.

Finally, the youth explore the diversity of a re-visioned school space by rewriting their bodies from an asset-based perspective informed by the LatCrit consciousness discussed at the summer camp.[11] But this time, they take black markers and strips of white paper and hold them below their smiling faces, now fully visible above handwritten messages that read "graduate," "successful," "productive," and "valued." While youth position their video as an asset-driven intervention in the STPP and a regime of normativities around sex, sexuality, gender, race, and disability, their video also reproduces an aspirational normativity. This linear progression from "delinquent" to "productive" does not imagine other possibilities and the perhaps dynamic ebb and flow that might lead to different outcomes. In this moment, we see the youth intervening in pathologizing representations from an asset-driven perspective, but this rather straight progression also reproduces a linearity that speaks to Berlant's view of aspiration: "the goodness of the good life now feels possible" (163) and assured, even if, like Muñoz's queer horizon, the "good life" is in sight but out of reach. Still, in the outward look from this present scene, a hopeful line of sight connects, in the moment, to utopic imaginations. For youth who are often told to wait until they grow up—that they will understand when they are older—imagining an awkward and imperfect future in the play of a present moment is a radical act, because anyone who is young and Other can see the promise of an adult future for what it really is: an illusion.

THE PLAYFUL, THE UNRULY, AND THE COALITIONAL

What is illuminated by the unruly performances of remixes in these coalitional media productions? Do the ephemeral markings on the bodies and the narrative remixes provide an "anticipatory illumination of a queer world" (49) as Muñoz describes? Can we see these videos as expressions of survivance, as well as what Muñoz recognizes as the youth's "need to imagine becoming Other in the face of conspiring cultural logics of white supremacy and heteronormativity" (80)?[12]

We can, of course, offer a critique of neoliberal and normative reproductions of the self and the rights-based discourses deployed in rhetorics of being "saved." After all, remix is a potentially, not inherently, unruly practice, and some rules are stickier—harder to shake—than others. Yet, in this particular case, students created remixes in a way that rejects the normalizing calls for the exceptional that they so often face in order to be counted. They thus practice a politics of refusal that is coalitional and radically open. Practiced in this way, remix rejects the inherent divisions of a system of meritocracy that imposes risks on queer youth who fail to make themselves legible according to a binary of narrowly defined options: either youth are extraordinary or exceptional in their successes and performed optimism or they are an at-risk pathological mix of immorality and doomed sexual consequences. Artfully rearticulated bodies and a bricolage of voices critically relocated to the mouths of an/Other further refuse notions of authenticity, exceptionalism, and singularity—an act of unruly radical plagiarizing as purposeful remix. And so we ask, can these multimodal productions be playfully read as both normative and anti-normative, both possible and impossible, as well as critical of the state and, therefore, as Muñoz suggests, as "sexual avant-gardist act[s]" (56)? Can we experience these videos as a "relational and collective modality of endurance and support" (Muñoz 91) as well as a "vast [storehouse] of queer history and futurity" (91)? We think so.

In this chapter we have attempted to honor the value of play—and unruly play—as well as the utopic potential of a queer futurity that works with and through aspirational normativities. Remixed participatory productions can help adult allies and youth work together to cocreate spaces for exploring and expressing desires that may be deemed unruly by the state. Yet, we must remain critically open to both the promises and the perils of such im/possibilities. We have to cocreate learning spaces where youth and adult allies can witness their productions, have room to dream (a radical act in light of dominant imaginations of straight white and settler colonial futurity), and also be playfully critical of their missteps and imperfections.[13] Thus, although inflected with neoliberal discourses and desires, the youth approach their dis/embodied and disordering—even disorienting—reconfigurations and rememberings through remixed stories, bodies, and spaces to challenge dominant cultural and colonizing logics of coherent and stable gendered and sexed beings, assumed anatomies, and desires to provoke new definitions of desiring subjects who long for knowledge/s and the right to access, share, produce, and claim them. And in playfully calling for and producing transgressive knowledges as sites of desire, they defy the regulatory aims of the neoliberal state while also calling on the state to save them through (access to) knowledge, information, and education.

NOTES

1. The Crossroads Collaborative is a think-and-act research, writing, and teaching lab addressing youth, sexuality, health, rights, and justice. Adela Licona codesigned and codirected the Collaborative with Stephen Russell as a result of a 2010 Ford Foundation grant.

2. We proceed with an understanding of the cautions expressed by scholars, such as Karma Chávez, who are skeptical of the utopic, particularly when it is an "alternative to politics" and divorced from material lives (Chávez 5). We move forward with attention to material lives and proceed, also, with an appreciation for the ways in which the utopic is imagined and pursued as part of the creative vision that informs the political activism of the youth with whom we worked.

3. For evidence of the successes of the TUSD MAS program, see Nolan L. Cabrera, Jeffrey F. Milem, and Ronald W. Marx's *An Empirical Analysis of the Effects of Mexican*

American Studies Participation on Student Achievement within Tucson Unified School District.

4. To clarify, while Horne in his letter urges the dismantling of the "ethnic studies program," as of this writing, supporters of HB 2281 have only targeted the MAS program. TUSD continues to offer students courses in African American studies and Asian Pacific American studies.

5. The US Supreme Court ruling on the unconstitutionality of state-level bans on same-sex marriage reads as "marriage equality" for some. Will abstinence-only courses continue to uphold so-called straight marriage as the only legitimate pathway to sex and sexuality? A radical queer collective, Against Equality, argues that such marriage equality affirms hetero- and homonormativities and their associated privileges, which may proliferate despite—perhaps because of—the SCOTUS ruling.

6. Grrrls Literary Activism, a project of Kore Press, partners with local organizations, activists, and scholars to encourage youth in their desires for justice-oriented artistic expressions.

7. Eon Youth Lounge is a drop-in space for queer, queer of color, and allied youth that encourages youth leadership and well-being by meeting their expressed needs through education, activism, and play ("About Eon Youth Lounge").

8. Crossroads Collaborative scholars and community partners have worked to contextualize and analyze different aspects of the 2011 "Youth. Art. Activism." summer camp, including its pedagogical design and continuing innovations. For a study guide on using Crossroad Collaborative remix practices in classroom and workshop contexts, see Coan et al.; Licona and Gonzales; Martin; Martin and Licona.

9. In a study supported by the Gay-Straight Alliance Network and the Crossroads Collaborative, queer youth and youth of color report feeling unsafe and surveilled by school administrators and faculty, and they note disparities in the application of disciplinary policies that disproportionately impact them. For more on the formal and informal policies and practices that constitute school push-out and the STTP, see Burdge et al.

10. Some argue that removing books like Rodolfo F. Acuña's *Occupied America* and Paulo Freire's *Pedagogy of the Oppressed* is not the same as banning them. But the prevailing sentiment among those who opposed the ban is well captured in these lyrics from "Bulls on Parade" by Rage Against the Machine: "they don't gotta burn the books they just remove 'em / while arms warehouses fill as quick as the cells."

11. Many of the summer camp materials collected by Gonzales and the youth advisory council were grounded in the kind of asset-based approach to literacy and critical pedagogy that has been theorized and advanced in LatCrit and Chicana feminist scholarship. Here, we draw on Dolores Delgado Bernal's understanding of an "asset-based" approach to education as one that recognizes and values the often devalued cultural,

linguistic, and everyday knowledges that youth of color bring to formal and informal educational contexts and that recognize youth as keepers and creators of knowledge.

12. For more on survivance, see Aretha Matt, *Reclamation and Survivance*; Malea Powell, "Rhetorics of Survivance"; and Gerald Vizenor, *Manifest Manners*.

13. Gonzales has gone on to codirect Spoken Futures, Inc. where she works with "an all-youth staff on three core programs, the Tucson Youth Poetry Slam, Liberation Lyrics and Kaleidoscope, as well as the La Pilita Cultural Center in Barrio Viejo" ("About"). Many of the youth we worked with for this project are affiliated with these programs as participants and leaders.

WORKS CITED

"About." *Spoken Futures*. www.spokenfutures.org/about/.

Acuña, Rodolfo. *Occupied America: A History of Chicanos*. 8th ed., Pearson, 2014.

Alexander, Jonathan, and Jacqueline Rhodes. "Queerness, Multimodality, and the Possibilities of Re/Orientation." In *Composing(media) = Composing(embodiment): Bodies, Technologies, Writing, the Teaching of Writing*, edited by Kristin L. Arola and Anne Frances Wysocki, 188–212. Utah State University Press, 2012.

Arizona State, House of Representatives. House Bill 2281. Arizona State 49th Legislature, 2nd reg. sess., 2010. www.azleg.gov/legtext/49leg/2r/bills/hb2281s.pdf.

"Arizona: UN Experts Warn against 'a Disturbing Legal Pattern Hostile to Ethnic Minorities and Immigrants.'" *James Anaya: Archive Former UN Special Rapporteur*, May 10, 2010. www.unsr.jamesanaya.org/statements/arizona-un-experts-warn-against-a-disturbing-legal-pattern-hostile-to-ethnic-minorities-and-immigrants/.

Berlant, Lauren. *Cruel Optimism*. Duke University Press, 2011.

Burdge, Hillary, Adela C. Licona, and Zami T. Hyemingway. *LGBTQ Youth of Color: Discipline Disparities, School Push-Out, and the School-to-Prison Pipeline*. Gay-Straight Alliance Network and Crossroads Collaborative, 2014.

Butler, Judith. *Bodies That Matter: On the Discursive Limits of "Sex."* 1993. Routledge, 2011.

Butler, Judith. *Gender Trouble: Feminism and the Subversion of Identity*. Routledge, 1999.

Cabrera, Nolan. L., Jeffrey F. Milem, and Ronald W. Marx. *An Empirical Analysis of the Effects of Mexican American Studies Participation on Student Achievement within Tucson Unified School District*. Report to Special Master Dr. Willis D. Hawley on the Tucson Unified School District Desegregation Case, 2012.

Chávez, Karma R. *Queer Migration Politics: Activist Rhetoric and Coalitional Possibilities*. University of Illinois Press, 2013.

Coan, Casely, Leah S. Stauber, Adela C. Licona, and the Crossroads Collaborative. "Let's Talk about Sex Ed: Study Guide." *Crossroads Connections* 3, no. 2 (2014): 1–6.

Delgado Bernal, Dolores. "Critical Race Theory, Latino Critical Theory, and Critical Raced-Gendered Epistemologies: Recognizing Students of Color as Holders and Creators of Knowledge." *Qualitative Inquiry* 8, no. 1 (2002): 105–26.

Eon Youth Lounge. "About Eon Youth Lounge." www.facebook.com/eonyouth/.

Fausset, Richard. "Alabama Enacts Anti-illegal-immigration Law Described as Nation's Strictest." *Los Angeles Times*, June 10, 2011. www.articles.latimes.com/2011/jun/10/nation/la-na-alabama-immigration-20110610/.

Freire, Paulo. *Pedagogy of the Oppressed*. 30th Anniversary Edition, Continuum, 2005.

Gordon, Avery. *Ghostly Matters: Haunting and the Sociological Imagination*. University of Minnesota Press, 1997.

Gutíerrez, Laura, Christina Hanhardt, Miranda Joseph, Adela C. Licona, and Sandra K. Soto. "Nativism, Normativity, and Neoliberalism in Arizona: Challenges inside and outside the Classroom." *Teaching Sex*, special issue of *Transformations: The Journal of Inclusive Scholarship and Pedagogy* 21, no. 2 (2010/2011): 123–48.

Halberstam, J. Jack. *In a Queer Time and Place: Transgender Bodies, Subcultural Lives*. New York University Press, 2005.

Haraway, Donna. "The Promises of Monsters: A Regenerative Politics for Inappropriate/d Others." In *Cultural Studies*, edited by Lawrence Grossberg, Cary Nelson, and Paula A. Treichler, 295–337. Routledge, 1992.

Horne, Tom. "An Open Letter to the Citizens of Tucson." *Arizona Department of Education*, June 11, 2007. Online at wayback.archive-it.org/645/20080716203152/https://www.ade.az.gov/administration/superintendent/AnOpenLettertoCitizensofTucson.pdf.

Jenkins, Henry, K. Clinton, R. Purushotma, A. Robison, and M. Weigel. *Confronting the Challenges of Participatory Culture: Media Education for the 21st Century*. MacArthur Foundation, 2009.

Licona, Adela C. *Zines in Third Space: Radical Cooperation and Borderlands Rhetorics*. State University of New York Press, 2012.

Licona, Adela C., and Karma R. Chávez. "Relational Literacies and Their Coalitional Possibilities." *Peitho: Journal of the Coalition of Women Scholars in the History of Rhetoric & Composition* 18, no. 1 (2015): 96–107.

Licona, Adela C., and J. Sarah Gonzales. "Education/Connection/Action: Community Literacies and Shared Knowledges as Creative Productions for Social Justice." *Youth, Sexuality, Health, and Rights*, special issue of *Community Literacy Journal* 8, no. 1 (2013): 9–20.

Licona, Adela C., and Marta Maria Maldonado. "The Social Production of Latin @ Visibilities and Invisibilities: Geographies of Power in Small Town America." *Antipode* 46, no. 2 (2014): 517–36.

Licona, Adela C., and Londie T. Martin. "Remixed Literacies and Radical Cooperation: Exploring Responsivity at Play in a Youth-Directed Media Project." In *Writing for Engagement: Responsive Practice for Social Action*, edited by Mary P. Sheridan, Megan J. Bardoph, Megan Faver Hartline, and Drew Holladay, 125–38. Lexington Books, 2018.

Martin, Londie T. *The Spatiality of Queer Youth Activism: Sexuality & the Performance of Relational Literacies through Multimodal Play*. PhD dissertation, University of Arizona, 2013.

Martin, Londie T., and Adela C. Licona, with the Crossroads Collaborative. "Youth and Legislation: Changing Conversations through Action Research." *Crossroads Connections* 1, no. 2 (2012): 1–4.

Matt, Aretha. *Reclamation and Survivance: Diné Rhetorics and the Practice of Rhetorical Sovereignty*. PhD dissertation, University of Arizona, 2011.

Muñoz, Jose Esteban. *Cruising Utopia: The Then and There of Queer Futurity*. New York University Press, 2009.

Powell, Malea. "Rhetorics of Survivance: How American Indians Use Writing." *College Composition and Communication* 53, no. 3 (2002): 396–434.

Rage Against the Machine. "Bulls on Parade." In *Evil Empire*. Epic, 1996.

Santos, Fernanda. "U.S. and Arizona Yield on Immigration." *New York Times*, May 30, 2014. www.nytimes.com/2014/05/31/us/us-and-arizona-yield-on-immigration.html.

Sullivan, Laura. "Prison Economics Help Drive Ariz. Immigration Law." *NPR*, October 28, 2010. www.npr.org/2010/10/28/130833741/prison-economics-help-drive-ariz-immigration-law/.

Sutton-Smith, Brian. *The Ambiguity of Play*. Harvard University Press, 1997.

Tuck, Eve. *Urban Youth and School Pushout: Gateways, Get-Aways, and the GED*. Routledge, 2011.

Vizenor, Gerald. *Manifest Manners: Postindian Warriors of Survivance*. Wesleyan University Press, 1994.

Warner, Sara. *Acts of Gaiety: LGBT Performance and the Politics of Pleasure*. University of Michigan Press, 2012.

14

ON DEMOCRACY'S RETURN HOME

THE OCCUPATION OF LIBERTY/ZUCCOTTI PARK

JOHN ACKERMAN AND MEGHAN DUNN

Place is the first of all beings, since everything that exists is in a place and cannot exist without a place.

—Archytas, Commentary on Aristotle's *Categories*

I am ready to go home now. I am ready. Very tired.

—Cherríe Moraga, *This Bridge Called My Back*

The call to action was first made on *Adbusters*—to "#OCCUPYWALL-STREET" by showing up with a tent at an undesignated location in lower Manhattan on September 17, 2008 (*Adbusters*). This call performed the symbolic and informational work of galvanizing attention, but it did so—first and foremost—by conjuring a territorial imaginary, a place (somewhere) that would enable those interested to organize. Soon enough the imaginary became real, corresponding with Liberty/Zuccotti (L/Z) Park: a thirty-three-thousand-square-foot expanse of privately owned city park adjacent to Ground Zero and Wall Street between Broadway, Trinity Place, Liberty Street, and Cedar Street. This location eventually was chosen by the members of the Occupy Wall

Street (OWS) Tactical Committee for its proximity to Wall Street, its "high-visibility," and the "affordances" allowed as a park not subject to city curfews (Schwartz). Within months, over six hundred in-kind occupations had sprung up around the world, dovetailing with events, movements, and revolutions abroad—"first in Tunisia and then in Bahrain, Libya, Syria, Yemen, and most notably in Egypt" (Osborn xi)—as word of OWS traveled quickly by mouth and by media through sites such as Twitter, Facebook, Instagram, and LiveStream. #OWS, #Occupy, and #occupywallst went viral as the movements' territories multiplied.

The motives for answering the call differ according to who is speaking, and from which locale, and then, according to which part of history matters most. It is now a matter of social and economic history in the United States that the banks and insurance companies of New York's financial district failed, and the global system shuttered and then in very real ways collapsed. Steve Eisman recounts from inside the New York financial culture how such a catastrophe could occur: "Wall Street mistook leverage for genius" enabled by a culture accustomed to unwavering and unchecked growth and income incentives. This desire and greed was structured through credit-default swaps between those who loan money—the big banks, like Citigroup—and those who insure those loans—big insurance companies, like AIG. Then came for Eisman the "irresistible force" of subprime loans upon which global credit was at least partially based. Housing loans with shaky foundations eventually hurt the banking industry, but they gave banks leverage in the public sphere because the industry could blame homeowners for their irresponsible desire to own a home instead of blaming themselves. Subprime loans, as is now commonly known, were marketed to those new to mortgage lending or to those whose personal finances could be leveraged to the point of precarity. The income inequality that persists today, as Olivier Blanchard in 2009 and then Joseph Stiglitz in 2013 pointed out, is still cloaked in the American ideal of self-sufficiency in the household (*The Price of Inequality*). The economic crisis, with its many causes, led to the Stock Market Crash of 2008, which in turn resulted in the widespread loss of public securities, currencies, investments, and homes. And when the government interceded, it was not directly on behalf of the American people who suffered those losses but, rather, to secure the banking, credit, and insurance industries "too big to fail" whose reckless practices and greed paved the road to no uncertain perdition. It is no wonder today, as Marlia Banning has shown, that resentment circulates: it has been manufactured through a neoliberal economic apparatus for political gain, while it also builds from the ashes of personal financial loss. It is easier to blame oneself, or to be blamed, than to blame an apparatus.

Economic harm that underwrote outrage and resentment led some people to speak out, march, and then to occupy public places; yet there were other motives, other exigencies, for why people took to the streets and for why encampments grew. Simon Rogers reported in *The Guardian* in 2012 that OWS in L/Z Park eventually spawned over fifteen hundred locations worldwide, pointing out that the phenomenon of occupation itself—residing with others in fragile territories—became a visible, traceable, and mutable reason to act. We know this to be true from our direct involvement with the movement; to be present in the moment was to be present in place both locally and globally. We know it through conversations on the street and by following the digital growth of Occupy locations around the world, and then assisted by Rogers and other journalistic accounts. And we looked for theoretical allegories to what we saw and felt. Someone may well act out in society, choosing a place to occupy, for the reward of what John Protevi describes as a "political physiology" that scales ever outward, a body politic that builds across "civic, somatic and 'evental'" layers (94). A political physiology takes form in a specific locale through what Nathan Schneider describes as a "diversity of tactics"—a term common to social resistance to name the violent and nonviolent means of aggregating, motivating, and broadcasting civil disobedience. The Occupy movement's unique contribution to this repertoire was the occupation of territory itself such that embodied, communal acts of occupation fostered a different realization of the self and community. As Occupy encampments spread like "fireflies setting wildfires" (as the expression goes in Occupy), the rhetorical message and motive for the movement shifted from "who will save us?" to *how* will we save [ourselves]?" (Hornbein), and then by implication to *upon what higher ground shall we stand?*

We refer to someone's territorial imaginary to honor the embodied, physical, and geographic exposures that enable a social imaginary to congeal. Public life as an imagined possibility manifests through these material exposures, and when people occupy a setting, to realize camaraderie or to pursue a common cause, they do so knowing they will return home with a territorial imaginary altered by new exposures with others. In a recent retrospective on Occupy Wall Street, the New York–based photographer Accra Shepp reports the whereabouts of a few of the four hundred people he met in 2011 to remind us that—as people formed alliances to express outrage at financial institutions housed just a few blocks away from the park—they also gathered simply to be together in one place, guided by an uncharted will to cohabitate with those presumably of common mind but from different locations. In Shepp's photo essay, people gathered out of fear of an uncertain future for loved ones or to provide legal assistance and health care. People came to argue through legal, civic, and religious channels that public space should be set aside permanently as a residence for the movement. They came because of student debt and undocumented legal status, and they came because they were homeless. They came to record history in the making by image and story, and they came to offer their crafts and trades (such as a set of stationary bicycles to power personal devices and reduce the carbon footprint). In all these accounts, they gathered for many reasons and with the implicit motive to return home soon, however that may occur, guided by public life as it was encountered in lower Manhattan.

Everyone went somewhere once the protests subsided. Some married while others traveled. Some turned more closely to art while others went back to school. Some protested other forms of social and environmental injustice while others opened businesses, in one case a restaurant that employs undocumented workers. Some turned to medicine, engineering, and the law, while others employed legal services to fight for their own citizenship. Judith Butler proposes in *Notes toward a Performative Theory of Assembly* that going home after a political assembling is no idle act. The one and the many assemble for causes but also for the benefit of "cohabitation" in precarious times and circumstances to share a common foreboding born out of real social and economic danger and indexed differently by gender, sexuality, and social standing. What one may well discover through public protest is the texture of a common experience of precarity, "a felt sense . . . lived as slow death, a damaged sense of time, or unmanageable exposure" (*Notes* 69–71). A commonplace sense of precarity reveals its sustaining nature upon the return home as the by-product of occupation, the consequence of living in common with strangers in time- and space-limited circumstances. Occupy Wall Street is treated as an exceptional moment in economic and democratic history; going home is not.

Wendy Brown comments on the difference between exceptional moments of publicity that oppose the totalizing economies of late capitalism, even though "we are everywhere *homo oeconomicus* and only *homo oeconomicus*" (33). Capitalism incarcerates those who aspire to some form of civic ideal or common cause of justice to the degree that we exist as human capital in all domains of public life and have been that way for a very long time. Yet Brown holds out that a counterfigure exists within all of us, a figure that she calls *homo politicus*, a "creature animated by and for the realization of popular sovereignty" (86). This personage—partial within all of us and burdened with a distant horizon for public fulfillment—refuses defeat, as we retain an irrevocable capacity to imagine and construct "the substance and legitimacy of whatever democracy might mean *beyond* securing the individual provisioning of individual ends" (87, emphasis added).

These figures are estranged at this stage of advanced capitalism, yet the nature of public resistance when it is deployed to occupy public spaces—when people stand, speak, and work together—could sponsor a recuperation of *homo politicus* that courts speech actions and even organizes civic resistance for the maintenance of everyday life. To assemble as "cohabitation"—and thus to bear witness to how someone else's precarity might resemble yours—fuses the quotidian with the political, reimagining ordinary public life in extraordinary circumstances and unapproved territories. Butler cautions those who witness the spectacle of protest to look beyond the uproar: "We miss something of the point of these public demonstrations if we fail to see that the very public character of the space is being disputed" (*Notes* 70–71). She urges us to ask the rhetorical question, "how it is that public assembly and speech reconfigure the materiality of public space . . . when crowds move outside the square, to the street or the back alley, to the neighborhoods where streets are not yet paved, then something more happens" (71). Public protest premised on occupation serves those who march and those who witness the marching by "bringing attention to the way that politics is already in the home, or on the street, or in the neighborhood, or indeed in those virtual spaces that are equally unbound by the architecture of the house and the square" (71).

The authors of this essay strove to recapture our sense of cohabited precarity even though we are living very different lives, with vastly different exposures to the causes of the movement. One of us without a mortgage but with burgeoning student debt took leave from graduate studies in Colorado to participate directly in the Occupy movement, as fieldwork for the dissertation and then as the best location to study emplacement that serves public resistance. The other of us, cocooned within his career, did not "occupy" places much more than the classroom or the local neighborhood, although in the summer of 2010 he took to the rhetoric of letters, phone calls, and legal maneuvering. His family bore the brunt of global economic collapse by losing a home in Ohio as a consequence of a devalued housing market in the region. If the outrageous ethics behind subprime loans brought some people to the streets to march in solidarity, it brought others into the threats and turmoil of the banking industry's piety and legal protections. The historical figures of *homo oeconomicus* and *homo politicus* seemed very real to us in writing this essay, because the former clearly dominates our economic selfhoods while we struggle to realize the most just sense of our political being. The aftermath of occupation invites these kinds of articulations of a shared sense of economic precarity in very different circumstances, realized by marching in the street and by fighting to protect sweat equity. Our territorial imaginaries were built through different circumstances and different stretches of time, but we achieved a "conjunctive" articulation of the political value of political and residential occupation that could be, then, carried forward in our lives (Grossberg 37).

This conjunctive tapestry for making do in the everyday fits well with Kelly E. Happe's characterization of the Occupy movement as the struggle to recuperate the bases for daily survival. Cooking, finding shelter, figuring communication, and asserting due processes, all were framed by the circumstantial attraction of helping each other to thrive. These *techne*, this *metis*, were on display as technical markers of quotidian survival; the rudiments of daily survival had to be imported and then reassembled for the sake of Occupy. In this sense, Occupy refurbished everyday life in the moment and then eventually for what it could become, opening the viewfinder to where and how *homo politicus* might transcend *homo oeconomicus*.

Neither Butler nor Happe foregrounds the materiality of public emplacement to the degree that we do for this chapter. Butler does nest the term "assemblage" with a collected sense of the self in relation to others and for an alliance among people, things, and geographies: "For the point is not that I am a collection of identities, but that I am already an assembly, even a general assembly, or an assemblage . . . from Deleuze" (*Notes* 68). Yet we need to go further to comment on how an assembled identity mutates from the known to the unknown and then to a newly embraced publicity that depends upon residence and occupation. Happe finds in Occupy, as one would, that parrhēsian speech enacts the phenomenon of precarity; yet for our purposes, the spaces occupied and the material circumstances before, during, and after Occupy are their own expression of solidarity.

The assembled lives and places that preceded the process of occupying Wall Street stretch the temporal and material horizon of possibility well beyond the expected duration of a political movement. An assemblage in this sense allows many disparate territorialities to overlap and morph, such that borders, boundary objects (in the case of L/Z park, the ordinary devices of daily living), and external relations of power can trade positions. These externalities from everyday life, as Manuel Delanda (*A New Philosophy of Society*) proposes, offer up different kinds of codes and expressions by trading on different territorial origins. Political change, as it occurs, builds through synchronic exchanges more than as a result of some historical event. Any instance of political occupation, from how one resides in a neighborhood to how one occupies a public place, carries within it the potential to reconfigure a territorial imaginary and a territorial circumstance. For each locale, sustained protest depends upon food that, in turn, depends on procurements and distribution routes, the wherewithal established elsewhere and imported for the protest community. While observers may take note of assembled bodies and powerful speeches, the presence of food (along with other daily needs) is what enables habitation to continue, and daily sustenance enables parrhēsian speech acts to occur. Henri Lefebvre (*Critique of Everyday Life*) proposed long ago that the roots of critical action lived within the residuum of the everyday, and it was from there that a sustained challenge to the ravages of advanced capitalism must occur.

Lefebvre's insistence that critical labor must inhabit the ebbs and flows of everyday life suggests that moments of public resistance from Ferguson to Charlotte, from Baltimore to Flint, will eventually lose their energy and fade from public life at least as social movements reported by the press and recorded as history. His grand lesson is that we do not lose the battle so much as it exposes the conditions for renewed political energy. All instances of public unrest and resistance carry in them the inevitability of returning home—the 1930s sit-down strikes in Flint, Michigan; the 1960s lunch counter sit-ins of the Civil Rights Movement; the occupation of Alcatraz in 1969 by Native American activists; the 2011 encampments of the Arab Spring and *acampanadas* of Spain's 15M movement and so on. Therefore, a more complete theory of performative assembly would need to employ a territorial imaginary that includes the return to the residua of everyday and to places where that "slow death" that Butler intoned could be met by an equally slow, yet vital, recovery. Where else but from familiar surroundings would one comprehend the slow violence of economic discrimination? What other grounding would provide the accoutrements for daily living to sustain a political movement premised on illegal territorial occupation? However exhausted by confrontation, those who protest publicly on the streets or privately in their homes are tired, as Moraga suggests in her epigraph, and they are ready to go home, and be home, so that they can start anew.

Some of the fieldwork of Meghan Dunn stood out to us as evidence of the employment of everyday life in service of the rhetorical desire and means to occupy a public place—and then to ready oneself to return home. A contemporary application of the *chōra*, as rhetorical invention, calls forth an imagined extension of public life, as a civic ideal that legitimates the material construction of that ideal. Choric invention for our purposes must be understood as a commonplace occurrence, open to anyone who was obligated or positioned to "move from ideas . . . to the sensible, active world" (Rickert 258). The chōra on display in civic life rekindles the possibility of territorial extension, from what serves as the known sense of public life toward the possible. According to Keimpe Algra: "in those cases where *chōra* should be translated as 'place/space' the idea is always that of an extension, whether two- or three- dimensional, which is occupied or which can be occupied" (33).

Field notes below document place-making as it unfolded in and around L/Z park in lower Manhattan along with a sample of the digital correspondence about the fact of occupation and the tactics supporting occupation. The reader may notice a shift in citational practices to include digital sources of interest primarily to occupiers, perhaps more so than to academic scholars; we include these so as to sketch something of the scale of the storm of inter-mediation that took place on the web as the movement spread across the ground. The rhetorical effects made visible through occupation carry forward the vicissitudes as well as the subtle achievements of everyday life that enabled encampments to occur, to adapt, and to be sustained. We close this essay by speculating on the return of *homo politicus* and publicity's recovery through occupation as cohabitation.

CHORIC OCCUPATIONS AND THE TERRITORIAL IMAGINARY

The chōra in antiquity is said to *precede* the rules, codes, properties, and laws that allow us, in retrospect, to assign form to invention. Edward Casey in *The Fate of Place* describes the chōra as something "at once locatory and yet not itself located, permanent and yet invisible, underlying and yet insubstantial" (37). In a sense this was true for lower Manhattan, because the residua of everyday life both preceded and exceeded the bounds of economic and governmental control. The chōra as we revisit it here through L/Z unfolds as three movements. The first appears as an imagined social space that takes hold of a public place, that is, a territorial imaginary from the possible to real premised first on the desire to occupy for a common good. Choric invention extends the presumed boundaries and territorial possibilities of public space. Once the territorial imaginary takes root, a second movement unfolds, a rhetorical becoming otherwise understood as the material realization of community that sustains daily living and serves as a political act. Both of these first two movements depend on the recuperation of everyday living, with its spatial content, and such a community discovers the limits, possibilities, and textures of its future existence. The third movement might be thought of as the shift from topos to logos, if topos can be considered a place as well as the seat of an argument. The movement toward logos is crucial because when the tents are removed, and people return to their everyday life, some sort of imprint must carry them forward, and the terms that index this movement are many—an "experimental agora," an "exemplar society" (terms from Boston's General Assembly); a "base of operations" or "base camp," a "micro-city," "hyper-city," and an "alternative polity," according to Jonathon Massey and Brett Snyder. In these grounded ways, the occupation of L/Z park moves through the catalytic process of territorial emergence—first imaging and occupying a public park, followed by the appearance of community as a space of becoming that fairly quickly results in a discursive terrain to accompany an alternative polity. We believe the pacing of these movements would not be possible were it not for the vitality of public life that preceded occupation, and these movements bode well for altered practices tumbling back into the quotidian once the movement recedes.

The geographic location—between Broadway, Trinity Place, Liberty Street, and Cedar Street in lower Manhattan—and physical features of L/Z Park were in many ways unspectacular. As Jon Stewart quipped, "apparently it's a park in lower Manhattan where people from Wall Street would go to smoke around noon." In other ways, however, the park that OWS took over and held onto for the 99 percent was originally the site of a different kind of spectacle and trauma. It was the place where Zuccotti—formerly known as Liberty Plaza Park before its reconstruction—was used as an emergency staging area by the Federal Emergency Management Association (FEMA) and the New York City Department of Design and Construction in the immediate aftermath of 9/11. Facing Ground Zero at its northwest corner, L/Z Park looks diagonally and directly into a void left by what is considered by many today (e.g., Morgan) to be the worst act of terrorism on US soil since Pearl Harbor at the dawn of World War II. During the World Trade Center recovery effort, the park's already compromised foundation cracked beneath the weight of emergency vehicles and equipment and required extensive renovation. Now lined with an orchard of fifty-four honey locust trees and five hundred twinkling lights, the renovations and "reimaginings" of old Liberty/new Zuccotti Park would be described by Governor Pataki as "an urban oasis" and "another symbol of the rebirth of downtown" (Brookfield Properties)—testimonies etched into the façade of One Liberty Plaza at 165 Broadway although few would know the park until OWS emerged in this location.

We find it consequential that the Occupy movement was framed as a response to economic crisis, yet it originated in what was once a place of triage and recovery after an attack on the symbolic pillars of Western economic dominance, an emergency staging ground situated just outside the immediate bounds where a national trauma took place. Because the chōra is characterized in Plato's *Timaeus* both as "the nurse of all becoming and change" (¶49) and as an outlying territory necessary for the *polis* to thrive, it is fitting, then, that the same grounds that served as the closest periphery to national trauma—the space nearest to, but *just outside* the range of disaster—would likewise give birth to a movement that operated outside the structures of power. As described by Massey and Snyder, it "prefigured in microcosm the alternative polity desired by many participants, modeling and testing modes of self-organization partly autonomous from those provided by the state and the market." As further detailed on maps of the park (see Saget and Tse), the given spaces and structures became a "temporary autonomous zone" to host a range of operational areas including three information tables/tents (one positioned on the northwest corner next to "Double Check" and one on the southeast corner under Di Suvero's "Joie de Vivre"); an assembly area; a library; a legal, media, and outreach zone; two art sections; zones for sanitation, cooking, sleeping, and medical aid; a comfort station; an art/flex section; a social area; and lastly, a sacred space.

The site of this sacred space was on the northwest corner of the park where granite benches encircled the lone London plane tree, the only tree to survive the aftermath of 9/11 and where Johnson's "Double Check" sculpture once sat. Some may remember this haunting figure from post-9/11 images, as many mistook the sculpture for a live person covered in dust and debris. The tree around which sacred space formed would later be called by occupiers "the sacred tree of Zuccotti" or "the tree of life" and by New York natives as 'The Survivor Tree' (see Daly's "A Tale of Two Trees"). Eventually, the park as a whole would be considered a sacred space, even called by some "a holy place." In fact, were it not for the intersections between L/Z Park and the "sacred" or "holy," there may not have been an encampment to speak of: protestors circumvented city law when members from Occupy Judaism erected a sukkah in L/Z—a "temporary [dwelling] in which Jews are commanded to live during the holiday of Sukkot" (Nathan-Kazis)—to commemorate the Israelites' exodus from Egypt. Thus, by observing a "higher law" outside the law of the city or the state, occupiers began to rewrite the social and spatial codes that had traditionally marked the use of public or privately owned public space.

In many ways, to occupy "higher ground" became synonymous with what it was to "occupy" in the first place. The territorial imaginary collectively looked for the best site for communal occupation, and places come equipped with their own resonances of history, energy, aesthetics, and technical and spatial affordances. Place affords much more than a geographic marker or an indication of status, according to numerous scholars (Casey; Massey). Given the economic instability in the world and in the lives of many who resided in the park, the political imperative sought a suitable location through which to comprehend the world's economic and social compressions, overlaps, and contiguous energies and dis/affiliations. In Michel Foucault's short essay "Of Other Spaces," he proposes that Western society has moved beyond (without awareness of) the ontology of an open space of conquest: colonization, conquests by military campaigns, methodical discoveries of new land, or even the buying and selling of space produced through capitalist exchanges (see also Lefebvre, *Production*). Foucault asserts that "Today the site (fixed, bounded) has been substituted for extension . . . defined by relations of proximity between points or elements" (23). Place was taken up and taken over by the occupiers through actions and demonstrations and without blessings or permits, and yet as a choric extension of the park, all of its affordances of shape, border, history, and use signaled a goodness of fit for those looking for cohabitation. We saw the relations of proximity imported by people from different walks of life collapse into a communal desire, will, and opportunity to occupy. After all, it was the unjust and unwise distribution of home spaces, coupled to subprime loans, that destabilized a global economic empire founded in economic conquest, calculated risk, resentment, and greed. The first move was to find a place on the ground where a reversal of fortunes was possible in a park nested ironically near the former Twin Towers.

Becoming Residential

In the weeks and months following the emergence of OWS, occupations arose in geographic locations (OccupyBoston, OccupyLSX, OccupyParis, OccupyPortland, OccupyHood), in conceptual and disciplinary realms (OccupyDesign, OccupyResearch, OccupyTheory, OccupyRhetoric, OccupyTheology), in regulatory and resistance domains (OccupyTheSEC, Strike Debt/Rolling Jubilee), in religions (OccupyBuddhism, OccupyJudaism, OccupyCatholics, OccupyHolySee), and eventually in disasters and events (OccupySandy, OccupyCentral, [Occupy]BoulderFloodRelief). Everywhere there existed a critical need to address a local crisis engendered by global circumstances. If it is true, as we have argued, that occupation displays a choric potential to take hold of a place and then invent its habitation, we can look to see how the residual energies and tactics, the routines and commonplaces allow habitation to occur.

The capacities of L/Z Park to engender everyday life converged as a native tactic and trope of reimagining and remaking the use of public space. Matt Mulberry, from the International Center for Nonviolent Protest, notes the tactic of occupation did not *begin* with Occupy, but "[occupation] stands out as a relatively new phenomenon when considered within the longer history of civil resistance movements, when the tactic or place of occupation seldom came to define the entire movement." However, as an American "take" or "fusion" on the Spanish *acampada* and the tactics of Tahrir (Castells), the occupation of L/Z would differ from its forerunners by seemingly serving as an end (a telos) in itself to establish an encampment that served as a site for society reinvented.

While this movement was not realized "in mass" until the raising of sukkahs by Occupy Judaism, it would appear (in retrospect) that a goal—from the beginning—was to occupy in the sense of holding possession or office: to dwell, to reside, to thrive. The park's affordances enabled a community to emerge, echoing the chōra as an "eternal and indestructible space" that can only be approached "as through a dream (*oneiropoloumen*)" (Rickert 270). In Susan Jaffe's commentary on life after OWS, "Clinton," a labor organizer who helped to plan OWS, noted, "I remember, I wish[ed] I had more of an imagination, because it seemed like whatever idea we had in that space we could make happen, and we did." The implication of the chōra's "odd passivity" and "fundamental indeterminacy," as Rickert notes, is that "while a beginning requires a place, the generative or *choric* aspects of that place remain indeterminate" (Rickert 251) and therefore open to possibility. Occupy Wall Street emplaced embodied dissent through a process of spatial extension from places lived prior to newly captured places shimmering with possibility. The call and cause to occupy part of the financial district did not necessarily determine what shape that occupation would take or where an occupation would emerge. The shape, contours, substance, and the interrelatedness of the assembled people would first extend the park beyond its intended purposes and then make it a receptacle for civic becoming.

Each strand or rhizome of the movement, each trajectory, was imbued with its particular physiognomy as if a movement can have a face, a bodily form, or a character within its discourse. Such characteristics of a place come to be known only within its conditions of emergence (Griffin). The imagined, the possible, resulted in a "political physiology" as we suggested earlier, a quite real circumstance of material assemblage scaled at the level of the body, civic life, and the iterative event taking on the generative properties of emergence in its ontological sense (Delanda, *Philosophy and Simulation*). Thus, while each occupation operated under the banner of Occupy, no two occupations would be alike—except through their capacity to be invented—emerging across information, people, and places. Each occupation came to reflect the local crises and emergent (albeit many *systemic*) issues and physiology that affected that area or region: be it water cutoffs in Detroit, fighting for direct democracy in Hong Kong, housing foreclosures in Atlanta, or even natural disasters like Hurricane Sandy in New York City. Demby writes, "Occupy Wall Street is streamed, tweeted, posted and reposted. It is a curiosity, a screen for projection, a spectator sport, everyone's favorite and most hated child. Yet people continue to come daily who earnestly want to join or to aid the effort. OWS has become a receptacle for the lost progressive hopes of a previous generation." Just as choric scholars contend that "what must be underscored here is the *necessity* for the *polis* to go beyond its boundaries to thrive (a reinforcement of *Timaeus's anagke* [necessity] in 47e)" (Rickert 259, emphasis in original), occupiers such as Suzhan E. would similarly contend that "creating new autonomous community zones is necessary for the survival of the movement." This capacity to reside was the zeitgeist for the movement, a mantle related to—yet different from—the opening call to speak out against economic aggression.

The Ideal City

For scholarly purposes, the chōra gestures to a cultural geography, "a specifically political dimension, being both the boundary of the city and what lies beyond the boundary" (Rickert 259), in material and discursive terms. Occupiers in kind answered the call to #OCCUPYWALLSTREET by building a community and a lexicon from daily conversations: what Massey and Snyder term an "experimental agora" or an "alternative polity" inside the city, but outside "the state." As a "little city" or "exemplar society" in "the big city" of New York City (our own terms), the occupation of L/Z Park could be said to have existed in (at least) two places at once. Referred to as the "epicenter" of the movement for those present, and in a scholarly vein as a "hypercity built of granite and asphalt, algorithms and information" (Massey and Snyder), the park was as much on the streets—locatable on a map—as it was an emergent conceptual bastion that existed outside the city's expressive coding.

As occupation first took hold of the idea of a public place, then tangibly occupied someone else's territory for its residential potential, those who occupied L/Z park began a process of democratizing their newly hewn public place with documents, protocols, and distribution networks. The park would provide a site for the New York City General Assembly (NYCGA) to emerge and convene, where dozens of Occupy groups came together to "organize and set the vision for the #occupywallstreet movement" (NYCGA) through consensus-oriented discussion. Functioning as the democratic and organizational nexus of OWS, the NYCGA defines itself as "an open, participatory and horizontally organized *process* through which we are building the capacity to constitute ourselves in public as autonomous collective forces within and against the constant crises of our times" (italics added). Some products of this solidarity, the "statement of autonomy" and the "declaration of the occupation of New York City," outline the foundational values and grievances associated with the movement; these documents are publicly available at the New York General Assembly's resource page. By this point in OWS's short history, the desire to reside has now become a gesture toward due process in governing.

As Massey and Snyder reported, each night for nine weeks straight, the NYCGA met at the eastern end of L/Z Park, "where a shallow crescent of stairs creates a modest amphitheater" beneath Suvero's sculpture named after the "joy of living." In this assembly area, participants would spend hours "work[ing] through issues of common concern—every word repeated by the assembly, which formed a 'human microphone' amplifying the speaker's voice—until they reached consensus." The "mic check" was another example of necessity giving rise to invention—and that invention being, in a sense, outside the law as a vernacular mode of resistance—where NPR reported that "the protesters have come up with a creative way around the no-amplification rule at the park. One person talks and the rest of the crowd repeats what they've said so everyone can hear" (Peralta). While getting around this law was not a primary motive, it was a product of necessity to the extent that voices needed to project to keep deliberation inclusive (Peralta). In fact, due to the number of "speaking bodies" participating in the deliberative process of the NYCGA, the meetings would necessitate or otherwise bring into being a facilitator selecting volunteers to #takestack and record meeting minutes (with members often live-tweeting critical takeaways and hashtagging movement terms) as well as to review the rules for prioritizing speakers. This process often involved demonstrating the nonverbal hand gestures "by which participants could signal agreement or dissent" (Peralta). These gestures would become one of the more recognizable "traits" of Occupy's vernacular logic: the ability to quickly assess the climate of a democratic body operating outside the political spaces typically "reserved" for civic life.

As illustrated in the NYCGA Guide, these gestures—part of an emergent vernacular discourse through which occupiers communicated by signal and sign—were designed both to "ensure everyone's voice is heard and every opinion is respected" and to quickly conduct a #tempcheck of the assembly: a way of determining the general "climate" or "leanings" of the participants on a matter of discussion. Eventually, these gestures—or "hippie finger wiggles" as Allah Pundit humorously called it—would inspire the creation of an online application, Loomio (Cassano) which was designed to help groups make decisions collaboratively online. As indicated in the Assembly Guide, the NYCGA began to produce smaller gatherings or groups known as "Working/Thematic Groups" that "focus on supporting specific initiatives or topics relevant to the movement that ranged from Food, Medical, and Legal Committees to Arts & Culture, Direct Action, Principles of Solidarity and many more" (NYCGA).

Democracy of a more pristine kind was clearly in the making, nothing of course that would overthrow the economic domination that brought many occupiers together, yet still a visible, livable gesture toward what an equitable democratic process would look like. The periphery of the occupation began to push these democratic gestures outward. The working/thematic groups in the park would eventually bleed over into a satellite space, the Deutsche Bank building at 60 Wall Street, to continue the labor of developing a functioning general assembly. As Massey and Snyder note of this space, "from morning to night [occupiers] used the tables, benches, chairs and wifi of the climate-controlled space as a purposeful, orderly, extension of the eastern end of Liberty Plaza, establishing commuting patterns that figured 60 Wall as the Occupy office."

Eventually, business owners supporting the movement would offer up vacant spaces and properties within the general vicinity of the park to OWS for temporary use, including a storage space that held the shipments of goods that were sent to OWS from across the country. Judson Church in Washington Square Park would eventually be used as a general "presentation" and meeting space, an in-solidarity space; so too would the Brecht Forum, 2 Beaver Street, and an office along Broadway that served as the "Occupy Office" (separate from 60 Wall Street) that was temporarily given to OWS by a company who gave OWS members the key code to their office. The use of these places/spaces "from morning to night" not only calls to mind an emergent chant of the movement—"All day, all week, Occupy Wall Street"—but the description of these satellite sites as a "purposeful, orderly extension of the eastern end" is in many ways a meta-demonstration of the way that an ideal city could be invented, terminologically and territorially designated as "an extension . . . which can be occupied" (33) as Algra proposed. The site of L/Z Park was first and foremost a choric "entry point" into the movement, first a place subsumed, then a receptacle of becoming, and then a city within a city with its own ethics and routines. No ideal city can exist for very long without discursive representation; and once residential life took hold, once the topological invention of a city space became visible for those in residence, the logos of occupation emerged to help sustain the residents' ideals for how cities might serve and honor the 99 percent.

RECOVERABLE DEMOCRACY

It seemed to us, the authors of this essay who are also residents within different kinds of occupied territories (the office, the home, the streets and social movements), that OWS exhibits a temporal movement common to every other political event in modern history. It morphed, it moved, from an imagined possibility of cohabitation to a more tangible physical and geographic realization of proximity as political event. Hoped-for territories became actual, localized, embodied geographies. And with them the opportunity arose for residential becoming, not just living side by side but a cohabitation that joyously and laboriously depended upon on quotidian practices of daily sustenance and survival. An ordinary, vernacular democracy emerged that was attuned to the generative capacities of L/Z Park and served as a catalyst for discursive identification. We have employed a late-modern rendering of the ancient notion of the chōra because of its capacity to engender new sorts of civic spaces and because the chōra, to us, honors the quotidian antecedents to civic renewal. The occupation of public places teaches us that to be *choric* is to be open and opportunistic toward the publicity that lurks within everyone's imaginary (i.e., we all want to be somewhere), a publicity equipped with basic routines and strategies, imported from a prior life lived in dire conditions of economic inequality.

Empirically speaking, we cannot report where thousands upon thousands of occupiers went once occupied territories were reclaimed by the state and once the movement dispersed. Yet from Shepp's portrayal, our engagements with OWS, our reflections upon daily living thereafter, and then from the commentary of many others, occupation does not end with expulsion or denial or defeat. There is no expulsion from political emergence if we understand that social unraveling by the hands of the powerful leaves in place the residue of political cohesion, nested in the everyday. In *Notes toward a Performance Theory of Assembly*, Butler makes the obvious, yet poignant point, that none of us, certainly not the "destitute," is ever outside spheres of exclusion or resistance. We who cohabitate (and we who govern) de-territorialize political potency if our viewpoint "disregards and devalues those forms of political agency that emerge precisely in those domains deemed prepolitical or extrapolitical" (*Notes* 78). As we have framed the invention of the ideal city from territorial imaginations and the occupation of public places, we suggest that an "unruly rhetoric" of occupation carries forward from the extrapolitical as an originary basis for an afterlife of civic, political resistance. The life lived before occupation refines itself toward the next chapter of quotidian occupation. It returns from whence it came, the residuum of everyday life, retrofitted for future encampments.

One could say—and many did—that the occupiers lost their residential rights through eviction from L/Z Park on November 15, 2011, when a surprise police raid was followed by a hollow gesture to civic democracy by then Mayor Michael Bloomberg: "Protesters have had two months to occupy the park with tents and sleeping bags, now they will have to occupy the space with the power of their arguments" (Schneider, *Thank You* 103). The mayor's rhetorical conceit is all too clear: if those who occupy do not return to public life and deliberation as deemed acceptable by those in power, then brute force will speed their expulsion from the public sphere. What the mayor's conceit does not recognize is that the occupiers will leave fully equipped. All assemblies of public insurrection eventually dissipate, but occupiers left with other values and practices to challenge the status quo. They took from Occupy something more vital than public address and the acumen for policy debates. Journalist Michael Levitin in *The Triumph of Occupy Wall Street* would write, "the movement that began in Zuccotti Park didn't disappear—it just splintered and regrouped around a variety of focused causes," and "ironic as it may seem, the impact of the movement that many view only in the rearview mirror is becoming stronger and clearer with time." Occupation splinters and regroups in city parks everywhere—in grocery aisles and college classrooms, in council chambers and boardrooms— it gains its fullest valence in the ordinary spaces of everyday life, because, as OWS so profoundly demonstrates, those ordinary spaces call on the 99 percent to speak and act in ways less bounded by the control and limits inscribed into our technological, economic, and spatial unconscious (Thrift).

The authors of this chapter are well aware of the sobering arguments that public assemblage has little chance to amount to much more than cathartic expressions of injustice. As Brown notes, "Neoliberalism . . . is best understood not simply as economic policy, but as a governing rationality that disseminates market values and metrics to every sphere of life and construes the human itself *exclusively* as *homo oeconomicus*. . . . [D]emocracy itself has been radically transformed. . . . [S]ubjects, including citizen subjects, are configured by the market metrics of our time as self-investing human capital . . . almost *exclusively* for their contribution to capital enhancement" (176–77, emphasis added).

We respect her descriptive clarity of the exclusivity built into economic domination, but we cannot abide by such depictions of human capital if, as Butler proposes, every sphere in public life *inclusively* could territorially reproduce itself through daily, residual, locatable practices—the streets, kitchens, trades, and arts where the lessons of occupation live on. Our desire in this essay for ethical civic action underscores the reemergence of a *homo politicus* who works tactically in the machinations of the quotidian and toward the inclination for assembled people to inhabit common spaces and to embrace the possibility of their own making. We understand that there will not be a second coming for the politically righteous, no second coming that "rights" the entire demos or flattens out economic distributions; yet we resist any depiction of those who protest, and then who go about their daily business, as naïve to their choric potential. We offer, in closing, that one value, one territorial commodity, open to all who engender unruly rhetorics, is the return to a familiar homeland enriched by unruliness. There will be direct costs and collateral fatigue, but just as real will be the lessons of fortitude, survival, adaptation, and resilience.

Ultimately, our goal in telling a choric tale of Occupy is to reinvest in the possibility of territorial recovery, even if the odds are stacked against the participants in the streets or those elsewhere who struggle to make ends meet. What follows Occupy can be taken as victory as it is retained in the global imaginary, and as it returns as a basis for progressive reform elsewhere. Writing for *Tidal Magazine*, Suzahn E. concludes, "we must project our vision of a just world onto the blank paving stones of public parks and into the silent hallways of abandoned schools . . . to turn our collective imaginary into a collective reality." If the world is as rife with precarity as Butler proposes and is as lost to neoliberalism as Brown proposes, those who resist will need to practice the reanimation of city spaces and to practice again and again the accoutrements of living—shelter, clothing, food, distributions, communication, ethics, and lawful behavior. These routines gather through the practice of occupation itself, a telos, a movement sometimes without clear demands other than to occupy, as Butler ("For and against Precarity") comments in 2011 very much in stride with Suzahn E.: "The reason it is said that sometimes there are 'no demands' when bodies assemble under the rubric of 'Occupy Wall Street' is that any list of demands would not exhaust the ideal of justice that is being demanded. . . . For when bodies gather as they do to express their indignation and to enact their plural existence in public space, they are also making broader demands . . . they are exercising a right to appear and to exercise freedom; they are calling for a livable life." Never to be taken from us.

WORKS CITED

Adbusters. "#OCCUPYWALLSTREET: A Shift in Revolutionary Tactics." July 13, 2011. www.adbusters.org/occupywallstreet/.

Algra, Keimpe. *Concepts of Space in Greek Thought*. E. F. Brill, 1995.

Banning, Marlia. *Manufacturing Uncertainty: Contemporary U.S. Public Life and the Conservative Right*. Peter Lang, 2013.

Blanchard, Olivier. "The Crisis: Basic Mechanisms and Appropriate Policies." Munich Lecture, Working Paper 09–01, CESifo Forum 1, December 29, 2008. www.imf.org /external/pubs/ft/wp/2009/wp0980.pdf.

Brookfield Properties. "Brookfield Properties Re-opens Lowe Manhattan Park Following $8 Million Renovation." Press Release, June 1, 2006. www.marketwired.com/press -release/brookfield-properties-re-opens-lower-manhattan-park-following-8-million -renovation-tsx-bpo-597554.htm.

Brown, Wendy. *Undoing the Demos: Neoliberalism's Stealth Revolution*. Zone Books, 2015.

Butler, Judith. "For and against Precarity." *Tidal Magazine: Occupy Theory, Occupy Strategy* 1 (December 2011). www.occupyduniya.wordpress.com/2011/12/09/tidal/.

Butler, Judith. *Notes toward a Performative Theory of Assembly*. Harvard University Press, 2015.

Casey, Edward. *The Fate of Place*. University of California Press, 1998.

Cassano, Jay. "An Occupy-Inspired App That Helps Groups Make Actual Decisions." Fast Company & Inc., April 16, 2014. www.fastcompany.com/3029132/fund-this/an-occupy -inspired-app-that-helps-groups-make-actual-group-decisions/.

Castells, Manuel. "The Disgust Becomes a Network." Translated by Hugh Green. *Adbusters*, August 2, 2011. www.adbusters.org/article/manuel-castells/.

Daly, Michael. "A Tale of Two Trees." *The Daily Beast,* November 5, 2011. www.thedaily beast.com/tree-of-life-and-survivor-tree-at-occupy-wall-street-a-history/.

Delanda, Manuel. *A New Philosophy of Society: Assembling Theory and Social Complexity.* Continuum, 2006.

Delanda, Manuel. *Philosophy and Simulation: The Emergence of Synthetic Reason.* Continuum, 2011.

Demby, Nicole. "Liberty Plaza. A 'Message' Entangled with its Form." Transversal Texts: #Occupy and Assemble, *EIPCP-European Institute for Progressive Cultural Policies,* October 2011. www.eipcp.net/transversal/1011/demby/en/.

Dunn, Meghan. *On Radical Grounds: A Rhetorical Take on the Emergence of #Occupy in Time, Place, Space.* Communication Graduate Theses & Dissertations, 60, 2015. www .scholar.colorado.edu/comm_gradetds/60/.

Eisman, Steve. "Don't Break Up the Banks. They're Not Our Real Problem." *New York Times,* opinion pages, February 6, 2016. www.nytimes.com/2016/02/07/opinion/dont -break-up-the-banks-theyre-not-our-real-problem.html.

Foucault, Michel. "Of Other Spaces." *Diacritics* 16 no. 1 (1986): 22–27.

General Assembly at Occupy Boston. December 2, 2011. We are the 99% Occupy Boston. www.wiki.occupyboston.org /wiki/Declaration_of_Occupation/.

Griffin, Leland. "The Rhetoric of Historical Movements." *Quarterly Journal of Speech* 2 (1952): 184–88.

Grossberg, Lawrence. *Cultural Studies in the Present Tense.* Duke University Press, 2010.

Happe, Kelly, E. "*Parrhēsia*, Biopolitics, and Occupy." *Philosophy and Rhetoric* 48, no. 2 (2015): 211–23.

Hornbein, Drew. "#OCCUPYWALLSTREET Year One: A Brief History of the Fastest Growing Start Up of All Time." Drew Horbein's Web Log, September 12, 2012. Accessed July 10, 2015, but no longer available.

Jaffe, Sarah. "Post-Occupied: Where Are We Now?" Occupy.com, May 30, 2014. www .occupy.com/article/post-occupied-where-are-we-now#sthash.wpme9a4g.dpbs/.

Lefebvre, Henri. *Critique of Everyday Life: From Modernity to Modernism.* Vol. 3. Translated by Gregory Eliot. Verso Press, 2005.

Lefebvre, Henri. *The Production Space.* Translated by Donald Nicholson-Smith. Wiley-Blackwell, 1991.

Levitin, Michael. "The Triumph of Occupy Wall Street." *The Atlantic,* June 10, 2015. www .theatlantic.com/politics/archive/2015/06/the-triumph-of-occupy-wall-street /395408/.

Massey, Doreen. *For Space.* Sage Publications, 2005.

Massey, Jonathan, and Brett Snyder. "Occupying Wall Street: Places and Spaces of Political Action." *Places Journal,* September 2012. www.placesjournal.org/article/occupying -wall-street-places-and-spaces-of-political-action/.

Moraga, Cherríe. "La Jornada: Preface, 1981." In *This Bridge Called My Back*, 4th ed., edited by Cherríe Moraga and Gloria Anzaldúa, xxxv–xliii. State University of New York Press, 2015.

Morgan, Matthew J. *The Impact of 9/11 on Politics and War: The Day that Changed Everything?* Macmillan, 2009.

Mulberry, Matt. "Physical Space and 'Occupy' Tactics: A New Trend in Civil Resistance?" OpenDemocracy.net, November 19, 2014. www.opendemocracy.net/civilresistance /matt-mulberry/physical-space-and-'occupy'-tactics-new-trend-in-civil-resistance/.

Nathan-Kazis, Josh. "Occupy-ing Sukkahs, across the Nation." Forward.com, October 13, 2011. www.forward.com/opinion/144381/occupy-ing-sukkahs-across-the-nation/.

New York City General Assembly (NYCGA). "#Occupy Wall Street NYC General Assembly: About." NYCGA.net, n.d. Accessed July 10, 2015, but no longer available.

Osborn, David. "Foreword." In *Understanding Occupy from Wall Street to Portland*, edited by Renee Guarriello Heath, Courtney Vail Fletcher, and Ricardo Munoz, xi. Lexington Books, 2013.

Peralta, Eyder. "Siding with Mayor, Judge Rules against Occupy Wall Street Protesters." NPR.org, The Two-Way, November 15, 2011. www.npr.org/sections/thetwo-way/2011 /11/15/142365231/siding-with-mayor-judge-rules-against-occupy-wall-street-encampment/.

Plato. *Timaeus* and *Critias*. Translated by Desmond Lee, Penguin Book, 1977.

Protevi, John. "Beyond Autopoiesis: Inflections of Emergence." In *Emergence and Embodiment: New Essays on Second-Order Systems Theory*, edited by Bruce Clarke and Mark B. N. Hansen, 94–113. Duke University Press, 2009.

Pundit, Allah. "Finally: Occupy Protester Explains the 'Twinkles' Hand Gesture." HotAir. com, October 13, 2011. www.hotair.com/archives/2011/10/13/finally-occupy-protester -explains-the-twinkles-hand-gesture/.

Rickert, Thomas. "Toward the Chora: Kresteva, Derrida, and Ulmer on Emplaced Invention." *Philosophy & Rhetoric* 40, no. 3 (2007): 251–73.

Rogers, Simon. "The Occupy Map of the World." *The Guardian*, September 17, 2012. Accessed July 10, 2015 but no longer available.

Saget, Bedel, and Archie Tse. "How Occupy Wall Street Turned Zuccotti Park into a Protest Camp." *New York Times*, October 5, 2011. www.nytimes.com/interactive/2011/10/05 /nyregion/how-occupy-wall-street-turned-zuccotti-park-into-a-protest-camp.html? _r=0/.

Schneider, Nathan. *Thank You, Anarchy: Notes from the Occupy Apocalypse*. University of California Press, 2013.

Schneider, Nathan. "What 'Diversity of Tactics Really Means for Occupy Wall Street." *Waging Nonviolence: People-Powered News and Analysis*, October 19, 2011. www .wagingnonviolence.org/feature/what-diversity-of-tactics-really-means-for-occupy -wall-street/.

Schwartz, Mattathias. "How Occupy Wall Street Chose Zuccotti Park." *New Yorker*, November 18, 2001. www.newyorker.com/news/news-desk/map-how-occupy-wall-street-chose-zuccotti-park/.

Shepp, Accra. "Occupy Wall Street: Where Are They Now?" *New York Times*, Exposures, September 17, 2016. www.nytimes.com/interactive/2016/09/17/opinion/Occupy-Wall-Street.html.

Stewart, Jon. "Occupy Wall Street Divided." *The Daily Show with Jon Stewart*. November 16, 2011. www.cc.com/video-clips/5510me/the-daily-show-with-jon-stewart-occupy-wall-street-divided/.

Stiglitz, Joseph. *The Price of Inequality: How Today's Divided Society Endangers Our Future*. W. W. Norton, 2013.

Suzahn E. "An Occupier's Note." *Tidal Magazine: Occupy Theory, Occupy Strategy* 1 (December 2011). www.occupyduniya.wordpress.com/2011/12/09/tidal/.

Thrift, Nigel. *Knowing Capitalism*. Sage Publications, 2005.

THEN COMES FALL

ACTIVISM, THE ARAB SPRING, AND THE NECESSITY OF UNRULY BORDERS

STEVE PARKS, WITH DALA GHANDOUR, EMNA BEN YEDDER TAMARZISTE, MOHAMMED MASBAH, AND BASSAM ALAHMAD

470,000 dead—an approximate total of individuals killed in the Syrian uprising.
—"World Report 2017," Human Rights Watch

11,000 people—an approximate total of the torture victims in Syria as of 2014.
—"Syria Accused of Torture," BBC News

What are the proper connections among an individual's tortured body, the barbarous acts perpetrated upon a civilian population, and the seeming logic of academic writing? How do we understand our responsibility as academics to develop ways of speaking that, in conjunction with activism, can blunt barbarity and produce an expansion of fundamental human rights? Or is the very question a sign of disciplinary arrogance?

For the past three years I have been fortunate to work with Middle Eastern and North African (MENA) activists and educators advocating for an expansive vision of democratic rights that include not only the right to vote but also a right to gender, religious, and economic equity. Beginning within US-based disciplinary scholarship in community publishing, this work produced a collection of essays entitled *Revolution by Love: Emerging Arab Youth Voices (RBL)* that focused on these individuals' involvement in the Arab Spring.[1] This collection offered personal testimony founded upon a sense of national identity and was premised on a rhetoric of hope. Today, in the aftermath of the Arab Spring, such rhetoric seems inadequate to the current moment. Consequently, a new rhetoric is now required that not only recognizes the complicated period of the post–Arab Spring, with its failures to broaden the number of stable independent democratic nations in the region but also validates the emergent anticolonial border struggles of formerly oppressed identities.

To make this argument, I begin with the production of *RBL*, then move to the work of a human rights defender in Assad's Syria, and finally conclude with the work of a coalition of Syrian activists (of which I am a member) that has created Syrians for Truth and Justice (stj-sy.com). In doing so, the essay moves from an examination of human rights arguments linked to an essentialized vision of national identity, to a Westernized framing of political rights, and then ultimately to a post-nationalist rhetorical framing of the human right to self-determination. It is this last definition, I believe, that places academics in solidarity with those struggling for a geographically and culturally informed definition of international borders. Although the actual practices of such a rhetoric are necessarily difficult, I would argue it is the unruly nature of such work that speaks to its vital importance.

Finally, the work discussed in this essay is the result of the collective efforts of those listed as authors as well as many other individuals. To mark this collaboration, we have chosen to list those who have direct editorial and organizational experience in the projects discussed as authors. Dala Ghandour, Emna Ben Yedder Tamarziste, and Mohammed Masbah worked on *RBL* and, along with myself, approved the section on that project. Bassam Alahmad worked on STJ and, along with myself, approved the section on that project. All conclusions drawn from these projects in the "Revolution by Bodies" section, however, should be attributed only to me.

REVOLUTION BY LOVE

In the immediate aftermath of the Arab Spring I had the opportunity to work with MENA educators and activists who were trying to understand the events that had just occurred. Many of them had spent years doing the slow grassroots work of building collectivities designed to produce an oppositional force against undemocratic and oppressive political regimes. They were now in the

United States, at Syracuse University, to learn how to expand their work toward building civil societies that could cement the progress that had seemingly been made.

Progress, however, is a tricky word. As the participants moved through the program, an uneasy sense of dissonance occurred between the attempts to provide civil society models premised upon US frameworks and the actual historical meaning of the United States in their countries. As a result, the participants were looking for an alternative space to articulate their collective vision. With the support of their university sponsors, I was contacted in my role as founder/editor of New City Community Press (newcitycommunitypress.com) to help them organize and publish their thoughts. The result was *RBL*.

Rather than rehearse the intricate history of that publication, the goal here is to read *RBL* as an attempt to create a rhetorical space in which to understand the work of democratic political reform in the MENA region within the context of a US global hegemony. What did these participants imagine to be the rhetorical moves necessary to gain support from the West for democratic reform while also acknowledging the United States' own complicated (and complicit) role in the region? And what unintended consequences might their imagined rhetorical stance, when taken on by hegemonic global powers, have produced in justifying state actions against these very goals?

Within this context it is important to begin by looking at how the United States is invoked in *RBL*. For instance, in the introduction the editors note:

> Simply put, this story reveals how young Arab women and men from the Middle East and North Africa, who come from very diverse backgrounds, regions, continents, share the same passion for their countries, *the same audacity of hope*, for a better tomorrow, the same dream of making their country proud of them. All of the writers who were committed to this project were deeply *convinced that one should not ask what their country can do for them, but rather what could they offer their countries*. In a world where barriers are constantly being erased, where virtual communication turns the world to a global village, what is this strange bond that ties this Arab youth to politics and public affairs? (*RBL* 1, emphasis added)

Later this argument continues: "[Our collective stories] could even give the reader a more nuanced understanding of the people who are behind this so-called phenomenon of the 21st century: The *Arab Spring*. This mysterious, catchy, used and reused phrase, in every current political analysis of the MENA was *made by the people, for the people*" (*RBL* 3, emphasis added). In effect, the Arab Spring is recast within terms that rhetorically resonate within the context of the United States. There is the invocation of a globally inflected multiculturalism free from consideration of economic or neocolonial contexts—"very diverse backgrounds, regions and continents, [that] share the same passion for their countries." There is Obama's "audacity of hope." There is Kennedy's "ask not what your country can do for you, ask what you can do for your country." And finally, there is Lincoln's Gettysburg's Address—"of the people, by the people, for the people"—invoked as a means to understand the framework by which young activists took to the streets.

Indeed, *RBL* is replete with instances where each of these hoped-for values is invoked by the collection's authors. Dala Ghandour discusses Beirut as a city that has historically been blessed with diverse cultures and heritages. Raghda Abushahla speaks to how Palestinian women tend to the graves of British soldiers from World War I. Each imagines a common understanding of humanity that can move across contentious religious, political, and international divisions despite the actual historical facts on the ground. Individuals also demonstrate the commitment to being personally engaged in working for political change. Mirelle Karam Halim discusses her work in sponsoring workshops for young Egyptians on democracy. Shadin Hamaideh highlights the sacrifices that men *and* women made in protesting for greater freedoms for all Arabs. Finally, Mohammed Masbah, along with all the writers, speaks of the need for collective action to foster more representative governments.

Interestingly, in light of the invocation of Lincoln, the writers do not speak of their actions as fostering a civil war against the government; none consistently invokes previous political activism based in other paradigms, such as anticolonial struggles. Almost without exception there is a commitment to their country as a framework that seems to transcend the colonial history that produced its political borders. In this way, an essentialized national identity where borders are seen as natural and not the result of Western colonial powers is invoked as a means to produce the possibility of a collective political movement for change.

And it is a national movement seemingly premised on the possibilities of new technology.[2] Throughout all the essays, there is a sense that social media played a fundamental role in the Arab Spring. Here it is useful to return once again to the introduction of *RBL*, specifically the following sentence: "In a world where barriers are constantly being erased, where virtual communication *turns the world to a global village*, what is this strange bond that ties this Arab youth to politics and public affairs?" (1, emphasis added). This belief in new technology is perhaps best represented by Ibrahim Shebani's involvement in the Libyan protests. His narrative begins with a Facebook message calling for an uprising, which leads to a series of cell phone calls to connect with friends, followed by additional Facebook posts featuring clips of political protestors—

all of which are designed to bring the nonvirtual bodies of Libyans to Benghazi to protest the arrest of the Busleem massacre lawyer in front of the security directory.[3] (Here Shebani also notes Gadhafi's use of digital cameras to videotape protestors.) The piece ends with Shebani, along with others, bringing a satellite dish to the site so as to broadcast images of the protests internationally, an effort he admits was already being somewhat achieved by cell phones. The piece ends with the following: "That was my mission of the day. People were happy to see the satellite. Finally, the world would witness our happiness, our liberation. I felt so proud to be part of this small mission" (*RBL* 29). Technology, coupled with mass protests by individuals, had won the day.

Taking these rhetorical strategies collectively, and at some risk of a loss of nuance, I want to highlight what I believe to be a symptomatic rhetorical argument surrounding the Arab Spring that was occurring in the US context. Succinctly stated it might go something like the following: Informed by models of US democracy, MENA activists used social media to bring together hundreds of thousands of individuals, creating a mass movement that ultimately toppled dictators and put the region on a (perhaps temporary) path to democracy. I would argue that such a rhetoric works to affirm cherished beliefs about the United States, technology, and democracy. Within this rhetoric, the borders in which these nationalist struggles occurred are taken out of the colonialist context in which many were created. That is, the rhetoric naturalizes a colonialist history while it simultaneously overlays a US-informed Western model of democracy on the region as a whole.

This is not to argue that *RBL* simply existed within such a rhetorical framework, that *RBL* only invoked but did not critique such a vision. Indeed, within the collection itself, the authors consciously manipulate the rhetoric for maximum impact on the reader. In the essay, "The Pearl of the Gulf," for example, Amal Mater begins by framing Bahrain in terms similar to those found in the other essays in the book:

> The pearl of the gulf is what Bahrain used to be called. Not only because it is a beautiful small island on the Arabian Gulf that used to depend on the pearl industry, but also because its people were well known for their kindness, openness, pureness like a shining pearl. Bahrain was always known for its tolerance and openness to other cultures and religions, and comparing to other neighboring countries, was advanced in terms of education, civil society and women's rights. It was well known throughout history that Bahrainis regardless of sect or religion were living in harmony and socializing with each other with mixed marriages, friendships, and neighborhoods. (*RBL* 11)

Mater then traces those values back through Bahrain's history—from Delmon, Tylus, and Awal, through being a British protectorate, to independence and the establishment of the Al Khalifa as the ruling family. It was soon after the new constitution was put into effect, she argues, that the ruling family of Al Khalifa in 1973 suspended the parliament in response to protests, instituted the States Security Law, and began the process of ruling through extraparliamentary procedures. Stating that Bahrain was "the first Gulf country that responded to the wave of democracy movements," Mater then details how the rhetorical construction of a social movement—one that was not "looking for democracy only for a better life in terms of jobs and economy, but also in terms of liberty and dignity" was confronted by national, regional, and international military violence, a violence that would sacrifice human rights aspirations on the altar of realpolitik (*RBL* 13).

Almost immediately after recounting Bahrain's identity, settling her narrative within the comfortable rhetorical framework of the book's introduction, Mater describes her work as an ophthalmologist at the only public hospital in the country. In response to the Arab Spring protests, she argues, the government responded violently, "killing over 80, injuring, detaining hundreds, and dismissing thousands from their jobs" (*RBL* 13). Moreover, in concert with Gulf Cooperation Council (GCC), a force created to protect Gulf states from "outside" invasions, the hospital was surrounded, troops then invaded and killed some protestors, and tortured others. Matel's husband, a member of parliament, was arrested and detained for months in an unknown location (Holmes). In attempting to understand the cause for such a brutal crackdown, for the introduction of the GCC, Matel notes the following: "Sadly, the Bahraini regime is supported not only by the GCC monarchies, but also largely by its ally, the United States. Bahrain is a strategic non-NATO ally for the United States, hosting the US fifth fleet" (*RBL* 17).

She further comments, "Unfortunately, democracy and human rights don't seem to come first in the foreign policy of the United States. What we see on the ground is that the stability is what really matters. As long as this regime guarantees the interests of the United States in security and oil, any change is considered worrisome" (*RBL* 17). She ends her piece with the hope that the citizens of the United States will compel the government to act differently— invoking US citizens and US nonprofit organizations as having a truer sense of democracy and human rights: "In contrast to our frustration with the US government, the Arab spring was an eye-opening experience to the wonderful dynamic American civil society. We were amazed by the huge support we got from the American democracy and human rights organizations" (*RBL* 18).

Within that context of a hegemonic US presence, Raghda Abushahla details her family's history in Palestine. Beginning with her mother's birth prior to the creation of Israel, Abushahla moves through a history of violence enacted on her family (and by association to Palestinians), "the 1948 War (Al-Nakba), the 1967 Six Days War, and the Operation Cast Lead on Gaza, the Intifada, the recurring Israeli invasions, the internal clashes and on and on" (*RBL* 104). Her family's story then gets translated into her father's and her own struggles to gain a passport, framed as legal recognition by the international community of their very existence, as they were shuttled between Egypt and Libya. With such an emphasis, Abushahla details the political instability of a Palestinian identity in a US dominated context—juxtaposing the family struggles with the use of US military power to punish Libya for the Lockerbie bombings, US support of Egypt, and US silence over the systemic oppression of Palestinians on the West Bank and Gaza by Israel. She writes, "Gazans are marked as terrorists and imprisoned in the Gaza enclave for so many years with severe shortages of money, electricity, fuel, and other essential life commodities. Nevertheless, a small percent of the Gaza population is in possession of weapons or rockets. The vast majority of the population were middle class people who suffered years of hardships and now live in poor conditions and aspire to survive" (*RBL* 90).

Ultimately, the *RBL* collection demonstrates that the earlier, somewhat idealistic rhetorical version of the Arab Spring does not fully account for deeper economic and geopolitical forces that are buffeting and damaging the possibilities that these democratic movements might be fully realized. The GCC, Israel, and the United States form a triad of forces clamping down on grassroots movements for democratic reform that move beyond limited constitutional revisions and that might challenge geopolitical alliances. There is seemingly no version of political reform that might entail the Fifth US fleet leaving Bahrain. Nor, does it appear, is there any version of reform that might move the geopolitical discussion of Israel toward an examination of that country's own human rights record or colonialist status. Indeed, it seems to be exactly at moments where such a possibility occurs that the formerly democratic bodies of protestors are marked as "unruly" and need to be made "proper," disciplined by these larger geopolitical forces that want to reduce the protestors' actions in meaning and actual possibility to the softened rhetorical narrative that brings together US visions of democracy and the power of technology.

In this sense, the rhetorical argument invoked in *RBL* represents the aspirations of those involved in political change and in its dark underbelly. For it is at the same moment when the writers invoke an essentialist national identity, a Westernized vision of democracy, and a faith in technology to tip the balance of global power that the writers also demonstrate how this same rhetoric, when deployed by Western powers minus the simultaneous critique of that very rhetorical stance, justified the international actions that led to the goals of the Arab Spring (again admitting a lack of nuance) being swept up into and limited by larger geopolitical forces.

In saying this, I am not discounting the power of this rhetorical model as an organizing structure at a given historical moment or diminishing the important work of individuals done within this framework—many of whom continue to work actually and rhetorically for more democratic societies. Rather, I am suggesting the need for US-based academics to recognize the historical specificity and limitations of any rhetoric that invokes an idealized view of "Western values" as a means to form alliances with MENA-based activists. Given the historical legacy that such a view inhabits (and how it is currently being enacted), it is not clear such a framework would be effective in supporting the work of activists in fostering fundamental democratic political change in the current moment. As is clear to everyone, the political terrain has only become more complicated in the interim between the publication of *RBL* and today.

REVOLUTION BY ARMS

Syria is not featured in *RBL*. The individuals from Syria who traveled to Syracuse chose not to participate in the book. With their families currently being held by the government and with government forces attacking their neighborhoods, they believed the act of publishing stories of resistance and democratic activism would put their families in danger of being arrested. For, although in the United States it seems that, in community publications, "disempowered voices" have become a trope almost devoid of political significance, for these Syrian individuals, "going public," having any association with Western organizations and rhetorics, would have real and dangerous consequences (a fact to be demonstrated below).

The Syrian "Arab Spring" protests began in March 2011. At first, the protests were in alignment with many of the demands seen across the region: increased democratic rights, systemic political reform, an end to emergency powers, and a crackdown on corruption. In the beginning there were also a few calls for the resignation of President Bashar al-Assad. Initially, the protests were peaceful both in intent and in government response. Then beginning March 18, the Syrian troops began to fire upon the crowds, such as in Daraa, and protestors began publicly to ask for Assad to resign. Assad soon claimed that the protests were sparked by outside agitators and hostile governments, but such arguments had little impact on the anti-Assad protestors who continued to grow in numbers, even as the violence increased. By the end of May, over one thousand civilians had been killed.[4]

During this same period, Syrian officers defected and created the Free Syrian Army, and in Turkey the Syrian National Council was formed. While consistently shifting policies in an effort to find "moderate allies," the United States has essentially aligned with the Free Syrian Army, a force that has been unable to overthrow Assad and, increasingly has been equally concerned with the rise of ISIS, which had been preceded by the emergence of numerous Islamic and Jihadist groups. In addition, the region of northern Syria controlled by Kurds declared itself the "Democratic Federal System of Northern Syria," while the Kurdish-controlled region of Iraq has named itself the Kurdish Regional Government. Slowly, then, the national borders of Syria and Iraq—drawn by the France and United Kingdom governments at the end of World War I as part of the Skyes Picot Agreement—are being reframed in terms outside the "existent nation" nationalism that marked a primary component of the Arab Spring. New borders and new nationalities seem increasingly likely.

It is within this context that organizations such as the Syrian Center for Media and Freedom of Expression emerged. The center was established in 2004 but became more active in 2011. As framed in its mission statement, the center was a "non-profit, independent" organization that was "not linked to any political, religious, partisan or economic side, [either] inside and outside Syria."[5] Its primary purpose was to use professional journalistic standards to report on the events in Syria. In articulating a framework for the center's mission, the organization invoked John Stuart Mill, the Magna Carta, the French Declaration of Human Rights, and the UN Universal Declaration of Human Rights. Like *RBL*, the center frames itself solidly within a Western framework of democracy and the belief in the political right to free speech within properly functioning nation-states.[6]

Given the critique of the romantic view of some of the rhetoric in *Revolution by Love*, it would be easy to understand the center's goals as being unaware of the ramifications of invoking such ways of speaking in the context of the actions of global powers, such as the United States and Great Britain, who might co-opt such rhetoric. (This seems particularly the case when both countries' support of human rights in Syria has been troubled at best.) Yet the history of the center reminds us that the danger of such rhetoric lies not just in its co-option of ends other than intended but also in the fact of its perceived alignment with Western powers.[7] Indeed, the center in Syria was violently shut down by the government for being "aligned" (rhetorically) with Western powers. Ultimately, the center had to relocate to Turkey—a country that today seems a complicated location to enact the principles of a "free press."

Indeed, individuals in this center, along with many other such journalists, were tortured by the Syrian government for seeming to align with rhetoric associated with Western powers and enacting the principles of a free press. Here it might be useful to listen to the voice of one human rights defender and activist employed by the center, who with his colleagues was arrested for being perceived as an "outside agitator" because of their use of Westernized arguments concerning human rights in their reporting:

> When they picked up all of us, I was working with others who were publishing about what is happening in Syria especially the number of people who demonstrated or the number of cities or places which had demonstrations. We were putting the information on our Facebook page, sending it to media centers, to channels, to everyone to say "This is exactly what happened."
>
> We were representing ourselves as internal opposition, doing it for our country. We were telling the people that we are not like the other people outside of Syria, who have a relationship with the West. Our narrative to the regime said we would not cooperate with people outside of Syria because the government considered all channels, all countries except Iran and Russia, enemies. So you cannot talk with the human rights commissions. You cannot talk to anyone. So we said, "We care about internal issues. We are from Syria. We stayed here. We didn't travel. But that we need some kind of reforms."
>
> We were working in the middle of Damascus. They stormed our office. There were about thirty people, snipers, with guns. They motioned to us with their Kalishnikovs. At first, I didn't think they meant to come to our office because we were working publicly. We were not doing any kind of arms. I thought they had come to the wrong place. Then they did kind of a drama, a theater. They acted like there was a real investigation. They asked a lot of questions. They saw our computers. They tried to discover something about us: "What are you doing here? Why are you publishing the news?" Then they brought a big bus and took all of us.
>
> Once on the bus, in each second, we were thinking thousands of things at the same time. But when we saw there was a bridge, and it was the bridge on the only road towards the Air Force detention center, we discovered *where* they are taking all of us. We just . . . we didn't talk. We just looked towards each other's eyes. This Air Force branch is very famous. It is worst branch around Syria. All of us were just saying, "Oh my god." I cannot describe it. It was very difficult.
>
> After they took us off the bus, they took our mobiles, keys, wallets, all things. They put something to blind our eyes and took us to a room on the base. By coincidence or not, our room was behind the investigation room. . . . While there, we saw how they hung the people from the ceiling by their hands with distance between their feet and the ground, which is very very awful. One of our friends,

in our room, they do it to him, hanging in our room for more than 24 hours. They chose him because he was a doctor. They said you are supporting terrorist people, giving them medical aid and support.

They interrogated us the first day, then, I don't know, maybe three or four days later. But they just repeat the same questions. When it was my time to go into the room, they asked me to take all my clothes off, then they closed the door. Our work was a little bit famous in Syria, so we were exceptional people to the investigator. He tried to present himself as an intellectual, knowing everything. He tried to make it kind of a discussion, like "Yes I understand the situation." He tried to be our equal but he was not. He was very stupid. He started asking us questions. "Why are you doing something like this? You are doing something against your country. From where are you getting the money?" You know many many questions. He argued the protests were not occurring because of anything the government was doing. His narrative was about all of our enemies, that everyone is against us because we are fighting Israel, the United States, because we are strong. You know, these kinds of very stupid things. . . .

After 28 days, we did kind of a hunger strike. We said, "You have to release us or transfer us to the Judge." And we told them, "See we are like activists. We know exactly how we can get our voice out. We can tell all people around the world what happened here." We did hunger strike for five days. They asked us to stop our hunger strike but we didn't. Then they transferred us to another security branch, which when compared with the Air Force branch, the Air Force was kind of a five star hotel.

When we arrived there, they did not ask us anything. They just started to beating us without any kind of question. They were just beating us with sticks, with electricity, with cables. Every night. We couldn't see anything. We were just like hearing our voices. I don't know how long each day they beat us because we are like so tired. They repeated that for six days.[8] They said, "We will teach you about doing hunger strikes in our places. You are not allowed to do something like this because other prisoners will see you and learn from you." After that, they didn't beat us every day, just every two to three days. They would come and choose some people, but it was not systematic.

In this branch, after 33 days, I don't know how or why, but they came and said my name and the names of two others. They said come with us and took us back to the Air Force branch and gave us our mobiles, wallets and money. Then they took us to the military police station. We stayed for one night and then they transferred us to the central prison. It was much better. There was like a doctor. There was food. There were new clothes. I was there 20 days. After they transferred us to the military base, then the prison, we thought will be released, the three of us, because in Syria if you are transferred from the secret detention center, that means you will be released.

Still, they didn't leave me go totally. They transferred us to the military court. The judge asked us, "If I release you will, will you remain in Damascus and attend the court again to face charges." I signed the paper saying I would attend, but after they did something like this, I prepared myself and left the country.

My hopes for the future? Maybe we can distinguish between what we wish and what we think. I wish Syria to be unified, to return to the same cohesion between all Syrians, but with a new political structure. But objectively, we are in a real civil war, a very brutal civil war. We are doing our best as activists, who demonstrated from the first day, to do our best to like stop this kind of killing, the human rights violations, and teach people about how can they live life together. But unfortunately the sound of guns, the sound of barrel bombs, of ISIS, is louder than our sound. We are weak. We are very weak. We wish to be loud, to be more strong. We wish to be more strong by having more people on our side. But, unfortunately, no, because unfortunately they are strong instead.

I think it is important for people to know that there are a million Syrians that want to lead a normal life like them. They are not killing or beheading. They can do a lot of focusing on this issue supporting Syrian people, activists, especially supporting peaceful activities and non-conflict resolutions. (Parks, "Interview")

The human rights defender's narrative shares many characteristics with those by the authors in *Revolution by Love*. There is a faith in social media to expose the truth of a situation and garner international support. There is also a faith that activism can act as a moral force to produce necessary political change. There is a belief that the citizens in the country share a common value to live in a nonviolent world and lead normal lives.

What is not part of the narrative is a faith in the possibility of Syria continuing on within its established borders. Today, reluctantly and with remorse, this individual has diminished hope for a unified restored Syria under the control of a democratically elected government. Indeed, with colonial borders being redrawn, with Syria becoming a battleground for Western global power struggles, and in a position where activists are "weak," "very weak," the individual has articulated the need for a new vision of "states" to be produced that seemingly rely less on Western(ized) visions of a political order of nation-states in service of the West. Instead of propping up such a network of nation-states, a new rhetorical and political model should work to tame the violence, eliminate the barbarous acts of too many of the principal actors, recognize the legitimate claims of unrecognized populations for governmental and territorial status, and restore a semblance of hope to the region and those who live there. This may or may not result in a "nation-state" named Syria. Most importantly, at this political juncture, this nuanced rhetoric of human rights must be developed so as to navigate a narrow political space between strategic use of Western visions of democratic and human rights while simultaneously muting the ability of global powers to use this same rhetoric to enforce political and economic solutions on the MENA region. As all of the above has demonstrated, it is a rhetoric that must be connected to bodies that can physically challenge the facts on the ground.

REVOLUTION BY BODIES

The above discussion provides two powerful lessons about activism in the current moment:

Bodies have returned to the public square.

Bodies are surrounded by and enact rhetoric.

In the above stories, individuals and collectives positioned themselves not only as part of the public sphere but also as physical entities taking up public space. The bodies were initially drawn together by emergent and traditional activist tools: cell phones and Facebook; workshops and training sessions; nongovernmental agencies and political parties. These individual bodies formed a common "political body" through a rhetoric that framed their actions as well as the counteractions of their opponents. Ultimately, these emergent political bodies demonstrated how a US- and Western-based rhetoric of democracy can both enable protests and generate oppression: the unruly body tortured in the name of nationalist and geopolitical interests. And so, the question emerges: Where is the space, and what is the work, of an unruly rhetoric, of unruly bodies, at the current moment?

In answering these questions, I would argue that an unruly rhetoric cannot draw upon an uncritical sense of US democracy, a rhetoric both invoked and then critiqued in *RBL*. For such a rhetoric is necessarily premised upon the United States' colonialist history in the region—a colonialism that is both geographic and economic. It is a rhetoric, regardless of its perhaps more expansive historical vision, that is now also premised upon the economic and military needs of the United States. It is deployed to justify an essentially imperialist dream premised upon an open market ideology that allows the exploitation of natural resources and of human beings. Such a rhetoric seems to me capable of supporting dictators or democracies with equal enthusiasm from Western powers, often with UN support (either overt or covert).

It is within this context that a post-*RBL* project has emerged. Working with Bassam Alahmad as well as three other Syrian activists, we are developing Syrians for Truth and Justice (STJ), a nonprofit that records the torture experiences of Syrians, some similar, some far worse than the above story. The documentation, however, will cast a much wider net than just nation-state actors. In addition to the Syrian regime, STJ will also record the atrocities of the Free Syrian Army, the PYD (Kurdish Forces), and Daesh/ISIS, among other military and militia forces. As an organization, STJ will not endorse a naïve vision of a "multicultural free space" but rather embed itself in a reality where minorities are singled out and where religious background or gender identity becomes cause for persecution. Supporting this work will be a network of citizen journalists in Syria who are documenting the current human rights abuses by all of the above actors.

Unlike the personal narratives of *Revolution by Love*, these stories will serve multiple purposes. A journalistic version of the testimonies and stories will be provided on the STJ website. This information will also be collected and categorized for potential use by nation-states, NGOs, and international human rights organizations and courts as evidence in attempts to seek justice for victims. STJ, that is, will work to integrate its findings into actual UN International Court actions. This same information will, we hope, be used to support a series of gatherings (or workshops) among Syrians both within and outside the country to begin a dialogue on the future of the terrain named "Syria," but which exists now only as a battlefield for global power struggles. These workshops will ask what a future society might look like, what values it might inhabit, what it might understand as its "borders."

Ultimately, I believe the United Nations should not become the assumed framework through which a collective future is imagined—particularly as new political structures such as the Democratic Federal System of Northern Syria continually emerge from within the borders of Syria/Iraq/Turkey.[9] For while it is strategic to call upon the UN International Court to punish perpetuators of human rights abuses, there also must be a strategy that will support the creation of new forms of political collectives that perhaps transcend current understandings of "nation-states" and their relationship to current hegemonic powers. This is particularly the case if new borders, new "nations," are to be constituted, which can move the Arab Spring activism from its initial hope and current conflicts to a newly restructured world order.

Here the work of Michael Lowy's framing of nationalism is useful to consider. Rather than seeing nationalist claims based upon an essentialized sense of soil or blood (as at times invoked in *RBL*), claims to national status, he argues, can be premised on the right of historic communities to self-determination (79). Under this logic, self-identified political collectives could claim a right to a legal status that could stand in contradistinction to the needs of the global powers, often enacted by the United Nations, or regional powers such as Israel. That is, the individuals and collectives that have inhabited "Syria" would be seen as having a right to imagine their own collective future outside of existing claims by third parties and international systems of governance. In casting a rhetoric for the current moment, one that pushes against human rights abuses and toward a future marked by new forms of "borders," then, this seemingly contradictory rhetoric of working within and against the current nation/international political structure must be developed.

For ultimately, this new rhetoric works to move beyond international, national, and regional bodies, toward a deep engagement with the formation and reformation of communities within the context of their right of self-determination. This rhetoric recognizes an ever-forming sense of continuity and identity by communities, which necessarily means the consideration of new forms of political organization, neither nation nor United Nations, but bodies and coalescing political bodies forming under an expansive vision of human rights liberated from "nation-state border" restrictions. In many ways, the attempt, in such a project, is to achieve a revolution that yet has no model because it imagines an international definition of human rights that moves the discussion of rights within existing nations to the populations whose identity has suffered most under previous attempts at national unity or colonialist nation building. It is a vision of regionalism (invoking Spivak's articulation of this concept) that works to articulate new subjectivities representing a diversity of identities under different democratic governmental/political regionalist structures—structures that do not have to align with U.S. interests to maintain power, structures that do not need the UN "sanction" to be seen as legitimate entities.[10] In recognizing the destruction of (neo)colonial borders, this rhetoric calls for a new political landscape to emerge.

It is, perhaps, a rhetorical reach to frame the STJ project in such a bold fashion. In reality, the project is the work of five individuals, operating within an international context replete with cross-border and intra-border violence, the ongoing persecution and political exile of hundreds of thousands of Syrian refugees, and acting within the global rivalry among the United States, Russia, and Iran. But sometimes, the power of rhetoric (however small its instantiation) lies in its ability to point bodies toward a utopian future that transcends the brutality of the present moment.

And in such work might be the beginnings of a truly unruly rhetoric.

NOTES

1. For scholarship in community publishing, see Steve Parks, "Sinners Welcome."

2. For a particularly pro-social media account of the Arab Spring in Egypt, see Wael Ghonim, *Revolution 2.0.*

3. In 1996 over twelve hundred political prisoners were executed on the same day, within several hours, inside the Busleem prison (Chulov and Smith; Franklin).

4. For an extended study of the civil war, see Reese Erlich, *Inside Syria*.

5. The center revised its mission statement and goals in response to the ongoing Syrian conflict as well as the discussed actions by Assad against their organizations. The text cited here is from their original mission statement. Their current organization framing is available at www.scm.bz/en/. Given that the earlier text is no longer available, I cite it at length in the article and accompanying footnotes.

6. Indeed, their organizational goals echo this belief in the need for free expression and a commitment to an international vision of human rights:

Disseminate the culture and consciousness of freedom of opinion and expression and belief and respect for the opinions of others and diversity and tolerance within the Syrian society and in collaboration with government agencies and civil society organizations.

Raise the normal theoretical and practical level for the media and journalists and workers in the field of freedom of expression and through seminars and workshops and training process and the publication of studies and research on freedom of opinion and expression sessions, encourage creative initiatives in this area and provide support Legal told reporters.

Review of legislation and local laws and regulations and to provide scientific proposals to align them with international standards on freedom of opinion and expression and human rights and to contribute in theory to build a state of law and institutions, civil society and democratic.

Publishing and dissemination of new cultural values within Syrian society, such as the abolition of discrimination against women and children's rights and environmental education and consumer protection and taking into account the special needs and psychiatric patients' rights and people living with AIDS and housing rights and minority rights and the right to development and personal freedoms and abolition the death penalty.

Adhere to international standards of a set of laws and charters and conventions and international declarations and international conventions on freedom of opinion and expression and human rights in order to bring about a fundamental change in cultural infrastructure and cultural and intellectual formation and social within the Syrian society and foundation to find a material cognitive learning [that] is consistent with the principles of freedom of opinion and expression and the International Bill of Human Rights and notes the social inequalities and cultural that characterize the Syrian components of society and trying to bridge the gap by focusing on the aspects of convergence and build on them and monitor changes and influences that contribute to the creation of a social dynamic and the analysis of its implications for the understanding of transitions in the course of civil society in Syria.

Discrimination in the relationship between states and societies between the level of governments and political interests that relations control and decisions and between peoples' level, which all share the humanitarian concern and highlight the positive effects of the interaction between people and intermingling among civilizations for the benefit of all mankind and to help support the dialogue of cultures.

7. The *RBL* authors were aware of the consequences of seeming to be aligned with the United States, even as they invoked elements of its history in the book. Many feared they would be branded as spies upon their return.

8. Lest we imagine the United States is not capable of similar actions, see the Senate Select Committee on Intelligence, *The Senate Intelligence Committee Report on Torture: Committee Study of the Central intelligence Agency's Detention and Interrogation Program.*

9. Here it should be noted that this new model does not imply that new governance structures within the existing borders of Syria are impossible, nor that recognition of historic communities within its borders cannot be negotiated or recognized under the correct politically negotiated system.

10. See Gaytri Spivak and Judith Butler, *Who Sings the Nation-State?*

WORKS CITED

Chulov, Martin, and David Smith. "Search for Tripoli Prison Massacre Victims Seeks to Heal Wounds." *The Guardian*, September 9, 2011. www.theguardian.com/world/2011/sep/09/search-victims-tripoli-prison-massacre/. Last accessed 2015. No longer available.

Erlich, Reese. *Inside Syria: The Backstory of Their Civil War and What the World Can Expect.* Prometheus Books, 2016.

Franklin, Stuart, "Abu Salim: Walls that Talk." *The Guardian*, September 30, 2011. www.theguardian.com/world/2011/sep/30/mass-grave-libya-prison-abu-salim/.

Ghandour, Dala, Emna Ben Yedder, Mohammed Masbah, Tamara Issak, Theresa Keicher, and Steve Parks. *Revolution by Love: Emerging Arab Youth Voices.* New City Community Press, 2012.

Ghonim, Wael. *Revolution 2.0: The Power of the People Is Greater than the People in Power/A Memoir.* Houghton Mifflin Harcourt, 2012.

Holmes, Amy Austin. "The Military Intervention that the World Forgot." *Al Jazeera*, 29 March 2014. www.america.aljazeera.com/opinions/2014/3/bahrainuprisingintervention saudiarabiaemirates.html/. Last accessed 2017. No longer available.

Lowy, Michael. "Why Nationalism." *Fatherland or Mother Earth? Essays on the National Question.* Pluto Press, 1998.

"Operaton Cast Lead." GlobalSecurity.org. www.globalsecurity.org/military/world/war /operation-cast-lead.htm.

Parks, Steve. Interview with Syrian Human Rights Journalist. June 15, 2015.

Parks, Steve. "Sinners Welcome: The Limits of Rhetorical Agency." *College English* 76, no. 6 (July 2014): 506–24.

Senate Select Committee on Intelligence. *The Senate Intelligence Committee Report on Torture: Committee Study of the Central Intelligence Agency's Detention and Interrogation Program.* Melville House, 2014.

Spivak, Gaytri, and Judith Butler. *Who Sings the Nation-State? Language, Politics, Belonging.* Seagull Books, 2011.

"Syria Accused of Torture and 11,000 Executions." *BBC News*, January 21, 2014. www.bbc .com/news/world-middle-east-25822571/.

"World Report 2017: Syria." *Human Rights Watch*, 2017. www.hrw.org/world-report/2017 /country-chapters/syria/.

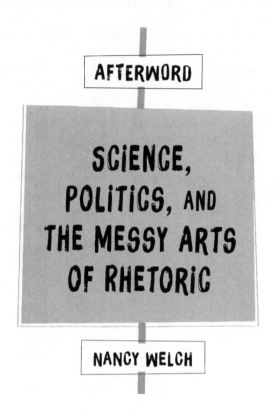

SCIENCE, POLITICS, AND THE MESSY ARTS OF RHETORIC

NANCY WELCH

Among the signs at the mass marches following the inauguration of Donald J. Trump were those proclaiming "What Do We Want? Evidence-Based Science! When Do We Want It? Following Peer Review!" I count those signs among my favorites, an unabashedly nerdy rebuff to the promotion of "alternative facts" in a "post-truth" age. Yet the evidence is already in: peer-reviewed findings and fact-backed arguments won't be allowed persuasive sway (on climate change, health care, immigration, affirmative action in university admissions, and more) or even much of a hearing outside the distortions of alt-Right and Fox News propagandists. Hence the need for National Parks Service and Environmental Protection Agency (EPA) employees to create "Alt-National Parks" and "Alt US EPA," circumventing the Trump administration's gag order (Davenport; Magill) and creating channels through which dissemination and advocacy might still take place.

A premise of this collection is that when political power and economic privatization combine to impede the circulation of critical perspectives and urgent social justice demands, people have turned to unruly means—means that, outside of subfields such as "social movement rhetorics," have received scant attention in composition, rhetoric, and communications scholarship and classrooms. The aim of this collection has been to bring specific accounts of rhetorical unruliness into the disciplinary spotlight, so that scholars and teachers can begin to examine, theorize, critique, and introduce students to what Marxist linguist Jean-Jacques Lecercle calls *la langue de bois* (the "wooden" or unabashedly oppositional language of mass protest). Under the banner of *la langue de bois*, we find such persuasive tactics as pot-banging protest, flash-mob theatrics, and space-claiming occupations that have proved necessary to expose and redress the exclusions and injustices otherwise tolerated by a procedural democracy.

To be sure, the favored neo-Aristotelian rhetorical foundations of many classrooms—aptly summed up by John Duffy as honesty in and accountability for one's claims and a willingness to consider counterclaims and contradicting evidence ("Post Truth")—remain vital to teach and to defend. But, suggest Jonathan Alexander and Susan C. Jarratt in the introduction to this volume, rhetorical scholars must grapple with the political if our work is to have much relevance, especially when the United States' highest officeholder dismisses as "fake news" all challenge to profit and privilege. Middlebury sociology professor Linus Owens argues, "The science is in: we won. But the politics is also in, and, sorry to say, but we've lost, and will continue to do so if we don't take a more active stance against this nonsense" ("Coming Together"). The nonsense Owens refers to is that of eugenicist Charles Murray whose coauthored *The Bell Curve* has long been discredited as pseudoscience but who has gained new license at colleges and universities to peddle his "psychometric" brand of racism under the warrants of free speech, academic freedom, and intellectual diversity. Hence Owens's point. We can win on the science (human activity is the driver of a warming planet; *The Bell Curve* is a piece of toxic junk) but lose on the politics—a president's welcome at Middlebury for Murray, a gag order for the EPA.

What gave Owens occasion to write these words wasn't simply Murray's visit to Middlebury but the widespread condemnation across the political spectrum of the audience's unruly response. The moment Murray began to speak, most members of the largely student and multiracial audience stood, turned their backs, and began to chant. When Murray abandoned the lectern and college officials spirited him to another venue for a closed-circuit broadcast, he was met in the parking lot by a smaller number of protesters. The confusing after-dark physical confrontation that ensued resulted in emergency-room treatment of a professor for a wrenched shoulder. (See "The Charles Murray Event at Middlebury College" for a roundup of reportage and commentary; see also "Middlebury Students" and Jiya Pandya, "Moving beyond Rhetorical Resilience," for student organizers' accounts.) "A Violent Attack on Free Speech," declared *The Atlantic* in a web article whose featured photographs and videos (scores of students, many of them racial minorities, wielding the weapons of cell phones, hand-made placards, and chant sheets), underscore the commentator's view that violence took place *inside* the auditorium the moment the audience refused to sit down, face forward, and listen (Beinart).

The Middlebury media coverage echoes the charges described in my chapter in this volume that were laid out against nuclear-power protestors and Bread and Roses strikers: the tactics of back-turning and chanting censured by liberals and conservatives alike as acts of alarming incivility; ubiquitous vague references to the parking lot's "outside agitators." In the torrent of op-eds that followed, the progressive Cornel West joined the conservative Robert George in calling for "a willingness to listen to and respectfully engage those with whom we disagree"; Bill McKibben (himself a Middlebury faculty member though he was not present at the event) counseled today's antiracist activists to take a lesson from the civil rights era by choosing "dignity" over "rage." Owens's initial blog post and subsequent coauthored essay are among the few faculty commentaries written in the students' defense: "If speech can justify a platform for Murray, it also justifies students talking back. We don't have to agree with the protesting students' tactics to still recognize that the nonviolent demonstrators were defending speech just as much as the people now rushing to condemn them" (Owens, Harper, and Goldberg-Safir; also Essig; Gannon).

I won't wade here into contemporary debates about free speech (though Murray's first-amendment rights were never in question; at no point did the state attempt to set limits on or punish him for his speech). Instead, I want to flag three critical questions that this event and the chapters gathered in this volume raise. These are critical questions with which we need to grapple if we are to include in the study of rhetoric those practices that might effectively respond to the current nonsense creating an increasingly dangerous world and an endangered planet.

First, what kind of rhetorical ethics are required in situations where the counsel to "listen respectfully and try to learn from a speaker with whom I disagree" (George and West) has become untenable? Of relevance here is the fact that, in a 2007 lecture at Middlebury, Murray opined without the least regard for the audience's students and faculty of color that affirmative action policies fail African American and Latinx students by allowing them entrance to elite institutions (Gee; Owens, Harper, and Goldberg-Safir). Recalling the word "faggot" written on his dorm-room door and swastikas on other doors following that visit, Middlebury alum Brian Pacheo wrote in a letter to the *New York Times*, "As a gay Latino, I find it troubling that students of color are continuously burdened to try to understand dissenting viewpoints that dehumanize us" ("To the Editor"). Scholarly and public discourse on rhetorical ethics emphasizes "rhetorical listening" (Ratcliffe), "rhetorical friendship" (Duffy, "The Good Writer"), or from Middlebury College's president, "rhetorical resilience" (Patton). But as the contributors to this volume suggest, such formulations of rhetorical ethics provide insufficient guidance in situations where one's would-be interlocutor is already pushing through a destructive plan (see Ackerman and Dunn; Anderson; Cloud; Mahoney; Parks; Sterne), has repeatedly failed to act on institutional or constitutional promises (see Mutnick; Rodríguez and Kuebrich; Trimbur), or denies civil rights and recognition (see Abraham; George and Mathieu; Martin and Licona; Peters; Rhodes; Welch). Between bearing Murray's words in silence or seeking to silence him, what were the other choices at hand for the predominantly African American students who organized the Middlebury protest? What responsibilities do we bear in rhetorical teaching to introduce students to a fuller range of choices and a contextually sensitive, politically efficacious ethics of decision-making about them?

These questions intertwine with a second critical question: What consideration should be paid not only to means but also to goals? Axiomatic among anarchist antifa (antifascist) and Black Bloc–identified activists organizing resistance to the Trump agenda is the expression "No platform for fascists." From this principle comes the strategy of "Shut it down," including when the alt-Right's ideological architects—Milo Yiannopolous, Ann Coulter, Richard Spencer, Charles Murray, and the like—come to town. At first glance, it might seem that the shut-it-down strategy falls in step with anti-Stalinist Russian revolutionary Leon Trotsky's famous assertion that "A means can be justified only by its ends" (49). Dropped out, however, is the second part of Trotsky's dialectical conception of the necessary relationship between means and ends: "But the end in its turn *needs to be justified*" (49, my emphasis). In his critically acclaimed hundredth-anniversary history of the Russian Revolution, *October*, China Miéville provides a brilliant illustration of that dialectical means-and-ends relationship. In the months between the February 1917 mass strikes that deposed the tsar and the October revolution, the Bolshevik party did not argue for a small minority to "take power," whether through armed insurrection or political maneuvering but, instead, sought, especially through the means of "patient explanation," to win the majority of workers, peasants, and soldiers to the need for socialist revolution and to prepare this majority not only for claiming political power but for the tasks of self-governance (Miéville, chapter 4).

Of course, Trump's tsar-like excesses notwithstanding, 2017 is not 1917. Yet the Bolshevik allegiance to mass democratic ends—those ends and not "no platform for tsarists" or even "All power to the soviets" holding primacy—can provide useful lessons. The axiom of "No platform for fascists," for instance, leaps past other, potentially more primary, goals—for instance, the goal of growing in numbers a confident and mass participatory movement that can effectively check the growth of the far Right. When elevated to unquestionable principle, the no-platform axiom also forestalls needed attention to social and political conditions—conditions that currently include (or included until the hoods came off in Charlottesville) the success of the alt-Right in casting its figures and groups as the dubious champions of social tolerance and nonviolence. Well-organized and highly confident "trolls," notes McKibben, stoke protest in their "campaign to discredit academia and multiculturalism." Hence, he argues, the Middlebury protestors unwittingly delivered a "gift" to the "bad guys" with university presidents, faculty, and commentators rallying around Murray as the victim and elevating him as a paragon of free-exchange virtue. "To put this bluntly, ya'll," wrote Owens two days after the protest, "we got played."

Yet if the strategy of "shut it down" and its accompanying tactics require contextual sensitivity and sober assessment, so too does McKibben's counterclaim that "shouting down someone . . . reads badly to the larger public, *every single time*" (emphasis in original). Not five months after the Middlebury controversy, for instance, Cornel West praised antifascist activists for physically intervening to defend West and a contingent of clergy from attack on the streets of Charlottesville. Had these activists with their defensive shields, clubs, and shut-it-down commitment not stepped in as Nazi street fighters set upon the clergy, West told *Democracy Now*'s Amy Goodman, "We would have been crushed like cockroaches" (Goodman; see also Lithwick). To give two more examples from my own campus: in the mid-1980s, amid growing disquiet over US proxy wars in Central America, students won broad approval for a mass noisy campaign that drove CIA recruiters from campus; more recently, the University of Vermont's environmental justice activists have garnered strong audience support and new movement members through disruptive tactics like mic-checking a speaker from Royal Dutch Shell ("Police Arrest"; "Climate Justice Activists").

As much as we might wish it to be, activism isn't, as McKibben asserts, a "science with fairly predictable rules: history has shown what does and doesn't work." A tactic that reads and works well in one set of circumstances may not work in another. The hecklers' veto that Middlebury students were rebuked for using in spring 2017 was widely applauded when used by University of Florida students against Richard Spencer in the fall's post-Charlottesville context. Science itself only appears predictable in retrospect, its hypothesis-methods-results narratives papering over messy untold tales of frustration (a result refusing replication) and surprise (a game-changing discovery one did not anticipate). Better, I think, is to understand activism as a messy rhetorical art. Doing so, we restore the specificity of each occasion that McKibben's advice would erase—the particular issue, the particular place, the particular differentials of power at play, all requiring complicated acts of judgment and the risk of mistake.

History matters to the pursuit of such an art, but its hail is for students of social movement and social justice rhetoric to consider in much more depth and with greater honesty the material, social, and political conditions in which arguments were made and received. Fuller historical investigation, for instance, contests the truism that civil rights activists were applauded for their dignity rather than lambasted and hounded as extremists. It is hard to find an image of greater dignity than in the bowed-head, bare-footed, raised-fist poses struck by John Carlos and Tommy Smith on the medal stand at the 1968 Olympics—or in the "take a knee" national anthem protests initiated by former San Francisco 49ers quarterback Colin Kaepernick. Yet these and other black athletes have suffered profound career consequences from sports officials enraged that they should use their public platforms to address racism, poverty, policy brutality, and war. Difficult to tease apart too are which forms of address—including the urban rebellions of the 1960s and the Ferguson and Baltimore uprisings of today—have proved most effective in focusing national attention on systemic racism, poverty, and police brutality and making possible any sort of progress. "Our impatience and rage is what has produced progress," argues Mychal Denzel Smith. "That we are still impatient and angry reflects not black people's failing but how far America still has to go" ("The Function of Black Rage").

This leads to the third critical question for teachers of rhetoric: at a moment when angry and impatient voices are all around and when the same tactics and claims are taken up by the Right as well as by the Left, how can we teach rhetorical discernment? Many students I teach don't see themselves as activists; they are, however, audience to public events and movements that seek to enlist their approval and support. What tools and practices do these students need to make discerning judgments about the near simultaneous occupations in 2016 at Standing Rock and at the Malheur National Wildlife Refuge, both occupations making claims, though for very different ends, about the role of the federal government on public land (see Welch and Scott)? At a moment when critical academics face harassment and dismissal for their academic, social media, and activist speech, what are the potential consequences when Evergreen State College students seek the dismissal of a biology professor for his opposition to affirmative action reporting requirements for new faculty hires (Jaschik)?

One answer to these questions of audience discernment can be found in McKibben's description of what took place in the short week between the announcement of Murray's invitation to Middlebury and the night of his address: the math faculty, for instance, sponsoring seminars to guide students in discerning why *The Bell Curve*'s statistical methods are "rubbish." Described here is a commitment to the creation of deliberative space undergirded by the traditional foundations of a rhetorical education: students learning to assess the evidence for and soundness of claims, investigating (stated and unstated) aims, and potential consequences. Depth examination of the alt-Right provocateurs, organizations, and intellectual architects who are now on campus tour can indeed reveal the noxious ecosystem within which they exist, and more, why they believe they can win a new generation of white male college students to white supremacy. (See Singal and the organization Hope not Hate for an undercover account of the alt-Right and the players and recruiting strategies of the "alt-Light.") But even as we cultivate and insist upon such deliberative spaces, we should not confuse or substitute them for political efficacy. The Moral Monday movement that chooses a press conference to contest voter ID laws (McKibben) seems unlikely to find in this tactic alone defense enough against voter disenfranchisement. As I write, dissident scientists face their latest test—at the limits of Alt US EPA as an effective advocacy and protest venue—with the Trump administration poised to suppress rather than release to the public the National Climate Assessment's comprehensive and also damning report about climate change (Friedman).

I won't attempt any fuller answers to these questions than what I've sketched and suggested above. Instead, I'll end with the hope, and expectation, that the conclusion of this volume and the high stakes of our political moment mark the beginning of earnest and far-reaching uptake of these and other questions about means and ends, ethics and discernment. "It's So Bad, Even Introverts Are Here" read another popular sign at the winter and spring 2017 marches. My hope is that this volume, *Unruly Rhetorics*, is among many hails for rhetorical scholars to join them.

WORKS CITED

Beinart, Peter. "A Violent Attack on Free Speech at Middlebury." *The Atlantic*, March 6, 2017. www.theatlantic.com/politics/archive/2017/03/middlebury-free-speech-violence /518667/.

"The Charles Murray Event at Middlebury College." *Middlebury College Newsroom*. www .middlebury.edu/newsroom/information-on-charles-murray-visit/.

"Climate Justice Activists Interrupt Dutch Shell Oil." *Rising Tide Vermont*, November 14, 2012. www.risingtidevermontinthenews.wordpress.com/2012/12/20/climate-justice -activists-interrupt-shell-oil/.

Davenport, Coral. "Federal Agencies Told to Halt External Communications." *New York Times*, January 25, 2017. www.nytimes.com/2017/01/25/us/politics/some-agencies-told -to-halt-communications-as-trump-administration-moves-in.html?mcubz=0/.

Duffy, John. "The Good Writer: Virtue Ethics and the Teaching of Writing." *College English* 79, no. 3 (January 2017): 229–50.

Duffy, John. "Post Truth and First-Year Writing." *Inside Higher Ed*, May 8, 2017. www .insidehighered.com/views/2017/05/08/first-year-writing-classes-can-teach-students -how-make-fact-based-arguments-essay/.

Essig, Laurie. "Talking Past Each Other on Free Speech." *Chronicle of Higher Education* 63, no. 29 (March 2017): B4.

Friedman, Lisa. "Climate Report Full of Warnings Awaits President." *New York Times*, August 7, 2017, A1.

Gannon, Kevin. "Middlebury, Murray, and the Problem of False Equivalence." *The Tattooed Professor*, March 16, 2017. www.thetattooedprof.com/2017/03/16/middlebury -murray-and-the-problem-of-false-equivalence/.

Gee, Taylor. "How the Middlebury Riot Really Went Down." *Politico*, May 28, 2017. www .politico.com/magazine/story/2017/05/28/how-donald-trump-caused-the-middlebury -melee-215195/.

George, Robert P., and Cornel West. "Truth Seeking, Democracy, and Freedom of Thought and Expression: A Statement by Robert P. George and Cornel West." *James Madison Program in American Ideals and Institutions*, Princeton University, March 14, 2017. www.jmp.princeton.edu/statement/.

Goodman, Amy. "Cornel West & Rev. Traci Blackmon: Clergy in Charlottesville Were Trapped by Torch-Wielding Nazis." *Democracy Now*, August 14, 2017. www.democracy now.org/2017/8/14/cornel_west_rev_toni[sic]_blackmon_clergy.

Hope not Hate. "The International Alternative Right." N.d. www.alternativeright.hope nothate.com/.

Jaschik, Scott. "Who Defines What Is Racist?" *Inside Higher Ed*, May 30, 2017. www.inside highered.com/news/2017/05/30/escalating-debate-race-evergreen-state-students -demand-firing-professor/.

Lecercle, Jean-Jacques. *A Marxist Philosophy of Language.* Haymarket Books, 2009.

Lithwick, Dahlia. "Yes, What about the 'Alt-Left'?" *Slate*, August 16, 2017. www.slate.com /articles/news_and_politics/politics/2017/08/what_the_alt_left_was_actually_doing _in_charlottesville.html.

Magill, Bobby. "The E.P.A. Gag Order." *New York Times.* January 27, 2017. www.nytimes .com/2017/01/27/opinion/the-epa-gag-order.html?mcubz=0/.

McKibben, Bill. "College Students Should Resist—Not Silence—Their Political Foes." *The Guardian*, March 10, 2017. www.theguardian.com/commentisfree/2017/mar/10/college -students-resist-not-silence-political-foes/.

"Middlebury Students: College Administrator, Staff Assault Students, Endanger Lives after Murray Protest." *Middbeat*, March 4, 2017. Last accessed August 8, 2017, but no longer available.

Miéville, China. *October: The Story of the Russian Revolution.* Verso, 2017.

Owens, Linus. "Coming Together and Coming Apart at Middlebury." *Middbeat*, March 7, 2017. www.middbeat.org/2017/03/07/coming-together-and-coming-apart-by-professor -linus-owens/.

Owens, Linus, Rebecca Flores Harper, and Maya Goldberg-Safir. "Divisiveness Is Not Diversity." *Inside Higher Ed*, March 17, 2017. www.insidehighered.com/views/2017/03/17 /professor-and-two-former-students-say-why-they-think-students-are-protesting/.

Pacheo, Brian. "To the Editor." *New York Times*, March 18, 2017. www.nytimes.com /2017/03/18/opinion/dealing-with-offensive-ideas-on-campus.html.

Pandya, Jiya. "Moving beyond Rhetorical Resilience." *Middlebury Campus*, March 9, 2017. www.middleburycampus.com/35354/opinion/moving-beyond-rhetorical-resilience/.

Patton, Laurie L. "Old Chapel: A Robust Public Sphere." *Middlebury Blog Network/ Middlebury Magazine*, May 9, 2017. www.sites.middlebury.edu/middblogs/tag/featured -dispatch/.

"Police Arrest 17 Students in CIA Protest." *United Press International*, October 29, 1987. www.upi.com/Archives/1987/10/29/Police-arrest-17-students-in-CIA-protest /7092562482000/.

Ratcliffe, Krista. *Rhetorical Listening: Identification, Gender, Whiteness.* Southern Illinois University Press, 2006.

Singal, Jesse. "Undercover with the Alt-Right." *New York Times*, September 19, 2017. www.nytimes.com/2017/09/19/opinion/alt-right-white-supremacy-undercover.html? action=click&pgtype=Homepage&clickSource=story-heading&module=opinion -c-col-right-region&region=opinion-c-col-right-region&WT.nav=opinion-c-col-right -region&_r=0/.

Smith, Mychal Denzel. "The Function of Black Rage." *The Nation*, April 1, 2014. www .thenation.com/article/function-black-rage/.

Trotsky, Leon. *Their Morals and Ours: The Class Foundations of Moral Practice.* Edited by George Novack. Pathfinder, 1969.

Welch, Nancy, and Tony Scott. "Between Equal Rights: Rhetorical Discernment in an Era of Climate Conflict." *Works & Days*, Thirty-Fifth Anniversary Retrospective, vol. 36, nos. 71–72, forthcoming.

CONTRIBUTORS

MATTHEW ABRAHAM is professor of English, specializing in rhetoric and composition and the teaching of English at the University of Arizona. His publications have appeared in *JAC: An Interdisciplinary Journal of Rhetoric, Culture, and Politics*; *Cultural Critique*; *South Atlantic Quarterly*; *College Composition and Communication*; and *Logos: A Journal of Modern Society and Culture*. Abraham is the coeditor of *The Making of Barack Obama: The Politics of Persuasion* (Parlor Press, 2013) and the editor of *Toward a Critical Rhetoric on the Israel-Palestine Conflict* (Parlor Press, 2015). Abraham's single-authored books are entitled *Out of Bounds: Academic Freedom and the Question of Palestine* (Bloomsbury Academic Press, 2014) and *Intellectual Resistance and the Struggle for Palestine* (Palgrave MacMillan, 2014). Professor Abraham is the coeditor of the symposium entitled "Independent Writing Programs in the Age of Austerity" in the September 2016 issue of *College Composition and Communication*.

JOHN M. ACKERMAN is jointly appointed in the Program for Writing and Rhetoric and the Department of Communication at the University of Colorado at Boulder. He teaches graduate courses on materiality and public space, agentive technologies, and participatory design. He currently writes about cultural and economic change in late-industrial neighborhoods premised on theories of rhetoric as everyday life. He brings qualitative and critical methods to bear on how economic performance, collective memory, and material circulation help to constitute resilient communities, along the Front Range in Colorado and in the Great Lakes industrial area.

JONATHAN ALEXANDER is Chancellor's Professor of English and Informatics at the University of California, Irvine, where he is also the founding director of the Center for Excellence in Writing and Communication. He is the author, coauthor, or coeditor of fifteen books, including *Writing Youth: Young Adult Fiction as Literacy Sponsorship*; *Literacy, Sexuality, Pedagogy: Theory and Practice for Composition Studies*; and the award-winning *On Multimodality: New Media in Composition Studies* and *Techne: Queer Meditations on Writing with the Subject* (both coauthored with Jacqueline Rhodes). Committed to interdisciplinary troublemaking, Jonathan Alexander works generally under the rubric of "writing studies" to explore the creation and uptake of "texts" as they perform different kinds of ideological work in specific contexts. He is currently the editor of *College Composition and Communication* (2015–19).

JOYCE RAIN ANDERSON is associate professor of English at Bridgewater State University. In addition to teaching first-year writing, cultural rhetorics, and Indigenous rhetorics, she coordinates ethnic and Indigenous studies and is the faculty associate for the Pine Ridge Partnership. She is also coeditor of the award-winning collection *Survivance, Sovereignty, and Story: Teaching American Indian Rhetorics*.

DANA L. CLOUD is professor of communication studies at Syracuse University. She teaches and conducts research in the areas of feminist, Marxist, and postmodern theory; social movements, particularly labor; race and gender in media; and rhetorical criticism. Her articles have appeared in *Communication and Critical Cultural Studies*; *Quarterly Journal of Speech*; *Critical Studies in Media Communication*; *Communication and Cultural Critique*; and numerous anthologies. She is the author of two books, *Consolation and Control in Popular and Political Culture: Rhetorics of Therapy* (Sage, 1999) and *We ARE the Union: Democracy and Dissent at Boeing* (University of Illinois, 2011). Her third book, *Reality Bites: Rhetoric and the Circulation of Truth Claims in US Political Culture*, is in press. She is a longtime activist for social justice.

MEGHAN M. DUNN's research investigates rhetorical and technological innovation, particularly emergent and disruptive information communication technologies (ICTs), in the international, humanitarian, and disaster sectors. She conducted a four-year study of the Occupy Movement where she attended to the vernacular communications and rhetoric of participants on the ground and in virtual forums. Her dissertation provided an empirical grounding to theory on the chora, where the tactic of occupation gestured to "inventive" or generative sites of economic and rhetorical activity. She is concurrently employed as an innovation research analyst with the Office of Information and Communications Technology at the United Nations and as adjunct assistant professor of humanities at the New York City College of Technology.

DIANA GEoRGE is emerita professor of rhetoric and writing at Virginia Tech and at Michigan Technological University. Throughout her career she has written on and taught about rhetorics of dissent, both visual and written. Her work has appeared in a number of collections and journals including *College Composition and Communication, College English, Cultural Studies,* and *Reflections.*

SUSAN C. JARRATT is emerita professor of comparative literature at the University of California, Irvine. She is the author of *Rereading the Sophists: Classical Rhetoric Refigured* (Southern Illinois, 1991) and coeditor of *Feminism and Composition Studies: In Other Words* (1998, with Lynn Worsham). Her essays on ancient rhetoric, historiography, gender, and pedagogy have appeared in *College English, College Composition and Communication, Rhetorica,* and other journals. She is currently serving as editor of *Rhetoric Society Quarterly* (2016–19).

BEN KuEBRICH is assistant professor of English and digital journalism at West Chester University. He lives in Syracuse, New York.

ADELA C. LICONA is associate professor of English, director of the University of Arizona's Institute for LGBT Studies, and vice chair of the graduate minor in social, cultural, and critical theory. She is also affiliated faculty in gender and women's studies, the Institute of the Environment, and Mexican American studies. Her research and teaching interests include cultural, ethnic, gender, and sexuality studies, race, critical rhetorics, community literacies, action-oriented and arts-based research, borderlands studies, space/visual culture, social and environmental justice, and feminist pedagogy. She has published in such journals as *Antipode, Transformations, Latino-Latin American Studies, Sexuality Research and Social Policy, Annals of the Association of American Geographers,* and *Critical Studies in Media Communication.*

KEVIN MAHONEY is professor of rhetoric and composition at Kutztown University, where he focuses on the intersections of rhetoric, activism, and digital media. Following the Tea Party electoral victories in the 2010 midterm elections and the Wisconsin Uprising in early 2011, Mahoney founded the progressive, activist media site Raging Chicken Press as part of building an independent media infrastructure in the state. His publications include *Democracies to*

Come: Rhetorical Action, Neoliberalism, and Communities of Resistance, coauthored with Rachel Riedner; "The Kairos of Authorship in Activist Rhetoric," coauthored with Seth Kahn, for the collection *Authorship Contested: Cultural Challenges to the Authentic, Autonomous Author*; and "You Can't Get There from Here: Higher Education, Labor Activism, and Challenges of Neoliberal Globalization" for the collection *Activism and Rhetoric: Theories and Contexts for Political Engagement.* He has written dozens of investigative articles on Pennsylvania politics for Raging Chicken Press. He lives in Perkasie, Pennsylvania, with his wife and two kids.

LONDIE T. MARTIN is assistant professor of digital rhetorics in the Department of Rhetoric and Writing at the University of Arkansas at Little Rock, where she teaches courses on digital narrative, web design, document design, and multimodal composition. As a feminist rhetorician and composer of multimodal work, she emphasizes in her interdisciplinary research the role of the body and sensate engagement in new media, performance, and activist contexts. In 2015 her coauthored webtext titled "Performing Urgency" was published in *Kairos: A Journal of Rhetoric, Technology, and Pedagogy* and won the journal's 2016 Best Webtext Award. She serves on the editorial board for *Feminist Formations,* a leading academic journal in women's, gender, and sexuality studies.

PAULA MATHIEU works as associate professor of English at Boston College where she directs the First-Year Writing Program. She teaches graduate and undergraduate courses in rhetoric, writing as social action, and writing pedagogy. She wrote *Tactics of Hope: The Public Turn in English Composition* and coedited three essay collections including *Circulating Communities* with Stephen Parks and Tiffany Roscoulp. With Diana George, she has written about the rhetorical power of the dissident press. She also most recently published on the intersections between writing and contemplative practice.

DEBORAH MUTNICK is professor of English, former director of writing at the Brooklyn campus of Long Island University, and current codirector of Long Island University's Brooklyn Learning Communities (LIUBLC). She is the author of *Writing in an Alien World: Basic Writing and the Struggle for Equality in Higher Education* (1996), recipient of the W. Ross Winterowd Award. She has published refereed articles and book chapters on basic writing, narrative, autobiography, critical pedagogy, oral history, and the intersection between geography and composition studies. In 2012 she received a National Endowment for the Humanities Digital Humanities Startup Grant for the Pathways to

Freedom Digital Narrative Project, which maps oral histories of Brooklyn civil rights activists in time and space using GIS, crowdsourcing, and other digital technologies.

STEVE PARKS is professor of English at the University of Virginia. He is the author of *Class Politics: The Movement for a Students' Right to Their Own Language* and *Gravyland: Writing beyond the Curriculum in the City of Brotherly Love*. His current book project is *Syria, Truth, Justice: The Rhetorical and Material Practices in the Struggle for Human Rights*. He is founder of New City Community Press (newcitycommunitypress.com) and cofounder and board chair of Syrians for Truth and Justice (stj-sy.com). Currently, he is serving as editor for the National Council of Teachers of English book series, Studies in Writing and Rhetoric.

JASON PETERS is assistant professor of English at California Polytechnic State University, San Luis Obispo. His work has appeared in *College English* and in the collection *Economies of Writing* (Utah State University Press, 2017).

JACQUELINE RHODES is professor of writing, rhetoric, and American cultures at Michigan State University. She is the author, coauthor, or coeditor of books and articles that explore the intersections of materiality and technology, including *Radical Feminism, Writing, and Critical Agency* (2005), *On Multimodality: New Media in Composition Studies* (2014), *Techne: Queer Meditations on Writing the Self* (2015), and *Sexual Rhetorics: Methods, Identities, Publics* (2015).

YANIRA RoDRíGUEZ is a PhD student in composition and cultural rhetoric at Syracuse University. She recently accepted a position as assistant professor of English and journalism at West Chester University.

JONATHAN STERNE is James McGill Professor of Culture and Technology at McGill University. He is author of *MP3: The Meaning of a Format* (Duke, 2012), *The Audible Past: Cultural Origins of Sound Reproduction* (Duke, 2003), and numerous articles on media, technologies, and the politics of culture. He is also editor of *The Sound Studies Reader* (Routledge, 2012) and coeditor of *The Participatory Condition in the Digital Age* (Minnesota, 2016). His current projects consider instruments and instrumentalities; mail by cruise missile; and the intersections of disability, technology, and perception. His next book, tentatively titled *Tuning Time: Histories of Sound and Speed*, is coauthored with Mara Mills. His website is at http://www.sterneworks.org.

JOHN TRIMBUR is professor of writing, literature and publishing at Emerson College. He has published widely in composition and writing studies, including the Braddock Award–winning article with Bruce Horner, "English Only and U.S. College Composition," and *Solidarity or Service: Composition and the Problem of Expertise.*

NANCY WELCH is professor English at the University of Vermont, where she also helped found the union representing full- and part-time faculty. She is the author, coauthor, and coeditor of books and articles exploring the impact of neoliberal privatization and austerity measures on public space, voice, and rights as well as the continued relevance of working-class means for organized resistance. Her article "'We're Here and We're Not Going Anywhere': Why Working-Class Rhetorical Action *Still* Matters" received a Richard Ohmann Award for Best Article in *College English.*

INDEX

NOTE: Page numbers in *italics* refer to figures.

feminism (*cont.*): blind spots of, 96; critical, 90, 98, 102; French, 31; mainstream, 91, 100; postmodern nature of, 97; radical, 31; SlutWalk and, 92–93, 93–94, 95–96; third world, 97; waves of, 91, 96–99; white, 18, 91, 100

Feminisms Matter (Bromley), 96, 98

feminist movement, 90, 92, 96, 97, 101; antiracist, 100; emergence of, 99

Feminist Rhetorical Practices (Royster and Kirsch), 90, 140

#feministarmy, 28, 40, 41; emergence of, 29–33; unruliness of, 31, 33–39

Ferguson, 89, 165, 210–11, 217, 221, 267, 305

filibustering, 16, 28, 30, 33–34, 36, 41, 155

First Nation, 49, 52, 53

Forni, P. M., 167, 168

fossil fuels, 48, 166, 171

Foucault, Michel, 12, 173, 270

Founding Fathers, 152, 153

fracking, 17, 50, 55, 122

Fraiberg, Steven, 76, 77, 85n4

free speech, 12, 139, 150, 157, 290, 302

Free Syrian Army, 290, 295

freedom of expression, 186, 197, 297n6

Freire, Paulo, 173, 215, 257n10

French, 235, 238; dialect of, 239; as minority language, 234; as national language, 240; purification of, 236

Fukushima, 107, 108

Furness, Zack, 66, 67

futurity, 102; queer, 20, 249, 256; settler colonial, 256

Garner, Eric, 211, 220, 224n15

Garza, Alicia, 209, 210, 211, 213–14; on African American murders, 212–13

Gaza, 72, 73, 74, 75, 77, 78, 80, 84, 186, 288; attacks on, 185, 192; deaths in, 81; mass destruction/death in, 184; occupation of, 185

#Gaza, 78, 79

GCC. *See* Gulf Cooperation Council

gender, 31, 90, 98, 100, 101, 159, 246, 250, 253, 264; normativities around, 255

geographies, 266; cultural, 273; embodied, 275; rhetorical, 245, 287

geopolitical forces, 173, 288, 289, 294

Ghost Dance, 47, 51

Giffords, Gabrielle: shooting of, 108, 109

Gilded Age, 18, 113, 120, 136, 158

Goldman, Emma, 129, 135, 137, 142

Gómez-Barris, Macarena, 52, 53

governance, 28, 36, 184, 298n9; international systems of, 296; self-, 304; student, 171

Gray, Freddie, 211, 213, 215, 225n15

Great Army of Tramps, 131, 133, 139, 142

Great Depression, 120, 128, 133, 136

Great Recession (2008–2009), 149, 157, 262, 265

Grosz, Elizabeth, 31, 40, 62

Grrls Literary Activism, 250, 257n6

Guardian, The, 89, 211, 223, 263

Gulf Cooperation Council (GCC), 287, 288

Happe, Kelly E., 12, 266

Haraway, Donna, 245, 246

harmony, 51, 67, 121, 286

Harper's, 113, 116

Hayes, Chris, 155, 156, 157

HB 2281: 247, 254, 257n4

health care, 31, 61, 112, 156, 263

hegemonic power, 27, 248, 295; cultural, 219; global, 284; political, 29

herstory, 209, 210

heteronormativity, 245, 248, 249, 252, 253, 255

heterosexual norm, 65, 246, 248

Hobo Colleges, 135, 142

Hobo News, The (IBWA), 18, 141, 142; circulation of, 137, 138, 140; as dissident counterpublic, 135–37; hobo problem and, 139; How and, 130, 131; masthead of, 143n3; stories from, 136; support for, 140

hoboes, 131, 133, 134–35, 140, 142–43; main stem of, 143n9; newspaper for, 135; number of, 136; population of, 135; problems with, 139

Hodge, Roger, 152, 153, 155

Holocaust, 74–75, 80

homeless, 18, 129, 135, 136, 141, 142, 143, 264; explaining, 133; as failed individuals, 134; justice for, 132

homo oeconomicus, 264, 265, 266, 277

homo politicus, 264, 265, 266, 268, 277

homophobia, 165, 222, 246

Horner, Bruce, 191, 195, 203n1, 204nn6–7, 204n9; letter from, 201–3

Horton, Myles, 159, 172

housing, 265; inattention to, 31; rights, 297n6

How, James Eads, 18, 129, 134, 141, 142; characterization of, 143n4; death of, 129, 130, 131, 132; *Hobo News* and, 140; honoring, 131, 132; Knights of the Road and, 131; mentions of, 143n5; story of, 131, 133, 139; work of, 132, 137–38, 139

Huckin, Tom: letter from, 198–99, 200–201; letter to, 199–200

Huffington Post, 37, 172

human rights, 219, 282, 288, 291; abuses, 295; defending, 293; democracy and, 287; framing, 283; nation-border restrictions and, 296; rhetoric of, 294; violation of, 293; vision of, 294, 297n6

hunger strikes, 49, 50, 52, 53

IBWA. *See* International Brotherhood Welfare Association

ideal city, 273–75

idealism, 77, 148, 153

identity, 32, 142, 176; assembled, 266; cultural, 230; diverse, 253; ethnic, 231; fixed class, 191; freedom of, 197; French, 236, 240; gender, 295; group, 8; linguistic, 235; mobilization of, 229; modernist oppositional, 97; national, 231, 283, 285, 288; performance and, 101; political, 175; racial, 222, 231, 247; sexual, 20; sociocultural, 231; trafficking of, 229; transnational, 240; tropes of, 249; women's, 31

ideology, 229; language, 235; open market, 294; praxis, 97